I AM DY

Sue Prideaux's first biography, *Edward Munch: Behind the Scream*, won the James Tait Black Memorial Prize. *Strindberg: A Life* was awarded the Duff Cooper Prize and was shortlisted for the Samuel Johnson Prize. Both Munch and Strindberg were influenced by Nietzsche.

www.sueprideaux.com

Further praise for *I Am Dynamite!*:

'Sue Prideaux's Nietzsche is a compelling, vulnerable and poignant figure; this biography is the liveliest and freshest account for a long time of one of the most overwhelming intellectual presences in the mind of modern Europe.' Dr Rowan Williams

'Terribly clever and steeped in the wild, doomed peculiarities of nineteenth-century Germania, it is a tremendous and reformative biography of a man whom popular history has perhaps done a disservice.' Hugo Rifkind, *The Times*

'In this witty and lucid new biography, we find not only an accessible introduction to Nietzsche's work but also an invaluable insight into the forces that helped to shape his ideas.' James Black, *Mail on Sunday*

'Splendid . . . a beautifully written, and often intensely moving, account of a life devoted to the achievement of intellectual greatness and the exploration of the conditions for its flourishing.' Jonathan Derbyshire, *Financial Times*

'Books about German philosophers generally score low on the entertainment count. Not *I Am Dynamite!*, which captures the utter oddness of Nietzsche and his circle.' Robbie Millen, *The Times* Books of the Year

'The picture she paints of Nietzsche's early time in Tribschen with the composer Richard Wagner and his wife, Cosima, who came to greatly appreciate the young professor, is, with the description of the silk-lined house and bucolic walks in the mountains, worthy of a Turner, and the book is laced with humour and the eye for a bon mot.' Hugo Drochon, *Irish Times*

'Prideaux emulates her subject by refusing to take anything for granted . . . If ever there was to be a popular biography of Nietzsche, this is it . . . [Prideaux] is a dogged, amiable guide and leaves you in no doubt whatsoever that her frail, footloose, ill-tempered subject was one of the most extraordinary people who ever lived.' Leo Robson, *Evening Standard*

'[An] approachable biography of a usually forbidding man . . . Nietzsche had plenty to overcome in his own life, which is vividly recounted in Ms Prideaux's wide-ranging and sensitive book.' *The Economist*

'Masterful . . . What sets Prideaux's biography apart from previous accounts of Nietzsche's life is its vibrant intimacy . . . Prideaux quite simply gets closer to Nietzsche than anyone before her.' *Los Angeles Review of Books*

---

by the same author

EDVARD MUNCH:
Behind the Scream
STRINDBERG:
A Life

SUE PRIDEAUX

I am Dynamite!

· A LIFE OF ·

FRIEDRICH NIETZSCHE

ff

FABER & FABER

First published in 2018
by Faber & Faber Limited
The Bindery, 51 Hatton Garden
London EC1N 8HN

This paperback edition first published in 2019

Designed by Faber
Printed and bound by CPI Group (UK) Ltd, Croydon, CR0 4YY

A CIP record for this book
is available from the British Library

ISBN 978—0—571—33622—7

8 10 9

To Georgia, Alice, Mary,
Sam and George

Become what you are, having learned what that is.

· CONTENTS ·

CONTENTS

· PLATES ·

· ACKNOWLEDGEMENTS ·

Many people helped me in different ways through this book's four-year journey. I am grateful to those I have met, and those I have not. To the Nietzsche scholars, dead and alive, who have clarified and translated the texts, in some cases clearing away later creative editorship to get back to Nietzsche's original, untangling the true from the false in the Nachlass, the literary estate.

Thank you to my editors in the UK and the US, Mitzi Angel and Tim Duggan, for setting off new trains of thought. To Nigel Warburton who has shown immense generosity and swung his hammer to great effect while overseeing the philosophy.

In Switzerland and Germany: Erdmann von Wilamowitz-Moellendorff of the Herzogin Anna Amalia Bibliothek in Weimar, Tanja Fehling of Klassik-stiftung.de, Professor Peter André Block and Dr Peter Villwock of the Nietzsche-Haus in Sils-Maria, and Katya Fleischer of the Richard Wagner Museum in Tribschen.

In the UK, thank you Felicity Bryan, Michele Topham and all the team at Felicity Bryan Associates. At Faber, special mentions go to Laura Hassan, Emmie Francis, Donna Payne, Anne Owen, Anna Davidson, John Grindrod and Sophie Portas. Thank you Eleanor Rees for the copy edit and Rachel Thorne for clearing permissions. Thank you Louise Duffett (relative of Harry Kessler) and the Classics Department of Godolphin School in London. Thank you Roger Lomax for casting your eye over the complications of nineteenth-century currencies, and Laura Sanderson for a hilarious session on aphorisms. I am grateful to the team at Andrew Nurnberg and, as always, to the omniscient staff of the London Library.

ACKNOWLEDGEMENTS

In the USA, in addition to Tim Duggan, thanks to George Lucas, William Wolfslau, and to Hilary McClellen for fact-checking.

Special thanks to Gillian Malpass, Christopher Sinclair-Stevenson and the late Tom Rosenthal, all of whom gave me courage and support at the very start, to Antony Beevor, Artemis Cooper, Lucy Hughes-Hallett and Sarah Bakewell for useful conversations, and to my family for tact, criticism, research, and tolerating the ghost about the house.

· A MUSICAL EVENING ·

> To escape from unbearable pressure you need hashish. Well, then, I
> need Wagner. Wagner is the antidote to everything German.
>
> *Ecce Homo*, 'Why I am so Clever', section 6

On 9 November 1868, the twenty-four-year-old Nietzsche recounted
a comedy to Erwin Rohde, his friend and fellow-student at Leipzig
University.

'The acts,' he wrote, 'in my comedy are headed:

1. An evening meeting of the society, or the sub professor.
2. The Ejected Tailor.
3. A rendezvous with X.

'The cast includes a few old women.

'On Thursday evening Romundt took me to the theatre, for
which my feelings are growing very cool . . . we sat in the gods like
enthroned Olympians sitting in judgement on a potboiler called *Graf
Essex*. Naturally I grumbled at my abductor . . .

'The first Classical Society lecture of the semester had been arranged
for the following evening and I had been very courteously asked if I
would take this on. I needed to lay in a stock of academic weapons but
soon I had prepared myself, and I had the pleasure to find, on entering
the room at Zaspel's, a black mass of forty listeners . . . I spoke quite
freely, helped only by notes on a slip of paper . . . I think it will be
all right, this academic career. When I arrived home I found a note
addressed to me, with the few words: "If you want to meet Richard
Wagner, come at 3.45 p.m. to the Café Théâtre. Windisch."

'This surprise put my mind in somewhat of a whirl . . . naturally
I ran out to find our honourable friend Windisch, who gave me more
information. Wagner was strictly incognito in Leipzig. The Press

knew nothing and the servants had been instructed to stay as quiet as liveried graves. Now, Wagner's sister, Frau Professor Brockhaus,[1] that intelligent woman whom we both know, had introduced her good friend, Frau Professor Ritschl to her brother. In Frau Ritschl's presence, Wagner plays the *Meisterlied* [Walther's Prize Song from Wagner's most recent opera, *Die Meistersinger*, premiered a few months earlier] and the good woman tells him that this song is already well known to her. [She had already heard it played and sung by Nietzsche, though its musical score had been published only very recently.] Joy and amazement on Wagner's part! Announces his supreme will, to meet me incognito; I am to be invited for Sunday evening . . .

'During the intervening days my mood was like something in a novel: believe me, the preliminaries to this acquaintance, considering how unapproachable this eccentric man is, verged on the realm of fairy tale. Thinking there were many people to be invited, I decided to dress very smartly, and was glad that my tailor had promised my new evening suit for that very Sunday. It was a terrible day of rain and snow. I shuddered at the thought of going out, and so I was content when Roscher[2] visited me in the afternoon to tell me a few things about the Eleatics [an early Greek philosophical school, probably sixth-century BC] and about God in philosophy. Eventually the day was darkening, the tailor had not come and it was time for Roscher to leave. I accompanied him so as to continue to visit the tailor in person. There I found his slaves hectically occupied with my suit; they promised to send it in three-quarters of an hour. I left contentedly, dropped in at Kintschy's [a Leipzig restaurant much frequented by students] and read *Kladderadatsch* [a satirical illustrated magazine] and found to my pleasure a notice that Wagner was in Switzerland. All the time I knew that I would see him that same evening. I also knew that he had yesterday received a letter from the little king [Ludwig II of Bavaria] bearing the address: "To the great German composer Richard Wagner".

'At home I found no tailor. Read in a leisurely fashion the dissertation on the Eudocia,[3] and was disturbed now and then by a loud but distant ringing. Finally I grew certain that somebody was waiting at the patriarchal wrought-iron gate; it was locked, and so was the front door of the house. I shouted across the garden to the man and told him to come in by the back. It was impossible to make oneself understood through the rain. The whole house was astir. Finally, the gate was opened and a little old man with a package came up to my room. It was six thirty, time to put on my things and get myself ready, for I live rather far out. The man has my things. I try them on; they fit. An ominous moment: he presents the bill. I take it politely; he wants to be paid on receipt of the goods. I am amazed and explain that I will not deal with him, an employee, but only with the tailor himself. The man presses. Time presses. I seize the things and begin to put them on. He seizes the things, stops me from putting them on – force from my side; force from his side. Scene: I am fighting in my shirttails, endeavouring to put on my new trousers.

'A show of dignity, a solemn threat. Cursing my tailor and his assistant, I swear revenge. Meanwhile he is moving off with my things. End of second Act. I brood on my sofa in my shirttails and consider black velvet, whether it is good enough for Richard.

'Outside the rain is pouring down. A quarter to eight. At seven thirty we are to meet in the Café Théâtre. I rush out into the windy, wet night, a little man in black without a dinner jacket.

'We enter the very comfortable drawing room of the Brockhauses; nobody is there apart from the family circle, Richard and the two of us. I am introduced to Richard and address him in a few respectful words. He wants to know exact details of how I became familiar with his music, curses all performances of his operas and makes fun of the conductors who call to their orchestras in a bland voice; "Gentlemen, make it passionate here. My good fellows, a little more passionate!" . . .

'Before and after dinner, Wagner played all the important parts of the *Meistersinger*, imitating each voice and with great exuberance. He is indeed a fabulously lively and fiery man, who speaks very rapidly, is very witty and makes a very private party like this one an extremely gay affair. In between, I had a longish conversation with him about Schopenhauer; you will understand how much I enjoyed hearing him speak of Schopenhauer with indescribable warmth, what he owed to him, how he is the only philosopher who has understood the essence of music.'

Schopenhauer's writings were at that time undervalued. Some universities were reluctant to recognise him as a philosopher at all, but Nietzsche was swept up in a whirlwind enthusiasm for Schopenhauer, having recently discovered *The World as Will and Representation* by chance, the same chance or, as he preferred to put it,[4] the same chain of fateful coincidences seemingly arranged by the unerring hand of instinct that had led up to this meeting with Wagner in the Brockhauses' salon.

The first link in the chain had been forged a month before the meeting, when Nietzsche heard the preludes to Wagner's two latest operas, *Tristan und Isolde* and *Die Meistersinger von Nürnberg*. 'Every fibre, every nerve in my body quivered,' he wrote the same day, and he set himself to learning the piano arrangements. Next, Ottilie Brockhaus had heard him play and relayed the news to her brother Wagner. Now the third link: Wagner's deep attachment to the obscure philosopher whose writings had been Nietzsche's comfort when he had first arrived in Leipzig, rootless and unhappy, three years previously.

'I [Nietzsche] lived then in a state of helpless indecision, alone with certain painful experiences and disappointments, without fundamental principles, without hope and without a single pleasant memory . . . One day I found this book in a second-hand bookshop, picked it up as something quite unknown to me and turned the pages. I do not know what demon whispered to me "Take this book home with you." It was contrary to my usual practice of hesitating over the purchase of books. Once at home, I threw myself onto the sofa with the newly won treasure and began to let that energetic and gloomy genius operate upon me . . . Here I saw a mirror in which I beheld the world, life and my own nature in a terrifying grandeur . . . here I saw sickness and health, exile and refuge, Hell and Heaven.'[5]

But there was no time, that evening in the Brockhauses' salon, to speak further of Schopenhauer, for what Nietzsche described as Wagner's spirals of language, his genius for shaping clouds, his whirling, hurling and twirling through the air, his everywhere and nowhere,[6] were hurtling on.

The letter continues:

'After [dinner] he [Wagner] read an extract from his autobiography which he is now writing, an utterly delightful scene from his Leipzig student days, of which he still cannot think without laughing; he writes too with extraordinary skill and intelligence. Finally, when we were both getting ready to leave, he warmly shook my hand and invited me with great friendliness to visit him, in order to make music and talk philosophy; also, he entrusted to me the task of familiarising his sister and his kinsmen with his music, which I have now solemnly undertaken to do. You will hear more when I can see this evening somewhat more objectively and from a distance. For today, a warm farewell and best wishes for your health. F.N.'

When Nietzsche left Professor Brockhaus's handsomely situated, solid, corner mansion, he was greeted at every corner by gusting wind and sleety snow on his chilly walk down to Lessingstrasse 22, where he rented a large, bare room from Professor Karl Biedermann, editor of the liberal newspaper *Deutsche Allgemeine Zeitung*. He describes his mood as one of indescribable elation. He had first discovered Wagner when he was at school. 'All things considered, my youth would have been intolerable without Wagner's music,'[7] he wrote, and the spell that the composer exercised over him would never release him. Wagner is the person who features more often in Nietzsche's writing than any other, including Christ, Socrates or Goethe.[8] His first book was dedicated to Wagner. Two of his fourteen books have Wagner in their title. In his last book, *Ecce Homo*, Nietzsche wrote that he was still searching vainly in every field of art for work 'as dangerously fascinating, with as weird and sweet an infinity as "Tristan"'.[9]

From an early age, Nietzsche's ambition had been to become a musician, but as an outstandingly clever pupil at an outstandingly academic school where words counted above music, he had reluctantly abandoned the idea when he was about eighteen. At the moment of this meeting with Wagner, he was not yet a philosopher but merely an undergraduate at Leipzig University studying classical philology, the science of classical languages and linguistics.

A good-natured, cultured, solemn, rather stiff young man, he was stout but not fat. In photographs it looks as if his clothes are borrowed; the elbows and knees are not in the right places and the jackets strain at the buttons. Short and ordinary in appearance, he was saved from nonentity by peculiarly arresting eyes. One pupil was slightly larger than the other. Some say the irises were brown, some grey-blue. They gazed out on the world with the blurred uncertainty of the extreme myopic but once focused, his glance was described as piercing, penetrating and unsettling; it made lies stick in your throat.

These days we know him from the photographs, busts and portraits of his later years when the mouth and most of the chin are completely obliterated by the great ram's horn moustaches, but photographs taken with his fellow students during his Leipzig University days show us that in an age of imposing facial hair, his was comparatively unimpressive. We can see that his lips were full and well shaped, a fact confirmed in later life by Lou Salomé, one of the few women who kissed him, and we can also see that his chin was firm and rounded. Just as preceding intellectual fashion had run to flowing locks and floppy silk bow ties to advertise Romantic credentials, so Nietzsche advertised his post-Romantic rationalism by emphasising the astonishing forehead, seat of the astonishing brain, and concealing the sensuous lips and determined chin.

Nietzsche was becoming increasingly unhappy as a philologist. In a letter written eleven days after the meeting with Wagner, he describes himself and his fellow-philologists as 'the seething brood of the philologists of our time, and every day having to observe all their moleish pullulating, the baggy cheeks and the blind eyes, their joy at capturing worms and their indifference to the true problems, the urgent problems of life.'[10] A further aggravation to his pessimism was that he was so exceptionally good at the moleish pullulating he despised that he would shortly be offered the Chair of Classical Philology at Basle University, becoming their youngest ever professor, but such glory had not yet arrived on the evening when Wagner treated him as an equal and indicated that he would be pleased to continue the acquaintance. It was an extraordinary honour.

Simply known as 'the Master', the composer was in his mid fifties and enjoying notoriety across Europe. His every move was reported in the press, as Nietzsche had discovered earlier that evening reading *Kladderadatsch* in the café. If Wagner visited England, Queen Victoria and Prince Albert graciously sought him out. In Paris, Princess Pauline Metternich arranged things. King Ludwig of Bavaria addressed Wagner as 'my adored and angelic friend' and was planning completely to remodel the city of Munich in honour of his music.

Ludwig died before the extravagant scheme could be realised (possibly murdered, to stop his wild building projects bankrupting his country) but we can still see the architect's plans: a new avenue cutting through the city centre, crossing the River Isar by a noble stone bridge reminiscent of Wotan's rainbow bridge leading to Valhalla in Wagner's *Ring*, and terminating in a huge opera house resembling the Colosseum sliced vertically in half with a couple of wings added either side. Wagner's music was, for King Ludwig, 'my most beautiful, supreme and only consolation', a sentiment often echoed by Nietzsche.

From his earliest days, Nietzsche was unusually sensitive to music. Family accounts of his childhood suggest that it was more important to him than speech: he was such a delightfully quiet toddler that his was the only presence his father, Pastor Karl Ludwig Nietzsche,[11] would allow in his panelled study while he worked on parish business and composed his sermons. Father and son would pass companionable hours and days in smooth monotony but, like many two- and three-year-olds, little Friedrich would sometimes be seized by violent paroxysms of rage, screaming and thrashing his arms and legs furiously. Nothing, then, would pacify him, neither his mother, nor toys, nor food, nor drink, but only his father lifting the lid of the piano and making music.

In a musical nation, Pastor Nietzsche was exceptionally accomplished at the keyboard; people would come for miles to hear him play. He was Lutheran pastor of the parish of Röcken, south of Leipzig, where J. S. Bach had held the post of director of music for twenty-seven years until his death. Karl Ludwig was known for his Bach recitals. More unusually, he was celebrated for his exceptional talent at improvisation, a talent that Nietzsche would inherit.

The Nietzsche ancestors were modest Saxon folk, butchers and cottagers who made their living in the area around the cathedral town of Naumburg. Karl Ludwig's father, Friedrich August Nietzsche, moved the family up the social scale on taking Holy Orders and he advanced his position further on marrying Erdmuthe Krause, daughter of an archdeacon. A woman of thoroughly Napoleonic sympathies, Erdmuthe gave birth to Nietzsche's father, Karl Ludwig, on 10 October 1813, a few days before the Battle of Nations, also called the Battle of Leipzig, in the immediate vicinity of the battlefield on which Napoleon was defeated. Nietzsche loved to tell the story. He thought of Napoleon as the last great immoralist, the last wielder of power without a conscience, the synthesis of superman and monster and this rather tenuous connection gave him, he fancied, a prenatal physio-psychological reason for his fascination with the hero. One of the unrealised ambitions of his life was to visit Corsica.

Karl Ludwig was, naturally, destined to follow his father into the Church. He attended nearby Halle University, which had long been renowned for theology. Here he learned theology, Latin, Greek and French languages, Greek and Hebrew history, classical philology and biblical exegis. He was not an outstanding student, nor was he stupid. He was known as a hard worker and he won a prize for eloquence. On leaving university at twenty-one, he took a tutoring job in the large city of Altenburg, some thirty miles south of Leipzig.

Karl Ludwig was a conservative and a royalist. These solid qualities brought him to the attention of the reigning Duke Joseph of Saxe-Altenburg, who appointed him to supervise the education of his three daughters, Therese, Elisabeth and Alexandra. Karl Ludwig was still in his twenties but he managed to execute the job admirably, and without a whiff of romantic entanglement.

After seven years of tutoring, he applied for the post of pastor of the parish of Röcken, on the fertile but treeless plain about fifteen miles southwest of Leipzig. In 1842 he moved into the parsonage with his now-widowed mother Erdmuthe. The parsonage stood cheek by jowl with one of the oldest churches in the province of Saxony, an ancient fortress-church dating from the first half of the twelfth century. Under Frederick Barbarossa, its tall, rectangular tower had doubled as a lookout over the extensive plain defended by the Knights of Kratzsch. Inside the sacristy there stood a larger-than-life stone effigy of one of the knights. It used to terrify Nietzsche as a little boy, when the sun caught its eyes of inlaid ruby glass, making them flash and glow.

On a visit to the parish of Pobles, the eye of twenty-nine-year-old Pastor Karl Ludwig was caught by the seventeen-year-old daughter of the local priest. Franziska Oehler was without much education but she had a simple and profound Christian faith and she desired no more glorious fate than to support her husband through this mortal vale of tears.

They married on his thirtieth birthday, 10 October 1843. Karl Ludwig moved his bride into the Röcken parsonage, where the household was dominated by Erdmuthe, now an uncompromising *materfamilias* of sixty-four who dressed in the forbidding bonnet and false side curls of the previous generation. She doted on her son, controlled the purse strings and further controlled the household by means of her 'delicate hearing', which demanded volume permanently be kept at *pianissimo*.

The other members of the household were the pastor's two sickly and neurotic elder stepsisters, Nietzsche's Aunts Augusta and Rosalie. Aunt Augusta was a martyr to domesticity, who would not allow newly married Franziska to be useful in the kitchen lest she spoil her difficulty. 'Leave me this one solace,' Aunt Augusta would say when Franziska offered to help. Aunt Rosalie was of a more intellectual bent; she martyred herself to charitable causes. Both aunts ailed from the widespread contemporary complaint of nerves and were forever five steps away from the medicine cabinet that never could cure them. This triumvirate of older women effectively rendered Franziska, the bride, useless in her own home. Fortunately, a few months after the marriage she found herself pregnant with Friedrich.

Friedrich Wilhelm Nietzsche was born on 15 October 1844 and christened in the Röcken church by his father, who named him after the reigning king, Friedrich Wilhelm IV of Prussia. Two years later, on 10 July 1846, a girl was born and named Therese Elisabeth Alexandra after the three Altenburg princesses whom her father had tutored. She was always known as Elisabeth. Two years later, another boy was born in February and named Joseph for the Duke of Altenburg.

The pastor was both pious and patriotic but he was not free from the nervous disorders that affected his mother and half-sisters. He would shut himself up in his study for hours, refusing to eat, drink or talk. More alarmingly, he was given to mysterious attacks, when his speech would abruptly cease mid-sentence and he would stare into space. Franziska would run over to shake him awake but when he 'woke' he would be oblivious to the interruption in his consciousness.

Franziska consulted Dr Gutjahr, the family doctor, who diagnosed 'nerves' and prescribed rest but the symptoms worsened until finally the pastor had to be excused his parish duties. The mysterious paroxysms were diagnosed as 'softening of the brain' and for months he was prey to prostration, agonising headaches and fits of vomiting, his eyesight deteriorating drastically into semi-blindness. In the autumn of 1848, aged thirty-five and married only five years, he took to his bed and his active life effectively ceased.

Franziska's life was stifling beneath Erdmuthe and the two neurotic aunts and the increasing debility of her husband. Dark frowns and covert signals passed between the adults in the parsonage but somehow Franziska managed to shield her children from the morbid atmosphere. Memoirs of their childhood days written by both Friedrich and Elisabeth each recount the liberty and lightness of being that brother and sister found in their seemingly limitless playground, encompassing the great church tower, the farmyard, the orchard and the flower garden. There were ponds overhung with willows into whose green caves they could creep to listen to the birds and watch the quick fish dart beneath the water's glossy surface. They felt that the grassy graveyard at the back of the house was 'friendly', but they did not play among its ancient stones on account of the three slitted dormer windows that were let into the roof on that side of the house and seemed to glare down like the all-seeing eyes of God.

Karl Ludwig's sufferings grew worse; he lost the power of speech, and finally his eyesight deteriorated into total blindness. On 30 July 1849, he died, aged only thirty-five.

'The parish had prepared a crypt of stone for him . . . Oh, never will the deep-throated sound of those bells quit my ear; never will I forget the gloomily surging melody of the hymn "Jesus, My Consolation"! Through the empty spaces of the church the sounds of the organ roared,' wrote the thirteen-year-old Nietzsche in a memoir of his childhood.[12]

'At that time, I once dreamt that I heard organ music in the church, the music I had heard during my father's funeral. When I perceived what lay behind these sounds, a gravemound suddenly opened and my father, wrapped in a linen shroud, emerged from it. He hurried into the church and returned a moment later with a child in his arms. The tomb yawned again, he entered it, and the cover closed over the opening. The stertorous sounds of the organ ceased instantly, and I woke. On the day that followed this night, Little Joseph suddenly fell ill, seized by severe cramps, and after a few hours he died. Our grief knew no bounds. My dream had been fulfilled completely. The tiny corpse was laid to rest in his father's arms.'[13]

The cause of Pastor Nietzsche's decline into death has been extensively investigated. Whether the pastor died insane is a question of considerable importance to posterity because Nietzsche himself suffered from symptoms similar to his father's, before he suddenly and dramatically went mad in 1888, when he was forty-four years old, remaining insane until his death in 1900. The considerable literature on the subject continues to grow but the first book, *Über das Pathologische bei Nietzsche*, was published in 1902, just two years after Nietzsche's death. Its author, Dr Paul Julius Möbius,[14] was a distinguished pioneering neurologist who had been specialising in hereditary nervous diseases from the 1870s onwards. Möbius was named by Freud as one of the fathers of psychotherapy and, importantly, he worked directly from Pastor Nietzsche's post-mortem report which revealed *Gehirnerweichung*, softening of the brain, a term commonly used in the nineteenth century for a variety of degenerative brain diseases.

The modern interpretation includes general degeneration, a brain tumour, tuberculoma of the brain or even slow bleeding into the brain caused by some head injury. Unlike his father, no post-mortem was performed on Nietzsche and so it was impossible for Möbius or any later investigators to produce anything like a post-mortem comparison of the two brains, but Möbius, looking wider, revealed a tendency to mental problems on the maternal side of the family. One uncle committed suicide, apparently preferring death to being shut up in the *Irrenhaus*, the lunatic asylum. On the paternal side, a number of Nietzsche's grandmother Erdmuthe's siblings were described as 'mentally abnormal'. One committed suicide and two others developed some sort of mental illness, one requiring psychiatric care.[15]

Before leaving this area of speculation altogether, the death of Nietzsche's baby brother must be touched upon. Joseph suffered from seizures before dying of a terminal stroke. One can come to no definite conclusion but there can be no doubt that the Nietzsche family was indeed affected by a strong tendency to mental or neurological instability.

Karl Ludwig Nietzsche was thirty-five when he died. Franziska was twenty-three, Nietzsche was four and Elisabeth three. The family was required to move out of the parsonage to make way for the new incumbent. Grandmother Erdmuthe decided to go back to Naumburg, where she had excellent connections. Her brother had been a preacher at the cathedral. She rented a ground-floor flat in Neugasse, a modest but respectable street of semi-detached houses. Erdmuthe took the front room for herself and installed Aunt Rosalie and Aunt Augusta in the room next door.

Franziska had a widow's pension of ninety thalers a year, plus eight per child. This was augmented by a small pension from the Altenburg Court but even taken together this was not sufficient for independence. She and the children were moved into the two worst rooms at the back of the house, where Nietzsche and his sister shared a bedroom.

'It was terrible for us to live in the city, after we had been living in the country for so long,' Nietzsche wrote; 'we avoided the gloomy streets and looked for the open spaces, like birds trying to escape from a cage . . . the huge churches and buildings of the market place, with its *Rathaus* [town hall] and fountain, the throngs of people to which I was unaccustomed . . . I was astonished by the fact that often these people did not know one another . . . among the most disturbing things to me were the long paved streets.'[16]

With a population of fifteen thousand, Naumburg was indeed an intimidating place for the children from the tiny hamlet of Röcken. Nowadays we know Naumburg as picture-book romantic, an illumination taken from a medieval Book of Hours, a cluster of pale towers rising from a meander in the River Saale, but when the Nietzsche family took up residence the Saale was no play-moat but a real defensive tool bristling with fortifications.

Two years before the family had come to live in Naumburg, the revolutions of 1848–9 had convulsed Europe in spasms of libertarian uprisings that had been abhorred by Nietzsche's dying monarchist father. Richard Wagner, on the other hand, had wholeheartedly supported the revolutionary era, which he expected to bring about a complete rebirth of art, society and religion. Wagner fought beside the Russian anarchist Mikhail Bakunin at the barricades in the Dresden uprising of May 1849. He financed the rebels' supply of hand grenades. When this was discovered he was exiled, which explains why he was living in Switzerland when the meeting with Nietzsche took place.

The Germany of the 1850s was the Germany of the Bund (1815–66), the confederation of states formed when the map of Europe was redrawn at the Congress of Vienna, following Napoleon's defeat. The Bund comprised thirty-nine autonomous German states governed by Princes, Dukes, Bishops, Electors and so on. This fragmentation into small, and small-minded, states meant that there was no national army, no common tax structure, no overarching economic policy and no real political authority. Despot jockeyed against despot, too short-sighted to see the advantages of unification. As an additional complication, the Bund also contained Czechs in Bohemia, Danes in Holstein and Italians in the Tyrol. Hanover was governed by the King of England until 1837, Holstein by the King of Denmark and Luxembourg was under the Dutch King. In 1815, when the Deutscher Bund was formed, Austria had been the dominant member of the confederation but as the century progressed and Austrian Chancellor Metternich's power waned, the large, mineral-rich state of Prussia became increasingly prosperous and bellicose under Chancellor Otto von Bismarck.

The city of Naumburg, in the province of Saxony, belonged to the King of Prussia. The fortress character of the city that Nietzsche remembers is not only down to frictions within the Bund but also from the days when it was threatened by France. Five heavy gates sealed the town at night. Only by dint of ringing loudly and presenting the night watch with a bribe could a citizen be readmitted. Nietzsche and his sister enjoyed expeditions in 'the fair mountains, river valleys, halls and castles' round about but they had to listen for the Watch Bell (which later he put into *Zarathustra* as 'the bell which has seen more than any man, which counted the painful heartbeats of our fathers'[17]) lest they experience the Hansel and Gretel horror of spending the night shut out.

Round Naumburg pressed the black Thüringer Wald, the Thuringian forest: Germany's ur-forest with its tombs of ancient heroes, dragon caves, dolmens and dark abysses that from the earliest days of German myths symbolised the irrationality and uncontrollability of the German subconscious. Wagner would appropriate it for Wotan's mental journey towards embracing chaos, resulting in the destruction of the old order through the death of the gods and the cancellation of all the old contracts. Nietzsche would characterise it first as daemonic and later as Dionysian.

Nothing could be more Apollonian, more necessary and logical, than the city of Naumburg itself. Down the River Saale flowed reason, prosperity and an impulse towards romantic conservatism. It had begun as a trading centre, a vital place of peace between ancient warring tribes. Over the years, this had developed into a medieval centre for German crafts and guild trade. Since the founding of the cathedral in 1028, Church and State had grown together harmoniously and reasonably throughout the centuries, particularly the Protestant centuries, so that when Nietzsche came to live in Naumburg it was a grand city of bourgeois solidity, a place of clean living. Its twin architectural marvels in the shape of the cathedral and the equally magnificent town hall demonstrated how prosperously Church and State could flourish if religious and civic virtue were allowed to become indistinguishable through harmonious cooperation within a materially comfortable, backward-looking society.

During the time that Grandmother Erdmuthe had been growing up in Naumburg, its religious circle had been governed by the plain Lutheran ideals of duty, modesty, simplicity and restraint, but her return to the city coincided with the Awakening movement, which valued fervency and sublime revelation over rational belief. People declared themselves born again. They denounced themselves in public as desperate sinners. This new-fangled behaviour did not suit the Nietzsche ladies, and while there was not the smallest deviation from the intention that Friedrich was to follow his father and his grandfather into the Church, there was no question of the family becoming part of such an unbuttoned ecclesiastical circle. Instead, they found their friends among the wives of Court functionaries and the wives of Justices of the High Court, a wealthy and powerful section of provincial society untroubled by new ideas.

Within the slow momentum of a conservative society moving at a slug-like pace, the two clergymen's widows Erdmuthe and Franziska, with their settled, though not particularly prosperous circumstances, fitted acceptably into the position of gentlewomen who could be useful to the establishment old guard, in exchange for discreet patronage. Nietzsche was far from chafing at priggish convention, a fact he ruefully acknowledges when he describes his childish Naumburg self as always behaving with the dignity of a thorough little philistine. But if the account he wrote describing the King's visit to Naumburg when he was ten years old shows no precocity of political thought, it certainly shows precocious literary talent:

'Our dear King honoured Naumburg with a visit. Great preparations were made for the occasion. All the school children were decked with black-and-white favours and stood in the market place from eleven o'clock in the morning awaiting the arrival of the Father of his People. Gradually the sky became overcast, rain poured down on us all – the King would not come! Twelve o'clock struck – the King did not come. Many of the children began to feel hungry. A fresh downpour occurred, all the streets were covered with mud; one o'clock struck – the impatience grew intense. Suddenly, about two o'clock, the bells began to ring and the sky smiled through its tears upon the joyously swaying crowd. Then we heard the rattle of the carriage; a boisterous cheer burst through the city; we waved our caps in exultation and roared at the tops of our voices. A fresh breeze set flying the myriad flags which hung from the roofs, all the bells of the town rang out and the vast crowd shouted, raved, and literally pushed the carriage in the direction of the cathedral. In the recesses of the sacred edifice a bevy of little girls in white dresses with garlands of flowers on their heads were arranged in the form of a pyramid. Here the King alighted . . .'[18]

In the same year, 1854, Nietzsche became passionately interested in the Crimean War. For centuries, the strategically important Crimean peninsula sticking out into the Black Sea had been a bone of contention between Russia and Turkey. It was currently in Russia's possession and now the troops of Tsar Nicholas I were fighting the forces of the Ottoman Empire and its allies, England and France. It was the first war to be covered by photographers. Thanks to the electric telegraph, reports were received from the front almost as they happened. Nietzsche and his school friends Wilhelm Pinder and Gustav Krug followed the campaigns avidly. Their pocket money went on lead soldiers, they pored over maps and built models of the battlefields, they shaped a pool to represent the harbour of Sebastopol and they made navies of paper boats. To simulate bombardments, they rolled pellets of wax and saltpetre, set them alight and threw them onto their models. It was tremendously exciting to see the fiery balls whizz through the air, hit a target and start a blaze. But one day, Gustav turned up at the toy battlefield with a long face. Sebastopol had fallen, he told them; the war was over. The furious boys vented their rage on their model Crimea, and the game was abandoned, but it was not long before they took up fighting the Trojan Wars instead.

Graecophilia was then running high in Germany, whose numerous little states were imagining a future and a greatness for themselves similar to the ancient Greek city-states. 'We became such passionate little Greeks,' Elisabeth wrote, 'that we threw lances and discs (wooden plates), practised the high jump and ran races.' Nietzsche wrote two plays, *The Gods on Olympus* and *The Taking of Troy*, which he performed before his family, persuading his playmates Wilhelm Pinder, Gustav Krug and his sister Elisabeth to take the other parts.

His mother had taught him to read and write when he was five years old. Boys' education started when they were six and in 1850 he was put into the Municipal School, attended by the children of the poor. His status-conscious sister Elisabeth states in her biography of her brother that this was because Grandmother Erdmuthe had a theory that 'Up to the age of eight or ten all children, even of very different social positions should be taught together; the children who came from the higher classes would thus acquire a better understanding of the attitude of mind peculiar to the lower orders.'[19] But this, according to their mother, was nonsense. He was there because they were poor.

Nietzsche's precocity, his solemnity, his precision of thought and utterance, together with his extremely myopic eyes which were constantly foundering in their effort to focus on physical objects, placed him firmly outside the pack. He was nicknamed 'the little Minister', and teased.

At Easter 1854, when he was nine, he was transferred to a school with the laborious title 'Institute with the Goal of a Thorough Preparation for the Gymnasium and other Higher Learning Institutions', a private crammer attended by the collective brood of sons of his own aspirational class. He felt much more comfortable here socially but the school was plainly overselling on its longwinded academic promises. At the age of ten he, together with Wilhelm Pinder and Gustav Krug, moved to the *Dom Gymnasium*, the cathedral school. Here he had to work so hard to make up for lost time that his studies permitted him no more than five or six hours' sleep a night. His descriptions of this time, like many other self-analytical passages, characteristically hark back to the death of his father. Again and again in Nietzsche's autobiographical accounts, whether he is writing as a child or even in the very last year of his sane life, he returns to the death of his father.

'By the time we went to Naumburg, my character began to show itself. I had already experienced considerable sadness and grief in my young life, and was therefore not as carefree and wild as children usually are. My schoolmates were accustomed to teasing me on account of my seriousness. This happened not only in the public school but also later at the institute and in my secondary school. From childhood on, I sought solitude, and I felt best whenever I could give myself over to myself undisturbed. And this was usually in the open-air temple of nature, which was my true joy. Thunder storms always made the most powerful impression on me: the thunder rolling in from afar and the lightning bolts flashing only increased my fear of the Lord.'[20]

During his four years at the *Dom Gymnasium* he distinguished himself in the subjects that interested him: German versification, Hebrew, Latin and eventually Greek, which at first he had found very difficult. Mathematics bored him. In his spare time he began a novel entitled *Death and Destruction*, composed numerous pieces of music, wrote at least forty-six poems and took lessons in the noble art of fencing that was so unsuited to his physical make-up but necessary to a position in society.

'I wrote poems and tragedies, blood-curdling and unbelievably boring, tormented myself with the composition of orchestral scores, and had grown so obsessed with the idea of appropriating universal knowledge and universal capability that I was in danger of becoming a complete muddle-head and fantasist.'[21]

But here the fourteen-year-old underestimates himself as he sums up his life to date, for he continues in that same piece of writing with a sharply critical analysis of his own poetry which he had started to write in his ninth year. The critique of his own juvenilia goes on interestingly to foretell the mood of Symbolist poetry, which he could not possibly have known about as it was just starting to be written in Paris by Baudelaire.

'I tried to express myself in more ornate and striking language. Unfortunately this attempt at gracefulness degenerated into affectation, and the iridescent language into sententious obscurity while every one of my poems lacked the chief thing of all – ideas . . . A poem which is empty of ideas and overladen with phrases and metaphors is like a rosy apple in the core of which a maggot lies hid . . . In the writing of any work one must pay the greatest attention to the ideas themselves. One can forgive any fault of style, but not a fault of thought. Youth, which lacks original ideas, naturally seeks to conceal this void beneath a brilliant and iridescent style; but does not poetry resemble modern music in this respect? It is on these lines that the poetry of the future will soon develop. Poets will express themselves in the strangest imagery, confused thoughts will be propounded with obscure but exceedingly high-falutin' and euphonious arguments. In short, works resembling the second part of *Faust* will be written, save that the ideas of this production will be entirely lacking. *Dixi.*'[22]

His quest to appropriate universal knowledge and universal capability was undoubtedly inspired by the example of Faust, as well as by polymaths like Goethe and Alexander von Humboldt. Like them, he studied natural history.

'Lizzie,' he said one day to his sister when he was nine years old, 'don't talk such rubbish about the stork. Man is a mammal, and brings his young into the world alive.'[23]

His natural history book had also taught him that 'The llama is a remarkable animal; it willingly carries the heaviest burdens, but when a llama does not want to go on, it turns its head round and discharges its saliva, which has an unpleasant odour, into the rider's face. If coerced or treated badly, it refuses to take any nourishment and lies down in the dust to die.' He felt that this description suited his sister Elisabeth completely, and for the rest of his life, both in letters and in conversation, he addressed her as 'Llama' or sometimes 'faithful Llama'. For her part, Elisabeth adored the intimate nickname and quoted its origin at every opportunity, though she omitted the bit about spitting malodorous saliva.

Gustav Krug's father owned 'a wonderful grand piano' that exercised a fascination over Nietzsche. Franziska bought a piano for him and taught herself to play so that she could teach him. Krug was a close friend of the composer Felix Mendelssohn. Whatever distinguished musicians were in town would collect in his house to play. Music floated out through the windows onto the street, where Nietzsche could stand and listen for as long as he liked. And so, as a boy, he became acquainted with the Romantic music of the time, the music that Wagner was rebelling against. These through-the-window-concerts raised Beethoven up to become Nietzsche's first musical hero but it was Handel who inspired him to his first musical composition. When he was nine years old, he composed an oratorio inspired by hearing Handel's 'Hallelujah Chorus'. 'I thought it was like an angelic song of jubilation, and that it was to this sound that Jesus ascended. I immediately resolved to compose something similar.'

Much of his childhood music survives, thanks to his mother and sister who preserved every scrap from the pen of their idolised boy. The purpose of his musical compositions was to express the passionate love of God that permeated the emotionally intense household, a love that could not be untwined from the morbid memory of his father whose spirit, they believed, watched over them. This was inseparable from the expectation that he himself would become 'just my father once again, and, as it were, a continuation of his life after his all-too-early death'.[24]

His women doted on him; he was everything to them. Elisabeth was extremely intelligent but, being a girl, her education was not a matter of scholarship but of learning accomplishments. She was taught reading and writing, a little arithmetic, enough French to be polite, dancing, drawing and a great deal of deportment. Every submission of the feminine to the superior sex caused her and her mother to rejoice in their inferiority. And he repaid them with becoming the superior little man they wished him to be. At home, if not at school, he had a high sense of his own importance. When Elisabeth was not 'the Llama' or 'the faithful Llama', she was 'the little girl' whom it was his duty to defend and protect. When he went walking with his mother or his sister he would walk five paces in front, to shield them from 'perils' such as mud or puddles, and from 'monsters' such as horses and dogs, of which they purported to be frightened.

The reports from the *Dom Gymnasium* showed that he was a diligent scholar. His mother had no doubt he had the capacity to fulfil her dreams and ambitions to follow his father into the Church. His devotion to theology made for excellent marks in the subject. Aged twelve and fervently religious, he beheld a vision of God in all His glory. It decided him to dedicate his life to God.

'In everything,' he wrote, 'God has safely led me as a father leads his weak little child . . . I have firmly resolved within me to dedicate myself forever to His service. May the dear Lord give me strength and power to carry out my intention and protect me on my life's way. Like a child I trust in His grace: He will preserve us all, that no misfortune may befall us. But His holy will be done! All He gives I will joyfully accept: happiness and unhappiness, poverty and wealth, and boldly look even death in the face, which shall one day unite us all in eternal joy and bliss. Yes, dear Lord, let Thy face shine upon us forever! Amen!'[25]

But even in the grip of this rather conventional religious enthusiasm he was concealing an extraordinary heresy in his private thoughts.

It is a basic tenet of the Christian faith that the Holy Trinity consists of God the Father, God the Son (Jesus Christ) and God the Holy Spirit. But twelve-year-old Nietzsche could not stand the irrationality of this construction. His reasoning pushed up a different Holy Trinity.

'When I was twelve years old I conjured up for myself a marvellous trinity: God the Father, God the Son, and God the Devil. My deduction was that God, thinking himself, created the second person of the godhead, but that to be able to think himself he had to think his opposite, and thus had to create it. – That is how I began to philosophise.'[26]

2

· OUR GERMAN ATHENS ·

> One repays a teacher badly if one remains only a pupil.
> *Ecce Homo*, Foreword, Section 4

When Nietzsche was eleven, his grandmother died, and at last his mother was free to set up her own household. After a few false starts, in 1858 Franziska and the two children settled in a corner house on Weingarten, a respectable, unremarkable Naumburg street. Nietzsche now had his own bedroom. He quickly fell into the habit of working till around midnight and getting up at five in the morning to resume. It was the beginning of a lifetime of what he called *selbstüberwindung*, self-overcoming, an important principle that he would develop further metaphysically, but for now what he was overcoming was devastatingly bad health. Harrowing episodes of headaches with vomiting and extreme eye ache might last as long as a whole week during which he had to lie in a darkened room with the curtains drawn. The slightest light hurt his eyes. Reading, writing and even sustained coherent thought were out of the question. Between Easter 1854 and Easter 1855, for example, he was absent from school for six weeks and five days. When he was in health, he pressed what he called 'the lofty majesty of the will' to push himself ahead of his classmates. Naumburg's *Dom Gymnasium* was no educational backwater but Nietzsche harboured the tremendous ambition somehow to attend Schulpforta, the foremost classical school in the German Bund.

'Pforta, Pforta, I dream only of Pforta,' he wrote when he was ten years old. Pforta was the insiders' slang for Schulpforta and his presumptuous use of the nickname conveys the depth of his yearning.

Pforta educated two hundred boys between the ages of fourteen and twenty, favouring boys whose fathers, like Nietzsche's, had died in the service of the Prussian Church or State. The entry selection process was not unlike the Prince's envoys travelling the length and breadth of the land looking to see whose foot would fit Cinderella's slipper. They arrived in Naumburg when Nietzsche was thirteen and were sufficiently impressed, despite his shaky maths, to offer him a place the following autumn.

'I, the poor Llama,' wrote Elisabeth with her customary drama, 'felt myself exceedingly badly used by Fate. I refused to take any food, and laid myself down in the dust to die.' Her decline was not due to envying her brother his first-class educational prospects but lamenting that he would be away from home for months at a time. Nietzsche himself was not without apprehension. As the day approached, his mother reported pillowcases wet with tears but during the daytime he maintained a masculine bravado.

'It was a Tuesday morning when I drove out through Naumburg's city gates . . . the terrors of a fraught night besieged me still, and the future ahead of me lay wrapped in an ominous grey veil. For the very first time I was to leave my parental home for a long, long period . . . My farewell had left me forlorn; I trembled at the thought of my future . . . the thought that from now on I could never give myself over to my own thoughts, that my schoolmates would drag me away from my most beloved preoccupations – this thought oppressed me terribly . . . every minute became more terrifying to me; indeed as I saw Pforta shimmering in the distance, it looked more like a prison house than an alma mater . . . Then my heart overflowed with holy sensations. I was lifted up to God in silent prayer, and a profound tranquillity came over my spirit. Yea, Lord, bless my entry and protect me too, in body and in spirit, in this nursery of the Holy Spirit. Send your angel, that he may lead me victorious through the battles I go to fight . . . this I beseech Thee, O Lord! Amen.'¹

Pforta's prison-like appearance was due to its origin as a Cistercian monastery. Occupying a secluded valley on a branch of the River Saale about four miles south of Naumburg, it was surrounded by walls twelve foot high and two and a half foot thick, enclosing seventy productive acres drizzled with the usual monastic accessories: carp pond, brew house, vineyard, hay meadows, arable fields and pasture, barns, dairy, stables, smithy, stone cloisters and any number of magnificent Gothic buildings. Like a blown-up version of his childhood home at Röcken, Pforta was an ecclesiastical fortress designed to withstand political buffetings, the most important of which, for Pforta, had been the religious wars of the 1500s and 1600s. When the struggle ceased and Roman Catholicism was flung out, the Prince-Elector of Saxony who had supported Martin Luther declared Pforta a *Prinzenschule*. It was one of the important Latin schools established in 1528 by Schwarzerd,[2] who had assisted Luther in translating the Old Testament into German. Schwarzerd added the teaching of Hebrew to the Latin and Greek that was already the basis for higher education, thus enabling scholars to read the great Hebrew texts first-hand rather than in translations that were so often politically or theologically skewed, a bold step against centuries of Church censorship, giving every scholar the means of independent analysis.

By the time Nietzsche entered the educational system it had been modified slightly by Wilhelm von Humboldt,[3] brother of the famous explorer, geographer and scientist Alexander. A friend of Schiller and Goethe, von Humboldt had been influenced politically by arriving in Paris shortly after the storming of the Bastille. 'I am now rather tired of Paris and France,' he wrote with surprising maturity for a young man of twenty-two, and concluded level-headedly that he was witnessing the necessary labour pains towards a new rationality. 'Mankind has suffered from an extreme and is obliged to seek salvation in another extreme.'

In charge of the reordering of German education between 1809 and 1812, von Humboldt combined exemplary rationality concerning contemporary events with first-hand experience of the classical heritage during a stint as Prussia's Ambassador to the Holy See. He envisioned a future for the German Bund modelled on the structure of ancient Greece: a system of small states existing diversely and creatively within artistic and intellectual unity. His theory is outlined in *Ideas Towards an Attempt to Determine the Limits of State Action*, a book that influenced

John Stuart Mill's *On Liberty*. Von Humboldt's guiding principle was that maximum freedom in education and religion should exist within a minimal State. Within that State the individual was everything, *ergo* education was everything. The final goal of education was 'a complete training for the human personality . . . the highest and most proportional development of the individual's powers to a complete and consistent whole'.[4] This complete and consistent whole combined two peculiarly German ideals: *Wissenschaft* and *Bildung*. *Wissenschaft* was the idea of learning as a dynamic process constantly renewed and enriched by scientific research and independent thought, so that each student contributed to the endlessly advancing sum of knowledge. It was the very opposite of learning by rote. Knowledge was evolutionary, and with it came *Bildung*, the evolution of the scholar himself: a process of spiritual growth through the acquisition of knowledge which von Humboldt described as an harmonious interaction between the student's own personality and nature, resulting in a state of inner freedom and wholeness within the greater context.

The question of wholeness and social morality was addressing the urgent contemporary problem of religious faith, as scientific progress wobbled the age-old certainties. Whatever stage the school pupil or university student had reached on the journey between Darwin and doubt, there was no denying the almost divine sanction bestowed on life by the canon of Western knowledge, from which a consistent version of truth, beauty, intellectual clarity and purpose had flowed through the centuries, regardless of what god was being worshipped at the time.

The sustaining force underlying civilisation was language, without which probably we cannot think and certainly we cannot communicate complicated ideas. Von Humboldt was himself a philologist and a philosopher of language. At Pforta, as at the other schools and universities under von Humboldt's reform, the highest disciplines were classical languages and classical philology, arts of scrupulous, backward-looking precision. Philologists were gods of impossibly small things, 'narrow-minded, frog-blooded micrologists' Nietzsche once called them,[5] and classical philologists were the gods of the education system, delving into Greek, Hebrew and Latin linguistics.

The Rector of Nietzsche's day described Pforta as a school-state: Athens in the morning, Sparta in the afternoon. It was a semi-monastic, semi-military regime, tough both mentally and physically. Nietzsche, who when he was at home had so treasured his own bedroom in which he could work to his own timetable, now slept in a dormitory of thirty boys. The day began at four in the morning with a simultaneous click of the unlocking of the dormitory doors that had been locked at precisely nine o'clock the night before (the parallel one can think of today is the loud, simultaneous clicking of the doors in the Bayreuth Opera House imprisoning the audience at the start of the performance and releasing them at the end). One hundred and eighty boys released, they rushed towards fifteen basins and a communal trough into which to spit after brushing their teeth. The day continued as Nietzsche set it down:

5.25	Morning prayers. Warm milk and bread rolls.
6.0	Lesson.
7–8	Study.
8–10	Lesson.
10–11	Study.
11–12	Lesson.
12	Collect table napkins and march into refectory. Roll call. Latin Grace before and after midday meal. Forty minutes free time.
1.45–3.50	Lesson.
3.50	Bread roll and butter, bacon dripping or plum jam.
4.0–5.0	Senior boys test junior boys on Greek dictation or mathematical problem.
5.0–7.0	Study.
7.0	March into refectory for supper.
7.30–8.30	Play in the garden.

8.30   Evening prayers.
9.0   Bedtime.
4. a.m.   The unlocking of the doors. A new day.

It was the most rigorous school day in Europe, as Madame de Staël approvingly observed; 'What is called study in Germany is truly admirable, fifteen hours a day of solitude and labour for years on end seem to them a normal mode of existence.'[6]

At first, Nietzsche was overwhelmingly homesick. 'The wind blew fitfully through the high trees, their branches groaned and swayed. My heart was in a similar condition.'[7] He confided in his tutor, Professor Buddensieg, who advised losing himself in his work and if that did not help he must simply throw himself upon the mercy of God.

He could see his mother and his sister once a week but only for a tantalisingly short period of time on Sundays after the school had been marched to and from church. Then he would hasten northward on the road winding between high, dark fir woods and leading to the village of Almrich. Meanwhile Franziska and Elisabeth would be scurrying southward towards him on the road from Naumburg. The family would have an hour together over a drink at the Almrich inn before he had to hurry back. Otherwise the Pforta boys' freedom consisted of the evening hour between seven thirty and eight thirty in the garden where scholarly debates in Greek or Latin over a gentle game such as bowls might develop into verbal duels fought in improvised Latin hexameters.

The boys were encouraged to speak to each other in Latin and Greek at all times. Nietzsche typically took things further, setting himself to think in Latin, and he probably succeeded because he did not complain of failing. They were not allowed newspapers. Politics, the outside world and the present were excluded as far as possible. The main body of the curriculum consisted of the literature, history and philosophy of ancient Greece and Rome and the German classics such as Goethe and Schiller. While excelling at these, he struggled with Hebrew, which he needed to take up Holy Orders; he found its grammar peculiarly difficult. He would never master English and, while he loved Shakespeare and Byron, particularly *Manfred*, he read both authors in German translation. The boys had eleven hours of Latin lessons a week, and six of Greek. He was an excellent student; sometimes, but not always, top of the class at the end of the school year. His average was regularly dragged down by paltry marks for mathematics, in which his interest remained faint, apart from a brief period when he became fascinated by the properties of the circle.

Sometimes the boys were taken on outings into the countryside. Then they dressed up in sports uniforms designed by Friedrich Ludwig Jahn, the rabid nationalist and father of the gymnastics movement, which was meant to foster a military *esprit de corps* among young men, whose coordinated wholesomeness would make a fine foundation for the emergent nation. Jahn coined the famous four Fs: *Frisch, fromm, fröhlich, frei* (brisk, devout, joyful, free), in which spirit expeditions were undertaken in military style. The boys were lined up to conquer the mountains with a marching band, singing, cheering, waving the school flag and giving three cheers for the King (now mad following a stroke), the Prince of Prussia and the school, before marching back home.

Swimming instruction was equally structured:

'The swimming trip finally took place yesterday. It was terrific. We lined up in rows and played cheering music as we marched through the gates. We all wore our red swim caps, which made a very pretty sight. But we young swimmers were very surprised when we were taken a long stretch down the river Saale to begin our swim, and all of us were afraid. However, when we saw the big swimmers approaching from a distance, and heard the music, we all jumped into the river. We swam in the very same order in which we had marched from school. In general, things went quite well; I tried my very best; but I was always in over my head. I also swam a lot on my back. When we finally got there, we were given our clothes, which had been brought along in a boat. We dressed in a hurry and marched in the very same order back to Pforta. It was really terrific!'[8]

Remarkably, in the light of such a beginning, swimming was to become a lifelong recreational delight. Not so acrobatics, which he undertook in a spirit of humorous desperation. His school friend Paul Deussen described his only acrobatic trick, to which he jokingly attributed great importance. It consisted in pushing his body legs-first between parallel bars and coming down on the other side. What other schoolmates accomplished in minutes, sometimes without even touching the poles, was hard work for Nietzsche, turning his face dark red, making him breathless and sweaty.[9]

Sweaty, unathletic, awkward, over-clever, Nietzsche was not universally popular. One of his classmates cut up a photograph of him and made it into a puppet that said and did ridiculous things but it was a characteristic of Nietzsche's personality that his vulnerability would always throw up devoted friends who took it upon themselves to protect him from the blows and buffets of an unkind world. His little circle of Pforta friends saw to it that the mocking marionette disappeared without its original being any the wiser.

His passion for music continued. He joined the school choir, which gave endless opportunities for group joy and military marching, but it is within this discipline of music that we can trace more easily than in his other school subjects – all based on the idea of self-realisation through submission to the group ethic – that he was succeeding in hanging onto the freedom of thought he had been so concerned he might lose when he was about to join Pforta. His teachers and fellow-pupils greatly admired his straightforward conventional skills on the piano and his proficiency at sight-reading, which was outstanding, but it was his dazzling keyboard improvisations that astounded them. While his father had been alive, people had journeyed far to hear him play. Now Nietzsche's schoolmates admired the same gift in him. When he embarked on one of his long, impassioned, free-flowing streams of melodic invention, they would cluster round the stocky boy with the thick spectacles and eccentrically long, swept-back hair, plumped ungracefully on the piano stool. Even those who found him insufferable were mesmerised by his virtuosity, as by a stage magician.

Stormy weather brought out the strongest inspiration in him and when thunder was rolling around, his friend Carl von Gersdorff thought that even Beethoven would have failed to reach such improvisational heights.

His religious devotion remained passionate and he did not swerve from the idea that he would follow his father into the Church. His confirmation took place in a maelstrom of religious fervour.

Confirmation day on Laetare Sunday of the year 1861 set a new bond between him and Paul Deussen, the school friend who had described Nietzsche's acrobatics. The confirmands walked to the altar in pairs to receive the consecration on their knees. Deussen and Nietzsche knelt side by side. They were filled with a holy, ecstatic mood and declared themselves quite ready to die immediately for Christ.

When the high-octane religious rapture subsided, it gave way to the same impartial examination of Christian texts that Nietzsche was used to apply to his Greek or Roman studies. He expressed his ideas in a couple of long essays entitled *Fate and History* and *Freedom of Will and Fate*, both showing his interest in the contemporary American thinker Ralph Waldo Emerson, who wrote extensively on the problem of free will and fate. Nietzsche concluded *Freedom of Will and Fate* neatly with one of his earliest aphorisms: 'Absolute freedom of will would make man into a god; the fatalistic principle would make him into an automaton.' He sets the same thought out rather more fully in *Fate and History*: 'Free will without fate is just as unthinkable as spirit without reality, good without evil . . . Only antithesis creates the quality . . . There will be great revolutions once the masses finally realise that the totality of Christianity is grounded in presuppositions: the existence of God, immortality, Biblical authority, inspiration and other doctrines that will always be problematic . . . we scarcely know whether humanity itself is but a stage or period in universal history, or . . . Is the human being perhaps no more than the development of stone through plant or animal? . . . Has this eternal becoming no end?'

Darwin's heretical theory of evolution leaps out in this speculation but for Nietzsche these thoughts were inspired by his reading of three thinkers who would preoccupy his creative thought for many years: Emerson, the Greek philosopher-poet Empedocles, and the German philosopher-poet Friedrich Hölderlin.

In 1861, he wrote a school essay entitled 'Letter to my friend, in which I recommend to him my favourite poet'. The favourite poet was Friedrich Hölderlin, who was then neglected and virtually unknown, though now he sits high in the pantheon of German literature. Nietzsche was given a low grade for the essay and advised by his teacher to 'stick to poets who are healthier, more lucid and more German'.[10] In fact, Hölderlin could hardly have been more thoroughly German but he did heartily dislike *über alles* nationalism. It was an attitude shared by seventeen-year-old Nietzsche and his essay points out that Hölderlin 'tells the Germans bitter truths which are, unfortunately, only too firmly grounded . . . Hölderlin flings sharp and cutting words at German barbarism. Yet this abhorrence of reality is compatible with the greatest love of his country, and this love Hölderlin did have in high degree. But he hated in Germans the mere specialist, the philistine.'[11]

Nietzsche's teachers disliked Hölderlin for what they regarded as his mental and moral unhealthiness. Hölderlin lost his mind towards the end of his life and this made him an unhealthy choice of subject matter. Combined with Nietzsche's delight in questioning the authority of reason, his teachers suspected in the boy a dangerous pessimism that was completely antithetical to Pforta's three guiding principles of *Wissenschaft*, *Bildung* and Lutheranism. Those three sacred principles ought to have provided adequate defence against any young Pforta student such as Nietzsche being attracted to the soul-shaking, godforsaken internal territory that Hölderlin explores:

'Oh, you wretches who feel all this, who, even as I, cannot allow yourselves to speak of man's being here for a purpose, who, even as I, are so utterly in the clutch of the Nothing that governs us, so profoundly aware that we are born for nothing, that we love a nothing, believe in nothing, work ourselves to death for nothing only that little by little we may pass over into nothing – how can I help it if your knees collapse when you think of it seriously? Many a time have I, too, sunk into these bottomless thoughts, and cried out; Why do you lay the axe to my root, pitiless spirit? – and still I am here.'[12]

During Hölderlin's last years he was occasionally, though erratically, capable of producing a startling insight, an oracular flash or a peculiarly disturbing phrase. He took up residence in a tower in Tübingen, where he became a tourist attraction, a stop on the Grand Tour of the Romantic age that loved nothing better than a ruinous tower full of owls inhabited by a human lightning rod for divine inspiration.

Nietzsche wrote that Hölderlin's 'grave of long madness', throughout which the poet's mind wrestled with the advancing night of insanity before finally expiring in dark mysterious funeral songs, ate into his own consciousness like the wave-beat of a troubled sea. His writing on Hölderlin reads hintingly as though he might already be almost half in love with the idea of surrendering his mind, if the consequence was the opening of the doors of revelation.

Hölderlin certainly did not strike the right note at Pforta. But despite his teacher's criticism and disapproval Nietzsche did not give up his interest in the poet.

Hölderlin had written a play about Empedocles (c.492–432 BC), and Nietzsche went on to do the same. According to legend, Empedocles ended his life by jumping into Mount Etna in the sure and certain expectation of emerging as a god, an expectation which brings to mind both Zarathustra emerging from the cave and Nietzsche losing his mind and believing himself translated into the god Dionysus. The theme of nascent godhood and god-touched insanity as a passport to godhood runs through the lives and thinking of Nietzsche, Hölderlin and Empedocles. By the age of seventeen, then, a pupil at the foremost German school devoted to the civilised cult of Olympic reason and clarity, Nietzsche was exploring the idea of emancipatory insanity and the validity of the irrational.

'To be alone, and without gods, this – this it is, is Death,' Hölderlin puts into Empedocles' mouth in the play and maybe in this we can trace the first whisper of the gigantic tragedy that Nietzsche would articulate in the death of God.

Little has survived of Empedocles' writings. The fragments that remain are shards of two epic philosophical poems, *On Nature* and *The Purifications*. *On Nature* is a beautiful creation poem reminiscent of Ovid's pastorals and of *Paradise Lost* but Empedocles was not merely a word-conjuror who reminds us of Ovid and Milton. He is important for being the first writer to name the four elements:

> Come! I will name the like-primeval Four,
> Whence rose to sight all things we now behold –
> Earth, many-billowed Sea, and the moist air,
> And Aether, the Titan, who binds the globe about.
> But come now, hear how 'twas the sundered fire
> Led life into the germs . . .[13]

Empedocles posits a universal round of things in which there is no creation and no annihilation. There is one form of matter which in its sum is unalterable and eternal, due to the mixing and unmixing of the two eternal, and eternally opposed, powers: Love and Hate. The tension between their opposition created the energy of the primal vortex, which Empedocles pictures as a Hieronymus Bosch-like nightmare whirlpool in which human body parts, 'heads, arms, eyes, roaming ghastly through space' are all looking for each other as they seek to become 'knit in all forms and wonderful to see'. Today these lines are interpreted as the first glimmering beginning of the theory of evolution.

From the fragmentary nature of Empedocles' literary survivals, Nietzsche learned brevity. He also learned how fragments free the mind to set off on endless journeys of speculation. It was to become an increasingly valuable power as the creative intervals between his bouts of illness became shorter, leaving him with the problem of how to communicate his thoughts speedily and to maximum effect before the next attack.

Another piece of work from this year following Nietzsche's confirmation is what he gleefully called his 'repulsive novelette'

Euphorion, a transgressive piece of teenage overwriting that flirts with sex and sin.

'When I wrote it, a burst of diabolical laughter exploded from me,' he boasts in a letter to a friend that he signs 'FWvNietzky (alias Muck) *homme étudié en lettres (votre ami sans lettres)*'.[14]

In the legend of Faust, Euphorion was the name given to the son born to Faust and Helen of Troy. In Nietzsche's Germany, Byron was popularly looked on as a modern-day Euphorion. So in writing in the first person as Euphorion, Nietzsche is striking a Faustian, as well as a Byronic, pose.

Only the first page of the novel survives. It opens with Euphorion in his study:

'"The crimson dawn plays in multichrome upon the sky, fizzling fireworks, how boring . . . Before me an inkwell in which to drown my black heart; a pair of scissors that I may grow accustomed to cutting my own throat: manuscripts for to wipe myself, and a chamber pot.

'"If only the Torturer will aim his micturition upon my grave – a Forget-me-not . . . methinks it is more pleasant to decompose in the moist earth than to vegetate under the blue sky, to scrabble as a fat worm is far sweeter than to be a human being – a walking question mark . . .

'"Across from me dwells a nun, whom I visit now and then in order to take joy in her excellent behaviour . . . Earlier, she was a nun, thin and fragile; I was her doctor and saw to it that she soon put on some weight. With her dwells her brother in common-law marriage; to me he seemed too fat and flourishing – I thinned him down – to a corpse . . ." At this point Euphorion leaned back a bit and moaned, for he suffered from a condition that affected the marrow of his spine.'[15]

Here, fortunately, ends the only surviving page of the manuscript.

There is another fragment that should not be omitted from the juvenilia. As a piece of writing it is usually regarded as a report on some sort of real experience, a vision or a sinister ghostly visitation, or even a preview of his insanity. As such, it is rightly treated as important but, given *Euphorion*, it might just as easily be another try-out in creepy experimental writing.

'What I am afraid of', he wrote, 'is not the terrible shape behind my chair but its voice; also not the words but the horribly unarticulated and inhuman tone of that shape. Yes, if only it spoke as human beings do.'[16]

At Pforta they were treating Nietzsche's ghastly episodes of chronic illness, his blinding headaches, suppurating ears, 'stomach catarrh', vomiting and nausea with humiliating remedies. He was put to bed in a darkened room with leeches fastened to his earlobes to suck blood from his head. Sometimes they were also applied to his neck. He hated the treatment. He felt it did him no good at all. Between 1859 and 1864 there are twenty entries in the sickness register lasting, on average, a week.

'I must learn to get used to it,' he wrote.

He was wearing smoked glasses to shield his sensitive eyes from the pain of light and there was not much cause for optimism from the school doctor, who predicted total blindness.

Spurred on by physical limitations and gloomy prognostications, he seized each productive moment. His appetite for work was prodigious. He added to his school workload by forming a literary brotherhood with his two childhood friends Gustav Krug and Wilhelm Pinder, who were still at the *Dom Gymnasium* in Naumburg, not having been selected for the Pforta elite. The three boys named their literary society 'Germania', probably in honour of Tacitus.[17] They held the inaugural meeting during the summer holidays of 1860, in a tower overlooking the Saale River. They swore many brotherly oaths and emptied a cheap bottle of red wine in toasts before flinging it down into the river below. Each swore to produce a piece of work every month: a poem or an essay, a musical composition or an architectural design. The others would then criticise it 'in a friendly spirit of mutual correction'.

Over three years, Nietzsche contributed some thirty-four pieces of work that varied from a Christmas Oratorio to 'Kriemhild's character according to the Nibelungen', to 'Concerning the Demoniacal Element in Music'. Nietzsche continued producing pieces of work long after the others had stopped. 'By what means may we be spurred to eager activity?' he wrote rather desperately in the Society's minutes of 1862.

The following year he became interested in a girl. Anna Redtel was the sister of a schoolmate. She had joined her brother on an outing to the mountains where she caught Nietzsche's eye by dancing prettily in a clearing. They danced together. She was a small, ethereal girl from Berlin, by all accounts charming, good-natured, cultured and musical. By her side, Nietzsche appeared big, broad-shouldered, vigorous, rather solemn and stiff. She played the piano well and their intimacy advanced on the piano stool as they played duets together. He sent her poems and he dedicated a musical rhapsody to her. When the time came for Anna to return to Berlin, he gave her a portfolio containing a number of his own compositions for piano. She thanked him in a graceful note and with that his first, gentle, introduction to love was over.

1864 was his last year at school. There was less extra-curricular activity. He must concentrate on producing an original and significant piece of work, a *Valediktionsarbeit*, in order to pass the *Abitur* exam, the entrance exam for university.

'So it came about that in the last years of my Schulpforta life I was working independently on two philological papers. In one, I aimed to give an account, from the sources (Jordanes, Edda, etc.), of the sagas of the East Gothic King Ermanarich, in their various ramifications; in the other, to sketch a special type of Greek tyrant, the Megarian . . . as I worked on it, it became a portrait of the Megarian Theognis.'[18]

Fewer than 1,400 lines survive by the sixth-century BC Greek poet Theognis of Megara. This gives Theognis something in common with Nietzsche's other subjects, Empedocles and Diogenes Laertius. It gave him great freedom. 'I have involved myself in a great deal of surmise and guesswork,' Nietzsche wrote of his work on Theognis, 'but I plan to complete the work with proper philological thoroughness, and as scientifically as I can.' Philological science and thoroughness did indeed triumph in *De Theognide Megarensi* (*On Theognis of Megara*). He wrote it in just a week at the start of the summer holiday. It comprised forty-two pages closely written in Latin and its brilliance astounded the philological pedagogues of Pforta. He ought to have devoted the rest of the summer holiday to mathematics but he couldn't be bothered and when he got back to school his exasperated maths teacher Professor Buchbinder wanted him to be refused the *Abitur*.

'As he has never shown any regular industry in mathematics, he has always gone backwards, so to speak, both in his written and in his oral work in this connection; so that he cannot even be called *satisfactory* in this subject,' scolded Buchbinder. But his grumbling was quashed by his fellow pedagogues, who asked, 'Perhaps you would like us to plough the most gifted pupil that Pforta has ever had?'[19]

'Got happily through,' cried Nietzsche on 4 September. 'Oh, the glorious days of freedom have come!' and he left Pforta in the school's customary flamboyant tradition, waving from the window of a garlanded carriage drawn by horses and attended by brightly uniformed postilions.

The school doctor's leaving report read: 'Nietzsche is a robust, compact human being with a noticeably fixed look in his eyes, short-sighted and often troubled by shifting headache. His father died young, of brain-softening, and was born to elderly parents; the son was born at a time when the father was already unwell. No bad symptoms yet, but the antecedents should be taken into account.'

Nietzsche's valedictory comment on Pforta was hardly more flattering:

'I lived a secret cult of certain arts . . . I rescued my private inclinations and endeavours from the uniform law; I tried to break the rigidity of schedules and timetables laid down by rules, by indulging an overexcited passion for universal knowledge and enjoyment . . . What I wanted was some counterweight to my changeable and restless inclinations, a science which could be pursued with cool impartiality, with cold logic, with regular work, without its results touching me at all deeply . . . How well taught but how badly educated such a student from a princely foundation is.'[20]

3

· BECOME WHAT YOU ARE ·

There are a hundred ways to listen to your conscience . . . But that
you feel something to be right may have its cause in your never having
thought much about yourself and having blindly accepted what has
been labelled *right* since your childhood.

The Gay Science, Section 335

Nietzsche was to call 1864 his wasted year. In October he enrolled as a
student at the University of Bonn. Playing the dutiful son, he entered
the theological faculty, though his greater interest was in classical
philology. His choice of Bonn had been decided by two celebrated
classical philologists on the teaching staff, Friedrich Ritschl and Otto
Jahn. He found the theology course boring and he missed his mother
and his sister. Bonn was some three hundred miles from Naumburg.
For the first time in his life, they were not within walking distance.
But even while missing them he was able to put the distance between
them to good, if dishonest, use. They still believed that he intended to
join the Church and he failed to disabuse them.

He decided that his life up till now had been parochial. The way to
rectify his ignorance of the world was to join a *Burschenschaft*, a student
fraternity. It was a movement that became horribly tainted by later
association with the Hitler Youth. But when it was founded, in 1815,
its purpose was to give shared, liberal cultural values to the generation
of German students across the aggregation of the Bund, though the
federation kept such a tight curb on the intellectual activity of the
Burschenschaften, in case the societies turned political and subversive,
that they didn't do much more than go for mountain hikes, sing songs,
fight duels and drink beer. Nietzsche joined the exclusive Franconia
fraternity expecting learned discussions and parliamentary debate but

found himself, instead, raising his tankard and roaring out fraternity drinking songs. Striving to fit in, he muddled himself into what he described as a strange imbroglio of bewildering movement and feverish excitability.

'After bowing in all directions in the most courteous way possible, I introduce myself to you as a member of the German Students' Association named the Franconia,' he wrote to his dear Mamma and Llama. Even they must have grown weary of his many letters describing the Franconia's outings which invariably started with a marching parade, all done up in their fraternity sashes and caps and singing lustily. Marching behind a hussar band ('attracted great attention') they usually ended in becoming extraordinarily merry at an inn or the hovel of some peasant whose hospitality and strong drink they condescendingly accepted. An unlikely new friend appears: Gassmann, editor of the *Beer Journal*.

A duelling scar was an essential badge of honour and Nietzsche took an unconventional approach to acquiring one. When he felt his swordsmanship was up to it, he went for a delightful walk with a certain Herr D., who belonged to an association that was on duelling terms with the Franconia. Nietzsche was struck by what a pleasant adversary Herr D. would make. He said to him, 'You are a man after my own heart, could we not have a duel together? Let us waive all the usual preliminaries.' This was hardly in accordance with the duelling code but Herr D. agreed in the most obliging way. Paul Deussen acted as witness. He reported the glistening blades dancing around their unprotected heads for about three minutes, before Herr D.'s blade hit the bridge of Nietzsche's nose. Blood trickled; honour was satisfied. Deussen bandaged up his friend, bundled him into a carriage, took him home and put him to bed. A couple of days and he was fully recovered.[1]

The scar is so small you cannot see it in photographs but it was a cause of enormous satisfaction to Nietzsche. He had no inkling how Herr D.'s friends laughed when he told them the story.

The Franconians frequented the brothels of Cologne. Nietzsche visited the city in February 1865, engaging a guide to show him the cathedral and other famous sights. He asked to be taken to a restaurant and maybe the guide thought he was too shy to ask for what he really wanted because he took him to a brothel instead. 'Suddenly I found myself surrounded by half a dozen creatures in tinsel and gauze who gazed at me expectantly. For a moment I stood absolutely dumbfounded in front of them; then, as if driven by instinct I went to the piano as the only thing with a soul in the whole company and I struck one or two chords. The music quickened my limbs and in an instant I was out in the open.'[2]

This is all we know of the incident but it resounds down Nietzschean literature and legend. Some believe that he didn't just play a few chords on the piano and leave it at that, but lingered for the usual purpose whereupon he contracted syphilis, from which his later mental and physical health problems stemmed. One reason for this is that in 1889, after he had lost his mind and was in the asylum, he said that he had 'infected himself twice'. The doctors assumed he was talking about syphilis. Had they looked at his medical records, they would have discovered that he had gonorrhoea twice, a fact he admitted to doctors while still in his right mind.

Thomas Mann makes the brothel incident pivotal in his enormous novel *Doctor Faustus*, in which Mann retells the Faust legend, reimagining Nietzsche in the title role. Mann takes the night in the brothel as the night that Nietzsche/Faustus sells his soul to the devil for the woman he desires. She becomes his obsession and his succubus. In earlier versions of Faustus, Helen of Troy customarily takes this role but Mann bizarrely replaces Helen with Hans Christian Andersen's Little Mermaid, a poor creature who in order to consummate human love must undergo terrible tortures: her tongue is cut out as the price of turning her fishtail into a human cleft and each step she walks on human feet cuts her like sharp-edged swords. Maybe this tells us more about Mann than it does about Nietzsche.

During the two terms Nietzsche spent at Bonn, music and musical composition remained his great passion. He wrote a full-length parody of Offenbach's *Orpheus in the Underworld* which won him the nickname 'Gluck' among the Franconia fraternity. He visited Robert Schumann's grave to lay a wreath and he became so indebted by the purchase of a piano that he could not afford the journey home to his mother and sister at Christmas. Observing that his money always ran out fast, 'probably because it was so round',[3] he sent in his place a volume of eight of his musical compositions (very Schubertian at this stage) expensively bound in lavender morocco and accompanied by wearisomely detailed instructions as to how his dear Llama was to play and sing them: seriously, mournfully, with energy, with a little flourish, or sometimes with great passion. Even *in absentia* he did not relinquish control over his doting women.

The Easter following the brothel incident, he was at home and he refused to take the sacrament of communion in church. Easter is an occasion of obligation for practising Christians and this was no faint gesture but a cause of fundamental terror to Mamma and Llama, for whom Nietzsche's apostasy was negating what they felt was the only real goal of this life on earth: the eventual reunification of them all with beloved Pastor Nietzsche in Heaven.

Nietzsche was not yet suffering a full-blown loss of faith, but he was harbouring grave doubts. As he sat in his student study, a shrine to his dead father whose photograph stood on the piano beneath an oil painting of Christ's deposition from the Cross, he was reading a book by David Strauss, *The Life of Jesus Critically Examined*, and making a list of twenty-seven scientific books he intended to read.

Along with his whole generation he was negotiating the shaky ground between science and faith, a problem in need of a solution. It seemed to be moving towards transferring blind faith in God to equally blind faith in scientists, who claimed to have discovered the mysterious nature of matter in something called 'the biological force', which accounted for the amazing diversity of the natural world.

A contemporary encyclopaedia explained the formation of the universe in an account that was not dissimilar from Empedocles:

'An eternal rain of diverse corpuscles which fall in manifold motion, consume themselves in falling, creating a vortex,' existing within the ether, which was 'a luminiferous medium with the nature of an elastic solid medium filling all space, through which light and heat are transferred in waves'. Light 'could not be explained in any other way', though it remained a puzzle 'how the earth could move through the ether at the rate of nearly a million miles a day. But if we consider that the shoemaker's wax is so brittle that it splinters under the blow of a hammer and that it yet flows like a liquid into the crevices of a vessel in which it is placed, and that bullets sink slowly down through it and corks float slowly up through it, the motion of the earth through the ether does not seem so incomprehensible.'[4]

The universe explained through shoemaker's wax; faith in science was becoming as irrational as faith in God. Strauss's book examined Jesus's life 'scientifically'. Nietzsche compared Strauss to a young philological lion stripping off the theological bearskin. If Christianity meant belief in an historical event or an historical person, then he would have none of it.

Llama demanded clarification. He wrote to her: 'Every true faith is indeed infallible; it performs what the believing person hopes to find in it, but it does not offer the least support for the establishing of an objective truth . . . Here the ways of men divide. If you want to achieve peace of mind and happiness, then have faith; if you want to be a disciple of truth, then search.'[5]

Too little had been achieved during his two terms at Bonn. He had got into debt and slept late. His collection of illnesses had been joined by rheumatism of the arm. He was sarcastic and peevish as he regretted the time and the money spent on the 'beery materialism' and 'mindless bonhomie' of the Franconia. Fortunately, a quarrel between the two philology professors Jahn and Ritschl became so vitriolic that Ritschl left Bonn to teach at Leipzig University. Nietzsche followed him.

The new beginning suited him well. Every morning he was up at five for a lecture. He founded the Classical Society, which agreed with him better than the Franconia fraternity. He turned a local café into 'a sort of philological stock exchange', and bought a cupboard to store its periodicals and papers. He joined the thriving Philological Society and gave papers in Latin on all sorts of obscure classical highways and byways; 'I have independently enlarged it by recently finding the evidence why the *Violarium* of Eudocia does not go back to Suidas but to Suidas' chief source, an epitome of Hesychius Milesius (lost, of course) . . .'[6]

He had the gift of bringing the dry subject to life, a rare talent in the field of philology. His talks were well attended. He was popular.

He was entirely free of philistine pedantry, one of his fellow-students recalled; 'I came away from his talks with the impression of an almost astounding precocity and confident self-assurance.'[7] He argued Homer against Hesiod and he excited the faculty by challenging the accepted idea that the *Odyssey* and the *Iliad* were folk-poetry written by several poets, arguing that it was inconceivable that such magnificent literary work should not be driven by one outstandingly creative individual. Ritschl praised his work on Theognis and he won a prize for an essay on Diogenes Laertius. He headed the essay with the line from one of Pindar's *Pythian Odes* that he would treasure all his life: 'Become what you are, having learned what that is.'[8]

Nietzsche was starting out on this road of becoming when fate intervened in the shape of the territorial ambition of Bismarck, whose expansionist policies were causing a succession of small wars designed to manoeuvre Prussia to the forefront of Germany at the expense of the Bund, and Germany, eventually, to the forefront of Europe. In 1866 Prussia had fought and won a short war against Austria and Bavaria. The Prussian army had invaded Saxony, Hanover and Hesse and declared that the German Confederation no longer existed. The following year, 1867, these issues were still rumbling on and Nietzsche was called up to serve as a private in the mounted section of a field artillery regiment stationed at Naumburg. He had taken some riding lessons but his experience of horses was not extensive.

'If some daimon were ever to lead you early one morning between, let us say, five and six o'clock to Naumburg and were to have the kindness to intend guiding your steps into my vicinity, then do not stop in your tracks and stare at the spectacle which offers itself to your senses. Suddenly you breathe the atmosphere of the stable. In the lanterns' half-light, figures loom up. Around you there are sounds of scraping, whinnying, brushing, knocking. And in the midst of it all, in the garb of a groom, making violent attempts to carry away in his bare hands something unspeakable . . . it is none other than myself. A few hours later you see two horses racing around the paddock, not without riders, of whom one is very like your friend. He is riding his fiery, zestful Balduin, and hopes to be able to ride well one day . . . at other times of the day he stands, industrious and attentive, by the horse-drawn cannons and pulls shells out of limber or cleans the bore with the cloth or takes aim according to inches and degrees, and so on. But most of all he has a lot to learn . . . Sometimes hidden under the horse's belly I murmur, "Schopenhauer, help!"'[9]

The artillerymen were taught to mount their horse at the run, flinging themselves boldly into the saddle. His short-sightedness made him a bad judge of distance and in March he misjudged the leap, crashing his chest onto the saddle's hard pommel. Stoically, he continued the exercise but that evening he collapsed and was put to bed with a deep chest wound. After ten days on morphine with no improvement, the army doctor opened up his chest; two months later his wound was still suppurating and refusing to heal. To his astonishment, a small bone came into view. He was told to bathe the cavity with camomile tea and nitrate of silver solution and to take a bath three times a week. This did not produce the desired result, and there was talk of an operation. The famous Dr Volkmann of Halle was consulted, and he recommended a salt-water cure at the brine baths of Wittekind. The little spa village was a gloomy place, rainy and damp, and his fellow-invalids were far from stimulating. To avoid their banal conversation, at mealtimes he sat himself next to a man who was deaf and dumb. Happily, the cure worked; the wounds healed, leaving only deep scars, and he was able to leave the depressing place.

In October he was declared temporarily unfit for active service and invalided out of the army until the following spring, when he was expected to come back for a month's gun hauling exercise, an activity hardly compatible with the successful completion of the healing of the wounds. On 15 October he celebrated his twenty-fourth birthday and three weeks later came the glorious first meeting with Richard Wagner, soon after which Nietzsche received the invitation to take up the Chair of Philology at Basle.

It was an astonishing offer; Nietzsche was still a mere student. He had spent two terms at Bonn University and two terms at Leipzig and he had no degree from either but his distinguished teacher Ritschl had recommended his outstandingly brilliant pupil for the post. He was offered the chair on 13 February 1869, and in order that he could take it up he was awarded his doctorate by Leipzig, without examination, on 23 March. In April he was appointed Professor of Classical Philology at the University of Basle with a stipend of three thousand francs.

Ecstatically proud to be the youngest ever professor to be appointed there, he spent some of the money on clothes, taking great pains to repudiate youthful fashions and selecting only those styles that would make him look older.

He had his reservations about the Swiss, suspecting them to be a race of 'aristocratic philistines', and about Basle, a wealthy, conservative society built on the ribbon trade, a place of impeccable parlours, infallible city elders and a small university of only 120 students, most of them studying theology.

The university insisted he give up his Prussian citizenship. They did not want him called back for further military service. They suggested he become a Swiss national, but while he revoked his Prussian citizenship he never fulfilled the requirements for Swiss citizenship. As a result he became stateless for the rest of his life, which he felt was certainly better than joining the ranks of the philistines.

'I would rather be a Basel professor than God,'[10] he said, and it was here that he discovered how much he enjoyed teaching. He was contracted to teach at the local secondary school, the *Pädagogium*, as well as at the university. He taught the history of Greek literature, ancient Greek religion, Plato and pre-Platonic philosophy, and Greek and Roman rhetoric. He made his pupils study Euripides' *The Bacchae* and write on the Dionysian cult.

His pupils 'seemed united in the impression they sat at the feet not so much of a pedagogue as of a living ephor [one of the magistrates in ancient Sparta who shared power with the king], who had leapt across time to tell them about Homer, Sophocles, Plato and their gods. As if he spoke from his own knowledge of things quite self-evident and still completely valued – that was the impression he made.'[11]

But this was not achieved without cost. One of his pupils describes Nietzsche's bad days, when it was painful to watch him struggle to give his lecture. At the lectern, his face almost touching his notebook despite the thick eyeglasses, the words would be produced slowly and laboriously, with long pauses in between. Unbearable tension built up as to whether he would be able to complete the task.[12]

His spirit was greatly stirred by the energy of the River Rhine. When pupils entered his classroom they often found him at the open window, mesmerised by its continuous roar. The grinding echo of the river against the tall walls of the medieval streets accompanied his walks through the town where he cut a stylish figure, a little under middle height (the same height as Goethe, he always claimed), stockily built, carefully and elegantly dressed, distinguished-looking with his large moustache and deep-set, rather pensive eyes. His grey top hat must have been part of his ageing strategy as it was the only one to be seen in Basle apart from one worn by a very old state counsellor from Baden. On bad days when his health was plaguing him, Nietzsche swapped the top hat for a thick green eyeshade to shield his sensitive eyes from light.

When Nietzsche had settled into Basle to take up the professorship, Wagner was living in Lucerne at the Villa Tribschen on the shores of the lake. Lucerne was a short train ride from Basle and Nietzsche was eager to take up his invitation to continue the conversation about Schopenhauer and to hear more of Wagner's Schopenhauerian opera, *Tristan und Isolde*.

Schopenhauer's philosophy is chiefly set out in the huge book *The*

World as Will and Representation (*Die Welt als Wille und Vorstellung*, 1818) in which he develops earlier thinking by Kant and Plato.

We live in the physical world. What we see, touch, perceive or experience is the representation (*Vorstellung*) but behind the representation lies the true essence of the object, the will (*Wille*). We are aware of ourselves, both in the perceptual fashion by which we know external things and, quite differently, from within as 'will'.

The representation is in a state of endless yearning and eternal becoming as it seeks unity with its will, its perfectible state. The representation may occasionally become one with the will but this only causes further discontent and further yearning. The human genius (a rare being) may achieve wholeness in the union of will and representation but for the rest of the human herd it is an impossible state in life, only to be achieved in death.

All life is yearning for an impossible state and therefore all life is suffering. Kant had written from a Christian standpoint which made the ever-imperfect, ever-yearning state of the empirical world bearable because some sort of happy ending could be anticipated if you tried hard enough. Redemption was always possible through Christ.

Schopenhauer, on the other hand, was heavily influenced by his study of Buddhist and Hindu philosophies with their abnegatory emphasis on suffering, destiny and fate, and on the fact that desires when satiated only give rise to fresh desires. The sense of flux at the noumenal (metaphysical) level of the will is resolved in a yearning for nothingness.

Schopenhauer is known as the pessimistic philosopher but for a young man such as Nietzsche who was finding Christianity increasingly impossible, he provided a viable alternative to Kant, whose influence dominated the German philosophical establishment, not least because Christianity was a vital component of the fabric of German society, enrolled by the State in the service of conservative, nationalist politics. This put both Nietzsche and Wagner in the position of outsiders, which of course they minded not at all.

Nietzsche had not read Schopenhauer uncritically. On the way he had studied F. A. Lange's *History of Materialism and Critique of its Meaning* in the Present (*Geschichte des Materialismus und Kritik seiner Bedeutung in der Gegenwart*, 1866), and he had made notes.

1. The world of the senses is a product of our organisation.
2. Our visible (physical) organs are, like all other parts of the phenomenal world, only images of an unknown object.
3. Our real organisation is therefore as much unknown to us as real external things are. We continually have before us nothing but the product of both.

Thus the true essence of things – the thing-in-itself – is not only unknown to us: the concept of it is neither more nor less than the final product of an antithesis which is determined by our organisation, an antithesis of which we do not know whether it has any meaning outside our experience or not.[13]

Within this free-fall unknowing, Schopenhauer struck a deep emotional need in him, giving him comfort. The proposition that all life is a state of suffering applied to him more than most, with his poor body in a constant state of chronic ill health and often great pain. Naturally it yearned for its ideal state. Likewise, he was in a state of yearning for his 'true being' that would make existence seem intelligible and thus justified. At this stage he was particularly confused as to what his 'true being' was. Schopenhauer told him that we cannot realise the oneness of our true being because our intellect constantly fragments the world – and how can it be otherwise, when our intellect itself is but a small part, a fragment of our representation?

Nietzsche was feeling this in the most personal way; 'The most irksome thing of all is that I am always having to impersonate someone – the teacher, the philologist, the human being,'[14] he wrote after taking up the Basle professorship, and it was hardly a surprising feeling given that he was a young man dressing like an old man to impersonate wisdom, an undergraduate impersonating a professor, an exasperated son impersonating a good son to his irritating mother, and a loving and dutiful son to the memory of his dead Christian father while in the process of losing his Christian faith. As if these everyday impersonations were not enough, there was the question of his statelessness, the formal identity within which all these impersonations existed. Utterly fragmented, he knew himself in the Schopenhauerian state of striving and suffering: a man far from understanding his true will let alone realising it.

Wagner on the other hand was, at least in his own opinion, such a long way down the road of Schopenhauerian thought as to have attained the status of genius. He felt so confident that his will and representation had become one that he and his mistress Cosima playfully addressed each other by Schopenhauerian love-names. He was *Will* (Will) and she was *Vorstell* (Representation).

For Schopenhauer, music was the one art capable of revealing the truth about the nature of being itself. Other arts such as painting and sculpture could only be representations of representations. This put them at two removes from the ultimate reality, the will. Music, however, being formless, in the sense of being non-representational, had the capacity directly to access the will, bypassing the intellect.

Since discovering Schopenhauer in 1854, Wagner had been studying how to compose what Schopenhauer calls 'suspension'. A piece of Schopenhauerian music must be like a life: moving from discord to discord, only resolved at the moment of death (in music, the final note of the piece).

The ear, like the shuddering soul, is endlessly yearning for the final resolution. Man is dissonance in human form; therefore musical dissonance must be the most effective artistic means of representing the pain of individual existence.

Composers who had gone before were wedded to observing musical form and obeying the ancestral rules: the formal, formulaic structure of the symphony for instance, or the concerto. Listening to them made you conscious of their individual contribution to music's historical continuity and development. If you knew the language you could easily place them on the historical line.

But Schopenhauer challenged the very idea of history, calling 'time' only a form of our thought. This freed Wagner from recognisable representation. Nietzsche described Wagner's *Zukunftsmusik* ('Music of the Future') as the triumphant culmination of all art because it was not concerned, like the others, with the images of the phenomenal world but rather spoke the language of the will directly. From the deepest source of its being, music was the will's most quintessential manifestation. And of all music, Wagner's exercised a spell over him that was becoming ever stronger; he could not keep a cool head when he listened to it, his every fibre quivered, his every nerve vibrated. Nothing else produced such a penetrating and lasting feeling of ecstasy in him. Surely what he was experiencing was the sensation of direct access to the will? He longed to renew his acquaintance with the Master.

When Nietzsche had been in Basle for three weeks, he felt he had university business sufficiently under control to be able to pay Wagner a visit. No matter that Wagner was more than twice his age and a world-famous figure whose casual invitation to visit had been extended some six months previously. On Saturday 15 May 1869, Nietzsche caught the railway train to Lucerne, got out and walked the path along the edge of Lake Lucerne leading to Wagner's house.

Built in 1627, Tribschen was, and is, thick-walled and imposing, an ancient manor house, almost a watchtower. Numerous symmetrical windows peer out from beneath a steep-sided pyramidal red roof. Sitting atop a rise, it dominates a triangular knuckle of rock that pushes bonily into the lake. Like a robber's castle it commands all approaches. Nietzsche could not scuttle up unseen but must arrive, like all visitors, discomfited beneath the windows' blank scrutiny. From within the house he could hear the agonising, soul-wrenching chord from the third act of *Siegfried* repeated again and again on a piano. He rang the bell.

A servant appeared. Nietzsche presented his visiting card and waited, feeling increasingly awkward. He was walking away when the servant came hurrying after him. Was he the Herr Nietzsche whom the Master had met at Leipzig? Yes indeed. The servant disappeared, reappeared. The Master was at his composition and could not be disturbed. Might the Herr Professor come back for lunch? Unfortunately, he was not free for lunch. The servant disappeared, reappeared. Might Herr Nietzsche come back the following day?

Nietzsche had no classes on Whit Monday. This time as he trod the intimidating approach, the Master himself came out to greet him.

Wagner adored fame and he adored clothes. He well understood the value of the image as vehicle for ideas. Today, greeting the philologist whose discipline was the understanding and continuity of the antique, he was dressed in his 'Renaissance painter outfit': black velvet jacket, knee breeches, silk stockings, buckled shoes, sky-blue cravat and Rembrandt beret. His welcome was warm, and genuine, as he led Nietzsche through the dazzling succession of rooms furnished in the opulent taste that the composer shared with his royal patron King Ludwig.

Many visitors commented that they found Tribschen too pink and over-endowed with cupids, but such an interior was something quite new and intoxicating to Nietzsche, whose life had been spent in self-denying, Protestant rooms. Tribschen's walls were covered in red and gold damask, or in cordovan leather, or in a special shade of violet velvet that had been carefully chosen to set off to best advantage the dazzling white marble busts of Wagner and King Ludwig. There was a carpet made of breast feathers of flamingos bordered with peacocks' feathers. Exalted high on a plinth stood a ridiculously fragile, elaborately curlicued beaker of ruby Bohemian glass presented to Wagner by the King. Mementoes of glory were hung like hunting trophies on the walls: fading laurel wreaths, autographed programmes, paintings of a muscle-bound, golden-haired Siegfried getting the better of the dragon, of breastplated Valkyries storming the skies like thunderclouds and of Brünnhilde bursting with joy as she awakened on her rock. Bibelots and precious objects lay trapped behind glass in vitrines, like pinned butterflies. Windows were muted by drifts of pink gauze and shimmering satin. The perfume of roses, tuberoses, narcissi, lilacs and lilies hung heavy on the air. No scent was too narcotic, no price too extravagant to pay for attar of roses from Persia, gardenias from America and orris root from Florence.

The creation of *Gesamtkunstwerk*, a total work of art integrating drama, music and spectacle, was itself a *Gesamtkunstwerk* involving Wagner's every physical sense, for, as he saw it, '. . . if I am obliged once more to plunge into the waves of an artist's imagination in order to find satisfaction in an imaginary world, I must at least help out my imagination and find means of encouraging my imaginative faculties. I cannot then live like a dog. I cannot sleep on straw and drink common gin: mine is an intensely irritable, acute and hugely voracious, yet uncommonly tender and delicate sensuality which, one way or another, must be flattered if I am to accomplish the cruelly difficult task of creating in my mind a non-existent world.'[15]

The room from whose window Nietzsche had heard the Siegfried chord floating was the Green Room, Wagner's composition room, a surprisingly small, masculine and workmanlike space within Tribschen's heavily operatic atmosphere. Two walls covered in book-shelves reminded one that Wagner was as much a man of words as of music who composed as many books, pamphlets and libretti as musical works. The piano was specially designed with drawers for pens and a table-like plane on which the sheets of the latest composition could be flung while the ink was drying on the paper. Visitors madly coveted these sheets and Wagner knew the value of autographing them and giving them out to the favoured influential. Over the piano hung the large portrait of the King. For some reason in Tribschen it was bad form to refer to King Ludwig by name. He was 'the royal friend'. He visited Tribschen alone and incognito, even spending the night, after which his bedroom was kept ever ready for his return. Tribschen was Ludwig's Rambouillet, his Marie Antoinette dairy. It took on much the same role for Nietzsche. He was the only person, apart from the King, to be given his own room in the house. During the course of the next three years he would visit Tribschen twenty-three times, and it would live in his thought forever as the Island of the Blessed.

King Ludwig, who was paying the bills, had given Wagner carte blanche to settle wherever his imagination might be free of all practical considerations as he concentrated solely on finishing the *Ring* cycle, which was the King's passion. Wagner had settled on this spectacularly picturesque site that took full advantage of Kant's principle of the sublime; 'a function of the extreme tension experienced by the mind in apprehending immensity and boundlessness, transcending every standard of sense and which rouses a sort of delightful horror, a sort of tranquillity tinged with terror which, accomplished through a transcendent scale of reference, a greatness comparable to itself alone . . . its effect is to throw the mind back upon itself – and thus we soon perceive that the sublime is not to be looked for in the things of nature but in our own ideas.'[16]

On this principle, the transcendent views from Tribschen's every window might trigger sublime inspiration in both Wagner and Nietzsche wherever they looked. Through the west-facing windows, where the sun set, rose the eternal snows of Mont Pilatus, originally a pre-Christian Nibelheim of legendary dragons and hobgoblins, renamed in a later, Christian age for Pontius Pilate who, banished from Galilee after the crucifixion of Christ, fled to Lucerne. Here, overcome by remorse, he climbed the seven-thousand-foot peak of the Pilatus, from which he flung himself into the little ink-black tarn that you can see below. Here lives his ghost, in silence and stillness complete. Local guides will tell you that the water itself is dead, pointing out as proof that its surface is always motionless and quite incapable of being ruffled by even the highest wind. Black pines surround the cursed spot. For centuries, no woodcutter dared venture there for fear of provoking the spirit to whom so many calamities were attributed, and so the pine trees grew up in tall peaks pressing round the little water and, incidentally, keeping the wind out and the water unruffled. In the fourteenth century a brave priest waded into Pilate's dark suicide lake and performed an exorcism. Nevertheless, locals remained wary and the numerous thunderstorms that bang and clatter round the mountain and swell sudden storms on Lake Lucerne remained attributed to Pilate's ghost. It was only after the 1780s that the *Frühromantiker*, pale young men with their minds in paroxysms of poetic metaphor, who valued Kantian sublimity and 'poetry of the heart' above all else, ventured onto the ill-omened mountain, where Pilate's pool surely made the ultimate suicide spot for many a young Werther hopelessly crossed in love.

By the time Wagner was inviting Nietzsche to join him on refreshing all-day hikes up the Pilatus, enterprising peasants had constructed a hostelry and were hiring out ponies for the ascent. Wagner and Nietzsche scorned this service. They conquered the rocky crags on foot, singing and philosophising all the way.

Should Nietzsche look through Tribschen's lake-facing windows, his eyes would sweep down the 'Robber's Park', a grassy, bouldery headland grazed by Wagner's horse Fritz, his chickens, peacocks and sheep, who dotted the ground sloping down to the lake's edge. Wagner and Nietzsche were both fond of swimming from the bathing ladder that cut the pale reflections of the run of snowy mountains on the far shore of the lake. The Rigi, at six thousand foot, is a little lower than the Pilatus but just as famous for being painted by J. M. W. Turner and for the curious lighting effect known as the 'Rigi ghost'. In particular conditions requiring brightness and mist, you can see the ghost clearly. It takes the shape of an enormous human figure like the silhouette of a giant in the vaporous sky above you. The giant is surrounded by a rainbow nimbus; in fact it is no ghost but your own figure projected onto the mist, as you discover when you stretch your arms out in wonder, upon which you see your movements gigantically reflected in the mist as in a magnifying mirror. Wagner used to dance and cut capers at his heavenly mirror image until the mist moved, and the puppet show was gone.[7]

On the lake's edge to the right of Wagner's bathing ladder was a little chalet roofed with wooden shingles, housing the boat. When Wagner needed to let off steam he would get his faithful servant Jacob to row him through the flocks of white Lohengrin swans that sailed the lake, far out to the echo spot where William Tell taunted his evil adversary Landvogt Gessler by shouting insults that rang round the mountains in endless mockery. Wagner liked to bellow obscenities in his rough Saxon accent. It made him roar with laughter when the echo shouted them back at him.

If the mood was still on him after Jacob had rowed him back, he'd shin up a pine tree and yell some more. Once he somehow scaled the smooth facade of the house and shouted from the balcony but that was an exceptional occasion because he wasn't raging against an enemy but against himself for having done something he was ashamed of.[18]

Wagner's domestic situation was in a muddle when Nietzsche paid his visit. His birthday was looming the following weekend and King Ludwig wanted to be with him on that significant day but Wagner was torn between spending the day with the King or with his mistress Cosima. Though she and Wagner had been together long enough for her to bear him two daughters and she was now pregnant by him for the third time, Cosima had only very recently left her husband to come to live with Wagner at Tribschen. Wagner was concealing her from the King for various reasons. The King was an ardent Roman Catholic who disapproved of adulterous relationships. He was a pale creature who adored Wagner more than anyone on earth. It was obviously never a physical relationship in any way beyond each of them falling to their knees to sob hot tears in tribute to each other, but it was a highly romantic one, at least on Ludwig's side.

Ludwig was jealous and possessive; he saw no reason why he should not be first-and-only to the genius he elevated to a sort of fetishistic idolatry while supporting him financially to a degree beyond reason, whipping his ministers and his subjects into a state of anxiety and suspicion that Wagner's Music of the Future, while emptying the State coffers, was hoodwinking their sweet, handsome, naïve young king and dressing him in the laughable garb of the Emperor's New Clothes.

Wagner and his mistress were already at the centre of a complicated emotional network of suppressed homo- and heterosexual loves, longings and social tensions into which Nietzsche would be swept. Cosima was the second of three illegitimate daughters born to the composer Franz Liszt and the Comtesse Marie d'Agoult. Wagner's own paternity was decidedly misty and when he needed a father figure, Liszt had filled the void both musically and practically. In 1849, Liszt had provided the money for Wagner to flee Dresden and helped him obtain a false passport. Since then he had stepped in financially to support Wagner's revolutionary new music over a sustained period. Liszt was both music-father and money-father to Wagner.

While Wagner was the better conductor, Liszt was the infinitely better pianist, effectively inventing the profession of international concert performer. He was worshipped as a demigod of the keyboard from Paris to Constantinople and most points between. Heinrich Heine coined the term Lisztomania for the mass hysteria he engendered. Women swooned and swayed like cornfields in his presence. They stole his cigar-ends from ashtrays and kept them as holy relics. They sneaked the flowers that adorned his concert platforms. Though there can never be any doubt of Wagner's vigorous heterosexuality (much to both his wives' fury there was practically a new young mistress for every opera) he would break into tears as he knelt to kiss Liszt's hand. In terms of sentiment and sentimentality, Wagner conformed to the conventions of an age of male-to-male hero-worship and unashamed emotion.

Cosima was not Liszt's favourite daughter. A gawky duckling of powerful personality, she was a long-faced *belle laide*, the physical image of her father. She shared his astonishing charisma, his height, his distinctive Roman nose and his etiolated looks which, handsome on a man, lent her a goddess-like unapproachability that was irresistible to certain intellectual men of short stature, including Wagner and Nietzsche.

At this Whit Monday lunch with Nietzsche, Cosima was still married to Hans von Bülow. Previously von Bülow had been one of Liszt's most promising pupils. Now he was Wagner's chief conductor. He was also, in this intimate tangle of musico-erotic relationships, King Ludwig's Kapellmeister.

Cosima had committed herself to marriage with von Bülow when she was still in her teens and had been swept away by a concert in Berlin conducted by him. The concert programme had included the first Berlin performance of Wagner's Venusberg music from *Tannhäuser*.

Von Bülow had proposed to her on the same night. Both of them were in love with Wagner and completely transported by his glorious music; one wonders who he was wooing and who she was accepting. Numerous accounts of von Bülow cast question on his sexuality. They seem to be borne out by the unusual letter he wrote to her father Lizst on the occasion of his engagement to Cosima:

'I feel for her more than love. The thought of moving nearer to you encloses all my dream of whatsoever may be vouchsafed to me on this earth, you whom I regard as the principal architect and shaper of my present and future life. For me Cosima is superior to all women, not only because she bears your name but because she resembles you so closely . . .'[19]

A year after their marriage, Cosima was in despair. She had made a grievous mistake. She requested one of her husband's close friends, Karl Ritter, to kill her. When Ritter refused, she threatened to drown herself in the lake and was only deterred when he said that if she did, he would have to do the same. The marriage continued with her making repeated attempts to contract fatal illnesses.[20] Both Cosima and von Bülow were passionate admirers of Wagner's music and one evening, Wagner noticed that she 'was in a strangely excited state which showed itself in a convulsively passionate tenderness towards *me*'.[21]

At that time Wagner was still married to his first wife, Minna, but on her death the situation unravelled itself. In the interval Cosima had borne von Bülow two daughters but that was no barrier to her bearing Wagner two more, while maintaining the sham marriage and becoming pregnant for a third time by Wagner.

When Nietzsche came to lunch at Tribschen, Cosima was eight months into expecting their third child, a fact of which the unworldly Nietzsche seems to have been totally unaware as he enjoyed the social sportiveness of the large household comprising Cosima's four daughters, a governess, a nursery maid, a housekeeper, a cook and two or three servants, young Hans Richter who was then Wagner's secretary, musical copyist and *maître de plaisir* in charge of organising concerts and entertainments, Wagner's huge, black Newfoundland dog, Russ, who now lies buried next to his master in Bayreuth, Cosima's grey fox-terrier to which she had given the name Kos so that nobody should shorten her own name to 'Cos', the horse Fritz, sheep, hens and cats, a pair of golden pheasants and a breeding pair of peacocks named Wotan after the father of the gods in German mythology who is the cause of all the trouble in Wagner's *Ring*, and Fricka after Wotan's shriekingly possessive wife, who had a certain amount in common with Cosima.

4

· NAXOS ·

Frau Cosima Wagner is the noblest nature by far that exists, and, in
relation to me, I have always interpreted her marriage with Wagner as
adultery.

Draft version of *Ecce Homo*

Frustratingly, there is no record of what Nietzsche and Wagner spoke
about over lunch. We gain little from Cosima's lukewarm diary entry:
'At lunch a philologist, Professor Nietzsche, whom R. first met at
the Brockhaus home and who knows R.'s works thoroughly and even
quotes from *Opera and Drama* in his lectures. A quiet and pleasant
visit.'[1] Wagner's enthusiasm for his guest seems to have been greater.
On bidding his visitor farewell he gave him a signed photograph and
pressed him to return. Three days later, he instructed Cosima to write
inviting Nietzsche for the coming weekend to celebrate the Master's
birthday on 22 May. Nietzsche refused, saying he was too busy
preparing his inaugural lecture on Homer, which was to be delivered
on the 28th. Wagner responded by urging him to come any weekend;
'Do come – you need only to send me a line in advance.'

The composer was fastening onto the philologist like a barnacle onto
the hull of the flying Dutchman's ship. While Nietzsche's enthusiasm
for Wagner is not terribly surprising, Wagner's enthusiasm for
Nietzsche is. Wagner's genius had an annihilating force to it. People
of interest were given the chance to be drawn into the charmed circle
or left in outer darkness; there was no middle ground. One acolyte
described himself as perfectly contented to be a footnote to Wagner's
private history, a factotum, a stick of intellectual furniture, but
Wagner saw the potential for rather more than a stick of furniture
in Professor Nietzsche, a rising man of intellectual influence who

was a passionate lover of Wagner's music and a superb classicist and philologist.

While Wagner was often flatteringly addressed as Professor Wagner, he was no such thing. His education was full of holes. He read neither Latin nor Greek but his great Artwork of the Future, the *Ring*, was conceived as a revival of Greek tetralogy as had been performed at the Greek festivals in the age of Aeschylus and Euripides. A re-inventor of classical drama who could only read the classics in translation might benefit greatly from Nietzsche's intellectual imprimatur.

In addition, Wagner was now nearing the completion of the *Ring* cycle and he was realising that it required rising young men such as King Ludwig and Nietzsche to champion it. The *Ring* was too forward-looking for old minds. Bright-eyed youth must drum up the money for this revolutionary theatrical work that needed huge sums, as well as considerable push, to bring it to the stage. Consisting as it did of fourteen hours of music performed over four days, it demanded the construction of an entirely new type of space in which it could be performed: an opera house designed something like a Greek amphi-theatre, but roofed in for a cold climate. Germany was full of Baroque and Rococo theatres but their acoustic was wrong and their theatrical spaces far too small for the hundred-strong orchestra that parts of the *Ring* require. Even today in London's Royal Opera House the harps and drums spill over into the boxes either side of the pit.

Nietzsche took up his open invitation to return to Tribschen at the very first opportunity after his lecture. He arrived on Saturday 5 June, apparently with no idea of Cosima's advanced state of pregnancy. Her diary for that day records that they spent a 'tolerable' evening. She said goodnight at about eleven, went upstairs and her labour pains began.

At three in the morning the midwife arrived, and at four o'clock, 'crying out in the most raging pain', Cosima bore Wagner his first son, whose lusty yells reached the Orange Salon where Wagner was waiting tensely. The boy arrived at the same time as the fiery glow of dawn blazed over the Rigi with a richness of colour 'never before seen'. Wagner dissolved into tears. Across the lake came the sound of the early morning Sunday bells ringing in Lucerne. Cosima took this as a good omen, a salutation to the boy who would be Wagner's son and heir, and 'future representative of the father for all his children' – all his children so far comprising four mere girls: Daniela and Blandine, Cosima's two legitimate daughters, and Isolde and Eva, whom the world believed were by her husband but who in fact had been fathered by Wagner while Cosima was still living with von Bülow.

Wagner spent the morning at Cosima's bedside holding her hand. He emerged at lunchtime to tell Nietzsche, the only guest in the house, the glorious news of Siegfried's birth. Nietzsche, remarkably, had remained innocent of the events of the night. Tribschen, while a large house, is not sprawling. Its rooms pile up on each other vertically. Noise travels up and down the staircase by which the midwife had been coming and going, in addition to which Cosima's labour was, by her own account, hardly any more silent than Siegfried's arrival. But nothing had struck Nietzsche as curious or unusual.

Be that as it may, Wagner now considered Nietzsche a fortunate presence sent by the gods. There being no such thing as coincidence, it was fate that had chosen the intelligent young professor to be Siegfried's guardian spirit. Wagner fantasised that when the time came for the boy to sally forth into the world, he would be tutored by Nietzsche, while Wagner and Cosima watched from afar; as Wotan, the father of the gods, watched the education of Siegfried, the young warrior hero of the *Ring*, who would redeem the world.

Nietzsche had the tact to leave soon after lunch, but Tribschen's will was indomitable and the very next day Cosima wrote thanking him for a book, enclosing two essays by Wagner and an invitation that he should bring them back on his next visit. Eight days later she wrote to von Bülow requesting a divorce. Eventually he granted it after much correspondence with her father, the libidinous Abbé Liszt, a devout if highly unorthodox Roman Catholic, who objected to his daughter imitating his own sexual freedom. Liszt was probably a little squeamish, too, on account of age. Cosima was thirty-one years old and Wagner, at fifty-six, was only two years younger than himself. As for von Bülow, he subscribed to the accepted Tribschen mythology, in which Cosima was the glorious Ariadne and von Bülow was Theseus – he was after all a mere conductor and pianist – but it was the musical genius Wagner, 'this wonderful man whom one must revere as a god', whose music was 'an act of deliverance from the sordidness of this world',[2] who was Dionysus. It was entirely in the natural order of things that a mortal man should cede his woman to a god. Wagner agreed.

Nietzsche would later subscribe to this ordering of the universe, elbowing out Wagner to take the place of the god for himself, but that was some way off. Now he spent the next few weeks following Siegfried's birth going about his teaching duties in Basle before returning to the Tribschen labyrinth, which held the stately Cosima and everything else that stimulated, excited and engaged him.

Engels lugubriously described Basle as a barren town full of frock-coats, cocked hats, philistines, patricians and Methodists.[3] Certainly it held nothing to rival the extravagant novelties of Tribschen. Nietzsche's inaugural lecture had been successful enough and he had a few interesting but hardly electrifying lectures to give on Aeschylus and the Greek lyric poets. There was, however, some interest to be found in Basle, in the person of his fellow-professor Jacob Burckhardt and in his lectures on the study of history.

Burckhardt and Wagner were to be the two great influences on Nietzsche's thinking over the next couple of years, during which he was marshalling his ideas towards his first book, *The Birth of Tragedy from the Spirit of Music* (*Die Geburt der Tragödie*). Both were about the same age that Nietzsche's father would have been had he lived. There the similarity ended.

No velvet berets adorned Burckhardt's close-cropped head, and there were no nationalist ideas inside it, either. It was said he would not endure Wagner's name being mentioned in his presence. Bony, brusque and brilliant, he was a neurotically private man who dressed anonymously and strongly disliked any form of pomp, pretension or fame. He lived in two rooms above a baker's shop and nothing pleased him better than to be mistaken for the baker.

A revolutionary in bourgeois clothing, Burckhardt founded his startling ideas on thorough scholarship conveyed with matter-of-fact simplicity which won him respect in the context of Basle's love of sober moderation. His telegraphically laconic style contrasted sharply with Wagner, the stormy, stylish artist of the sublime, who was viewed with great suspicion as he went vagabonding around Europe, sponging on kings and conducting international cultural upheavals from the fastness of Tribschen's rocky promontory.

The inky-fingered Burckhardt making his way through Basle's Old Town in his black suit and soft black hat was one of the beloved, unremarkable assurances that all was well in the city, and working to routine. If he was carrying a big, blue portfolio under his arm, so much the more interesting: it meant he was on his way to teach. His lectures were enormously popular. Burckhardt spoke without notes, using informal, everyday language. He delivered his words as if he were just thinking out loud, but it was said that even his pauses and spontaneous asides were carefully rehearsed in his rooms above the baker's shop.

Burckhardt and Nietzsche developed the pleasant habit of walking to an inn some three miles out of town to take a meal and some wine together. As they walked they talked of the ancient world and of the new, and of 'our philosopher', as they called Schopenhauer, whose pessimism chimed with Burckhardt's view that European culture was falling to a new barbarism in the form of capitalism, scientism and the centralisation of the state. In the age of the unifications of Germany and Italy, Burckhardt condemned the modern, monolithic state as 'worshipped as a god and ruling like a sultan'. Such a structure could, he felt, only give rise to what he called *terribles simplificateurs*, demagogues armed with all the potentially terrible weapons provided by industrialisation, science and technology.

Burckhardt believed in nothing, but saw this as no bar to behaving ethically. He heartily disliked the French Revolution, the United States, mass democracy, uniformity, industrialism, militarism and railways. Born in the same year as Karl Marx, Burckhardt was an anti-capitalist who raged against what he called 'the whole power and money racket',[4] but he was also an anti-populist, a conservative pessimist who earnestly believed that the masses should be saved from themselves, particularly from their own inclination to enthrone mediocrity and to cheapen taste, bringing everything down to what he and Nietzsche agreed was the vulgarity and confusion of popular culture.

Burckhardt and Nietzsche were both haunted by the coming spectre of war between France and Germany. Napoleon had been the *terrible simplificateur* of France, now Bismarck had pulled on Napoleon's hob-nailed jackboots to become the *terrible simplificateur* of Germany. Napoleon had used his military conquest of Europe as a weapon of cultural imperialism and it was obvious to Burckhardt that Bismarck was preparing to behave just as badly. All tyrants suffered dangerously from the Herostratic impulse, Burckhardt believed, referring to Herostratus the Ephesian who set fire to the Temple of Artemis at Ephesus, destroying that iconic symbol of culture for no better reason than the wish that his name should go down in history to the end of time.

Wagner, who was always a believer in ideological structures, hugely admired Bismarck and German nationalism, while Burckhardt, who was devoted to Europeanism, saw the disproportionate rise of any one country as imperilling the cultural whole. Wagner saw Jews and Jewish culture as an outside element that could belong to no European nation and that could only dilute precious native elements. Burckhardt saw Jewish culture as a universal leavening of European bread.

Nietzsche believed that nothing distinguishes a man more from the general pattern of the age than the use he makes of history and philosophy.[5] Burckhardt's interesting view was that history coordinates and hence is unphilosophical, while philosophy subordinates and hence is unhistorical. This idea of his that a philosophy of history was a nonsensical contradiction was one of the chief differences between him and his contemporaries. Another was his hatred of the obliteration of the individual within the state. While the other major historians such as Leopold von Ranke were increasingly concerned with the objective forces of politics and economics, Burckhardt believed strongly in the force of culture and in the effect the individual could have on history. He also questioned the fashion for seeing history as a process of collecting facts from documents and delivering an 'objective' account. He questioned the very notion of objectivity: 'To each eye, perhaps the outlines of a given civilisation present a different picture . . . the same studies which have served for this work might easily, in other hands, not only receive a wholly different treatment and application, but lead also to essentially different conclusions.'[6]

For both Burckhardt and Nietzsche, the Hellenising of the world had been the most important event. The object of the modern age was not to cut the Gordian knot of Greek culture after the manner adopted by Alexander, and then leave its frayed ends fluttering in all directions. It was, rather, to bind it up: to weave the pale outline of Hellenism into the culture of modern times. But while previous scholars such as Goethe, Schiller and Winckelmann had achieved such neo-classical weaving by presenting Greece as the ideal otherworld – calm, serene, perfectly proportioned and essentially imitable as long as you knew the classics – Burckhardt wrote a series of books revising this rose-coloured, flattened, idealising of the classical world and of its first imitator, the Renaissance.

The bloodthirstiness of decadent Rome was already well known but Burckhardt, in his succession of books and lectures on the ancient world and on the Renaissance, demonstrated that extreme barbarity was no cultural hiccup occurring only when a civilisation was on the slide into decadence; rather it was a necessary part of the fabric of creativity. Burckhardt is often called the father of art history, with Bernard Berenson and Kenneth Clark cited among his distinguished children, but unlike his followers, who depicted Renaissance Italy as an idealised intellectual Arcadia, Burckhardt's *The Civilisation of the Renaissance in Italy* includes hair-raising tales of the little Italian city-state courts, tales of torture and barbarity that would not disgrace Caligula, or the daughters of King Lear. Burckhardt's history did not deny the Dionysian, the hard, cruel underbelly-impulses from which arose the absolute necessity to create its opposite: clarity, beauty, harmony, order and proportion.

Burckhardt was a neurotically private man as well as a neurotically modest one, and Nietzsche was disappointed that their long walks and talks failed to develop into a warm and close friendship such as he had with Wagner, but while Wagner was incapable of a relationship that did not involve high degrees of passionate feeling – be they positive or negative – Burckhardt was essentially a repudiator of warmth, a complicated man for whom disinterest and freedom from emotional influence were necessary in order to perceive the highest ethical truths.

Nietzsche passed an intoxicating summer between his intense debates with Burckhardt and the rain of invitations to come to Tribschen, where he and Wagner and Cosima composed a well-balanced triangle of cleverness, high seriousness and mutual admiration.

'At Wagner's house the days passed in the most charming fashion. Hardly would we enter the garden than our arrival was greeted by the barking of an enormous black dog, accompanied by children's laughter from the steps, while at the window, the poet-musician would shake his black velvet beret in a signal of welcome . . . No, I cannot recall seeing him seated, even once except at the piano or table. Coming and going through the large room, moving this chair or that, searching his pockets for a misplaced snuffbox or his eyeglasses (sometimes they had become hung up on the pendants of the chandeliers, but never in any case on his nose), grasping the velvet beret that hung down over his left eye like a black cockscomb, rubbing it between his clenched fists, then thrusting into his waistcoat only to take it out again and replace it on his head – all the while talking, talking, talking . . . He would let fly with great outbursts: sublime metaphors, puns, barbarities – an incessant stream of observations flowing in fits and starts, alternately proud, tender, violent or comical. Now smiling ear to ear, now turning emotional to the point of tears, now working himself up into a prophetic frenzy, all sorts of topics found their way into his extraordinary flights of improvisation . . . Overwhelmed and dazed by all this, [we] laughed and cried along with him, sharing his ecstasies, seeing his visions; we felt like a cloud of dust stirred up by a storm, but also illuminated by his imperious discourse, frightful and delightful at once.'[7]

It was a sublime accolade when Wagner told Nietzsche, 'I now have nobody with whom I can take things up as seriously as you, with the exception of the Unique One [Cosima],'[8] and it was high praise indeed when the icy Cosima said she regarded him as one of the most important of their friends.

This was a difficult time for Cosima. Her husband was not immediately granting her a divorce, she was publicly living in sin with a baby to prove it and she was in an overwrought, morbid state. Wagner's eye was already straying towards the beautiful Judith Gautier, who was seven years younger than her. The survival of baby Siegfried was absolutely necessary to the security of Cosima's position. The baby's every slightest childish complaint caused her disproportionate terror and plunged her into morbid meditations on death.

During this first summer, Nietzsche made six visits to Tribschen. They gave him his own room, an upstairs study. They christened it the *Denkstube* ('the Thinking Room') and Wagner became cross if he did not come often enough to use it.

What could be more inspirational than to sit at his work while listening to Wagner working on the third act of *Siegfried*? What privilege beyond compare to overhear the strange stop-start compositional process floating up the stairwell on the scented air: the Master's footsteps calm or agitated as he paced the room, his raspy voice singing a snatch, followed by a short silence as he darted to the piano to try out the notes. Silence once more as he wrote them down. Later in the evening would come the calm moment when Cosima would sit by the cradle inking in the day's score. During the day, if there was no work for her to do, she and Nietzsche would picnic in the woods with the children and watch the play of the sun on the waters of the lake. Their private name for it was 'the star dance'.

Tribschen supplied him with other, everyday domestic delights that he had never experienced before. At home, his mother and his sister waited upon him as a demigod, but Wagner and Cosima thought nothing of getting him to run errands and do their most banal shopping. He was proud to be set little tasks.

Once, just as he had returned from his usual Sunday visit to Tribschen, he asked one of his students casually where he might find a good silk shop in Basle. Nietzsche eventually had to admit to his student that he had undertaken to shop for a pair of silk underpants. For reasons best known to himself, Wagner wore tailor-made silk underwear. This important commission filled Nietzsche with anxiety. Directed to the daunting shop, he squared his shoulders manfully, observing before going in, 'Once you've chosen a God, you've got to adorn him.'[9]

Nietzsche climbed the Pilatus alone, taking as his reading matter the essay 'On State and Religion' in which Wagner proposed that religious education be replaced by cultural education, an heretical proposal which so roused Pilate's remorseful ghost that the mountain was shaken by an unusually ferocious electrical storm. White snakes of lightning darted across the sky. Thunder shook the ground. Down below in the Tribschen villa, Wagner's superstitious servants shook their heads and wondered what on earth the Professor was doing or thinking up there to have provoked such fury.

When Nietzsche and Wagner climbed the Rigi and the Pilatus together, they often discussed the development of music in Greek drama. Soon Nietzsche would write about this in his first book, *The Birth of Tragedy from the Spirit of Music*, but before that he would give two public lectures on the subject during the early months of 1870. They were, he wryly reported to Wagner, mostly attended by an audience of middle-aged mothers whose desire to broaden their minds seemed to have been baffled by the complexity of the subject. This was hardly surprising, given that Nietzsche was enlarging on ideas that Wagner had been developing over twenty or so years, the length of time it took him to write the cycle of four operas that make up *Der Ring des Nibelungen* (*The Ring of the Nibelung*).

Wagner began writing the *Ring* when he was a fiery young revolutionary in his mid thirties, and he didn't complete it until he was sixty-one, by which time he was an internationally revered figure and a friend of kings. But the ideals behind the *Ring* never swerved from the revolutionary spirit of its birth. In 1848, known as the Year of Revolutions, Wagner had been ripe for the conflagration sweeping the continent when the peoples of Europe had taken to the streets demanding electoral reform, social justice and an end to autocracies. Wagner had played an active part manning the barricades in the Dresden uprising, which was quickly crushed. A warrant was issued for Wagner's arrest and he fled, reputedly disguised in women's clothing, to Switzerland where he began work on the *Ring*. At that time, Wagner had not yet come across the work of Schopenhauer and he was subscribing to the philosophy of Ludwig Feuerbach who inspired the Young Germany movement, which called for the unification of Germany, the abolition of censorship, constitutional rule, the emancipation of women and, to a certain extent, their sexual liberation. In *The Essence of Christianity* Feuerbach proposes that man is the measure of all things. The idea of god is an invention of man, a lie that has been perpetuated by the ruling classes to subdue the masses throughout history.

Today one hardly thinks of Wagner as a political progressive and the *Ring* as designed to liberate the arts from the stranglehold of Church and Court and give opera back to the people, but that is exactly what it was. Wagner explains as much in the three essays he wrote at the start of his political exile, during which he observed five years of (comparative) musical silence while working out his ideas for the artwork of the future. The first two essays, 'Art and Revolution' and 'The Artwork of the Future', were written in 1849, soon after he was exiled from Germany for his revolutionary activities.

When Wagner started out on a career in music, unless you were a virtuoso instrumentalist like Liszt (which Wagner certainly was not; 'I play the piano like a rat plays the flute'), the only way to get on was to become Kapellmeister, director of music, to one of the many small courts that then made up the Bund. Wagner thus became Kapellmeister to the Court of Saxony under Friedrich August II, a perfectly civilised despot taken in the context of his peers. But the yoke of court service inevitably meant musical constipation to a go-ahead young Kapellmeister. The taste of the princes of the German courts was seldom forward-looking and often turned on a whim, such as a performance being shortened because the prince had toothache.

What Wagner experienced at court infuriated him. Society paid his musical offerings about as much attention as they gave the noisy clattering of knives and forks while they got on with the real business of the evening, flirting and gossiping over their elegant suppers, and flitting from box to box.

The greatness of music must be recognised and restored! The theatre must become the focus of communal life as it had been in ancient Greece and Rome. The great Plato had written how 'rhythm and harmony find their way into the inward places of the soul, on which they mightily fasten'. Wagner would restore it to something more than accompaniment to gossip and the wielding of eating irons.

His new music of the future would touch the soul while not necessarily referencing the Supreme Being, doubt of whose existence had taken possession of Wagner's own soul. The opera of the future would be relocated within the greater cultural picture; it would occupy an important place in public life. The theatre of ancient Athens had only opened on days of special festivity, when the enjoyment of art was at the same time a religious celebration. Plays had been presented before the assembled populations of town and country, who were filled with high expectations of the loftiness of the works to be performed, so that Aeschylus and Sophocles could produce the most profound of all poems and be certain of their appreciation.

The *Ring* cycle took the form of such an (imagined) Hellenised music-drama, a tragic cycle equivalent to the *Oresteia* but based on specifically German myths and legends and, as such, designed to represent, and indeed to shape, the post-Napoleonic pan-German spirit. Through his new opera form, Wagner imagined himself purging German culture of alien elements, specifically, anything French and anything Jewish. Things French were *non grata* because the French were basically frivolous in their preference for elegance over sublimity. Additionally, they were an ever-present reminder of Germany's national humiliation by Napoleon. Things French also reminded Wagner of his own personal humiliation in 1861, when Paris's riotously hostile reception to his opera *Tannhäuser* turned him into a Francophobe for the rest of his life.

Anything Jewish had also to be swept away. Anti-Semitism was inseparable from Wagner's nationalist agenda; his essay 'Judaism in Music' is horrible to read today. Working out his ideas concerning the authenticity of German music, he was convinced that nineteenth-century art and civilisation had been corrupted and debased by capitalism. Capitalism was epitomised by Jewish bankers and traders throughout Europe. Conveniently, he ignored the fact that Jews had been squeezed into the financial sector by being barred from other trades and professions by law. Wagner's anti-Semitism, like his Francophobia, was also fired by personal reasons. He was jealous of Jewish composers, such as Meyerbeer and Mendelssohn, who were experiencing far greater success than himself.

The *Ring* cycle comprises four operas whose narrative, continuous and circular as a ring, demonstrates the inevitability of consequences upon action. The storyline is based on the great German myth of the Nibelungen, in which the ancient Norse gods behave quite unlike the Judeo-Christian God but very much as Greek gods. They are capricious, unfair, lustful, deceitful, and entirely human. Their legends, as related by Wagner, have all the appeal of a soap opera.

The anonymous medieval epic the *Nibelungenlied*, dating from *circa* 1200, was already a potent symbol in the struggle for German national identity and seen as a text that illustrated the distinctive *Volksgeist*, the spirit of the German people. Nationalistic ideology permeates Wagner's *Ring*, an artwork that has come to be written in stone for some 150 years, during which the pilgrimage to Bayreuth in full evening dress has become a sacred and unchanging capitalist – and sometimes political – ritual. But we must give Wagner the credit for conceiving his juggernaut quite differently. Its purpose was not to become a behemoth but to be the inspirational springboard for the artwork of the future. It was to be performed at a festival for the *Volk*, the ordinary people, just like the early festivals in ancient Greece. He envisioned the *Ring* itself as an ephemeral and transitional artwork. 'After the third [performance], the theatre will be demolished and my score burned. To the people who enjoyed it I shall then say: "Now go away and do it yourself."'[10] Rather a magnificent sentiment towards something that ate up decades of his life and thought and being.

On Nietzsche's long ascents of the mountains round about Tribschen together with the Master, they thumped out the idea of the *Ring* festival as a revival of the Anthesteria, the annual four-day festival in honour of Dionysus. Beneath them shone the waters of Lake Lucerne, where Cosima and the children swam among the swans. Cosima in her billowing white gown had all the grace of a swan herself, according to one of an important group of summer visitors, all writers, who made the pilgrimage to Tribschen from Paris.

While the 1861 Paris *Tannhäuser* had been a notorious fiasco, it had also had a great effect on the French avant-garde. The Symbolist and the decadent movements took great heed of Baudelaire's essay 'Wagner and *Tannhäuser* in Paris',[11] drawing attention to the opera's open exploration of the idea of sexuality and spirituality being antithetical yet mutually dependent, and also to Wagner's miraculous technical achievement of synaesthetic crossing of the senses between words and music in his *Gesamtkunstwerk*.

Now three ardent Parisian Wagnerians arrived at Tribschen in the shape of Catulle Mendès, decadent poet, playwright, novelist and founder of the literary journal *La revue fantaisiste*, his wife Judith Gautier, and Villiers de l'Isle-Adam, founder of the Parnassian movement, which jettisoned Romanticism for a neo-classical revival. Parnassianism never got far, as it was overshadowed by the much more successful Symbolist movement.

Villiers de l'Isle-Adam, a slightly built man, made his entrance to Tribschen wearing the padded 'Hamlet' tights he wore when he wished to have beautiful legs. Catulle Mendès had no need of costume to make an impression; he was often called the handsomest man of his generation. His looks were compared to a blond Christ but his personality was cruel, perverse and destructive; Maupassant called him 'a lily in urine'.[12]

Judith Gautier was in her twenties and the daughter of the poet and critic Théophile Gautier. She made her entrance as a *Parnassienne* with singular gusto, having jettisoned corsets and crinoline for loose drapery in the antique style that left her amplitude unfettered. It was Judith who had proposed the visit. Her husband Catulle's alcoholism was making him an increasingly unreliable breadwinner and Judith had turned herself into a journalist and successful author of highly charged romantic novels set in a Mysterious Orient she had never visited. The purpose of the trip to Tribschen was for Judith to write a colourful piece on Wagner at home, to be published in France.

Judith was a goddess of instinct and Dionysian sensuality: tall, dark, pale, intensely theatrical, overflowing 'with the buxom figure and nonchalance of an Oriental woman. One ought to see her lying on a tiger-skin and smoking a narghile,' said the Provençal poet Théodore Aubanel, who found her poetry 'diabolically nebulous' but her person 'wonderful' and her concocted orientalism perfectly irresistible. She made a speciality of loving much older men. She had already been the mistress of Victor Hugo, who was eleven years older than Wagner. Judith well knew the effect of lowering her long-lashed, languid eyelids, soulfully exhaling a suspiration of heavily perfumed Tribschen air and stroking the soft, slithery fabrics that Wagner loved.

'On more than one occasion,' Catulle Mendès reported, 'our morning visit caught him [Wagner] in that odd costume that legend has often since attributed to him: dressing gown and slippers of gold satin, brocaded with pearl-coloured flowers (for he had a passionate love of luminous fabrics, spreading out like flames or spilling out in splendid waves). Velvets and silks were in abundance in the salon and in his study, freely dispersed in swelling heaps or torrential trains in no particular relation to the furnishings – simply for the sake of their beauty and to enchant the poet with their glorious warmth.'[13]

When Judith went back to Paris, Wagner wrote her letters that began, 'Beloved Amplitude'. Often he enclosed shopping lists of the soft fabrics and heavy scents they both adored. She posted them to a different address so that Cosima should not discover. The enchantment of Wagner and his music was a religion for Judith, an ecstatic state of grace, as it was for Cosima. Both used the same self-abasing tears and hyperbolic tributes in their worship of the Master – 'the sounds he creates are the sun of my life!' and so on. But the two acolytes couldn't have been more different. Tightly corseted at all times, Cosima was described by Count Harry Kessler as 'all bones and will-power . . . a John the Baptist by Donatello', and by her dentist as a woman whose disdain of obstacles standing between her and her purpose was truly striking.'[14] In contrast to Judith's free-flowing Dionysianism, Cosima's control over Wagner was Apollonian, strictly intellectual, often admonitory. This summer, Cosima's diary records a ferocious programme of reading aloud most of Shakespeare's plays to each other, and playing Beethoven and Haydn piano duets. She was an accomplished pianist and a stern critic. Wagner feared her censure like a child. He endured agonies when Cosima refused him sex.

Though Wagner and Judith had not become lovers, Cosima's instincts required no actual misdemeanour to have taken place. Meanwhile, her cerebral, chaste and utterly correct relationship with Nietzsche grew closer and stronger. Unfortunately, she burned the correspondence between herself and Nietzsche, and so we must rely on her diary, which she wrote not as an intimate journal but as a future public document for the enlightenment and instruction of her children and posterity. Over the period of Judith Gautier's visit, it merely describes Nietzsche as a well-formed, cultured and pleasant man. Judith Gautier and her party are referred to as 'the Mendès people'.

On returning to Paris, Judith wrote an article on the Wagners at home that would not have disgraced *Hello* magazine. Cosima was horrified by the invasion of their privacy and the vulgarity of Judith's breezy exposure of the small, everyday details of their private life.

In breaks from composing, Wagner would take himself off with the dogs to hike up a mountain, or to a favourite antiquarian shop in Lucerne. While the Master was out of the house, Nietzsche was permitted to play on the Master's piano. He played well, even in this exalted context, and with greater emotional abandonment than Wagner, whose mind was always technically engaged. Nietzsche would work himself up into a trance-like state while playing, arousing in Cosima (Liszt's daughter after all) a state of hallucinatory intoxication.

The longer and more frenziedly he played, the tighter she felt gripped by 'a sense of fear and trembling', noting that it released the demonic in her. For Cosima, as for Nietzsche, music accessed the realm of divine ecstasy. Everyday life, she said, suddenly became unbearable compared to it. When Wagner was out, they tried several times to conjure up the underworld by Nietzsche playing frenziedly at the piano as a prelude to summoning the forces of the occult.[15]

That Christmas of 1869, Nietzsche was invited to spend the holiday at Tribschen. He was the only outsider, the only guest. He had never known a Christmas like it.

Wagner and Cosima observed an elaborate Christmas ritual. Cosima was a devoted Roman Catholic and Wagner a confirmed atheist, but year after year they collaborated to enchant the children. On Christmas Eve, they followed the old German tradition of St Nicholas, the gift-bringer, and Knecht Ruprecht, who threatens to thrash or abduct naughty or disobedient children.

Nietzsche helped Cosima set up the theatre in which the ritual would be enacted. Together they decorated the tree. When all was in place, the nursemaid Hermine ran to the children, telling them she could hear *such* roaring! Then Wagner appeared, dressed up as Knecht Ruprecht, roaring at the top of his voice and spreading terrible alarm. Gradually the children were pacified by gifts of nuts that Cosima had spent much of December gilding. The Christ child appeared, distracting the children from the disappearance of their father. Silence fell and the atmosphere became mysterious as the Christ child beckoned them down the dark staircase to the gallery. The whole household followed in a silent procession. At last they came to the tree, dazzlingly lit by candles. Presents were exchanged and Cosima led the children in prayers.

The following week appears to have been one of great happiness and great closeness between Nietzsche and Cosima. Her diary is blank following the entry for 26 December. It only resumes on 3 January, noting that she has not written in it for a whole week and that she spent most of the time with Professor Nietzsche, who left them yesterday.

On 18 July 1870, Cosima's marriage to von Bülow was at last dissolved. Nietzsche was invited to be a witness to her marriage to Wagner in the Protestant church in Lucerne on 25 August, but he was unable to attend. By that time, war had broken out between France and Prussia, as Nietzsche and Jacob Burckhardt had feared it would.

When Napoleon III's France declared war on Bismarck's Prussia on 19 July 1870, Nietzsche was in Basle, in bed with a sprained ankle, and his sister Elisabeth was looking after him. The natural course would have been to send her back to their mother in Naumburg but this was neither safe nor possible in the chaos immediately following the declaration of war.

'On the 19th of July, war was declared,' Elisabeth wrote, 'and from that day onwards the most incredible confusion prevailed in Basel. German and French travellers poured in from all sides, on their way to join their regiments at home. For a whole week it seemed almost impossible for the incoming crowds to get even a night's shelter in Basel. The railway stations were chock-full night after night, and those people who were unable to endure the suffocating air, would hire flies for the whole night.'[16]

Nietzsche accompanied Elisabeth for a brief visit to Tribschen before they continued to Mount Axenstein. Here they put up in a large hotel. While pondering his future, he wrote the essay 'The Dionysian Worldview' ('*Die dionysische Weltanschauung*'), relating Schopenhauer's philosophy to the spirit of Greek tragedy, and he wrote several drafts of a letter to the President of the Board of Education at Basle:

'In view of the present state of affairs in Germany, you will not be surprised at my request to be allowed to discharge my duty towards my native land. It is with this object that I appeal to you in order through your kind mediation to solicit a leave of absence, for the last weeks of the summer term, from the honourable Board of Education at Bâle. My health has now so far improved that I could without any fear of the consequences help my fellow-countrymen either as a soldier or as an ambulance attendant . . . in the face of Germany's awful cry that each should do his *German* duty, I confess that I could allow myself to be bound by my obligation to Bâle University only through painful compulsion . . . And I should like to see the Swiss who would consent to being kept to his post under similar circumstances . . .' The last sentence was crossed out in the final draft.[17]

On 9 August, he wrote to Cosima telling her of his intention to go to war. She replied the same day that she thought it was far too soon to volunteer. Anyway a gift of a hundred cigars would be more useful to the army than the presence of a dilettante. It was typical of the briskness that made her celestial in the eyes of Nietzsche and Wagner, and rendered them both helpless at her feet.

The university authorities released him with the stipulation that as he was to all intents and purposes a Swiss citizen he should not go back to his old regiment but take the non-combatant role of ambulance attendant.

Nietzsche travelled to the city of Erlangen on 12 August to receive training as a medical orderly in its large hospital. His fortnight's training course was not even finished before he had to deal with a trainload of the badly wounded: dead and dying children and adults.

On 29 August, four days after Cosima's marriage to Wagner, Nietzsche made an eleven-hour march to tend the wounded on the battlefield of Wörth, where the Germans had won a great victory at a terrible cost. Almost ten thousand Germans lay dead on the battlefield among eight thousand French corpses.

He wrote to his mother of the terribly devastated battlefield, 'scattered all over with countless mournful remains and reeking with corpses; today we go to Hagenau, tomorrow to Nancy, and so forth, following the Southern Army . . . For the next few weeks, your letters cannot reach me, for we are continuously on the move and the mail travels extremely slowly. One hears nothing now of military advances here – no newspapers are being printed. The enemy populations here seem to be getting used to the new state of affairs. But then they are threatened with the death penalty for the least offence.

'In all the villages we pass through there is hospital after hospital. You will hear from me again soon; do not worry about me.'[18]

2 September found Nietzsche tending the wounded on a hospital train travelling from Ars-sur-Moselle to Karlsruhe. The journey lasted three days and two nights. He described it in a letter to Wagner, dated 11 September.

'*Lieber und verehrter Meister:* So then your house is completed and firmly established in the midst of the storm. Far away though I was, I kept thinking of this event and wishing blessings upon you, and it makes me very happy to see, from the lines written me by your wife, whom I dearly love, that it was finally possible to celebrate these festivities [the wedding and Siegfried's christening] sooner than we suspected when we were last together.

'You know what stream it was that tore me away from you and made me unable to witness such holy and longed-for observances. My work as an auxiliary has come provisionally to an end, unfortunately through sickness. My many missions and duties brought me close to Metz [then under siege]. In Ars sur Moselle we took charge of casualties and returned with them to Germany . . . I had a miserable cattle truck in which there were six bad cases; I tended them, bandaged them, nursed them during the whole journey alone . . . I diagnosed in two cases gangrene . . . I had hardly delivered my transport at a Karlsruhe hospital when I showed serious signs of illness myself. I reached Erlangen with difficulty, to give various reports to my group. Then I went to bed and am still there. A good doctor diagnosed my trouble as, first, a severe dysentery and, then, diphtheria . . . Thus after a short run of four weeks, trying to work on the world at large, I have been thrown back once more upon myself – what a miserable state of affairs!'

Throughout the first critical week in Erlangen, Nietzsche was in danger of dying. He was treated with silver nitrate, opium and tannic acid enemas, the normal treatment of the time, the effect of which was to ruin the patient's intestines for life. After a week, his life was out of danger and he was sent to his mother and Elisabeth, who were still living in the childhood home in Naumburg. In terrible pain and constantly vomiting, he began the unfortunate lifetime habit of self-administering the drugs that temporarily alleviated the symptoms while further damaging his constitution. It has been suggested that Nietzsche contracted syphilis as well as diphtheria and dysentery from nursing the wounded in the railway carriage. Like the whole question of whether Nietzsche had syphilis, it is unverifiable one way or the other.

During his convalescence, he plunged himself into preparing lectures and seminars for the coming term and keeping in touch with friends by letters which never refer to the gruesome battlefield memories that must have haunted his days and nights. Nietzsche was suffering from wrecked bowels, jaundice, insomnia, vomiting, haemorrhoids, a constant taste of blood in his mouth and whatever psychological horrors the battlefields had smudged onto his brain. Unlike Wagner and Cosima, who almost every morning related their dreams to each other before Cosima religiously recorded them in her diary, Nietzsche did not confide his dreams to posterity. However, he does permit himself to express a violent disgust for militarism and philistinism in general, and for Bismarck's Prussia in particular.

'What enemies of our faith [culture] are now growing out of the bloody soil of this war! I am prepared for the worst and at the same time confident that here and there in the mass of suffering and of terror the nocturnal flower of knowledge will bloom.'[19]

'Fatal, anti-cultural Prussia' was to blame: far from reviving the creative spirit of ancient Greece, Bismarck was turning it into Rome: philistine, brutal, materialistic, an engine of wholesale murder and endless barbarities.

Nietzsche was outraged by the bloodthirstiness and cynical brutality of the Prussians in deliberately starving the French in the Siege of Paris, which lasted from the September when he fell ill, until the following January.

His horror at the barbarism of war was not confined to the Prussians. No sooner had a new French government been formed than the Paris Commune rose against it and behaved just as badly against its own people as the Prussians had done. It embarked on bloody and indiscriminate slaughter: clergy, prisoners and innocent passers-by were cut down. War was made on culture too. Monuments were smashed and overthrown. The museums and palaces of Paris, including the Tuileries, were looted and burned in a vengeful, pointless frenzy of Herostratic destruction. It was reported incorrectly in the Basle newspapers that the Louvre had also been destroyed. At such appalling news of deliberate cultural genocide, both Burckhardt and Nietzsche rushed out into the street in search of one another. On meeting, they embraced, heartbroken and speechless.

'When I heard of the fires in Paris, I felt for several days annihilated and was overwhelmed by fears and doubts,' wrote Nietzsche; 'the entire scholarly, scientific, philosophical, and artistic existence seemed an absurdity, if a single day could wipe out the most glorious works of art, even whole periods of art; I clung with earnest conviction to the metaphysical value of art, which cannot exist for the sake of poor human beings but which has higher missions to fulfil. But even when the pain was at its worst, I could not cast a stone against those blasphemers, who were to me only carriers of the general guilt, which gives much food for thought.'[20]

Come Christmastide, he was once again invited to Tribschen. In the eyes of his hosts, he had grown heroically into the philosopher-warrior but his experience of the battlefield had opened a great chasm between him and them. It had confirmed Nietzsche as a committed European, while Wagner and Cosima were ablaze with vengeful, celebratory nationalism. Wagner was even refusing to read letters sent to him written in French.

On Christmas morning, ravishing sounds came pulsing through the scented air of the house. Wagner had secretly smuggled Hans Richter and a fifteen-piece orchestra onto the staircase. They played the *Siegfried Idyll*, then nameless, dubbed the 'staircase music' by Cosima's daughters.

'Now let me die,' Cosima exclaimed to Wagner on hearing it.

'It would be easier to die for me than to live for me,'[1] he replied.

The exchange was typical of the elevated plane on which Tribschen conversation was exhaustingly and unrelentingly conducted, often punctuated by sobs and tears. The Christmas interlude continued on this high level of intensity for Cosima, who wrote that it was as if the *Siegfried Idyll* had transported her life into a waking dream. She felt a euphoric melting of boundaries, an unawareness of bodily existence, supreme happiness, the highest bliss, as if she had at last attained the Schopenhauerian goal of dissolving the boundaries between will and representation.

Cosima was delighted with Nietzsche's birthday gift, the manuscript of *The Birth of the Tragic Concept*, an early draft of *The Birth of Tragedy*. In the evenings, Wagner read passages aloud. He and Cosima praised it as being of the greatest value and excellence.

Wagner and Cosima were giving no gifts this Christmas, as a tribute to those still experiencing the hardships of war. Nietzsche had not been forewarned. He arrived laden with the essay for Cosima and little things for the children. For Wagner he had thoughtfully chosen a copy of Dürer's great engraving *The Knight, Death and the Devil*, an image that since its creation in 1513 had been taken as a nationalist rallying point, a significant symbol of German faith and German courage in adversity. Wagner accepted it with great pleasure. For him, the German knight took on the double symbolism of being his hero Siegfried who, in the plot of the *Ring*, rides to the redemption of the world, and also standing for himself. Wagner riding into the musical arena mounted on the Music of the Future: the knight who will renew the spirit of German culture which, smothered by philistinism and multiculturalism, one day will be called, like Siegfried, to destroy dragons of imported culture. It was a well-thought-out present.

Nietzsche stayed eight days, again as the only guest. One evening he read out his essay on the Dionysian attitude, which they then discussed. Another, Wagner read out the libretto for *Die Meistersinger*. Cosima records that she and Nietzsche enjoyed the sublime experience of Hans Richter playing music from *Tristan* for the two of them alone. They held a discussion on the comparative merits of E. T. A. Hoffmann and Edgar Allan Poe, and they agreed on the profundity of the idea of looking upon the real world as a spectre, which Schopenhauer remarks is the mark of philosophical capacity. One day was so cold that Nietzsche experienced the unaccustomed domestic happiness of a cosy invasion of his Thinking Room, the *Denkstube*, by the entire family. It was the warmest room in the house. They conducted their readings and conversations in flattering *sotto voce* so as not to disturb the Professor at work.

On New Year's Day 1871, he left them to return to Basle. Nietzsche had finally resolved that he would act on his disinclination for philology and his growing inclination for philosophy. In January, he wrote another long letter to the president of the university board,[22] putting forward the unorthodox suggestion that he transfer to the Chair of Philosophy at Basle, which had just then fallen vacant. He went on to suggest that his friend Erwin Rohde take over the Chair of Philology in his place. Rohde and Nietzsche had studied together under Ritschl at Bonn and Leipzig but as Nietzsche had no philosophical qualifications to his name and Rohde was a mere *Privatdozent* (visiting lecturer) at Kiel University, the authorities found Nietzsche's proposals surprising.

The thought of going back to teach philology induced a kind of spiritual narcolepsy in him. All January, his health was bad. The doctors insisted on a complete rest in a warm climate. His sister was sent for.

When she had nursed him to something approaching health, the two of them embarked on a journey of convalescence in the Italian Alps.

'The first day,' Elisabeth writes, 'we only reached Flüelen, because the stage-coach, the running of which the heavy falls of snow had interrupted for a whole fortnight, could resume its regular service only on the following morning. In our hotel we came across Mazzini, who, under the assumed name of Mr Brown, was travelling in the company of a young man.' Giuseppe Mazzini was a crony of Garibaldi. He had been sentenced to death in his own country and he spent much of his exile scheming to bring about a unified republic in Italy. Like so many of the international republicans and anarchists of the time, Mazzini found refuge in London, from where he planned the invasion and conquest of Italy by all the political émigrés living there. The otherwise feisty revolutionary Jane Carlyle hastened to excuse herself, because of a tendency to seasickness, but nobody else objected. The plan was to proceed from England in balloons, a practical method for steering them having just been invented. Mazzini felt, with some justice, that such a campaign would throw the Bourbon tyrants of Italy into a state of consternation.[23]

'This noble fugitive,' Elisabeth continues, 'bowed down with age and sorrow, who could enter the fatherland he loved so deeply only in secret and under an assumed name, struck me as an extraordinarily stirring figure. The whole of this journey across St Gotthard in tiny little sleighs built to carry only two persons, was undertaken in such beautiful weather that the gloomy scenery as well as the winter landscape of gold, blue and white, struck us as indescribably beautiful. The intellectual companionship of Mazzini, who graciously joined the two of us at all the stations, and an accident which terrified us while we were descending the zig-zag road leading from the dizzy heights of St Gotthard into the valley of Tremola, as if on wings (a small sleigh immediately in front of us fell with its passengers, coachman and horse, more than 200 feet into the depths. Fortunately no one was hurt, thanks to the soft snow) – all these things combined lent this journey a peculiar and never-to-be-forgotten charm. The following phrase of

Goethe's, which Mazzini repeatedly quoted in his foreign accent to the young man who accompanied him, became thenceforward a favourite life-maxim with my brother and myself: *Sich des Halben zu entwöhnen und im Ganzen, Vollen, Schönen resolut zu leben.* ['Ban compromise and live resolutely in that which is whole, full and beautiful.'] Mazzini's farewell words were very touching. He asked me whither we were bound. I replied, "For Lugano, which from all accounts is a sort of Paradise." He smiled, sighed a little and said, "For youth Paradise is everywhere."[24]

On 12 February they reached Lugano, where they fell into the serene, Magic Mountain-like lucid dreaminess of the bourgeois grand hotel of the time. Elisabeth noted down every minor notable, the most distinguished in her eyes being Count von Moltke, brother to the great Field Marshal. There were drawing-room games, theatrical performances, concerts and pleasant excursions to the nearby beauty spot Mount Bré. As a twenty-seven-year-old bachelor and professor, Nietzsche was much sought after and lionised. Stylishly he climbed Mount Bré higher than the rest of the party. Drawing a copy of *Faust* from his pocket, he read from it, 'while our eyes wandered over the magnificent spring landscape, and grew intoxicated with the overflowing riches of the world. At last he let the book drop, and – with his melodious voice began to discourse upon what he had just read and upon the things around us, just as if we had shed all our empty northern narrowness and pettiness, had grown worthy of higher feelings and higher aims, and with greater courage and lighter wings, could now, with all our energy, ascend to the highest pinnacle to meet the sun.'[25]

Unfortunately, von Moltke caught a cold while taking a trip on the lake. 'To the general dismay of all our party, [he] died', Elisabeth noted, but this did not long dent her cheeriness; 'What happy, and cloudless days were these three weeks in Lugano – all around us we had the scent of violets, the sunshine, and the beautiful air of the mountains and of spring! – I can still remember how we joked and laughed; with wanton spirits we participated even in the fun of the carnival. At Mid-Lent we were invited by an Italian nobleman to Ponte Tresa. When

I now recollect how we Germans from the Hôtel du Parc[26] danced together and with the Italians on the open market-place there (I can still see Fritz quite vividly in my mind's eye, merrily dancing a round dance), the whole thing strikes me as a real carnival dream.'

While Elisabeth was writing of merry peasant dances, her brother was writing his first book, *The Birth of Tragedy from the Spirit of Music*, describing the conclusions he had reached during the years of thinking in a non-philological manner about the origin and aim of Greek tragedy and its enduring importance for the present and the future of culture.

5

· THE BIRTH OF TRAGEDY ·

Almost everything we call 'higher culture' is based on the
spiritualisation and deepening of cruelty. Cruelty is what constitutes
the painful sensuality of tragedy.

Beyond Good and Evil, 'Our Virtues', Section 229

The impact of Nietzsche's first book, *The Birth of Tragedy from the Spirit of
Music*, has proved far greater than the narrow and time-bound concerns
that drove Nietzsche to write it. The book originated partly as a young
man's impassioned attack on the cultural degeneration of his day, and
partly as a manifesto for the cultural regeneration of the newly unified
state of Germany through the vision of Richard Wagner. It endures as a
revolutionary perception of the elusive transactions made between the
rational and the instinctive, between life and art, between the world
of culture and the human response to it.

The book's famous opening tells us that, just as procreation depends
on the duality of the sexes, so the continuing development of art and
culture down the ages depends on the duality of the Apollonian and
the Dionysian. Like the two sexes, they are engaged in a continual
struggle interrupted only by temporary periods of reconciliation.

He identifies the Apollonian with the plastic arts, particularly
sculpture but also painting, architecture and dreams, which, at
that pre-Freudian time, did not represent the messy eruption of
guilty subconscious effluvia, but still held their ancient significance
as prophecy, enlightenment and revelation. The qualities of Apollo
can be summed up more or less as the apparent, the describable: in
Schopenhauerian terms corresponding roughly to 'representation'. The
world of Apollo is made up of moral, rational individuals, those who
exemplify 'the *principium individuationis*, whose gestures and gaze speak

to us of all the intense pleasure, wisdom and beauty of "semblance".[1]

The arts belonging to Dionysus are music and tragedy. Dionysus the twice-born son of Zeus was perceived in ancient Greece as both man and animal. He represented an enchanted world of extraordinary experience transcending existential boundaries. The god of wine and intoxication, of drink and drugs, of ritual madness and ecstasy, god of the fictional world of the theatre, of the mask, of impersonation and illusion; he is the god whose arts subvert the normal or individual identity of his followers as they are transformed by them.

Music and tragedy are both capable of erasing the individual spirit and awakening impulses which in their heightened forms cause the subjective to dwindle into complete self-oblivion, while the spirit is mystically transported to a transcendent state of bliss or horror. In Attic tragedy one of the names of Dionysus was 'the Eater of Raw Flesh'. Only through the spirit of music can we understand the ecstasy involved in self-annihilation. One thinks of today's rock festival-goers, or of Nietzsche describing his response to *Tristan* as having laid his ear against the heart of the universal will and felt the tumultuous lust for life as a thundering torrent. He illustrates the point to his own contemporaries by a reference with which they would be familiar: the frenzied throngs that had roamed medieval Germany in a mania of singing and dancing, the so-called singers and dancers of St John and St Vitus. (Wagner had referred to them elliptically in *Die Meistersinger von Nürnberg*.) In them, Nietzsche recognised the Bacchic choruses of the Greeks. Intoxication, music, singing and dancing were the activities in which the *principium individuationis* was lost. Here was the Dionysian response to the pain of life.

Where did the Greeks' pessimism, their attraction towards the tragic myth, towards the fearful, the evil, the cruel, the Eater of Flesh, the orgiastic, the enigmatic and destructive, begin? The genius of Greek tragedy, he tells us, is that through the miracle of the Hellenic will, the Apollonian and Dionysian are coupled. The pre-Socratic Greek playwright is an Apollonian dream artist and a Dionysian ecstatic artist at the same time, and this is achieved through the chorus.

The chorus represents the origin of tragedy and it is a representation of the Dionysian state. The introduction of the chorus is a negation of naturalism. Nietzsche warns against the culture of his own day: 'With our current veneration for the natural and the real, we have arrived at the opposite pole to all idealism, and have landed in the region of waxworks.'[2]

To understand the death of Greek tragedy, we have only to consider the Socratic maxims: that virtue is knowledge, that all sins arise from ignorance, and that the happy man is the virtuous man.

In this basically optimistic and rational formula lies tragedy's extinction. In post-Socratic plays the virtuous hero must be dialectical. There must be a necessary and visible bond between virtue and knowledge, between faith and morality. Socrates reduces the transcendental justice of Aeschylus to 'the flat and impudent principle of poetic justice'.

Socrates is 'the mystagogue of science' in whose eye the lovely gleam of madness never glowed. Socrates instigated the 'unimaginable, universal greed for knowledge, stretching across most of the cultured world, and presenting itself as the true task for anyone of higher abilities. [Socrates] led science on to the high seas, from which it could never again be driven completely . . . for the first time, thanks to this universality, a common network of thought was stretched over the whole globe, with prospects of encompassing even the laws of the entire solar system.'[3]

People are held fast by the Socratic delusion that pleasure in understanding can heal the eternal wound of existence. 'Anyone who has experienced the intense pleasure of a Socratic insight, and felt it spread out in ever-widening circles as it attempted to encompass the entire world of appearances, will forever feel there can be no sharper goad to life.'[4]

But this is to ignore that the world is more than a replica of phenomena. There also exists the Dionysian, the Will. And so, 'In this late period of Socratic culture, man . . . remains eternally hungry.' Reduced to rationality, Alexandrian man is basically 'a librarian and proof-reader, sacrificing his sight miserably to book-dust and [printing] errors'.[5]

Is our flight into science and scientific proof perhaps a kind of fear, an escape from pessimism, a subtle, last resort against truth? Morally speaking, is it a sort of cowardice and falsity?

The problem of science must be faced. Science was a post-Socratic problem in Greece, Nietzsche observes, as it remains a problem in post-Darwinian Europe. By faith in the explicability of nature and in knowledge as a panacea, science annihilates myth. As a result, 'We fall into a senile, unproductive love of existence.'

Never has there been a period in which culture was more enfeebled. When the disaster that is slumbering in the womb of theoretical culture gradually begins to frighten modern man, the only salvation for culture will be to break open the enchanted gate leading into the Hellenic magic mountain.[6]

Who holds the key to the magic mountain? Whose power is strong enough to break down the gate? Schopenhauer and, inevitably, Wagner. Opera, in short, with its marriage of words and music presents the new tragic art form in which the Dionysian and Apollonian are reunited.

Wagner's music of the future is based on the necessary revival of tragic myth (German rather than Greek) and dissonance. His use of musical dissonance reflects and acknowledges the dissonance of man's soul and the tension within him between Will and Representation, between Apollonian and Dionysian.

Who, Nietzsche asks, can listen to the third act of *Tristan und Isolde*, 'this shepherd's dance of metaphysics', without expiring in a spasmodic unharnessing of all the wings of the soul? How could anyone 'fail to be shattered immediately'?[7] A Dionysian experience if ever there was one and a fully German one, mythically speaking.

In some hitherto inaccessible abyss the German spirit still rests and dreams, undestroyed and Dionysian in strength, like a knight sunk in slumber; and from this abyss the Dionysian rises to our ears.

In *Tristan* (here things become complicated) the Dionysian is, in reality, in the service of the Apollonian. The highest goal of tragedy is when Dionysus speaks the words of Apollo and Apollo, finally, the words of Dionysus. Thus is the highest goal of tragedy, and of all art, attained.

Having quoted copiously from the libretto of *Tristan*, the book concludes with an imagined meeting between a modern man and an ancient Greek who go together to the tragedy to sacrifice to both deities. While *The Birth of Tragedy* is a book that is more about culture than about how people should lead their lives, it does introduce us to ideas that Nietzsche would return to as his philosophy developed. The concept of human nature's duality, expressed in *The Birth of Tragedy* by the Apollonian and the Dionysian, and the crucial need to confront the illusion of certainty provided by science would occupy his thoughts for the rest of his active life.

When he had finished the first draft of the book he fled the melting snows of Lugano for Tribschen, surprising Cosima by suddenly appearing at breakfast on 3 April. She remarked that he looked very run-down and she persuaded him to stay for five days. He read aloud his manuscript, which was then entitled *The Origin and Aim of Greek Tragedy*. Cosima and Wagner were delighted. Much of the text was a drawing together of their exchanges of ideas over the past couple of years. Besides, how could they fail to be captivated by the proposal of national cultural renewal through Wagner's music?

Suddenly, everyone and everything at Tribschen was Apollonian or Dionysian. Wagner had a new love-name for Cosima: she was now his 'Apollonian spirit'. He was already Dionysus in the love triangle but Nietzsche's book had added a new understanding to the role. Wagner incorporated the terms 'Apollonian' and 'Dionysian' into the address he was writing 'On the Destiny of Opera', which he was scheduled to deliver in three weeks' time to the Academy of Sciences in Berlin. After that, he had an appointment for a private talk with Bismarck. The cultural direction of the German *Reich* was on its way.

But while this was flattering to Nietzsche, he was discovering himself more of a Burckhardtian, more of a European than Wagner.

He could not condone Wagner's exultation at the sufferings of Paris under Prussian siege. Wagner referred to Paris as 'that kept woman of the world' and rubbed his hands in glee that she was at last getting her comeuppance for her mistress-like light-heartedness, her preference for elegance over seriousness and her 'Franco-Jewish trivialisation of culture'.

'Richard would like to write to Bismarck requesting him to shoot all Paris down,'[8] Cosima noted, but Nietzsche took a different view: he was overcome with pity for the innocents of Paris and horror at his own country for the imposition of such suffering.

The Tribschen soundtrack was unsettling, if not downright disagreeable, to Nietzsche's ears. The children were singing the catchy new *Kaisermarsch* that Wagner had composed in honour of the new Emperor, and the Master was reading aloud his new poem in praise of the Prussian army that besieged Paris. What Nietzsche saw as a barbaric tide of cultural erasure, Wagner saw as a tide of cultural renewal. Wagner's point of view was that if you are not capable of painting pictures again, you are not worthy of possessing them. Shorn of Wagner's ugly nationalism, this was surely the truly Dionysian, truly creative original viewpoint, compared to Nietzsche's merely historic, merely Apollonian inclination to preserve the cultural edifice.

We know that while Nietzsche was at Tribschen, he made changes to *The Birth of Tragedy* at Wagner's suggestion but we do not know exactly what they were. After 'making the children happy with a green snake',[9] he departed for Basle to tinker further with the text, to change its title and to add a long dedication to Wagner.

In Basle, only bad news awaited him. The vacant Chair of Philosophy had been filled by a suitable candidate. Nietzsche realised how naïve and inappropriate he had been in putting forward his own Musical Chairs suggestions.

'What idiocies I committed! And how sure I was in all my schemes! I cannot hide behind the bed-screen of my sickly state; obviously it was an idea born of a sleepless night of fever, and with it I thought I had found a healing remedy against sickness and nerves.'[10] Instead of which he must remain one of the wriggling brood of philologists investigating the grammatical minutiae of the ancients without ever confronting the compelling problems of life. His philological duties were a terrible distraction from the greater task. He must place his hopes in the publication of the book finding him recognition as a philosopher. Then he might be able to change direction.

Meanwhile, his anxiety and his health were such that the kindly Basle authorities lightened his teaching load. His sister Elisabeth moved to Basle to look after him. It was no hardship for Elisabeth to leave Naumburg, where she was leading the constrained life of a spinster, living in their mother's house and devoting herself to good works.

At the end of April, Nietzsche sent off the opening part of *The Birth of Tragedy* to a Leipzig publisher. Months passed without even an acknowledgement. His authorial insecurity was fuelled by the absence of Wagner and Cosima. The gods had deserted the Island of the Blessed and were travelling through Germany in their quest to find a place to build the festival theatre to stage the *Ring*. There could be no flight to Tribschen for intellectual support. Besides, even had he been to hand, Wagner was in no position to give support to anybody else because he too was in a sustained state of tension and insecurity. Despite Wagner's strenuous efforts to prevent him, King Ludwig had mounted a disastrous production of *Das Rheingold*, the first opera in the *Ring* cycle. Impatient to see it on stage, the King had backed a staging that was premature and desperately badly thought-out. It fulfilled Wagner's worst predictions, and the fallout from the hopeless production included the King severing direct connections with Wagner, who now had no idea whether Ludwig would carry on financing the *Ring* project. This made it peculiarly frustrating that on their trip through Germany, Wagner and Cosima identified Bayreuth as the perfect place to build their opera house, if only they had the money.

A medium-sized town in northern Bavaria, Bayreuth was served by a railway that could deliver the audience to the door. The setting was marvellously, mythically German. It was the highest point on a huge plain fertile with crops and cattle. A historic Baroque palace in a landscaped park represented the triumph of Apollonian intellect, while a good-sized grassy hill dominating the plain was crying out to be crowned by the Dionysian presence of an opera house.

At Whitsuntide, Wagner and Cosima returned to Tribschen full of hope. They summoned Nietzsche to join them. Whitsun was an emotionally charged time for the three of them. It could never pass without the sacramental memory of Siegfried's birth in 1869, the occasion that had sealed their mystical triumvirate.

Now, a mere two years later, loss loomed. If the cultural project succeeded, which Nietzsche must hope it would, Wagner and Cosima would leave Tribschen permanently for Bayreuth. His days on the Island of the Blessed were numbered. On which day was the ripple of the star dance destined to live only in retrospect? His uncertainty and emotional fragility were aggravated by the publisher failing to make up his mind whether or not to publish *The Birth of Tragedy*. In June, Nietzsche could stand the tension no longer. He demanded the manuscript back. Without telling the Master, he sent it to Wagner's publisher, Ernst Wilhelm Fritzsch.

At the beginning of September, Cosima wrote to Nietzsche to ask him to recommend somebody to accompany the son of Princess Hatzfeldt-Trachenberg on a very grand tour of Italy, Greece, the East and America. There were many good reasons for Nietzsche to volunteer. It would see some sort of resolution to a long and tension-filled summer. It might improve his health (his doctors were always recommending warmer climes). It would be a neat escape from the Chair of Philology. It meant that he would at last set eyes on Rome and the classical world. This so excited him that he chattered to his university colleagues about the project before anything was settled. Also – it seemed to be what Cosima wanted, or why had she mentioned it to him? But he had hopelessly misread Cosima, who was never one to hint when she could command. Cosima was scandalised by the idea of him giving up the serious role of professor to take up the frivolous one of *cicerone* to a princeling. When she communicated this, Nietzsche was consumed with the shame of having made a fool of himself in her eyes and in the eyes of the university. Fortunately the university saw it differently. When he announced his intention to stay, they raised his salary by the considerable sum of 500 francs, to 3,500.

In October he celebrated his twenty-seventh birthday. A month later he wrote a delirious letter to Carl von Gersdorff, his old school friend from Schulpforta, to let him know that 'the excellent Fritzsch' had accepted the book and promised to publish it in time for Christmas.

'The design is settled,' Nietzsche jubilantly told von Gersdorff, 'to be modelled on Wagner's *The Object of Opera* – rejoice with me! This means there will be a glorious place for a nice vignette: tell this to your artist friend and give him my most amicable regards as well. Take out the Wagner pamphlet, open the title page, and calculate the size which we might give:

The
Birth of Tragedy
from the Spirit of Music
by
Dr. Friedrich Nietzsche
Professor of Classical Philology
Leipzig Fritzsch

'I have at present the greatest confidence that the book will have tremendous sales and the gentleman who designs the vignette can prepare himself for a modicum of immortality.

'Now some more news. Imagine, my dear friend, how strangely those warming days of [our] reunion during my vacation came at once to fruition in me in the form of a longish composition for two pianos, in which everything echoes a beautiful autumn, warm with the sun. Because it connects with a youthful memory, the opus is called *Echo of a New Year's Eve: With Processional Song, Peasant Dance, and Midnight Bell*. That is a jolly title . . . At Christmas this music will be a present and a surprise for Frau Wagner . . . I had composed nothing for six years, and *this* autumn stimulated me again. When properly performed, the music lasts twenty minutes.'[11]

His euphoria did not last long. The woodcut artist who was to be immortalised by the vignette botched the job and another artist had to be found. The good Fritzsch set the text in a smaller type than Wagner's *The Object of Opera* so the book, at 140 pages, was slimmer and looked less important than Nietzsche had hoped, more like a booklet. Also, Wagner was angry with him for going to his publisher without first asking him. It made it look as if the two of them were colluding, as if Nietzsche were Wagner's tame propagandist.

He declined the invitation to spend Christmas at Tribschen, giving as his reason that he needed time to think out a new course of lectures on the future of educational institutions, but he could have done that just as well in the *Denkstube*. In fact, as he admitted confidentially to Erwin Rohde, he needed time to collect himself for Wagner's verdict on the piece of music he had sent. '[I] am excited as to what I shall hear about my musical work.'[12]

Nietzsche thought of himself as a composer of some talent and he glowed warmly in expectation of Wagner's admiration. When eventually Hans Richter and Cosima sat down at the Tribschen piano to play the duet to a listening Wagner, the Master fidgeted throughout the twenty minutes it took to perform. The piece was typical of Nietzsche's piano compositions at this period, a pot-pourri of Bach, Schubert, Liszt and Wagner. Bitty, over-emotional and short on development, his compositions invariably ignite the idea that had he lived later he might have found success as a composer of incidental music for the silent cinema. However much Wagner and Cosima laughed in private, they concealed their small opinion of the piece. She thanked him for the 'beautiful letter' accompanying the gift but made no mention of the music itself.

Alone in Basle over Christmas, Nietzsche was helped by an unexplained house painter to open a large crate that had arrived from his mother. Franziska was now quite prosperous, having profited from legacies on the death of the aunts, which provided her with the funds to purchase the whole of the Naumburg house and rent out bits of it to lodgers.

This Christmas, in missionary spirit, Franziska had decided to send her religiously wavering son a large Italian oil painting of the Madonna. During the solitude of the long days of Christmas, Nietzsche had plenty of time to compose a letter of thanks that includes a description of how very conventionally he had arranged his living quarters: 'Naturally the *Madonna* will be over the sofa; over the piano there will be a picture by Holbein, the big Erasmus . . . with Papa Ritschl and Schopenhauer above the book table beside the stove. Anyway . . . I thank you most heartily . . . it seems as if such a picture were drawing me involuntarily toward Italy and – I almost believe you sent it to me to lure me there. The only answer I can give to this Apollonian effect is through my Dionysian one – through the New Year's Eve music – and after that, through the Apollonian-Dionysian double effect of my book, which will be published at the New Year.'

The letter goes on to thank her for the good comb, hairbrush, clothes brush, 'except it is somewhat too soft', nice socks and large quantity of delicious gingerbread in festive packaging.[13] At the same time he wrote another letter in tones of gleeful transgression to his childhood friend Gustav Krug telling him to expect *The Birth of Tragedy* in the New Year and warning him, in very much the same tone and language that he had used as a seventeen-year-old to warn the friend to whom he had sent his 'repulsive' obscene novel *Euphorion*, 'Oh! It is naughty and offensive. Read it secretly, closeted in your room.'[14]

One cannot read his letters this Christmastime without pitying him for the uncertainty that was swirling around him. Nobody was being straightforward. Everybody, including himself, was pretending; everybody was wearing a mask, showing one face to one person, one to another. He had temporarily forgotten the guiding admonition of Pindar that he had adopted during his student days, 'Become what you are!'

At last the book emerged from the publisher's. On 2 January 1872, he was able to send it to Wagner with an accompanying letter describing it as delayed by 'the powers of fate, with which no eternal bond can be woven . . .'

'On every page, you will find that I am only trying to thank you for everything you have given me; only doubt overcomes me as to whether I have always correctly received what you gave.

With the warmest thanks for your love, I am, as I have been and shall be,

Your loyal Friedrich Nietzsche.'

It was the most naked, most openly affectionate letter he had ever written. Fortunately, on receipt of the book, Wagner wrote by return of post:

'Dear Friend!

I have read nothing more beautiful than your book. Everything is superb! . . . I told Cosima that after her it is you who come next in my heart, and then, after a long distance, it is Lenbach, who has made such a strikingly lifelike portrait of me! Adieu! Come very soon to us and then there will be Dionysian merriment!'

Cosima wrote an ecstatic letter praising the book unreservedly. She found the text profound, poetic and beautiful. She told him that it gave her all the answers to the questions of her inner life. The sentiment she expressed was genuinely felt: in the privacy of her diary she calls the book 'really splendid' and describes herself and Wagner almost tearing the volume in two as they vied for physical possession of it.

Nietzsche sent a copy to Liszt, who also responded kindly, saying, among much else, that he had never found a better definition of art. More praise piled up in the shape of letters from ladies and gentlemen of rank, barons and baronesses who did not necessarily understand the book but who wrote an assortment of platitudes to show they were in the camp of Wagner and King Ludwig *contra mundum*. There was nothing from any professional philosopher or philologist and there was no review in the press. He waited nervously. There spread around the book the most oppressive and uneasy public silence. 'It feels', he said, 'almost as though I had committed a crime.'

However, there was solid intellectual distraction in the task of delivering the lectures on education whose writing had prevented him spending Christmas at Tribschen. The Basle Academic Society had a great tradition of public lectures. Each winter a programme of thirty or forty lectures was open to an audience of all comers. About three hundred people turned up for Nietzsche's first lecture on 16 January, listened with great approval and came back for more.

The series *On the Future of Our Educational Institutions* took as its subject the direction that should be taken in the vital field of education in the newly founded *Reich*. Much ground covered in *The Birth of Tragedy* was reused in the lectures. Criticism of the sterile culture of the present age was followed by the suggestion it be replaced by a regeneration of 'the Germanic spirit' of the past.

Nietzsche structured the lectures like Platonic dialogues between a student and a teacher, making them relevant to his audience by putting current political points of view into their mouths; arguing Marxist theory against a return to the aristocratic radicalism of ancient Greece.

The student argues for the greatest possible expansion of education. The net should be cast as wide as possible. Utility should be made the object and goal of education. The greatest possible enabling of pecuniary gain would equal happiness for all.

The philosopher argues for a return to education for its own sake and for the sake of upholding the highest ethical morals. Expanded education produces enfeebled education. The state's dilemma is that the bond between intelligence and property demands rapid education so that a money-earning creature may be produced with all speed. Man is allowed only the precise amount of culture which is compatible with the interests of gain.

He had said the unsayable: that the state did not want brilliant individuals but cogs in the machine, specialists who had been educated just sufficiently to contribute uncritically and subserviently, an inexorable result of which was the perpetuation of intellectual mediocrity. We hear an echo of Nietzsche's perambulating conversations with Burckhardt in his rant against the newspaper stepping into the place of culture, and his exasperation that even the greatest scholar must avail himself of newspapers: 'this viscous stratum of communication which cements the seams between all forms of life, all classes, all arts, and all sciences and which is as firm and reliable as the newspaper is, as a rule'.[15]

The series of lectures was to run to six, but by the time he had delivered the fifth, his health had broken down. This, together with his inability to close the argument by moving in the last lecture from theory to concrete suggestions for educational reform, meant that the series was never completed. All five lectures had been popular and well attended. He received an offer to take up the Chair of Classical Philology in the northern town of Greifswald but the last thing he wanted was another chair in philology. What he wanted was to move to a chair in philosophy.

The enthusiastic students of Basle misinterpreted his 'No' to Greifswald. Thinking it signified his undying loyalty to Basle, they visited him with a proposal to hold a torchlight procession in his honour. He turned it down. A few days later the University of Basle raised his salary to four thousand Swiss francs in recognition of his 'outstanding services'.

Eight days after Nietzsche had delivered the first lecture, Wagner called on him in great distress. He wondered how he could prevent Nietzsche's book being 'killed by silence'.[16] But even deeper ran Wagner's concern for himself and for his life's work. It looked as if his dream was yet again collapsing. First, the town council of Bayreuth had offered him the site on which to build the opera house, then it had transpired that the council did not own the land, and the man who did refused to sell them the plot. And after that, things had gone from bad to worse: King Ludwig's secretary had checked the sums. Wagner was even worse at finance than he was at singing in tune and the building costs had somehow risen alarmingly from three hundred thousand thalers to nine hundred thousand. The money was to have been raised by the formation of subscription-paying Wagner Societies wherever enthusiasts could be found. Many societies had been formed across Germany and abroad, even as far as Egypt, where the Khedive, flushed with the idea of integration with Europe (he had recently invited Henrik Ibsen among others to the opening of the Suez canal), contributed. The responsibility for coordinating the diverse Wagner Societies' funds had been taken on by two fine-sounding bigwigs, the Barons Loën from Weimar and Cohn from Dessau, but they had only managed to raise somewhere between twelve thousand and twenty-eight thousand – at least this was what they said, but Wagner was convinced that Baron Cohn, whom he called 'the Court Jew', was sabotaging the enterprise for vile, Semitic reasons.

Wagner was in despair; he was almost ready to abandon the whole project. He could not sleep. His digestion was chaotic. He was haunted by the idea that King Ludwig would die or go mad. Then the money would dry up completely and the *Ring* project and the cultural regeneration of Germany would die with him. Wagner was calling on Nietzsche as his first stop on his final, despairing fundraising tour.

Seeing the Master in such a wretched state, Nietzsche impulsively offered to give up everything to tour the German fatherland, delivering fundraising lectures. Wagner dissuaded him. It was Nietzsche's job to remain in Basle and consolidate his reputation by completing his lecture series, whose real and important ambition was to effect a change in Bismarck's education policy. On the back of the successful lectures, which Nietzsche planned to publish as a book, he was secretly preparing a memorandum to send to Bismarck, pointing out the Chancellor's shortcomings in the field of education and suggesting reforms as a model for cultural renewal, 'to show how disgraceful it is that a great moment has been missed for founding a truly German educational institution which would regenerate the German spirit . . .'[17] In the event the book was never published and the memorandum never sent. It was an ill-conceived project in the first place; Bismarck never responded positively to a wagging finger.

Wagner continued on his way to Berlin, leaving Cosima alone to console herself with Nietzsche's book and a tub of caviar that Wagner had sent from Leipzig.[18] Had Nietzsche followed his quixotic impulse to throw up the university and roam the *Reich* for Wagner, he would have found himself redundant within the month. Wagner's trip was an overwhelming financial success. The victory over France had created a nationalistic mood that made him and his agenda immensely appealing. He was received with acclamation in Berlin and Weimar. Bayreuth offered him an even better piece of land, as well as another large plot close to the opera house, where he and Cosima could build a fine villa to make their home.

Late March, and the snows were melting. Wagner had come back from his triumphant tour and Nietzsche was invited to spend the Easter holiday together with them at Tribschen. Again he was the only guest. He arrived on Maundy Thursday with the burden of a hundred francs weighing down his pockets. It was an Easter betrayal of sorts, smacking of Judas's thirty pieces of silver. The money had been given him by Hans von Bülow, an expert in emotional manipulation, who would never cease to find exquisite ways of tormenting Cosima and those who loved her. Von Bülow had paid a visit to Nietzsche in Basle just before Easter. He had praised *The Birth of Tragedy* to the skies before charging him with the embarrassing task of delivering the money as an Easter gift to his daughter Daniela, who was living at Tribschen with Cosima and Wagner.

The weather that Easter weekend was as changeable and unsettled as their emotions as they stood at the jagged brink of separation, immersed in regret beyond words. They were leaving the Island of the Blessed. If leaving Tribschen did not actually signify what Wotan calls *das Ende*, the twilight of the gods, there was no doubt it marked the end of an enchanted period of godlike mutually inspired creativity that had seen the creation of one child and four masterpieces: *Siegfried*, *Götterdämmerung*, *The Siegfried Idyll* and *The Birth of Tragedy*. They all knew they were at the end of the idyll.

Wagner took Nietzsche out for what would turn out to be their last walk through the Tribschen landscape. In the evening Nietzsche read them his fifth lecture. The following day while Wagner worked, Nietzsche and Cosima set out for a walk along the Robbers' Path. For such walks, Cosima was wont to wear pink cashmere richly trimmed with lace and, to protect her fair complexion, a large Tuscan hat decorated with pink roses. Behind her paced the gigantic coal-black Newfoundland dog Russ, dignified, heavy, and inevitably reminiscent of the familiar spirit in the Faust legend. As they traced the shore of the silver lake, they spoke of the tragedy of human life, of the Greeks, the Germans, of plans and aspirations. Like the brush of a great wing, a cold wind signalled the arrival of a sudden storm that chased them back indoors, where they read fairy tales by the fire.

On Easter Sunday, Nietzsche helped her hide eggs in the garden for the children to find. In their pale Easter dresses, the children looked like a clutch of cygnets scuttling about the shoreline, searching the emerald reeds for the concealed eggs, and emitting little cries on making a discovery. Cradling the decorated eggs in interlocked fingers, the children bore them back to Cosima.

In the afternoon, Nietzsche and Cosima played duets at the piano. A rainbow rose in the sky. Universal symbol of hope and blazing aspiration, the rainbow was of even deeper personal significance to the two of them, for in the *Ring* Wagner uses the rainbow as the bridge that connects the world of mortals to the realm of the gods. Only by passing over the rainbow bridge can the transition be made from one world to the other.

At lunchtime the three of them talked of a different connectivity between gods and mortals: the fashionable pastime of spiritualism. Cosima was privately a great believer in the supernatural. She writes in her diary of lying in bed at night hearing creaking and knocking sounds in the old house and interpreting them as signals from the spirit world: messages from mortals that she once knew or from dead dogs that she once loved. But in Wagner's presence she pretended a greater scepticism so as not to look foolish in his eyes. Wagner himself was not interested in signals sent via the expansion and contraction of bits of wood, but he did pay heed when the gods tried to catch his attention by grander means such as a rainbow, or a thunderclap, or the moon struggling to get clear of a black ribbon of flying cloud, or the Northern Lights spreading their luminous curtains over Tribschen's sky. Over lunch, Wagner gave them the rational refutation of spiritualistic manifestations and Cosima declared it all a fraud. Nevertheless, in the evening they all had a go at table turning. It was a conspicuous failure.

On Monday morning Nietzsche had to return to his university duties. After the Professor had left them they both felt out of sorts, ill and depressed. Even the irrepressible Wagner expressed himself in the grip of disgust, sorrow, worry and fear of not being equal to the tremendous task ahead. Cosima retired to bed.

A series of misunderstandings, or maybe fate, dictated that Nietzsche should turn up at Tribschen to bid his farewell to the Master three days after the Master had finally left for Bayreuth. He found Cosima in the middle of packing up a house that was no longer the place that had changed his entire perception of how a life could be lived. The rooms had lost their heavy enchantment: the atmosphere, once narcotic, now smelled fresh, alpine and faintly of lake water. The rouged air of their private world had turned bright with sunlight. Flowing spaces that had been dematerialised by muffled light entering through rose-coloured gauzes had lost their soft mystery and now were harsh, sleek and solid. Windows that had been given the rapture of fantasy by curtains bunched and swathed, caught in the chubby hands of gilded cherubs and garlands of delicate pink silk roses, had reverted to flat glass rectangles. Wagner's apocalyptic vision which had transformed every domestic interior into a stage set had been replaced by mere fresh-looking cubes harbouring no mystery at all. The rich wall-coverings of violet velvet and stamped leather wore ugly mouse-coloured shapes where the icons of their faith had once hung. Blurred U shapes marked the ghosts of laurel wreaths. Blank rectangles memorialised the pictures of breastplated Valkyries, of King Ludwig looking young and noble, of scaly corkscrewing dragons, and of Genelli's *Dionysus Sporting with the*

Apollonian Muses that Nietzsche had contemplated so often during the time he was developing his thoughts into *The Birth of Tragedy*.

Nietzsche could not cope with the emotion. Just as on the overwhelming occasion when he had found himself overcome with horror and anguish in the brothel, he fled to the grand piano. He sat at the keyboard improvising, while Cosima moved with majestic solemnity through the rooms, supervising the servants in the melancholy task of packing up Tribschen's treasures. Extemporising, he poured out his poignant love for her and for her husband, for the radiance they had created together and shared over the period of three years, for rapturous memory and for the long forever of future yearning.

His loss was not yet complete but nothing could prevent it slipping away. It felt, he said, like walking among a future ruin. Cosima talked of 'eternal times now past'. The servants were all in tears; the dogs followed the humans about like lost souls and refused to eat. Nietzsche left the piano stool only to assist Cosima in sorting and packing the objects that were too precious to entrust to the servants: letters, books, manuscripts and, above all, the musical scores.

'Tears hung heavily in the air. Ah! it was desperate! These three years that I have spent in close relationship to Tribschen, and during which I have made twenty-three visits to the place – what do they not mean to me! If I had not had them, what should I now be!'[19] And in *Ecce Homo*, he added: 'None of my other personal relationships amounts to much; but I would not give up my Tribschen days for anything, days of trust, of cheerfulness, of sublime chance, of *profound* moments . . . I do not know what other people's experience of Wagner has been: no clouds ever darkened our skies.'

It was said that afterwards he could never speak of Tribschen without a break in his voice.

On return to Basle, he became ill with shingles in his neck and was unable to write the sixth and final lecture. There was no new book for Fritzsch to publish and the fog of silence continued to envelop *The Birth of Tragedy*.

Nietzsche had written a letter to his beloved teacher Professor Ritschl, the classical philologist whom he had followed from the University of Bonn to the University of Leipzig and whose portrait now hung above his book table by the stove. 'You will not grudge me my astonishment that I have not heard a word from you about my recently published book,'[20] began his ill-judged letter, which continued in the same juvenile tone.

Ritschl had not written because he could not find anything agreeable to say. He thought Nietzsche's letter displayed megalomania. He thought *The Birth of Tragedy* was ingenious claptrap. He peppered the margins of his copy with exclamations like 'megalomania!', 'rakish!' and 'dissolute!' But he worded his reply so tactfully that Nietzsche took no offence at the suggestion that the text was less scholarly than dilettante and the observation that he did not regard the individualisation of life as retrogressive, when the alternative would seem to consist of dissolving the sense of self into self-oblivion.

The other father figure whose opinion mattered was Jacob Burckhardt, who was equally tactful and elusive in his response. So much so that Nietzsche apparently believed that Burckhardt was thrilled and fascinated by the book, but in fact Burckhardt was offended by the book's thesis, its intemperance, its stridency of tone and by its proposal that the serious post-Socratic scholar was nothing more than an indiscriminate collector of facts.

And still there was silence! 'People have kept quiet now for ten months, because all actually think they are beyond and above my book, that it is not worth talking about.'[21]

The Wagners had not been gone from Tribschen a month before he received an invitation to join them for the laying of the foundation stone of the opera house in Bayreuth. Things had moved forward at an impetuous speed. Cosima had quickly put Tribschen behind her. Here in Bayreuth she was flourishing as never before. 'It is as though all our lives before were only a preparation for this,' she wrote. Wagner crowned her sentiment by kneeling at her feet while bestowing on her a new name: the Markgräfin (Margravine) of Bayreuth.

Cosima had always been a snob. They were living in the Hotel Fantaisie, which was owned by Duke Alexander of Württemberg and bounded by the gracious grounds of his castle, Schloss Fantaisie. The pages of her diary begin to read like the Almanach de Gotha. Double- and treble-barrelled dukes, princes and princesses swarm the pages. Her favours were curried by all. Lesser aristocrats, counts and countesses, pushed themselves forward by whatever means they could. Count Krockow presented Wagner with a leopard he had shot in Africa. Countess Bassenheim embroidered little blouses for the infant Siegfried. Cosima accepted every tribute with Markgräfin-like graciousness.[22]

The ceremony of the laying of the foundation stone took place on 22 May, Wagner's fifty-ninth birthday. Nearly a thousand musicians, singers and guests descended on the small town of Bayreuth, which had never seen such numbers. Guesthouses, inns and restaurants ran out of food and drink. The usual supply of horse-drawn carriages was soon exhausted. Odd vehicles belonging to the fire brigade and sports clubs were pressed in to help transport the distinguished up to the Green Hill. The sky bulged low grey clouds. Rain came in torrents. Soon, horses and pedestrians were toiling ankle-deep in oily brown mud. It was fortunate King Ludwig was not present.

The King was seen more and more infrequently these days. His day was wont to start with breakfast at seven in the evening in a tiny room lit by sixty candles, after which his night was usually spent gliding through his moonlit gardens in his swan-carved sleigh to snatches of Wagner's music performed by concealed musicians. He was still nursing the tiff with Wagner over premiering *Das Rheingold* without the composer's approval, but he did send a message of gracious approbation to Bayreuth. Wagner placed it in a precious casket which, with due ceremony, was laid into the foundation while the band played the *Huldigungsmarsch*, the march of homage that Wagner had written for King Ludwig some years earlier.

Like the god Wotan who smote the ground three times in the *Ring*, summoning fire and all sorts of fateful consequences, Wagner smote the foundation stone three times with a hammer. After pronouncing a blessing, he turned away moist-eyed and pale as death according to Nietzsche, who was given the great honour of riding back to town with him in his carriage.

Nietzsche was still on tenterhooks for artistic judgement on the piano duet he had sent Cosima at Christmastime. Neither Cosima nor Wagner had said a word, and he decided to send it to von Bülow.

On the occasion in Basle when von Bülow had given Nietzsche the hundred francs to deliver to Daniela, the conductor had told him that he was so impressed by *The Birth of Tragedy* that he carried it about everywhere and recommended it to all and sundry. Might he, von Bülow requested, dedicate his next book to Nietzsche? How could the young professor not accept such flattery? Surely this exchange might assure him of some degree of praise from von Bülow when he sent him the piece of music, which had now been orchestrated and entitled the *Manfred Meditation*.

At the very least, Nietzsche could expect von Bülow to favour him with the usual assortment of platitudes that professionals dole out when amateurs seek their opinion. But *Schadenfreude* ran deep and strong in the conductor and he delivered his verdict with unsparing cruelty. He wrote that he made no secret of his embarrassment at having to pass judgement on the *Manfred Meditation*. It struck him as 'the most extreme in fantastical extravagance, the most unedifying and least uplifting, the most anti-musical thing that I have come across in a long time in the way of notes put down on paper . . . More than once I had to ask myself: is this all some awful joke? Did you perhaps intend a parody of the so-called Music of the Future? Is it with conscious intent that you express an uninterrupted scorn for all the rules of tonal connection, from the highest syntax to the usually accepted orthography? . . . Of the Apollonian element I have not been able to discover the smallest trace; and as for the Dionysian, I must say frankly that I have been reminded less of this than of the day after a bacchanal [i.e. a hangover].'[23]

Both Wagner and Cosima thought von Bülow had been unnecessarily cruel but they felt no inclination to console their dear friend by sending him a few lines that might impugn their devotion to pure truth. When Cosima relayed von Bülow's words to her father Liszt, he shook his white head sadly and said that the judgement seemed despairingly extreme, but he too felt disinclined to soften the blow.

Nietzsche took three months to recover. Eventually he managed a letter to von Bülow: 'Well, thank God, that is what you have to tell me. I know quite well what an uncomfortable moment I have given you and to compensate for it let me tell you how useful you have been to me. Just think, since my music is self-taught, I have gradually lost all discipline in it; I have never had the judgement of a musician on it; and I am truly happy to be enlightened in such a simple way as to the character of my latest period of composition.'

He excuses his presumption in entering the 'dangerous, moonstruck region' of emotional turmoil, ascribing it to his impulse to honour Wagner, and he pleads with von Bülow not to put down this 'kind of *otium cum odio,* with this altogether odious way of passing my time' to Nietzsche's infatuation with the *Tristan* music. 'The whole thing, as a matter of fact, is a highly instructive experience for me . . . I shall try, then, to take a musical cure; and perhaps I shall remain, if I study Beethoven sonatas in your edition, under your tutelage and guidance.'[24]

A brighter note was struck when the first article appeared on *The Birth of Tragedy.* Nietzsche's friend Erwin Rohde managed to place a favourable piece in the *Norddeutsche Allgemeine Zeitung.* It can hardly be called a review. It simply repeated Nietzsche's argument concerning the death of the sacred and the mystical through the cruel consistency of Socratic thought, his concern at the creeping cultural vandalism by socialist barbarians and the mantra that Wagner's reinvention of the pantheon of Germanic gods was providing the firm foundation for the cultural revival of the German nation.

Nietzsche was ecstatic. 'Friend, friend, friend, what have you done!' He ordered fifty printed copies of the article but he had little time to enjoy it. Ulrich von Wilamowitz-Möllendorff, an old Pfortean and a fellow philologist, quickly knocked out a thirty-two-page pamphlet satirically entitled *Zukunftsphilologie!* (*Philology of the Future!*), a play on Wagner's term *Zukunftsmusik* ('Music of the Future'). Headed by a punchy quotation from Aristophanes which implicitly condemns *The Birth of Tragedy* as a delicacy for a catamite, it goes on to condemn the book as a bad piece of philology and a piece of Wagnerian fluff. Wilamowitz puts forward the case for strict interpretation of the past through the 'scientific' means of philology rather than Nietzsche's approach as a 'metaphysician and apostle'. Wilamowitz upholds the common view of the Greeks as 'eternal children, innocently and unsuspectingly enjoying the beautiful light'. The idea that the Greeks needed tragedy was 'a pile of rubbish! What a disgrace! . . . Nietzsche knows less about Homer than a Serb or a Finn.' The concept of an artistic alliance between Apollo and Dionysus was as ridiculous as a union between Nero and Pythagoras. The cult of Dionysus rose not from consciousness of the tragic but from 'the wine harvest, the crushing of grapes, the cheerful consumption of the new, rousing beverage'. He goes on to discuss the music of ancient Greece, a subject on which Wilamowitz is on as shaky ground as Nietzsche himself. Neither of them could have any idea what ancient Greek music sounded like. His summing up attacks Nietzsche for gross ignorance, gross errors and lack of devotion to truth. He demands that Nietzsche step down from the teaching of philology.

Cosima dismissed the whole dispute as 'not suitable for the public' but Wagner quickly leapt to Nietzsche's defence in an open letter published in the same newspaper on 23 June. His entirely predictable article was enlivened by the terrific observation that Wilamowitz-Möllendorff wrote like 'a Wisconsin stock-market news-sheet', a comment that surely sheds an interesting light on Wagner's own reading habits.

Nietzsche had taken two mortal hits from von Bülow and Wilamowitz-Möllendorff. Together they were enough to destroy his future prospects as a composer, as a classicist and as a philologist but the last was the least important. He had long been seeking an escape from philology. Maybe, amongst the diverse existing interpretations of *The Birth of Tragedy*, the book can be read as the suicide note of a philologist.

Eventually, *The Birth of Tragedy* became one of Nietzsche's bestselling books. But of the eight hundred copies printed and published in 1872, only 625 sold over the next six years.[25] The damage had been done to his reputation. When the new academic year started, Nietzsche discovered that only two students had enrolled for his course of lectures on philology, and neither was a philologist.

6

· POISON COTTAGE ·

The illness gave me the right to change all my habits completely;
it permitted, it *required* me to forget . . . My eyes alone put an end
to any bookworm behaviour, in plain language: philology: I was
redeemed from the 'book' . . . the *greatest* blessing I ever conferred
on myself! – That lowermost self, buried and silenced by constantly
having to listen to other selves (– and that would certainly mean
reading!) slowly woke up, shyly and full of doubts, – but it finally
started talking again.

Ecce Homo, 'Human, All Too Human', Section 4

In the autumn of 1872, Wagner invited Nietzsche to Bayreuth to
celebrate Christmas and Cosima's birthday, as they had been used to at
Tribschen. Nietzsche refused; no philology students at all had signed
up for the next semester and he could not face the shame. Instead, he
went home for the holiday to Naumburg where Franziska and Elisabeth
would no more see *The Birth of Tragedy* as a failure than they would
mention his inability to compose a decent piece of music, to finish the
lecture series on education, or to attract more than two students to his
New Year's course at the university.

His Christmas-cum-birthday present for Cosima cost him long, hard
work. Even so it arrived too late for both occasions. She was relieved
to discover it was not a musical manuscript but a literary one, albeit
one with an unpromising title: *Five Prefaces to Unwritten Books*. The first,
'On the Pathos of Truth' ('*Über das Pathos der Wahrheit*'), took the form
of a parable: a star is inhabited by clever animals who have discovered
truth. The star dies and the animals with it. They die cursing truth,
for it has revealed to them that all their previous knowledge has been
spurious, as man will also realise, should he ever discover truth.

The second preface dealt with the future of German education. The third was a profoundly pessimistic meditation on the Greek state and the problem raised by the fact that it was founded on slavery. Is not, Nietzsche asks, this nineteenth-century Iron Age civilisation of ours also constructed on slavery? Is the terrible fact of the necessity of a slave class the vulture that eternally gnaws at the liver of the Promethean culture-monger?

The fourth preface addressed Schopenhauer's relevance to present-day culture. The fifth concerned Homer's reportage of war. All January he waited in vain for some critique, or even some acknowledgement.

If he was hurt by her silence, he had no idea how much he had hurt and disappointed Wagner by choosing to spend Christmas elsewhere. Twice since moving to Bayreuth, once in June and once in October, Wagner had sent him intensely affectionate letters effectively consecrating Nietzsche as his son. On account of his own age (Wagner would soon be sixty), his relationship with his son Siegfried must be more that of a grandfather than a father. Nietzsche must be the generational link, son to one and father to the other.

Wagner and Cosima spent an appalling Christmastide without him. Finances had collapsed again, leaving the part-built opera house teetering on the brink of collapse. They felt forsaken by King Ludwig, who was now almost completely invisible to all as he ordered ever more extravagant decorations for his fantastic palaces, and dealt with his ministers concerning state business through his favourite groom. Wagner suspected the same groom of blocking his communications to the King. His feeling of isolation at Ludwig slipping away from him was heightened by Nietzsche's refusal to spend Christmas with them. It was seen as desertion and disloyalty and taken very deeply to heart.

Wagner had planned that over Christmas he would present Nietzsche with a scheme to restore Bayreuth's fortunes by starting some sort of periodical, a magazine or a news-sheet with Nietzsche as editor and contributor (he could publish as many articles as he liked and that would surely please him). Its purpose would be to publicise and raise funds for Bayreuth. Instead of which, Professor Nietzsche sent five random and pointless prefaces to five never-to-be-written books, none of which bore any relation at all to Wagner or his problems. 'They did not restore our spirits,' Cosima notes acidly in her diary, which goes on to record a mournful holiday dogged by anguish, anxiety and ill health, so that the two of them found themselves for the first time in their marriage quarrelling over whether the dog was too dirty to come into the house. Night after night, Wagner was tormented by a truly terrifying series of nightmares. When he awoke he would calm himself by thinking of Nietzsche. But Nietzsche thought of himself only in the role of disciple. He had no understanding of the Master's very real need of him and no idea that Wagner and Cosima saw his absence as a betrayal. When Cosima at last sent a letter on 12 February, Nietzsche was astonished at her reference to a breach between them: he had not even suspected such a thing.

In reparation he started on a book to present to Wagner on his sixtieth birthday in May. This would surely heal the wound. But before that came the summons to spend Easter with them. This time he obeyed smartly, bringing *Philosophy in the Tragic Age of the Greeks* (*Die Philosophie im tragischen Zeitalter der Griechen*) tucked under his arm and his friend Erwin Rohde, who was now professor at Kiel.

Cosima's initial delight at entertaining two professors quickly waned. Rohde, while a good, solid friend to Nietzsche, was hardly a festive character. His presence did nothing to lighten Bayreuth's gloom. On top of this, Nietzsche insisted on reading his work aloud over several evenings, leaving long pauses for thoughtful discussion. Wagner found himself deathly bored and he was further exasperated when Nietzsche was inspired by a thunderstorm to treat them to a performance of his latest musical composition. 'We are a little vexed by our friend's music-making pastimes, and R. expatiates on the turn music has taken,' Cosima noted grimly. Nietzsche in his turn was not at all amused by Wagner's proposal that he and Rohde should become newspaper propagandists for Bayreuth. Given the number of scornful words Nietzsche had written deploring newspaper culture, the suggestion was insulting.

The Tribschen years had unquestionably been the most satisfying period of Nietzsche's life. The steady rhythm of those early years of his promising professorship shuttling between the Basle classroom and the Master's inner sanctum had conferred upon him a sunlit interval of good health such as he had never before enjoyed, nor ever would again. But the plodding Easter vacation that he and Rohde passed together in Bayreuth had not recaptured a scintilla of the glory days. It had been a hollow mockery, a pitiful simulacrum.

On his return to Basle his health broke down. At first his eye- and head-aches only prevented him from following his evening custom of sitting down to read and write lecture notes in his red leather-covered notebook, but with every day that passed the intensity and insistence of the pain grew greater. By the time a month had gone by, he found himself incapable of even attempting such work. His doctor advised that he rest his eyes altogether.

Light was agonising. Mostly he sat in a darkened room behind tightly drawn curtains. Sometimes he would venture out of doors, protecting himself against the light with a sunshade, thick-lensed green-tinted spectacles, and a beak-like green visor overhanging his forehead. His fellow-Baslers passed like Platonic shadows in front of his cave. As far as they were concerned, this was convenient. They could pretend they had not seen the problematic professor, and ignore him.

He was an embarrassment. He had acquired such a bad reputation that it was damaging the standing of the university. A philological professor at the University of Bonn had told his students that Nietzsche was an enemy of culture and a wily imposter and *The Birth of Tragedy* was utter nonsense and totally useless.[2]

Nietzsche was renting rooms at Schützengraben 45. Other rooms in the house were let out to Franz Overbeck,[3] newly appointed Professor of New Testament and Church History at the university, who was writing his first book, *On the Christian Quality of Theology Today*, and Heinrich Romundt, who was writing his doctoral thesis on Kant's *Critique of Pure Reason*. On their walks to and from the university the three ambitious young academics would often stop in at a bar called

Das Gifthüttli ('Poison Cottage'), named for the fact that it stood on the site of a defunct arsenic mine. Gleefully the trio adopted the transgressive name for their own house. But plans to revolutionise society must be put on hold until his health recovered.

He summoned his sister Elisabeth to look after him and sort out the practical household chores. Secretarial help arrived in the shape of his old friend Carl von Gersdorff, who had championed him through Schulpforta days. Von Gersdorff came to Basle from Sicily where he had contracted malaria but there was nothing wrong with his eyes. He would read the material for Nietzsche's lectures aloud to him; Nietzsche would then learn by heart any quotations he wished to use. The process left von Gersdorff of the opinion that the stifling of Nietzsche's physical sight conferred an even greater clarity of inward focus. Both his material selection and his delivery were improved by the laboriousness of the work, which left Nietzsche speaking more clearly and eloquently, and with more concentration.[4] Nietzsche agreed: 'The illness gave me the right to change all my habits completely; it permitted, it *required* me to forget . . . My eyes alone put an end to any bookworm behaviour, in plain language: philology: I was redeemed from the "book" . . . the *greatest* blessing I ever conferred on myself! – That lowermost self, buried and silenced by constantly *having* to listen to other selves (– and that would certainly mean reading!), slowly woke up, shyly and full of doubts, – but it finally *started talking again.*'[5]

The system worked, but it did nothing to halt the march of increasing pain. His oculist Professor Schiess prescribed eye drops of atropine (deadly nightshade) to relax the eye muscles. Doubling the size of his pupils, the drops made it impossible for him to focus at all. The world became a dancing blur. He was even more dependent on von Gersdorff, who said that the glistening, dark pools of Nietzsche's eyes made him look very frightening.

With Elisabeth taking charge of the household and von Gersdorff acting as amanuensis, Nietzsche could experience intellectual freedom without suffering the appalling loneliness of the hermit of the intellect. The book for Wagner's birthday swiftly became a thing of the past, as his unfocused eyes roamed wider horizons. He plunged into making lists. He would write a whole series of *Untimely Meditations* (*Unzeitgemässe Betrachtungen*). They would set out his thoughts on the nature of culture in the modern world in general, and the *Reich* in particular. 'Untimely' is a small and overlooked word in English but for Nietzsche *unzeitgemässe* was a word of great stature. It meant standing outside time forward and time backward: outside current fashion and outside the drag-anchor of history, too. He defined it as standing strong and firmly rooted in his own power, the seeker of truth with his gaze always fixed beyond all that is ephemeral. He made a list of the subjects that he, the untimely one, would write about. He intended to publish two *Meditations* a year until he had covered the entire list. He kept adding and subtracting subjects but the constant core included:

David Strauss
History
Reading and Writing
The One Year Volunteer
Wagner
Secondary Schools and Universities
Christian Disposition
The Absolute Teacher
The Philosopher
People and Culture
Classical Philology
The Newspaper Slave

The first *Untimely Meditation* to be written was 'David Strauss, the Confessor and the Writer'. David Strauss was a theologian and Kantian philosopher who forty years previously had had a tremendous success with his two-volume book *The Life of Jesus* (*Das Leben Jesu*), a purportedly 'scientific' investigation into Jesus Christ as an historical character. The book was a scandal and a sensation. It was translated into English by George Eliot (whom Nietzsche enjoyed presenting as typical of the

British race: sexually peculiar and intellectually slack). The Earl of Shaftesbury condemned it as the most pestilential book ever vomited out of the jaws of Hell. When Nietzsche had read Strauss's book during his school days at Pforta he had written to his sister saying that if he was asked to believe in Jesus as an historical character it was of no interest to him at all, but as a moral teacher, that was a different matter worthy of the deepest investigation.

Strauss was now nearing seventy. He had recently published a follow-up book, *The Old and the New Faith* (*Der alte und der neue Glaube*), which again achieved great popularity. The book fitted the mood of the time by pioneering with almost manic cheerfulness the idea that it was possible to exist in the modern world as a new breed of *rationalist* Christian, a fundamental contradiction if ever there was one – impossible within the definitions either of rationality or of faith. As Nietzsche observed: if one breaks out of the fundamental idea, the belief in God, one breaks the whole thing to pieces. A revolution in belief requires a revolution in morality, a consequence that appeared to have eluded Strauss in what Nietzsche, with evident enjoyment, crushingly referred to as his 'portable oracle for the German philistine'.[6]

He sent the manuscript off to the publisher before embarking on a summer holiday with Romundt and von Gersdorff in Chur, a little Swiss alpine resort famous for restorative lake bathing and other 'cures'. Every day the three friends hiked for four or five hours, Nietzsche in his green glasses and peaked sun visor. The cool, clear air gave sharp edge to thought. Several hundred metres below their hotel gleamed the Caumasee, a pretty little lake. 'We dress and undress to the insistent croaking of a huge frog,' noted von Gersdorff. After swimming, the three would sprawl on velvety moss and larch needles, while his friends read aloud to Nietzsche from Plutarch, Goethe and Wagner.

Rohde and von Gersdorff had read the proofs of the *Untimely Meditation* very carefully on Nietzsche's behalf but when they received the first copies in early August, they made the humiliating discovery that it was almost as full of misspellings and typographical errors as Strauss's work that Nietzsche had criticised for the same fault.

Nevertheless, the arrival of the advance copies of the book was an occasion to be celebrated solemnly and ceremonially. They took a bottle of wine down to the shore of the lake where, on the slanting face of a rock, they solemnly engraved 'U.B.I.F.N. 8/8 1873' (*'Unzeitgemässe Betrachtung* 1. Friedrich Nietzsche, 8 August 1873'). Then they flung off their clothes and swam out to the little islet in the middle of the lake, where they found another rock to engrave with their initials. Then they swam back, poured a libation over the first rock, and declared, 'Thus we commemorated the Antistraussiad. Now let the adversaries advance. Let them all go to the devil!'[7]

Strauss died the following February. Nietzsche noted it in his diary. He was pricked by his conscience that his savage attack had hastened the end of a fellow author but his friends assured him that the book had cast no shadow over Strauss's last months. Strauss did not even know about the book, they told him. This was not true. Strauss had known. He had been puzzled, but found no need to be upset: the world had taken far more notice of his bestselling books than of this gadfly sting by an unknown and little-regarded author named Friedrich Nietzsche.

When Nietzsche returned to Basle for the autumn semester there had been no improvement in his physical condition. He still could not read or write for himself. In mid-October, Wagner sent him a request to write a rallying call to the German nation. Bayreuth was in desperate need of more money. Nietzsche felt so unequal to the task that he dictated a letter to Erwin Rohde asking him to write the thing for him, 'in Napoleonic style'. Nietzsche's letter to Rohde was impish and sarcastic. It made fun of Wagner, who had now decided that he was a victim of a communist plot to sabotage Bayreuth. An early move in the plot, Wagner believed, was that the communists were trying to take over the publishing house of Fritzsch, in order to muzzle his own and Nietzsche's writings.

'Is your strong manly heart beating against your ribs?' runs Nietzsche's letter to Rohde. 'After such events I no longer dare to put my name to this letter . . . thinking only in terms of bombs and counter-bombs, we sign only pseudonymous names and wear false beards . . .'[8]

Rohde refused to ghost the pamphlet, and so Nietzsche had to dictate it. Such was his determination that he had it ready for the Master in plenty of time for 31 October. This was Reformation Day, an occasion celebrated throughout Lutheran Germany. It commemorated the day in 1517 that Martin Luther had nailed his ninety-five theses to the church door. It was vital to Wagner that he should present his cultural appeal on that significant date, when it would go out to all the representatives of the Wagner Societies across Germany and the wider world.

His appeal delighted the Master, but when Wagner passed it on to the Wagner Societies, they found Nietzsche's pamphlet so hectoring, so tactless and so combative that they immediately rejected it and composed their own, milder form. Nietzsche's never saw the light of day.

Wagner's warm response encouraged Nietzsche to undertake a little adventure on his own. He was still venturing into the world gingerly, green-swathed against the light, but he risked a train journey to join the Master for the Reformation Day celebrations.

It was quite like the old days. Over an immensely jolly dinner, Nietzsche entertained them with the real story of the communist threat to Fritzsch's publishing house.

A mad and wealthy widow named Rosalie Nielsen, a political comrade of Mazzini and a woman, apparently, of terrifying ugliness, had read *The Birth of Tragedy*. It had ignited such a passion for the author in her breast that she had appeared in Basle and descended upon him. To his great alarm, she announced herself as a servant of the cult of Dionysus. He had shown her the door. She had threatened him. Eventually she had been persuaded to return to Leipzig, where she had decided to buy out Fritzsch, presumably with the aim of ownership and complete control over her hero's books, a plan that was frightening enough in itself but achieved terrifying proportions on the discovery that she had close ties with the Marxist International, who were now claiming Nietzsche as politically one of their own.

Wagner laughed longer and more heartily over this than he had all year. Days after Nietzsche told him the story, he was still chuckling and shaking his head.

Returning to Basle, Nietzsche wrote the second *Untimely Meditation*, 'On the Uses and Disadvantages of History for Life', which would be published the following year, 1874. Addressing the relation of history and historiography (the writing of history) to life and culture, it pointed out that the German obsession with the past was disabling action in the present.

The essay distinguished between three uses of history: the antiquarian which seeks to preserve the past, the monumental which seeks to emulate it, and the critical which seeks to liberate the present. All three must be held in a delicate balance to achieve the suprahistorical: an orientation towards eternally valid examples of the past, together with a deliberate forgetting of the past in the interests of the present.

Nietzsche had been pursuing a concentrated study of the latest books on scientific subjects such as the nature of comets, the history and development of chemistry and physics, the general theory of movement and energy, and the construction of space.[9] They had led him to return to the hobbyhorse he had been riding through the previous *Untimely Meditation* on David Strauss: nagging at the great question of science and religion, and excoriating his contemporary theologians for undermining the very faith they professed, by seeking to reconcile the two. It was one of the great questions of the age, and one he would never relinquish.

He coined a new word to describe the effect of science: *Begriffsbeben* ('concept-quake'). 'Life itself caves in and grows weak and fearful when the concept-quake caused by science robs man of the foundation of all his rest and security, his belief in the enduring and the eternal. Is life to dominate knowledge and science, or is knowledge to dominate life?'[10] To be sure, mankind climbed, or thought he climbed, up to heaven on the sunbeams of scientific truth, but science-heaven was as much a necessary lie as its religious counterpart. Eternal truth belonged no more to science than to religion. Each new scientific discovery had a habit of exposing previous eternal scientific truths as fictions. Truth was pulled into a new shape as the filaments of the spider's web became stretched and distorted, or even pulled apart altogether.

The last few pages conclude with advice for the young. To cure them of the malady of history he unsurprisingly recommends that the way to sort out the unruliness of existence is to look to the Greeks, who gradually learned to organise the chaos by following the advice of the Delphic oracle: become what you are.

He sent out the first printed copies to his most valued critics. Jacob Burckhardt followed his usual pattern of dodging a meaningful critique by pleading modesty: his poor old head had never been able to ponder so deeply the ultimate foundations, aims and desires of historical science.

Erwin Rohde provided the most constructive response, pointing out that while the thoughts were brilliant, Nietzsche must look to his style which must become less peremptorily insistent, and to the construction of his arguments which needed to be more fully developed and backed up by historical examples rather than each idea striking the mind individually and leaving it to the puzzled reader to make the connections.

Wagner passed the booklet on to Cosima with the comment that Nietzsche was still very immature; 'It lacks plasticity, because he never quotes examples from history, yet there are many repetitions and no real plan . . . I don't know anybody to whom I could give it to read, because nobody could follow it.'[11] He left it to Cosima to write their response. Characteristically, she wrote without compromise and with no thought for the author's feelings. The book would only appeal to a small public, she told him, and she put forward stylistic criticisms that made him furious.

Nietzsche became depressed. The *Meditation* on Strauss had received a couple of reviews for exactly the opposite reason of its 'untimeliness': it had been noticed because it was a fashionable topic. The 'History for Life' *Meditation* had no fashionable appeal. Great sales were not expected and none materialised. His publisher was making sour faces at the idea of continuing the series.

His mother's forty-eighth birthday fell in February 1874. His customary greetings for health and happiness were hardly cheerful. He told her not to follow the example of her esteemed son who had started to ail far too early in life. He went on pathetically to compare his life to that of a fly: 'The goal is too far away, and even if one ever reaches it, most often one's powers have been used up in the long search and the struggle; when one reaches freedom, one is as exhausted as an ephemeral fly when evening comes.'[12]

Wagner decided it was time for Nietzsche to brace up. He should either marry, or write an opera. Doubtless the latter would be so frightful that it would never get produced. But who cared? If the wife were rich enough it would hardly matter.[13] Nietzsche must enter the world, he must quit the little court he had created about himself, the circle of useful intelligent men subservient to him and the adoring sister-queen-consort-housekeeper on call whenever he needed her. A little more balance would be in order. It was a shame von Gersdorff was a man, or Nietzsche could have married him. Wagner and Cosima had come to a conclusion of probability concerning the intensity of Nietzsche's relationships to his male friends. They were liberal about such things. It did not worry them, nor could they see why it should stand in the way of him marrying.

'. . . Ach, my God, why must Gersdorff be the only male among you? Marry a rich wife! Then you can travel and enrich yourself . . . and compose your opera . . . What kind of Satan made you only a pedagogue!'[14]

This was Wagner at his most robust. Too robust for one who had described himself as an exhausted fly in the evening of its life. Nietzsche was not up to such red meat. He told Wagner that he would certainly not be coming to Bayreuth in the summer. He was planning to spend it in the refined air of some very high and isolated Swiss mountain while composing the next *Meditation*.

Wagner thought this a bad idea. He insisted that Nietzsche's presence in Bayreuth would be invaluable over the summer. King Ludwig had finally found himself so tormented by the intolerable idea that he should not see the *Ring* staged to the Master's sublime vision that he had extended a loan of one hundred thousand thalers. There would be a great deal for Nietzsche to do.

Like Wotan's Valhalla, the opera house was rising stone upon stone. The summer was to be devoted to auditioning singers and instrumentalists, constructing stage sets and inventing machinery – the Valkyries must *fly*, the Rhinemaidens somehow must *swim*, the dragon must *breathe fire* without burning down the house.

How could Wagner be so insensitive as to imagine that his delicate health could support a summer of such high commotion? How could his head stand it? Besides, he did not want to be further nagged about marriage, a topic his mother seldom relinquished.

7

· CONCEPT-QUAKE ·

It is truly wondrous how two souls simply live next to each other in this man. On the one hand, the strictest methods of well-schooled scientific research . . . On the other hand this fantastic-rhapsodic, overly brilliant, excessively head-over-heels-into-the-unintelligible Wagnero-Schopenhauerian, art-mystery-and-religious, giddy enthusiasm.

> Professor Friedrich Ritschl commenting on Nietzsche to Wilhelm Vischer-Bilfinger, Chairman of the Governing Council of the University of Basle, 2 February 1873

Nietzsche would soon reach thirty with only some little-read writing and a fading reputation as a philologist prodigy behind him. It was hardly impressive when compared to Jesus Christ, who at thirty was embarking on a three-year ministry that would quake the earth. Nietzsche's father had died at thirty-five and it had always been in his mind that he would die at the same age, but now he wondered whether he would last so long. Mortality was rattling the walls of the fortress; the machine was breaking down. Health crises alternated with 'cures'. Both would often result in ghastly convulsive reactions and the vomiting of blood. On several occasions he thought his last hour had come. There were times when he found himself longing for death.

Medical theory of the time, like religious theory, swung between witch-doctory superstition and scientific thought. Nietzsche's distinguished doctors diagnosed chronic gastric catarrh accompanied by an abnormal amount of blood in the body causing a dilation of the stomach and vascular engorgements resulting in the head being insufficiently supplied with blood. Leeches, cupping and Spanish fly were joined by shaky fashionable cures such as Carlsbad salts, electrotherapy, hydrotherapy, massive doses of quinine and a new miracle drug called 'Höllenstein solution'. None of them, Nietzsche felt, did any good at all.

He joined, in his words, the chlorotic and weak-nerved folk from all over the world as they shuffled around from spa to spa. He read medical and physiological texts voraciously and yet, for all the miracle cures he tried, and which he knew did him no good, it was the one area in which he suspended his analytical rigour. He was as credulous as a newspaper reader believing in horoscopes. But somewhere inside himself he knew: 'People like us . . . never suffer just physically – it is all deeply entwined with spiritual crises – so I have no idea how medicine and kitchens can ever make me well again.'[1]

Probably the worst effect on his health was produced by the best-regarded stomach specialist of the time, Dr Josef Wiel, whose clinic in Steinabad Nietzsche would attend in the summer of 1875. He was prescribed the usual enemas and leeches but the real novelty was Wiel's 'miracle-working' diet: meat, and only meat, four times a day. Wiel even gave him cookery lessons so he could pursue the monotonous diet after he had left the clinic.

Whenever he returned to Basle to resume work, he summoned Elisabeth to come and look after him. Every time that Elisabeth left their mother's side, Franziska complained strenuously to both children, making them feel undutiful and guilt-hagged. Nietzsche would later baptise the feeling *Kettenkrankheit* ('chain-sickness') when he felt his mother or his sister yanking on his chain.

Franziska was jealous of Elisabeth escaping the humdrum Naumburg round to look after her brother and mix with his circle of friends. Nevertheless, her son's health was so poor that she had no choice but to allow Elisabeth to look after him for four months in 1870, for six months in 1871, for several months apiece in 1872 and 1873 and for the summer of 1874. Finally, in August 1875, brother and sister set up house together in an apartment in Spalentorweg 48, just down the road from Poison Cottage, where Romundt and Overbeck remained close to hand.

Writings about Nietzsche often contain sentences such as 'Brother and sister were almost too close,' or 'The siblings loved each other almost too much,' sentences that pay tribute to the fact that sensationalist literary hoaxes die hard.

In the year 2000, some fifty years after its first publication in 1951, and exactly a century after Nietzsche's death, a book purportedly by Nietzsche called *My Sister and I* was still being reprinted. 'The Boy who grew up in a house full of Manless Women', runs the advertisement for the book. 'The Strange Relationship between Nietzsche and his Sister, suppressed for fifty years, Revealed At Last in the Philosopher's own Confession. The story of a famous Brother and terrifyingly ambitious younger Sister who grew to love each other Physically as Children and continued to do so in maturity – to the exclusion of all other Men and Women. One only has to read a few Pages of this Breathless Book to Realise why it has been Hushed Up all these years. Quite simply, and in Fearful Earnest, the 19th century's Greatest Philosopher tells how he was gradually led into this Extraordinarily Dangerous Love-trap which kept him from marrying and caused the Suicide of his sister's Only Husband. MY SISTER AND I was written in an asylum in Jena. Undoubtedly it was his studied Revenge on his family for refusing to let him publish an Earlier and much tamer Confession, entitled *Ecce Homo*, which did not appear until ten years after his Death. MY SISTER AND I had to wait over fifty years because it could not be made Public until all the actors in the Great Drama had Passed Away.'

It is a loathsome tale, right from its start, with Elisabeth creeping into his bed and 'the administration of her fat little fingers' occurring for the first time on the night of the death of their little brother Joseph. As Elisabeth was aged two at the time, and Nietzsche four, logic and reason are left behind at the outset. But then, good sense often finds itself trumped by sensationalism once scandal is abroad. The great scholar Walter Kaufmann unpicked the book philologically with great skill but it took years before it was unmasked as a forgery, product of the industrious fraudster and gaolbird Samuel Roth,[2] whose anonymous or pseudonymous publications included *Lady Chatterley's Husbands* (1931),

The Private Life of Frank Harris (1931), *Bumarap: the Story of a Male Virgin* (1947), *I Was Hitler's Doctor* (1951) and *The Violations of the Child Marilyn Monroe* by 'Her Psychiatrist Friend' (1962).

Roth also produced several short-lived erotic reviews given to publishing sexually explicit passages from contemporary authors without their permission. It drove the writers of the day mad with fury and it resulted in a protest signed by 167 of them, including Robert Bridges, Albert Einstein, T. S. Eliot, Havelock Ellis, André Gide, Knut Hamsun, Ernest Hemingway, Hugo von Hofmannsthal, James Joyce, D. H. Lawrence, Thomas Mann, André Maurois, Sean O'Casey, Luigi Pirandello, Bertrand Russell, Arthur Symons, Paul Valéry and William Butler Yeats.[3]

My Sister and I is still being published. The author's name on the cover still reads 'Friedrich Nietzsche' with no mention of the real author. Even today, having purchased the book, it takes a certain amount of investigation to arrive at the truth.

Elisabeth was a clever and intelligent girl. Franziska criticised her for being too clever, like her brother. Elisabeth's sex, her upbringing and her mother were her tragedy.

Had she been born a boy things would have been very different but there were no *Gymnasien* for girls until the end of the century. While Nietzsche's educational years at Pforta had been spent roaming the world of ideas in a rigorous search for truth and self, Fräulein Paraski's school for young ladies in Naumburg had been busy instilling the exact opposite in Elisabeth. It was Fräulein Paraski's job to overlay a girl's individuality and to equip her instead with a synthetic identity, pressing her into the sugar-coated mould of the perfect marriageable maiden, a *tabula rasa* prepared to take the impress of whatever husband should rule her future. A lexicon of the time gives the definition of *Frau* (woman): 'Woman *complements* the man; the unification of the two is the definitive example of divinity in man. He is the elm, she is the vine; he strives upward, full of strength and marrow; she is delicate, scented, with an inner glow, easy to bend . . .'[4]

A clever Naumburg maiden must pretend to be a muddle-headed shallow-pate if she were to snare a husband. It was not nice for a girl to be too clever. Elisabeth carried on the pretence all through her life. In fact, the convention suited her well. Her clever brother offered her numerous opportunities for self-education but she never took advantage of them. It was too uncomfortable, too disturbing. Even when she was in her seventies she was described as 'a flapper at heart who enthuses over this or that person like a seventeen-year-old', the same observer adding that Elisabeth possessed a robust and lifelong determination to resist intellectual demands, she was a snob who loved few things more than curtseying to members of the aristocracy and, in short, she was the embodiment of precisely what her brother fought against.[5]

Grandmother Erdmuthe had given their mother Franziska no adult role, no responsibility, nothing to be or to become, but to follow the pietistic habit of viewing herself as helpless as a child in the matter of free will. Everything that befell, whether good or evil, was the Will of the Heavenly Father Above. Second only to God came the male sex. All three generations of Nietzsche women were exceptionally wilful and strong-willed but they all maintained possession of super-clean consciences that they were 'good children' within the Church and the patriarchy.

Nietzsche knew his Llama was an intelligent female and he treated her as such. In this, he was unusual for his time. All his life he valued intelligent women, making close and enduring friendships with them. He only fell in love with clever women – starting with Cosima. He disliked ignorant and bigoted women.

Nietzsche had always treated Elisabeth as a thinking individual and tried to encourage her independence of thought. He attempted to make her into a writer of clear prose; 'If only she could learn to write better! And when she narrates something she must learn to leave out all the "ahs" and "ohs".'[6] He compiled reading lists for her. He encouraged her to improve her mind. He recommended (fruitlessly) that she learn languages. He wanted her to attend university lectures as an *Hörerin*, a listener; the only way a woman could get into the lecture theatre.

Franziska was implacably opposed to any such course. If Elisabeth were to become a domestic embellishment, she must steer clear of any independent thought or activity. She must keep house for her mother in Naumburg, attend tea parties, teach Sunday School and ply her needle at the Darning School for the Children of the Poor.

Given the opportunity of a proper education, Elisabeth would probably not have seized on it. All her life she enjoyed her own idea of femininity, positively embracing the role of helpless, ignorant female, and realising how it could excuse her from taking ultimate responsibility for her actions and her beliefs. While she was still a schoolgirl Nietzsche had written to her from Pforta confessing his religious doubts and pressing her to investigate her own ideas, and she had shied away from confronting the issue: 'Since I cannot forget my Llama nature, I'm completely confused and prefer not to think about it, because I just come up with nonsense.'[7] It was a theme she would repeat, with variations, whenever more was demanded of her than she was prepared to give: retreating into femininity in all its mysterious banality and girlish gaucherie and often pleading that she was 'just a dilettante'. Elisabeth never wanted to be mistaken for one of those feminist 'New Women', whom she scornfully described as 'fighting for the rights of trousers and the political rights of voting cattle'.[8]

The apartment in Spalentorweg where Nietzsche and Elisabeth set up house together in 1875 is described by the student Ludwig von Scheffler. He had come to Basle to study under Jacob Burckhardt but soon transferred to the classes given by Nietzsche, who 'captivated and confused' him by his lectures and by 'his mysterious psyche'. As von Scheffler describes them, the two professors' styles could not have contrasted more greatly.

In Burckhardt's studio above the baker's shop, books occupied the floor space on every side of a dilapidated old sofa where Burckhardt sat. Unless the visitor wanted to stand throughout, he had no choice but to build a tottering pile and take a seat on it.

Nietzsche's apartment billowed with deliciously soft armchairs, genteelly protected by lace antimacassars. Ornaments and flower vases teetered on terrifyingly fragile tables. Rosy light entered windows muffled by coloured gauze. Indistinct watercolours drifted pale walls. It gave von Scheffler the feeling of being a guest in the house of a delightful girlfriend rather than that of a professor.[9]

The difference between the two professors was equally extreme in the lecture theatre. Burckhardt was given to exploding into the room mid-speech, like an incendiary device blasted off by the fire of thought. They called him the Laughing Stoic. Clearly he wasted no thought on his outward appearance: close-cropped hair, unfashionable suits and carelessly arranged linen.

Nietzsche entered the lecture theatre humbly, so unobtrusive as to be almost unnoticeable. His manner was quiet. His hair and moustache were carefully brushed, his clothes were neatly arranged. It was obvious he paid attention to fashion, which then favoured pale-coloured trousers, a short jacket and a light-coloured necktie.

But for all his outward conventionality, Nietzsche was the one to snare von Scheffler. When he heard Nietzsche's reinterpretation of Plato, he no longer believed in the fable of 'sunny, cheerful Greece'. He knew he was listening to a true interpretation and it made him long to know more.

In the face of Germany's widespread passion for the Hellenic, Nietzsche's harsh lesson of the brutality of the antique had a bewildering effect on the majority of his pupils. Though it captivated von Scheffler, it emptied the classroom. In the summer of 1874 Nietzsche's course on Aeschylus' *Choephoroi* (*The Libation Bearers*) attracted only four students, and they were not in the front row of distinction. Nietzsche described them as 'university cripples'. One of them was an upholsterer, who had only been learning Greek for a year.

His seminar on Sappho was cancelled due to lack of participants and his course on rhetoric was cancelled too. It left him with plenty of time to write the third *Untimely Meditation*, 'Schopenhauer as Educator', an essay in eight sections published in 1874. Famous for its misleading title, it hardly deals with Schopenhauer's philosophy at all and instead is more interested in the moral example of the philosopher who voluntarily takes upon himself the suffering involved in being truthful.

The educator must help the student realise his own character. The whole point of life is not to be an imitation. Nevertheless, three types of men may be considered by the student who is on the quest for transfiguration of the soul. 'Rousseauian man' is the man of greatest fire. Like Typhon, the monster serpent who lives under Etna, Rousseauian man is sure of producing the greatest popular revolutionary effect, such as the French Revolution. Then there is 'Goethean man'. He is an example intended for the few. He is contemplative in the grand style and misunderstood by the crowd. Finally there is 'Schopenhauerian man': the truthful man who gives a metaphysical significance to his every activity.[10]

Nietzsche also writes appreciatively of Schopenhauer as a great stylist who expressed his thought in a personal voice, using clear prose. He sets only Montaigne above Schopenhauer in terms of capacity for expressing truth with elegance. This was obviously an example that Nietzsche took to heart, for the Schopenhauer *Meditation* is remarkable for the change in his own prose style. His previous written work had rightly been criticised by Wagner, Cosima and Rohde for its stiff, didactic style, its lack of clarity and its arrogant disregard for sequential argument but now, in this volume, his writing took on both the elegance of Schopenhauer and the humanity of Montaigne.

Whereas his advice to those seeking truth had up to now always ended with the gnomic and rather unhelpful utterance of the Delphic oracle that truthfulness and authenticity could only be achieved by becoming something vaguely and mistily named as the self, now he deserted Greece and dared draw on his own thought and experience to give practical guidance. 'Let the youthful soul look back on life with the question: what have you truly loved up to now, what has drawn your soul aloft, what has mastered it and at the same time blessed it? Set up these revered objects before you and perhaps their nature and their sequence will give you a law, the fundamental law of your own true self.'[11]

The text of 'Schopenhauer as Educator' is also lighter, playing with words, delighting and seducing with numerous elegant aphorisms, of which a few:

'One has to take a somewhat bold and dangerous line with this existence: especially as, whatever happens, we are bound to lose it.'[12]

'The objective of all human arrangements is through distracting one's thoughts to *cease to be aware of life*.'[13]

'The artist is related to the lovers of his art as a heavy cannon is to a flock of sparrows.'[14]

'[The state] never has any use for truth as such, but only for truth which is useful to it.'[15]

'The state wants men to render it the same idolatry they formerly rendered the church.'[16]

'The waters of religion are ebbing away and leaving behind swamps or stagnant pools; the nations are again drawing away from one another in the most hostile fashion and long to tear one another to pieces. The sciences, pursued without any restraint and in a spirit of the blindest *laissez faire*, are shattering and dissolving all firmly held belief; the educated classes and states are being swept along by a hugely contemptible money economy,'[17] a thought related to the notes that, while writing about Schopenhauer, he was simultaneously jotting down on Wagner, as he observed the juggernaut that was the Bayreuth publicity machine rolling forward on its wheels of gold.

Finding both subjects difficult, he decided to take a little holiday in the village of Chur, where he ran into a group of acquaintances that included a pretty girl from Basle called Berta Rohr. Nietzsche wrote to Elisabeth that he had 'almost decided' to propose to her. Whether the 'almost proposal' was to please Wagner remains moot but the question of marriage was very much on his mind. His two childhood friends Wilhelm Pinder and Gustav Krug had recently become engaged and Nietzsche, left behind, had been weighing the merits of marriage. He had come down against the potential interruption to work, but he did not have total confidence in his decision.

Wagner continued to insist that Nietzsche visit him over the summer.

At last, on 5 August, Nietzsche arrived in Bayreuth. Immediately on arrival he fell ill and took to his bed in an hotel. Wagner was himself overworked and run down, but he arrived in person to transport Nietzsche to Wahnfried, the newly completed mansion close by the opera house that was to be the family home. Once installed there, Nietzsche immediately felt better.

Originally Wagner had named the house Ärgersheim ('Annoyance House') on account of all the aggravation the building project had cost him but it was a petulant name to hand down to posterity. One evening, when he was standing on the balcony under a silver moon with his arms round Cosima's waist, the two of them gazing down on the capacious vaulted tomb in the garden where they planned to spend eternity together, alongside their pet dogs (Russ was the first to be buried there, predeceasing his master), he renamed the house Wahnfried ('Peace from Illusion').

Inscriptions either side of Wahnfried's massive portal read '*Sei dieses Haus von mir benannt*' ('Let this house be named by me') and '*Hier wo mein Wähnen Freiden fand*' ('Here where my foolish fancies found peace'). But peace and freedom from illusion were far from what Nietzsche discovered in that place.

In style and character Wahnfried could not have contrasted more greatly with the romantic seclusion and intimacy of Tribschen. Wagner/Wotan had built his Wahnfried/Valhalla on a godlike scale. Foursquare and imposing, the house more resembled a town hall than a home. The grim facade, dressed with forbiddingly large blocks of stone, was almost devoid of ornament. All attention focused on a semicircular balcony of papal proportions where Wagner might put in an appearance on solemn occasions, such as premieres, or his birthday, or simply make an appearance to wave cheerily at marching bands passing beneath, playing selections from his operas.

'A man who gives pleasure to thousands should be allowed a modicum of pleasure,' he said and for all his revolutionary roots, he had built himself a palace in the royal tradition of intimidatory architecture.

The visitor entered though a centrally placed front door ornamented with a made-up coat of arms in stained glass and an allegorical painting of the Artwork of the Future for which the five-year-old child Siegfried Wagner stood model. The vast entrance hall extended up through all the floors of the house to a skylight. Pompeiian red walls provided a vibrant background to the pantheon of marble busts and statues of the household gods, both human and mythical: Siegfried, Tannhäuser, Tristan, Lohengrin, Liszt and King Ludwig. Wagner and Cosima were raised on plinths sufficiently high for them to look down on everybody else.

In the hall, large enough for auditions and rehearsals, Nietzsche recognised the specially modified Bechstein piano, which had been a gift from King Ludwig. In Tribschen it had taken up most of the little green study that was the thinking heart of the house. Here it was dwarfed by a large organ, a gift from the USA. Continuing straight through the hall, tall doors gave on to an even bigger room, a hundred square metres in area. This was the family drawing room and library. Its decorative scheme had been designed by the Munich sculptor Lorenz Gedon, one of King Ludwig's favourite decorators, an expert in melding the neo-medieval with neo-Baroque on a grand scale. Heavily carved bookcases reached two thirds up the walls towards the deeply coffered ceiling from which hung a monster chandelier. Round the outer rim of the ceiling ran a garishly painted frieze of the coats of arms of all the cities which boasted Wagner Societies. The broad, flat strip running between the top of the bookcases and the multicoloured coats of arms was frenetically patterned by a floral wallpaper cluttered with portraits of the family and other notables. The far end of the room opposite the entrance doors extended into a semicircular rotunda of one storey, whose roof provided the floor of the much-beloved balcony. Floor-length windows, an over-curtained orgy of satin and velvet, arced around another grand piano, this one a gift from Steinway and Sons of New York. As Wagner sat here to play to his family in the evenings, he did not look out onto nature's sublime heights of the Rigi and the Pilatus as he had at Tribschen. Here his gaze followed a very different view, a green garden vista that led to the man-made sublimity of his own awaiting grave.

On Nietzsche's first evening at Wahnfried, Wagner took to the piano to entertain his guests by playing some of the Rhinemaidens' music from *Götterdämmerung*. In retaliation, maybe, for Wahnfried's monumental *folie de grandeur*, Nietzsche produced the score for Brahms' *Triumphlied*, which he had heard in concert and admired. It could not have been more tactless. Ten years earlier, Wagner and Brahms had quarrelled over the return of a manuscript score of *Tannhäuser* that Wagner wanted back. What had started as a small quarrel had leapt the bounds of reason. As Wagner sat in his splendid room looking over the score that Nietzsche had produced, he laughed out loud, commenting that Brahms' incomprehension of a *Gesamtkunstwerk* was total. The very idea of setting the word *Gerechtigkeit* (justice) to music was absurd!

The *Triumphlied* score was a noticeable object, being bound in red. Throughout the following week, every time Wagner walked past the piano the red rectangle glared at him and he would shove it away under something else. Every time he came back, Nietzsche had replaced it. Finally, on the Saturday, Wagner sat down to the piano to play it, and the more he played the angrier he grew. He called it a meagre composition: Handel, Mendelssohn and Schumann 'wrapped in leather'. Driven by wifely fury, Cosima noted in her diary with ungenerous glee that she had heard dismal things about Nietzsche at the university, that he only had three or four students and had virtually been excommunicated.[18]

Wagner was as irked by Nietzsche's perceived musical disloyalty to him as Nietzsche was irked by Wagner's materialism (which, after all, was nothing new). Truly the Master had given in to the contemptible money economy they had once, together, excoriated. Bayreuth was a world away from the free, democratic festival of cultural renewal that their shared idealism had originally envisioned.

Both mourned the loss of previous intimacy. Nietzsche was no longer the sole companion of the Master but merely one in the large international crowd flowing unceasingly through Wahnfried's vast and echoing halls in the interest of realising the project. The first festival was due to take place the following year. It was a staggeringly short time to allow for the completion of the opera house, the final orchestration of the score and the discovery, recruitment and rehearsal of singers who were capable of both acting and singing on an heroic scale. In the end it all took a year longer, opening in the summer of 1876.

During Nietzsche's visit, Wahnfried was loud with Wagnerian themes being hummed, sung, played and yodelled by potential Valkyries, Rhinemaidens, gods and mortals. Money men were received, town worthies fed and flattered. Designs were rolled and unrolled. By the end of the week the atmosphere had become so frosty between Wagner and the neglected Nietzsche that he wilfully insulted Wagner by saying petulantly that the German language gave him no pleasure and he would rather converse in Latin. He left at the end of the week, nerve-racked, tense and insomniac. 'The tyrant', he wrote in his notebook, 'acknowledges no individuality other than his own and that of his most trusted friends. Great is the danger for Wagner.'[9]

He did not have a great deal to look forward to on his return to Basle, where his thirtieth birthday was marked by muted celebration. The best birthday gift was the arrival of thirty copies of the newly printed 'Schopenhauer as Educator' *Untimely Meditation*. He forwarded a copy to Wagner, who quickly responded with a gratifying telegram: 'Deep and great. Boldest and newest in the presentation of Kant. Truly comprehensible only to the devilishly possessed.'[20] Hans von Bülow liked it too. His enthusiastic letter of thanks went some way to repairing the breach between them caused by his savage critique of Nietzsche as a composer of music. Von Bülow praised it as brilliant and expressed the opinion that Bismarck ought to quote certain passages in Parliament.

Nietzsche immediately felt better. Equal even to going home to Naumburg for Christmas. He didn't pack his workbooks, only the scores of his compositions. He spent a happy holiday reinforcing his belief in his musical talent, rewriting and improving his pieces and playing them to Franziska and Elisabeth, who made for a rapturous audience. During this quiet musical interlude, even Naumburg sermons had no capacity to spoil his good humour or upset his health, though there was cause enough for worry in the fact that Wilhelm Vischer-Bilfinger, the Chairman of the University Council, had died that year. It was Vischer-Bilfinger who had originally recommended Nietzsche for the Basle professorship. He had acted as his mentor and protector ever since. Nietzsche's long absences from teaching provoked by his ill health meant that his recent contribution to the university had been slight. His controversial publications had hardly added to the lustre of the institution. Nevertheless, his spirits remained high and maybe this had something to do with an idea he had put forward in the *Meditation* on Schopenhauer: that only freedom could liberate genius, only a philosopher who had no affiliation to any institution could think with any authenticity. A break from Basle would confer the same freedom on him.

Cosima wrote Nietzsche a charmingly tactful and well-mannered letter explaining that she and Wagner must embark on yet another fundraising trip, this time to Vienna. There was no one to whom they would be happier to entrust their most precious treasures – their children – than Elisabeth. Might she find it in the goodness of her heart to take up the burden of residence in Wahnfried and act as mother to her daughters and little Siegfried while they were away? Was it indelicate to request that Nietzsche put the proposal to his sister? Franziska grumbled mightily at such a demand on her daughter's time but Elisabeth would brook no obstacle. This was ascent on the social ladder. In the event, Elisabeth made a great success of the visit, using it to lay the foundation for a position in the household that was more than a servant but less than a friend, something like an occasional lady-in-waiting.

The winter of 1874–5 was cold and snowy. Between December and February, Nietzsche was severely ill. Fortunately he only had easy work to do for the *Pädagogium*. He turned his thoughts to the next *Untimely Meditation* whose subject, he had decided, would be 'Art'. He would base it on his own first-hand experience of Wagner. But before he could put this plan in hand, he was struck by two great 'earthquakes of the soul' that would derail his health for the rest of the year.

The first concerned Heinrich Romundt, his close friend and his amanuensis in Poison Cottage, whom he considered almost an extension of his own brain. Now Romundt announced that he was intending to become a priest in the Roman Catholic Church. Nietzsche felt it like a deep wound. Was Romundt in his right mind? Might he be cured by some sort of medical treatment, such as cold baths? Why, of all churches, had Romundt chosen the Roman Catholic? It was the most absurd of all the Christian denominations, with its superstitious relics, its bones and skulls paid for by the sales of indulgences. Five years previously it had overstepped even these medieval absurdities by elevating the Pope to infallibility. The Roman Church was the tinkle of bells on a fool's cap. Was this how Romundt repaid years of close friendship, of reasoning and philosophising together?

The few weeks that Romundt remained in Basle were painful to all parties. Romundt was tearful and inarticulate. Nietzsche was furious and uncomprehending. The day Romundt left for the seminary, Nietzsche and Overbeck conducted him to the station. He kept begging them for forgiveness. After the porters had closed the train doors, they saw him wrestling with the window, trying to lower it to say something to them as they stood on the platform. The window would not budge and their last sight of him was his strenuous physical effort to tell them something that they would never hear, while the train slowly pulled away.

Nietzsche immediately succumbed to a headache that lasted thirty hours, with frequent vomiting.

The second earthquake of the soul to shake Nietzsche's foundations came from his other Poison Cottage housemate. Franz Overbeck became engaged to be married. Romundt had left him for superstitious faith, Overbeck was leaving him for love. Was there anyone remaining for whom he counted as first in the world? Only his mother and sister; a lowering thought. But love might rescue loneliness. With Overbeck's example fresh in mind, he embarked upon a little romantic adventure.

In April 1876, he heard that a certain Countess Diodati who lived in Geneva had translated *The Birth of Tragedy* into French. This made her worth hunting down. He took a train. On arrival he discovered that the Countess was shut up in a lunatic asylum but her absence was more than made up for by the renewal of his acquaintance with Hugo von Senger, the director of the Geneva Orchestra and an enthusiastic Wagnerian. Senger gave piano lessons. Among his pupils was an ethereal twenty-three-year-old Livonian greatly admired for her beauty and delicacy. Her name was Mathilde Trampedach.

Nietzsche was only in Geneva for a short week. High on his list was a pilgrimage to the Villa Diodati, where Byron had once lived. Mathilde was one of the party. During the carriage ride along the shore of the lake, Nietzsche enlarged on the Byronic theme of freedom from oppression. Mathilde unexpectedly interrupted him with the comment that she found it odd that men should expend so much time and energy on the question of lifting purely external constraints when it was the internal constraints that really hampered them.

It was an argument that fired Nietzsche's soul. On their return to Geneva he took to the piano to treat her to one of his tumultuous and dramatic improvisations. The recital finished, he bowed low over her hand and shot an intensely penetrating look into her eyes. Then he went upstairs to write her a proposal of marriage.

'Muster all the courage of your heart,' he began, 'so as not to be afraid of the question I am going to ask you. Will you be my wife? I love you and feel that you already belong to me. Not a word [to anyone] about the suddenness of my feelings! At least they are innocent; so there is nothing that needs to be forgiven. But I would like to know if you feel as I do – that we have never been strangers at all, not for a moment! Do you not also think that in our association each of us would be better and more free than either could be alone – and so *excelsior*?

Will you dare to come with me as one who is striving with all his heart to become better and more free? . . .'[21]

He had no way of knowing that Mathilde was, in fact, secretly in love with her piano teacher, the much older Hugo von Senger. Doggedly she had followed him to Geneva in the hope of becoming his third wife, an ambition she eventually realised.

8

· THE LAST DISCIPLE
AND THE FIRST DISCIPLE ·

> They both wanted to sever the friendship at the same time, one
> because he thought himself too much misunderstood, the
> other because he thought himself understood too well — and both
> were deceiving themselves! — for neither of them understood
> himself well enough.
>
> *Daybreak*, Book IV, Section 287

The pressing task for 1875–6 was to complete the next *Untimely Meditation*. His publisher wanted to keep up the momentum of publishing one every nine months. He made a stab at writing on philology but We Philologists did not progress. What more did he have to say about the historical reductionist approach and its consequent insensitivity to the true sources of artistic inspiration? He returned to the subject of Art.

He would write a new *Untimely Meditation* on a subject that now held great interest for him: individual genius and the effect it can have on the culture of an age. Thanks to his long and close relationship with Wagner, nobody could be better qualified to apply the magnifying glass to genius. The fourth *Untimely Meditation* would be called 'Richard Wagner in Bayreuth' and it would serve a double purpose: as the next *Meditation* and as a trumpet-blast *Festschrift* marking the opening of the inaugural Bayreuth Festival.

'Richard Wagner in Bayreuth' is only some fifty pages long but it took him the best part of a year to write. The writing limped along on uneven legs, not for his usual reason of the difficulty of getting things down on paper but because tension between his head and his heart was taking him on a long journey of understanding. The process of writing a celebration of the composer's genius made Nietzsche realise the very necessity of freeing himself from Wagner. The dangerous influence of the beloved composer could hardly be overstated: Nietzsche's own becoming required the overcoming of Wagner, and this set up great emotional conflict within him.

Nietzsche had long hymned the sublime power that Wagner's music exercised over his senses but now he realised how it robbed him of his free will. The realisation filled him with a growing resentment against the delirious, befogging metaphysical seduction that once had seemed like the highest redemption of life. Now he saw Wagner as a terrible danger, and his own devotion to him as reeking of a nihilist flight from the world. He criticised Wagner for being a romantic histrionic, a spurious tyrant, a sensual manipulator. Wagner's music had shattered his nerves and ruined his health; Wagner was surely not a composer, but a disease?

He could not possibly put thinking of this kind into the work for publication: such thoughts would render *The Birth of Tragedy* completely invalid. And so while writing about Wagner's genius, the *Meditation* morphed, as he would acknowledge later, into an analysis of his own genius, and a meditation on the future use to which he might put it.

The previous *Meditation* on Schopenhauer had identified the Rousseauian genius whose nature is as primordial as that of the serpent Typhon beneath Etna's volcano.[1] Wagner was such a life force, and this was what Nietzsche aspired to be himself: an insatiable rebel, careless of his own safety and the safety of the world, a cultural innovator whose thought would initiate vast concept-quakes. It was exciting to think that the visionary upheavals of such geniuses as Wagner (and himself), while wreaking inevitable destruction, were essential to the salvation of humankind from stagnation and mediocrity.

The essay reprises themes first sounded in *The Birth of Tragedy*. In the name of Wagner he again takes up his own thoughts on the death of veneration for the Dionysian through the imposition of relentlessly rationalist theories of law, state and culture, leading to his present age in which the *Bildungsphilister*, the educated philistines, reign smug in their certainties, so that all active cultural spirit is used towards propping up the party walls of the great semi-detached edifices of economy and power — substantially buttressed by the power of the newspapers, which Nietzsche again decries as shallow props to the newspaper reader's ego while undermining his soul. Real culture, such as Wagner's (and by implication his own), carries a subterranean current of purification, enlargement and ennoblement of the spirit together with its inevitable role of iconoclasm. The essay ends with desperately overwritten passages of extravagant praise for Wagner: his glance casts 'beams of sunlight which suck up moisture, congregate mist, spread thunderclouds . . . He has surprised nature that he has seen her naked: so that now she seeks to conceal her shame by fleeing into her antithesis,'[2] and so on. But Nietzsche cannot resist smuggling in a few sly digs. Comparing Wagner's astonishing self-belief to Goethe's; his 'is perhaps an even more "presumptuous" nature than Goethe, who said of himself: "I always believed that I had everything; they could have set a crown upon my head and I would have thought it quite in order."'[3] The *Meditation* ends unequivocally on the statement that Wagner is not, in fact, 'the seer of a future, as he would perhaps like to appear to us, but the interpreter and transfigurer of a past'.[4]

Nietzsche was reserving the role of seer of the future for himself.

'Richard Wagner in Bayreuth' was never a successful piece of writing. Bristling with filial resentment and insincerity, it goes back to his previous stiff writing style, employing much earnest analysis and none of the warmth and wit of the previous *Meditation* on Schopenhauer. All the time he was composing it, he was suffering the tortures of the parricide: his head, eyes and stomach giving him no peace. Every day for several hours he experienced a sensation akin to seasickness. On average he was spending thirty-six hours every fortnight in bed in complete darkness, often in such agony that he was unable to think. He had lost the two friends who until now had devotedly taken dictation: von Gersdorff had departed for his estates and Romundt for the seminary, but the secretarial solution arrived in April, in the energetic shape of a wild-haired twenty-two-year-old Saxon composer named Johann Heinrich Köselitz. He was blessed with the most beautifully clear, calligraphic handwriting.

While studying counterpoint and composition in Leipzig, Köselitz had read *The Birth of Tragedy*. It had left him and his fellow student, Paul Heinrich Widemann, 'reeling with delight'. They were modest enough to confess that they did not understand the book entirely but they felt strongly that they had come up against a mind that spoke with interpretative force the like of which they had never experienced before. 'When Nietzsche had the Apollonian and Dionysian forces finally destroyed by utilitarian rationalism (as expressed by Socrates), we suspected why a sprouting and blossoming of great art is almost impossible under the domination of our culture of knowledge and reason . . . *The Birth of Tragedy* is a mighty protest of artistic and heroic man against the will-weakening, instinct-destroying consequences of our Alexandrian culture.'[5]

'Schopenhauer as Educator' had deepened their enthusiasm. 'For while our contemporaries understood "culture" to mean approximately Bentham's ideal of a maximisation of general comfort (the ideal of Strauss and all socialists since More), Nietzsche suddenly appeared among them like a lawgiver out of thunderclouds teaching that the goal and summit of culture was to produce genius.'[6]

Köselitz took to referring to Nietzsche as 'the great revaluator'. Impetuously he travelled to Basle, determined to meet him and to study under him.

Having no idea what Nietzsche looked like, he made calls at the bookshops where one could buy photographs of local beauty spots and personalities. To his dismay, the glass case devoted to university professors did not include a likeness of his hero. His enquiry was met with 'Professor Nietzsche? Is there anybody here by that name?', a reaction probably not entirely due to Nietzsche's patchy reputation at the university but also down to his dislike of what he called being 'photographically executed by the one-eyed Cyclops . . . I try, each time, to prevent the disaster, but the inevitable always occurs – and out I come, eternalised anew as a pirate or a prominent tenor or a boyar . . .'[7]

Köselitz was a neck-or-nothing Wagnerian and when they did eventually meet, Nietzsche lent him the uncompleted Wagner *Meditation*. Köselitz's characteristic tempestuous enthusiasm persuaded Nietzsche that it should be completed, and that he was the man to help. Between the end of April and the end of June he took down the last three chapters from dictation, as well as making a fair copy in his beautiful copperplate of the whole ninety-eight pages. When the proofs came back from the publisher, the diligent Köselitz corrected them. Finally, two magnificently bound volumes were ready to send to Wagner and Cosima in late July, which was the final rehearsal period before the formal opening of the festival, on 13 August.

In the thick of last-minute preparations, Wagner could not possibly have had a moment to read the book, but it was a marvellous gift to receive at a turbulent time. He responded quickly and enthusiastically by telegram: 'Friend! Your book is prodigious! But how have you discovered so much about me? Now come quickly and accustom yourself to the impacts [of the *Ring*] through the rehearsals.'[8] Wagner forwarded the second copy to King Ludwig, who professed himself equally enchanted by Nietzsche's text.

Before Nietzsche could think of responding to Wagner's imperious summons to Bayreuth, he received a letter from Erwin Rohde, announcing his engagement. Friendship alters with the glance of a bride, and now three of his closest old friends had moved on to matrimony.

Nietzsche's feelings were not straightforward. He wrote a warm letter of congratulation to Rohde that included the speculation that compared to his friends he was perhaps at fault but marriage must encompass compromise and unacceptable accommodation with human mediocrity that he was not prepared to make. During the night following the receipt of Rohde's letter he composed a maudlin poem entitled 'The Wanderer',[9] which pictures him striding through a mountain landscape at night and hearing a bird singing sweetly. Like the woodbird in Wagner's *Siegfried*, it can talk. On interrogation it informs him it is not singing for him, but for its mate.

On 22 July, he undertook the strenuous journey to Bayreuth, arriving two days later. He reported to Wahnfried the following day. Cosima barely noted his arrival in her diary. The frantic scramble of final rehearsals is always a stressful period for any theatre but this was more so than usual, because the money men had taken the horrifying decision to sell tickets to the rehearsals. Like a prolonged and ill-judged public striptease, every flaw and wrinkle was being exposed to the public gaze. But every day that passed was costing around two thousand marks, and it was a way of recouping some of the expense.

'Much vexation,' Cosima records. Wagner had a terrific argument on stage with the choreographer and the designer. Singers walked out and new ones had to be hired. Herr Unger, who was singing Siegfried, the young hero of the *Ring*, was hoarse – or was it just an excuse? A prominent Valkyrie displayed 'an excess of ungainliness and gracelessness'. The villain Hagen had forgotten his words. The only workshop that could make a dragon capable of breathing fire, waving its tail and rolling its eyes was in England. The dragon was shipped in three parts to be fitted together on arrival but only two arrived in Bayreuth. The neck had been sent to Beirut, the capital of Lebanon. The smoke machine was inadequate. Scenery collapsed to reveal husky workmen in shirtsleeves lounging around as they waited to make scene changes. The singers wanted curtain calls. Wagner would not allow them: they would break the magic spell holding the audience in thrall. In a self-interested but nevertheless democratic gesture, Wagner admitted the fire brigade to a rehearsal free of charge, causing an important member of the management committee to resign. The dress rehearsal was torture. Wagner had employed a painter of historic subjects to design the sets. They were so historically accurate and so meticulously executed that they acted as leaden boots, anchoring the tale firmly in the dimension of pernickety representation and making it impossible for the imagination to get off the ground, let alone soar.

Cosima loathed the costumes; 'reminiscent throughout of Red Indian chiefs and still bear[ing], along with their ethnographic absurdity, all the marks of provincial tastelessness. I am much dismayed by them.'[10] So dismayed that Wagner put Siegfried's horn to his head and charged the unloved costume designer, bellowing like a bull.

Cosima's woes multiplied with the arrival of Judith Gautier, the cynosure of all eyes as she went about the streets of Bayreuth in Paris's very latest fashion: the sailor suit. Wagner's infatuation for Judith, kindled at Tribschen, still blazed. He hid it very badly from Cosima. Whether or not Judith granted the final favour is debated but this hardly mattered. She was installed in a house that Wagner visited far too often, their liaison was steamingly erotic and gossip flew. Everyone was saying she was his mistress. It was a terrible humiliation for Liszt's ugly-duckling daughter. She had been through fire for Wagner, and now another was his muse, his inspiration and his love. Without these things Cosima felt erased. She writes of feeling 'non-existent' and 'dead'. Throughout the festival she drew herself up to her considerable height, raised her large-nosed, imperious profile, styled her hair in a medieval-looking pigtail suitable for a queen of the Nibelungen, gowned herself in the flowing white silk of a bride and, in the role of queen of Bayreuth, acted the pluperfect hostess.

While the festival buzzed with the Gautier scandal, the same society that once had heaped humiliation and scorn on Cosima as Wagner's mistress was now jockeying for her notice. Bayreuth was the place to be; Wagner the man to be seen with. All society was pleading at Wahnfried's door, and Cosima was the doorkeeper. Resplendent in her quasi-medieval garb with a large fan in her hand (Bayreuth was enduring the usual August heatwave that ensures much fainting in the opera house), Cosima stood frigidly erect and majestic, receiving the hundreds of visitors that had come from all parts of the world to see and be seen. It was a magnificent revenge on the society that had once scorned her, and on the Frenchwoman.

On the day that Nietzsche arrived, he was one of five hundred visitors flowing through Wahnfried. A mere professor, he had a very low place in the pecking order. Matters of etiquette were being observed as only parvenus observe them. Cosima had four ruling monarchs to deal with, numerous princes and princesses, grand dukes, grand duchesses, archdukes, archduchesses, dukes, earls, counts, countesses and lesser ranks. To prevent insult and scandal they must all be received in correct order of precedence. Commoners waited in anterooms, speaking in hushed voices, as in church.

King Ludwig wished to attend the festival incognito. He scheduled his arrival for mysterious midnight, to be met secretly by Wagner and conveyed in a carriage to Bayreuth's splendid Hermitage Palace, where the King thought he would stay 'unnoticed'. Beneath scudding clouds and a fugitive moon, the two men bared their souls while the carriage wound its way between the fantastical follies, fountains, and gloomy grottoes of the palace's moon-silvered park. For Wagner, this was one of the very few purely spiritual moments throughout the entire festival, a moment of compensation for the materialism and hullaballoo, a reconnection with the proper spirit, inspiration and purpose of his life's work.

But relations with monarchs are notoriously fragile. The King had insisted he wanted no public ovations during his stay in Bayreuth, but was furious to be taken at his word. However, theatre came first with King Ludwig, even before acclamation. He attended the dress rehearsal of *Das Rheingold* on 28 July. Despite the lack of ovation, the royal ear found the music utterly sublime. On his return to the Hermitage he commanded the park to be lit by flares and invisibly peopled by musicians playing Wagner's music from behind bushes, while the illuminated fountains were made to throb in time to the music.

As Nietzsche had foreseen, the first Bayreuth festival was a world away from a new Aeschylus forging a revival of the tragic spirit that would rescue European culture from stagnancy and mediocrity. Originally envisioned as so much more than a physical event: a metaphor for German culture, an image of the future and pattern for modernity, it had, as he had concluded in his *Meditation*, turned into something far lesser: a cowardly continuation of the old order, a compromise and a delight to the *Bildungsphilister*.

Bitterly, Nietzsche noted 'the entire loafing riff-raff of Europe' was treating the Bayreuth festival as just one more occasion to be added to its aimless perambulation on the annual round of its social calendar. He was repulsed, too, by the presence of numerous anti-Semites finding gratification in the *Ring*'s crude blueprint for racial struggle between the dark, misshapen dwarves of the underworld and Wotan's blond-haired progeny. Siegfried's eventual triumph delighted them, as it would delight Hitler on his first visit in 1923, after which he set to work on *Mein Kampf*.

Dom Pedro II, the Emperor of Brazil, arrived at Wahnfried on the evening following the dress rehearsal. His imperial presence considerably lightened the gloom cast by the flaws in the staging and the disappointing costumes. The King of Württemberg came low down in the hierarchy of monarchy; nevertheless his presence was also a source of satisfaction. The German Emperor himself, Kaiser Wilhelm, graciously attended the first two operas, clapping with his hands while calling out through smiling teeth to his adjutants, 'Frightful! Frightful!' Regretfully he discovered himself unable to stay for the final two operas in the cycle.

Though Wagner had told Nietzsche that he would have his own room at Wahnfried as he had at Tribschen, there was no question of his staying there. Instead, he was in the cheapest lodgings he had been able to find. They were right in the middle of town. The ceilings were low and the weather was baking.

Bayreuth was then a town of some twenty thousand inhabitants. Wagner's new opera house held an audience of 1,925. Three separate cycles of the four operas of the *Ring* were to be performed. This meant altogether an influx of some 5,775 lucky gods in possession of tickets to enter Valhalla, bringing along their households numbering thousands of spouses, children and servants. Then there were the professionals: the performers, singers, musicians, stage technicians, carpenters, seamstresses, laundresses, tradesmen and servants of all sorts. No public event is complete without the opportunistic uninvited. Ladies of the night, moustachioed adventurers in knickerbockers, pickpockets, street urchins, day-tripping gawkers, and a considerable number of peasants who had walked in from the local farms and fields to see the spectacle. All jostled together on the baking, arid pavements. The tumult was intolerable. Nietzsche could not even take civilised refuge in his lodgings, where the heat and smell built up like the disgusting atmosphere inside a roasting oven.

For Tchaikovsky, as for many other visitors, the chief preoccupation was finding food: 'The tables d'hôte prepared in the inns are not sufficient to satisfy all the hungry people,' he wrote. 'One can only obtain a piece of bread, or a glass of beer with immense difficulty, by dire struggle, or cunning stratagem, or iron endurance. Even when a modest place at a table has been stormed, it is necessary to wait an eternity before the long-desired meal is served. Anarchy reigns at these meals. Everyone is calling and shrieking, and the exhausted waiters pay no heed to the rightful claims of an individual. Only by the merest chance does one get a taste of any of the dishes . . . As a matter of fact, throughout the whole duration of the festival, food forms the chief interest of the public; the artistic representations take a secondary place. Cutlets, baked potatoes, omelettes – all are discussed much more eagerly than Wagner's music.'[11]

The theatre was much too bright for Nietzsche to watch from the auditorium. Instead he was given a dark little cupboard-like room close to the stage. It was stiflingly hot. His arrival coincided with rehearsals for the fourth and final opera, *Götterdämmerung*, in which the end of the world takes place. The hundred-piece orchestra drawing the picture of the apocalyptic fall of Valhalla and the destruction of the old gods produced a sheer volume of sound that was probably unprecedented in musical history. 'I did not like it at all . . . and I had to get out . . .'

He liked receptions at Wahnfried even less. He attended one, where he was remarked on as miserable and wordless, and he never attended another.

It is one of the repeating patterns of Nietzsche's life that whenever he was at his lowest, a saviour always emerged to take loving care of him. Now salvation appeared in the figure of Malwida von Meysenbug, a wealthy, ageing anarchist, three years younger than Wagner but of the same revolutionary generation.[12] Malwida's autobiography, *Memoirs of an Idealist*,[13] made her something of a personality at Bayreuth.

Malwida admired the composer greatly and her apartment in Rome was arranged around his marble bust. She was the daughter of a Prussian nobleman; a rejection at a ball had turned her from a member of high society into a determined agent for society's destruction. Like Wagner, she was exiled following the rebellions of 1848–9, in her case for smuggling letters written by the first of many revolutionaries she fell in love with. Her exile took her to north London, where she settled among the cluster of exiled Russian anarchists and where, though she would have preferred to become his wife, she became the tutor to the two daughters of the widowed Alexander Herzen.[14]

Malwida was sufficiently reputable in the world of revolutionaries that during Garibaldi's hugely popular visit to London to radicalise the English and form 'a floating Republic [of ships] always ready to land where there was fighting for freedom to be done',[15] he invited Malwida to breakfast on board his vessel, which was moored on the Thames. When she arrived by rowing boat, 'an armchair covered with a pretty rug was lowered, on which I was pulled up. Garibaldi received us on board in a picturesque costume – a short grey tunic, a gold embroidered red cap on his blond hair, and weapons in his broad belt. His sailors, with dark brown eyes and skin, were gathered on deck likewise in picturesque costumes.' Oysters were served and 'the jolliest and most delightful conversation followed . . . All the sailors seemed to idolise him and one could not help feeling the poetic charm of his personality . . .'[16]

Now a harmless-looking plump little woman in her sixties, with white hair drawn back beneath a scrap of expensive lace, at heart Malwida had lost none of the bloodthirstiness of her days as a young anarchist. Still she delighted in the example set by the Paris Commune

— there would have been fireworks had she and Jacob Burckhardt ever met. She was no humanist but a mystic who believed in an unspecified power for good standing outside the world, a force that could not be found in any laboratory, let alone in a test tube. It gave the human spirit boundless possibilities that made men and women capable of turning themselves into gods, and therefore they were obliged to do so.

Malwida still retained the naïve and direct manner of the determined revolutionary. Her soft blue eyes, much praised, still saw only what she wished to see. High-minded myopia filtered out those aspects of human behaviour irreconcilable with her idealism. All her relationships with the revolutionaries that she wrote about in her memoirs had remained platonic; she was always the housekeeper, much as she would have liked to be the influential mistress. It is difficult not to see her as an adoring adjunct of strong men, more pliant than she would have liked to believe: a monied 'useful idiot', in the Leninist sense. Nowadays she saw her mission as encouraging young 'Pioneers of Freedom', and she decided she had found the next in Nietzsche.

The two of them had first met in May 1872 in Bayreuth, at the laying of the foundation stone, since when they had kept up a courteous correspondence. She had admired his writings and he had extended warm sympathy when one of Herzen's daughters had married a man of whom Malwida's revolutionary heart could not approve.

Malwida saw the physical distress that Nietzsche's inferno quarters caused him, and she gave him daily refuge in the cool shade of her garden. She fed him unlimited sympathy and a soothing diet of milk. He took long swims in the waters of the little river that flowed through the garden. It was a regime that did him so much good that it even revived his adoration of the music he was listening to in the theatre. He had to admit that his soul could not help but submit, even though all the rest of the Bayreuth brouhaha was intolerable.

On 3 or 4 August, Nietzsche fled Bayreuth without telling anybody, not even Malwida. He took the train to Klingenbrunn, a tiny village in the Bavarian forest. He stayed there only a few days but it did him good. He returned in time for the opening night on 13 August, adhering to the plan to meet his sister in Bayreuth, together with his dear friends Rohde and von Gersdorff, all of whom had paid considerable sums for their tickets and accommodation.

A magic love potion is often a plot device in Wagner's operas, and now it was as if all three friends had drunk deeply.

Carl von Gersdorff fell 'madly, insanely, Byronically' in love with a young Italian countess named Nerina Finochietti. He proposed precipitately and spent subsequent months disentangling himself from her family's rapacity.

The recently engaged Erwin Rohde flirted outrageously, if clumsily, with every female they encountered, to the considerable embarrassment of his companions.

Nietzsche himself was struck helpless on meeting a pretty blonde, named Louise Ott. Musicality gave her something in common with his previous loves. Louise was an excellent musician with a good touch on the piano and a very sweet singing voice. When she and Nietzsche met, they talked of everything, but she omitted to tell him she was married. By the time he learned, the damage had been done. Louise's banker husband did not share her passion for Wagner and so he had been left at home in Paris, and she was attending the festival in the company of her young son Marcel. It seems that the *coup de foudre* struck both Nietzsche and Louise equally strongly and deeply.

'Everything was dark around me when you left Bayreuth,' he wrote to her; 'it was as though someone had removed the light. I first had to pull myself together, but that I have now done, and you can take this letter in your hand without apprehension. We want to hold fast to the purity of the spirit that brought us together.'[17]

'How good it is', she replied three days later, 'that a true, healthy friendship can spring up between us so that we can think of each other so directly from the heart without our conscience forbidding it . . . Your eyes, however, can I not forget: your deep, loving gaze still rests upon me, as it did then . . . Make no mention of our letters to each other — Everything that so far has come to pass will remain between us — it is our sanctuary, for both of us alone.'[18]

A year later, almost to the day, he wrote a passionate letter telling her he had felt her presence so vividly that he had glimpsed her eyes. Louise was pregnant again but she replied almost immediately, saying that this was not surprising, as she had been recollecting their brief time together; 'I relived everything and found myself so rich – so rich – because you had given me your heart.'[19]

9

· FREE AND NOT SO FREE SPIRITS ·

> But if science provides us with less and less pleasure, and deprives
> us of more and more pleasure through casting suspicion on the
> consolations of metaphysics, religion and art, then that mightiest
> source of joy to which mankind owes almost all its humanity will
> become impoverished. For this reason a higher culture must give
> to man a double-brain, as it were two brain-ventricles, one for the
> perceptions of science, the other for those of non-science: lying beside
> one another, not confused together, separable, capable of being shut
> off; this is a demand of health.
>
> *Human, All Too Human*, 'Tokens of higher and lower culture',
> Section 251

The university granted Nietzsche a year's leave of absence with pay, starting in autumn 1876. It even released him from the last teaching duties he had been keeping up at the *Pädagogium*. This meant complete freedom. Malwida von Meysenbug invited him to spend the winter in Sorrento, and he accepted.

His publisher was pressing him for the next *Untimely Meditation*. He told him it was well under way. This was not true, though he had an idea in his head that was nagging to get onto the page. Provisionally he gave it the title 'The Ploughshare' ('*Die Pflugschar*'). As the sharp blade of the ploughshare cuts the soil cleanly, severing the roots of the choking weeds that will strangle the useful shoots, so the book would cut out the weeds that so far had choked his original thought, namely his erstwhile idols Wagner and Schopenhauer.

Obviously the complicated railway journey to Sorrento with its train transfers and luggage-herding would be too much for him to undertake on his own, so he arranged for two friends to accompany him. One was a philology student named Albert Brenner, a tubercular twenty-year-old, prone to depression and poetry, whose parents had faith in the curative properties of wintering in the south. The other was the twenty-six-year-old philosopher Paul Rée, whom Malwida had met in Bayreuth. Rée's first book, *Psychologische Beobachtungen* (*Psychological Observations*) had attracted some attention, and he was on the verge of publishing another. He would be an excellent addition to the Sorrento circle, which Malwida planned as a philosophico-literary salon. She had always dreamed of existing in some sort of community of idealists and she looked forward to the coming winter as a laboratory for fertile thought. Malwida herself was planning to write her first novel. That winter she did, in fact, produce a novel called *Phädra*, a three-volume saga of tangled family relations intended to illuminate the quest for individual freedom.

On 19 October 1876, Nietzsche and Brenner boarded a train that would pass through the Mont Cenis tunnel, a recent engineering marvel, before taking them onward to Turin.

They found themselves sharing their first-class carriage with a pair of elegant and intelligent ladies, Claudine von Brevern and Isabella von der Pahlen. Nietzsche fell into one of his romantic flurries as he and Isabella talked intensely throughout the journey. They exchanged addresses before parting for the night, which was to be spent, as it happened, in the same hotel. In the morning, the ladies were to embark on a different train and Nietzsche got up to see them off, but on his way to the station he was smitten by such a searing headache that he had to be supported by Rée back to the hotel.

At Pisa he stopped to see the famous tower and at Genoa he saw the sea for the first time in his life. Thereafter the city became associated in his mind with Columbus, Mazzini and Paganini. It was the city of explorers, founders, innovators; the city of souls who were brave enough to set sail on uncharted seas in the hope of discovering new worlds. Nietzsche paced the heights surrounding Genoa, imagining himself into the mind of the great Columbus who, in discovering the New World, had doubled the earth's possibilities at a stroke.

From Genoa they took a steamer to Naples. It was to be his first entry into the classical world. He was given no time to mark the solemn moment. Instead, he must waste all his consciousness and thought on outwitting the aggressive urchins who haggled and hustled and quarrelled over his luggage like thieving magpies. It was intolerable to arrive with such utter lack of decorum into the world that he had imagined all his life. Malwida restored his humour by an evening carriage ride along the curving Bay of Naples from the wooded promontory of Posillipo (Pausilipon to the ancient Greeks) towards the looming cone of Vesuvius with the island of Ischia rising from the wine-dark sea.

'Storm clouds had gathered majestically over Vesuvius, from the lightning bolts and gloomy dark red of the clouds a rainbow formed; the city glistened as though it were built of pure gold,' wrote Malwida. 'It was so wonderful that the gentlemen were well-nigh intoxicated with rapture. I never saw Nietzsche so lively. He laughed aloud from sheer joy.'[1]

After two days in Naples, they continued to Sorrento. Nothing had prepared him for the journey through the architecture of the south. With their ochre and tangerine walls crumbling, and their plaster peeling, the jumble of faded, unkempt classical ghosts demanded a whole shedding of rigidity. It was unsettling in contrast to the Swiss and German architecture he had known all his life, with its stringently organised structures symbolising generational incarnations of correctitude and tidy civic virtue.

Malwida had rented the Villa Rubinacci, a foursquare stuccoed villa a little distance from the town of Sorrento. The villa was set in vineyards and olive groves. The three men had first-floor rooms overlooking the terrace. Malwida and her maid Trina were on the second floor, where there was also the salon. This room was large enough for the free spirits to gather together, and whirl into synchronised inspiration.

Nietzsche's first letter home, on 28 October, deliberately excluded his mother and sister from anything he had found profound or significant. Indeed, it was written with such cartoonish schoolboy naïveté that even Franziska and Elisabeth must have found it irritatingly uninformative. 'Here we are in Sorrento! The whole trip here from Bex took eight days. In Genoa I was ill. From there we took about three days for the sea journey, and – look! – we were not seasick.'[2] And so on. But for himself he wrote differently, confessing that he shuddered at the thought that he might have died without seeing the Mediterranean world.

On visiting Paestum he reflected: 'In the case of everything perfect, we are accustomed to abstain from asking how it became: we rejoice in the present fact as though it came out of the ground by magic . . . We still *almost* feel (for example in a Greek temple such as that at Paestum) that a god must one morning have playfully constructed his dwelling out of these tremendous weights: at other times that a stone suddenly acquired by magic a soul that is now trying to speak out of it. The artist knows that his work produces its full effect when it excites a belief in an improvisation, a belief that it came into being with miraculous suddenness; and so he may assist this illusion and introduce those elements of rapturous restlessness, of blindly groping disorder, of attentive reverie that attend the beginning of creation into his art as a means of deceiving the soul of the spectator or auditor into a mood in which he believes that the complete and perfect has suddenly emerged instantaneously.'[3]

The free spirits fell into a routine. They passed their mornings in complete freedom. Nietzsche swam every day the sea allowed, and walked, and worked. They came together at the midday meal. In the afternoon they took sociable walks through the surrounding citrus groves, or they went further afield on donkeys, and then there was much merriment over young Brenner, whose long legs almost reached the ground alongside his mount's. In the evening they all had dinner together. Then they would go up to the sitting room for stimulating conversations founded on a programme of common study. Rée and Brenner took it in turns to read aloud to Nietzsche and Malwida, who also had weak eyesight.

They began with Burckhardt's lectures on ancient Greek culture, then went on to Herodotus, Thucydides and Plato's *Laws*, followed by *Thought and Reality* by Afrikan Spir, a Russo-Ukrainian philosopher and metaphysician who had served in the same battalion as Tolstoy during the siege of Sebastopol in 1854–5. Spir's philosophical system is based on the demand for absolute certainty. What matters is not truth but certainty. The only unconditionally true proposition is the law of identity: A = A. Nothing in the realm of becoming (*Geschehen*) is truly self-identical. We must postulate an ultimate reality, although we can say nothing about it except that being self-identical, it must exclude plurality and change. Spir claimed that this provided a logical demonstration for what Plato and Paramides had grasped intuitively. It is odd that Spir wielded a strong influence on Nietzsche at this time, for Spir was a deist and, like Schopenhauer, a metaphysician, while Nietzsche's other strong interest was in the rationalist French moralists Montaigne, La Rochefoucauld, Vauvenargues, La Bruyère, Stendhal and Voltaire.

Rée called himself an evolutionary ethicist and it was almost certainly he who introduced the French rationalists to the reading programme. Voltaire would have been anathema in Nietzsche's Schopenhauerian days but so dramatic was the turn his ideas took over this winter that when his new book was eventually written he would dedicate it to Voltaire. Playfully, he referred to his new thinking as 'Réealism'.

Paul Rée was five years younger than Nietzsche. He was the son of a wealthy Jewish businessman; he had no need to earn his living and he became something of an eternal student, attending several universities, where he variously studied law, psychology and physiology. He had achieved his doctorate in philosophy the previous year. He was about the same unimpressive height as Wagner and Nietzsche. He was almost handsome, with brown, wavy hair and a kindly diffidence that explained the cats-paw that strong women, such as Elisabeth Nietzsche and Lou Salomé, would make of him in the future. Rée suffered from some minor, unexplained chronic health problem but he suffered more from lack of drive and self-confidence.

Like Nietzsche, Rée had taken part in the Franco-Prussian War and been wounded, but he saw this as no barrier to enjoying French culture. His cosmopolitan outlook appealed to Nietzsche's ambition to be a good European rather than a good citizen of the *Reich*. The friendship with Rée lasted around six years, between October 1876 and 1882, during which time they produced literary works that influenced each other both in style and thought. Both took the ancient Greeks as a starting point for thinking about the philosophical concerns of their own times as they struggled to come to terms with the post-Darwinian reorganisation of human knowledge.

Rée set out his basic principles in his doctoral dissertation of 1875:

1. Human actions do not depend on free will.
2. Conscience does not have a transcendental origin.
3. Immoral means are often praiseworthy for the sake of a good end.
4. There is no progress in human affairs.
5. Kant's categorical imperative is not suited to a practical doctrine of morals.[4]

It was Rée's declared intention to treat moral feelings and concepts as a geologist treats the formations of the earth, taking the Darwinian doctrine of natural selection as a general theoretical framework and replacing metaphysical speculation with scientific naturalism.

With no belief in free will, there could be no belief in moral responsibility. The very idea of blame or transgression was mistaken, because it assumed that someone could have acted differently.

In the final analysis, Rée's detached, even cynical, outlook repudiated any intention, or indeed any possibility that it might edify, instruct, justify, uplift or transcend. And so, being shorn of metaphysics, it was even more pessimistic than Schopenhauer, but it was Rée's naturalistic doctrine on these ideas that moved Nietzsche away from the metaphysical romanticism of Schopenhauer and Wagner towards a positivistic, scientific viewpoint. This new direction was heavily influenced by Rée seeking to explain moral feelings by reconstructing their historical or pre-historical development, in what he called his 'evolutionary ethics'.

Rée's explanation of the moral sense was this: just as children develop their ideas through daily experience, parental example and acquired habit, so the human race has, over time, developed a moral nature which is handed on. Rée's thinking on the acquisition of morality followed Darwin's evolutionary ethic set out in *The Descent of Man*. It is possible that Nietzsche only knew the work of Darwin second-hand, through such as Rée.[5] Nietzsche's capacity to read English was certainly doubtful. However, we do know that he had direct knowledge of Darwin's article 'Biographical Sketch of an Infant'.[6] It is a short piece, concerning the early display of moral sense. Darwin describes meeting his son William, aged two, coming out of the dining room. William was looking bright-eyed with 'an odd unnatural or affected manner'. The child had stolen some sugar. Darwin concluded that the child's feeling of discomfort stemmed from his frustrated desire to please, even as he experienced his newly acquired ability to correlate past and future events. It was not due to fear of punishment, as the child 'had never been in any way punished'. For Rée, the article bore out the second principle in his doctoral thesis: that conscience does not have a transcendental origin. Nietzsche was to write a whole book about this, exploring what he called the genealogy of morality.

Rée carried about a copy of La Rochefoucauld's *Maxims* in his pocket. He was a great concoctor of aphorisms himself, such as 'Teaching alters our behaviour, not our character,' and 'Religion arises from fear of nature, morality from fear of human beings.'[7]

Rée's doctoral thesis contained the brave and surprising statement that 'There are gaps in this essay, but gaps are better than stopgaps,' and there were plenty of gaps in the aphorisms he favoured as a means to deliver thought. Aphorism was a curiously unscientific technique for one who called himself an evolutionary ethicist, for surely it is a property of scientific proof that it travels transparently from A to B, while the aphorism, as Nietzsche observed, is the great launch-pad for conjecture; 'An aphorism, properly stamped and moulded, has not been "deciphered" when it has simply been read; rather, one then has to begin its *exegesis*.'[8]

Nietzsche was inspired to imitate Rée's elegant French aphoristic style. Brevity held great attraction for him because the periods when he was capable of reading or writing were becoming ever briefer. 'This neuralgia goes to work so thoroughly, so scientifically, that it literally probes me to find how much pain I can endure, and each of its investigations lasts for thirty hours.'[9] He could not always find an amanuensis to take down dictation and a well-thought-out aphorism took a very little time to commit to paper.

The first ones he jots down in his notebook read with all the insight of fortune-cookie mottoes: 'Motherhood is present in every kind of love; but not fatherhood.' 'To see something as a whole one must have two eyes, one of love and one of hate.'[10] With improvement came frustration with the German language. Compared to the French language, German was a lumbering leviathan. Its cumbersome construction was completely unsuited to brevity. Anyone attempting to write aphoristically in German soon encounters the problem that its constructions cannot be cut off as sharply and wittily as they can be in French or in English. Detached auxiliary verbs tumble on and on like an avalanche, ruining concision and blunting the point. Nevertheless, he derived great enjoyment from persisting, and the book that he was working on, *Human, All Too Human,* would eventually consist of almost 1,400 aphorisms or aphoristic paragraphs.

The Wagners were also wintering in Sorrento, in the Hotel Vittoria, close to the Villa Rubinacci. The only contact between Nietzsche and Wagner since the Bayreuth Festival had been in September, when the Master had written out of the blue to request Nietzsche to buy some silk underwear in Basle and post it to him. When he received the letter, Nietzsche had been so ill that he was unable to put pen to paper but he organised for the underwear to be purchased and posted, and he dictated a long and affectionate letter to accompany it. The letter expressed unaffected delight at being of service: the little commission had brought back fond memories of the happy times at Tribschen.[11]

As soon as Malwida's party had arrived in Sorrento, they had lost no time in calling on the Wagners at the nearby Hotel Vittoria. They found Wagner suffering from a mood of the blackest melancholy. The sustained effort of the festival had been exhausting. But worse, far worse, had been the festival's imperfections. He was in a state of sustained fury. Everything had been botched. He *must* correct the artistic faults in next year's festival. Could there even be a next one when the inaugural festival had left him with debts of 140,000 marks? He had written to King Ludwig proposing an ingenious plan to foist the debt onto the *Reich* but the King was following his usual course of avoiding anything he found difficult by simply not replying to letters.

The two parties coincided in Sorrento over the period of a fortnight. We learn, mostly from Malwida, of the wind in the olive groves, of daily sightseeing expeditions, of evening parties lit by shooting stars and of the lapping of phosphorescent waves on the shore, but we learn nothing meaningful concerning Nietzsche's conversations with Wagner. Cosima's diary mentions Nietzsche briefly on the first day, as seeming much run down and concerned with his health.[12] She wastes no politeness on Rée, whose 'cold and precise character does not appeal to us; on closer inspection we come to the conclusion that he must be an Israelite'.[13] She does not mention Nietzsche further but it might be that he was simply too ill to be present. October was a bad month for him. Following a 'quite desperate attack', he travelled to Naples to consult Otto von Schrön, a professor of optics, who prescribed that all would go much better if he married. This was quite possibly a euphemism for having sexual intercourse and Rée implies that he took the advice and slept with prostitutes while in Naples or when he got back to Sorrento. Malwida took the professor's advice at its innocent face value and happily embarked on a flurry of matchmaking. Together she and Nietzsche made a plan, which Nietzsche outlines in a letter to Elisabeth.

'The plan which Frl. von Meysenbug says must be kept firmly in view, and in the execution of which you must help, is this: We convince ourselves that, in the long run, my Basel University existence cannot continue, that to carry it through at best would mean abandoning all my important projects and still sacrificing my health completely.' The way out was to marry an affluent woman. '"Good *but* rich," as Frl. von M. said, this "but" making us laugh out loud . . . With this wife, I would then live for the next few years in Rome, which place is suitable for reasons alike of health, society and my studies. This summer the plan should be carried out, in Switzerland, so that I could return to Basel in the autumn a married man. Various "persons" are invited to come to Switzerland, among them . . . Elise von Bülow from Berlin, Elsbeth Brandes from Hanover. As far as intellectual qualities are concerned, I still find Nat[alie] Herzen the most suitable. You did very well with the idealisation of the little Köckert woman in Geneva! All praise and honour to you! But it is doubtful; and money? . . .'[14]

He listed the most important quality (after money) in a wife as being a woman with whom he could hold intelligent conversation into old age. On this score he marked Natalie Herzen as undoubtedly the outstanding candidate. The Russo-Jewish daughter of the widowed Alexander Herzen, Natalie had been brought up and educated by Malwida, who looked on her and her sister as foster daughters. While Natalie was sufficiently intelligent she was not rich, so there was no need for Nietzsche to concoct an escape route. It is difficult to imagine him contemplating marriage with anything but panic. When he received a letter from his train flirtation, Isabella von der Pahlen, expressing the hope that they might meet in Rome, sudden illness intervened, for a second time as far as Isabella was concerned, and he found himself too ill to reply directly to her letter, though not too ill to instruct his publisher to send her the *Untimely Meditations* with his compliments.

Nietzsche seems to have been particularly susceptible on trains. The next train journey he took he was dazzled by a young ballerina from a Milan theatre; 'O, you should have heard my Italian! If I had been a pasha, I would have taken her to Pfafers with me, where, whenever intellectual occupations failed, she would have been able to dance for me. I am still sometimes rather angry with myself for not having stayed at least a few days in Milan for her sake.'[15] But soon he admitted, 'Marriage, though indeed very desirable, is the most *improbable* thing — I know that *very* clearly.'[16]

The Wagners departed Sorrento on 7 November but before that, on All Souls' Day, which fell on the 2nd, the two house parties took a walk together before spending the evening in each other's company. In her biography of her brother, Elisabeth Nietzsche (who was never in Sorrento) tells the world that, on that day, her brother and Wagner had a mighty quarrel that led to them never meeting again. Cosima does not bear this out. She was there, after all, and her diary entry for the day is brief and tranquil. But this example of Elisabeth exercising her talent for fabrication must be included at this point in the narrative because her biography of her brother is an obvious port of call for any researcher, and indeed her untrue version of events influenced scholarship concerning Nietzsche's life for decades. Just as Elisabeth's fabricated account of her father's death was designed to draw attention from the possibility of syphilis in the family, so her story of the quarrel with Wagner was designed to conceal the real reason for the breach, which came later and centred round medical secrecy and sexual scandal that Elisabeth desperately wished to conceal.

'On the last evening together [in Sorrento],' Elisabeth writes, 'Wagner and my brother took a wonderful walk along the coast and up the heights, where a glorious view of sea, island and bay is obtained.

'"An atmosphere of farewell," said Wagner.

'Then he suddenly began to speak of *Parsifal* [the new opera he was composing, which took the Christian theme of the knights of the Holy Grail as its subject matter]. It was the first time he had dilated upon this work, and he did so in a remarkable way, outlining it not as an artistic creation but as a religious, a Christian experience . . . He began to confess to my brother various Christian emotions and experiences, such as repentance and atonement, and all manner of leanings towards Christian dogmas . . . He [Nietzsche] could regard Wagner's sudden change of front only as an attempt to come to terms with the ruling powers in Germany, who had now grown pious — his sole aim being material success. While Wagner talked on and on, the last gleam of sunshine vanished on the sea, and a slight fog, together with growing darkness, crept over the scene. In my brother's heart, too, darkness had arisen . . . What disillusionment! Malwida could only remember that my brother was much depressed all that evening and retired to his room early. He had a presentiment that Wagner and he would never meet again.'[17]

This is a complete fabrication from first to last but it stood as the truth until 1981, when the Wagner scholar Martin Gregor-Dellin told the real story.

When Nietzsche had arrived in Sorrento, Wagner had become concerned for Nietzsche's lamentable state of health and he wrote to a doctor friend, Otto Eiser, who advised that Nietzsche be given a proper clinical examination. On his return from Italy, Nietzsche went to Frankfurt to be examined by Eiser and an ophthalmologist named Dr Otto Krüger. This was the first time he had been examined thoroughly, and they spent four days over it. They diagnosed changes in an interior portion of the eyeball called the *fundus oculi*, which can be syphilitic in origin. They also discovered very severe damage to both retinas. This contributed to the severity of the headaches, which were not in fact caused by 'stomach catarrh' but by 'a predisposition in the irritability of the central organ', whose origin they diagnosed as excessive mental activity. He must work less, make a programme of relaxation from work, take quinine and wear blue spectacles. To Nietzsche's relief, they discounted a tumour of the brain.

Masturbation was then widely believed to cause severe eye problems such as Nietzsche suffered from, and Wagner sent a woefully indiscreet letter to Dr Eiser, voicing his suspicions. 'In assessing N.'s condition, I have long been reminded of identical or very similar experiences with young men of great intellectual ability. Seeing them laid low by similar symptoms, I discovered all too certainly that these were the effects of masturbation. Ever since I observed N. closely, guided by such experiences, all his traits of temperament and characteristic habits have transformed my fear into a conviction.'[18] Wagner saw further evidence for his theory in the advice that the doctor in Naples had given: that Nietzsche should marry, i.e. regularise his sex life.

Dr Eiser replied: 'In discussing his sexual condition, N. not only assured me that he had never been syphilitic but replied in the negative when I questioned him about strong sexual arousal and abnormal satisfaction of the same. I only cursorily touched on this latter point, however, and cannot therefore attach too much weight to N.'s remarks on the subject. As against this, I find it more cogent that the patient speaks of gonorrhoeal infections during his student days, and also that he recently had intercourse several times in Italy on medical advice. These statements, whose truth is certainly beyond dispute, do at least demonstrate that our patient does not lack the capacity for satisfying the sexual urge in a normal manner; a circumstance, which, though not inconceivable in masturbators of his age, is not the general rule . . . I concede that my objections are all far from watertight and open to rebuttal by your long and exhaustive observation of our friend. I am bound to accept your assumption all the more readily because I, too, am led by many aspects of N.'s comportment and behaviour to regard it as only too credible.'

Eiser went on to say that there had been cases of recovery by neurotic, hysterical patients who had been debilitated by masturbation but this was not possible after such a degree of damage and deterioration to the eyes. Nietzsche's eyesight was past restoring. Eiser ruled out both syphilis and chronic nephritis (kidney disease) as the cause of the trouble.

As for the headaches, 'Such pathological irritability of the nerve centres can most certainly be brought into a direct causal nexus with the sexual sphere, so the solving of the masturbation question would here have a most important bearing on diagnosis – although, given the well-known tenacity of the vice, I myself would be dubious of any method of treatment and its success.' Dr Eiser gave Wagner the same advice that Nietzsche had been given by Dr Schrön: there was hope that Nietzsche's general condition – eyesight apart – might improve a little if he could contract a happy marriage.'[19]

It was not, as Elisabeth said, their differences over the religiosity of Wagner's *Parsifal* libretto that caused the final breach between the two men who loved and valued each other so very much. It was Nietzsche's eventual discovery of this well-intentioned, but crushing, correspondence.

· HUMAN, ALL TOO HUMAN ·

The thinker – and similarly the artist – who has put the best of himself into his work, experiences an almost malicious joy as he watches the erosion of his body and spirit by time. It is as if he were in a corner watching a thief at his safe, while knowing that it is empty, his treasure being elsewhere.

> *Human, All Too Human*, 'From the Souls of Artists and Writers',
> Section 209

'To Malwida von Meysenbug

Lugano, Sunday morning [13 May 1877]

Human misery during a sea journey is terrible, and yet actually laughable, which is how my headaches sometimes seem to me when my physical condition may be excellent – in brief, I am today once more in the mood of serene crippledom, whereas on the ship I had only the blackest thoughts, my only doubts about suicide concerned where the sea might be deepest, so that one would not be immediately fished out again and have to pay a debt of gratitude to one's rescuers in a terrible mass of gold . . . I was wearing my strongest glasses and mistrusted everyone. The customs boat came laboriously by, but I had forgotten the most important thing, which was to register my luggage for the railway journey. Then began a journey to the fabulous Hotel Nationale, with two rogues on the coach box, who wanted to force me to get off at a miserable *trattoria*; my luggage was continually in alien hands, and there was always a man gasping under my suitcase ahead of me . . . The arrival was awful and a whole retinue of hoodlums wanted to be paid off . . . I crossed the Swiss frontier, in a downpour of rain, there was a single flash of lightning, followed by loud thunder. I took it as a good omen.'

He had misread the runes. Once back in Switzerland, there was little to exercise his self-mocking humour. The mild climate of Italy had failed to effect the hoped-for magic on his health, and while the sociability in the Villa Rubinacci had been agreeable and intellectually stimulating, it had not resulted in a book. With the *Untimely Meditations*' failure either to bring about a revitalisation of German culture or to sell (the greatest number sold being about ninety copies of 'Richard Wagner in Bayreuth' to the captive audience of thousands at the inaugural Bayreuth Festival), he wrote to his publisher Schmeitzner, 'Shouldn't we consider the *Untimely Meditations* finished?'[1] Schmeitzner objected, but Nietzsche had moved on from the *Meditations*' original and rather fussy list of topics and was concentrating on the new book that had its beginnings back in Klingenbrunn when he was taking his brief respite from Bayreuth. The titles 'The Ploughshare' and 'The Free Spirit' had evolved into *Human, All Too Human*, subtitled *A Book for Free Spirits*. He described it as a monument to a crisis. Its subject is the human condition. Reason is its lodestar. The language is not violent, didactic, boastful or obscure but personal, lucid and elegant. It is probably his most lovable book.

Everywhere he looked, he saw the inadequacies of both the Enlightenment and Romanticism to fill the void left by the collapse of traditional ways of thinking. A clean start was needed, 'free of phantoms and a hermit's shadow play'. Free, in his case, of nostalgic glorification of the culture of ancient Greece, of Schopenhauer, of Wagner, of division of the world into will and representation. The book would mark his development from philologist and cultural commentator to polemicist. It was not a book written for philosophers. It was a book for enquiring spirits willing to examine cultural, social, political, artistic, religious, philosophical, moral and scientific questions free from preconceptions, assumptions and all the other fictions that had been used over the ages to limit real freedom of thought. He would survey the phenomenal world with Voltairean eyes, accepting that the noumenal world is not only inaccessible but also of no everyday significance to man. He would be the spirit that has become free in the taking possession of itself, the heir to the Enlightenment. He blared his intent on the title page by dedicating the book to Voltaire. It was a showy act of defiance against Wagner.

He divided the book up into sections:

Of First and Last Things
On the History of the Moral Sensations
The Religious Life
From the Souls of Artists and Writers
Tokens of Higher and Lower Culture
Man in Society
Woman and Child
A Glance at the State
Man Alone with Himself.
Among Friends: an Epilogue

Each section consisted of numbered aphorisms or aphoristic paragraphs. 'Of First and Last Things' begins robustly by pointing out the congenital defect in the fundamental thinking of all previous philosophers: they saw human nature as an *aeterna veritas*, an eternal truth. Man hovered before them as something unchanging through all turmoil, a secure measure of things. But everything the philosopher asserts is basically no more than a statement about man observed throughout a very limited time span.[2] Man has evolved. There are no eternal facts, nor are there any absolute truths. Everything essential in human development occurred in primeval times, long before those four thousand years with which we are more or less familiar. Man probably hasn't changed much more in these years. But the philosopher sees 'instincts' in present-day man and assumes that they belong to the unchangeable facts of human nature. On this basis he takes them to provide a key to the understanding of the world in general.[3] But understanding of the world is not to be reached through anthropomorphism or homocentricity.

Religious, moral and aesthetic sensibilities belong only to the surface of things, though man likes to believe that they touch the heart of the world. This is because they are the things that give meaning to his life, making him deeply happy or unhappy. So he deceives himself in the astrological delusion, believing that the starry sky revolves around his own fate.[4]

The origin of metaphysics and culture lies in dreams. Primordial man thought he could come to know a second real world in dreams. This is the origin of all metaphysics. Without dreams, man would have found no occasion to divide the world. The separation into body and soul is connected to these ancient beliefs about dreams. So is the assumption of a spiritual apparition; that is the origin of all belief in ghosts and probably also in gods.[5]

Metaphysical assumptions are passionate errors of self-delusion. Nevertheless, Nietzsche is willing to concede that there might be a metaphysical world as one can hardly dispute the possibility of it. But even if the existence of a metaphysical world were demonstrated, it is certain that knowledge of it would be the most useless of all knowledge: more useless even than the knowledge of the chemical composition of water must be to the sailor in danger of shipwreck.[6]

The sections on logic and mathematics read like a non-mathematician's revenge: logic rests on assumptions that do not correspond to anything in the real world.[7] The same applies to mathematics, which would certainly not have originated if it had been known from the beginning that there exists no exactly straight line in nature, no pure circle nor any absolute beginning.[8] We remember Nietzsche's abysmal school reports for mathematics at Pforta as he tells us that the laws of numbers were invented on the basis of the initially prevailing error that there are various identical things, but actually nothing is identical. The assumption of multiplicity always presumes that there is *something* which occurs repeatedly. This is erroneous. We invent identical entities and unities that do not exist. In another world, a world that is *not* our idea, the laws of numbers are completely inapplicable. They are valid only in the human world.[9]

The section entitled 'On the History of the Moral Sensations' comes with warnings. Psychological observation must be the basis of free thought. Mankind cannot be spared the horrible sight of itself on the psychological operating table, with its knives and forceps.[10] He reinforces this warning by referring to La Rochefoucauld: 'That which the world calls virtue is usually nothing but a phantom formed by our passions to which we give an honest name so as to do what we wish with impunity.'[11] Man the super-animal ('*Das Über-Tier*') wants to be lied to. Social instincts grew out of shared pleasures and a common aversion to danger. Morality is an official lie told to keep the super-animal in order.

'A Glance at the State' observes that government by the ruling orders imperils freedom and verges on despotism; but when it comes to the masses, one must accustom oneself to this regrettable necessity as to an earthquake. Here he quotes Voltaire: 'When the populace becomes involved in thinking, all is lost.'[12]

The intentions of socialism cannot be faulted but the whole of the old culture has been built on force, slavery, deception and error. As products and heirs of the totality of this past, we cannot repudiate ourselves, and we may not wish away a single part of it. 'What is needed is not a forcible redistribution but a gradual transformation of mind: the sense of justice must grow greater in everyone, the instinct for violence weaker.'[13]

He writes on religion with adamantine self-confidence. Here he treads far surer ground than science, statecraft or mathematics. His scriptural aphorisms ring with Biblical cadences.

He takes specific verses from the Bible and delights in demolishing them. St Luke chapter 18, verse 14, for example, reads: 'For every one that exalteth himself shall be abased and he that humbleth himself shall be exalted.' Nietzsche writes, 'Luke 18, verse 14 improved: He that humbleth himself wants to be exalted.'[14]

Belief in 'the higher swindle' that is religion, and that includes belief in the ideal, is in danger of being replaced by a blind belief in science which, through its promise of certainty, is becoming elevated to the status of religion. The man who wishes to attain freedom of spirit must apply analytical and critical interpretation to religion, science and the ideal. Free spirits of this kind do not yet exist but one day they will: Nietzsche describes them coming slowly towards him, emerging like phantasmagoria out of the mist of the future. Wanderers upon the earth, they know themselves as travellers to a final destination that does not exist. But this does not blight their lives; on the contrary, their liberation lies in taking pleasure in uncertainty and in transience; they welcome the mysteries of every new dawn for the evolution of thought that it will bring.

Nietzsche called *Human, All Too Human* a monument to a crisis: not only was it the crisis of an ideological breach with Wagner but also the crisis of disgust at his past ten years of dusty scholarship. Looking back, he felt angry that he had been propelled too soon into a calling he was not suited to: philology had given him a feeling of emptiness and hunger that he had only managed to satisfy through Wagner's opiate spell. But a musical opium dream was no way to assuage reality. *Human, All Too Human* marks the start of his philosophical journey in search of the free spirit, the man whose existential hunger can be satisfied despite the absence of the ideal, or the divine, and even despite his own susceptibility to sublimity in music.

Human, All Too Human is the first book written in Nietzsche's aphoristic style of numbered sections. Driven to write in this staccato way by his appalling health, he had turned his affliction into an advantage. Through writing, he had learned that the aphorism is a provocation, a springboard, a stimulus to further and deeper questioning. The book marks the beginning of his emergence as a truly original stylist, and thinker.

He sent the completed text of the first volume (there would be one more) to his publisher Schmeitzner in the middle of January 1878. With it came a list of detailed instructions. The book *must* be published in time to honour the centenary of Voltaire's death on 30 May. It must not be advertised in any way. It must be published pseudonymously so that those factions that had already taken sides for or against Nietzsche would not be prejudiced for or against the book.

The name of the author to appear on the cover must be 'Bernhard Cron'. Nietzsche included a biography of the fictitious Cron to be printed in the publicity material.

'Herr Bernhard Cron is, so far as is known, a German from the Russian Baltic provinces, who of late years has been a continual traveller. In Italy, where among other things he devoted himself to philological and antiquarian studies, he made the acquaintance of Dr Paul Rée. Through the latter's agency he came into contact with Herr Schmeitzner. As his address for the next few years is subject to constant changes, letters should be forwarded to Herr Cron's publisher. Herr Schmeitzner has never seen him personally.'[15]

Schmeitzner refused absolutely. A book of aphorisms by Herr Bernard Cron would attract no attention at all, while a volte-face by the author of *The Birth of Tragedy* was an event. He wrote bracingly to Nietzsche, 'Whoever allows himself to speak in public is obliged also to contradict himself in public, as soon as he changes his opinions.'[16] Schmeitzner ordered a print run of a thousand copies, disregarded Nietzsche's ban on advertising and priced it at ten marks. This made it the most expensive book in his catalogue, an indication of high expectations.

Nietzsche's name appeared on the title page, voluntarily shorn of the title Professor, of which he had once been so proud. In late April Nietzsche sent out twenty-eight complimentary copies. Paul Rée's came with the inscription, 'All of my friends are in agreement that my book was written by you or originated from your influence. And so I congratulate you on your new authorship! . . . Long live Réealism!'

Jacob Burckhardt liked the book. He called it a sovereign publication that would increase the amount of independence in the world, but he and Rée were the only enthusiasts. The other recipients of complimentary copies were the close circle who had followed Nietzsche into the Wagnerian-Schopenhauerian labyrinth. They variously felt betrayed, baffled or repelled. Rohde asked, 'Can one remove one's soul and suddenly replace it by another? Can Nietzsche suddenly become Rée?' It was a question that was also puzzling the rest of the faithful few who had bravely supported *The Birth of Tragedy*. 'I want no adherents,'[17] he answered sternly when they expressed their doubts.

An anonymous correspondent sent him a bust of Voltaire from Paris with a note saying, 'The soul of Voltaire pays his respects to Friedrich Nietzsche.'[18] Maybe it came from the beautiful Louise Ott, whom he had fallen in love with during the Bayreuth Festival. They were still keeping up a wistful correspondence following her return to her banker husband in Paris. Or maybe Wagner had arranged to have it delivered from Paris. He was fond of a joke.

The book had arrived at Wahnfried on 25 April. The dedication to Voltaire aroused feelings of surprise. After a quick look through it, Wagner decided it might be kinder to the author if he didn't read it. Cosima, however, did. She observed in it 'much rage and sullenness', and something even worse than the influence of Voltaire, namely a microcosm of the whole Jewish conspiracy to take over Europe. Paul Rée was Jewish, a fact she had sniffed out within minutes of making his acquaintance in Sorrento. Cosima's explanation for *Human, All Too Human* was that 'Finally Israel intervened in the form of a Dr Rée, very sleek, very cool, dominated by [Nietzsche], though actually outwitting him – the relationship of Judea and Germany in miniature.'[19] And she made the dramatic gesture of burning Nietzsche's letters.

Wagner himself responded publicly to the book in *Bayreuther Blätter*, the newspaper-cum-propaganda sheet that he had succeeded in setting up. When Nietzsche had turned down the editorship of the paper, Wagner had appointed Hans von Wolzogen in his place. He was an anti-Semite and a second-rate intellectual who had wormed his way into Wahnfried by means of building a showy villa nearby and plying Wagner with flattery. Though Nietzsche famously despised newspaper culture and had rejected the post, he was jealous of von Wolzogen's editorship. It was a powerful position.

Wagner's article was ostensibly one in a general survey of the relation between art and the public in Germany. In fact it was a defence of himself and of Schopenhauerism, of the concept of the metaphysical and, above all, of the idea of artistic genius, of which he considered himself the prime European example. He deplored the rise of the model of scientific knowledge with its heavy emphasis on chemistry and unintelligible equations. He blamed this for the spread in sceptical intellectuality. Repudiation of metaphysics had led to questioning the very notion of all things human, including genius. Such a denial of genius's privileged access to the mystical inner essence of reality was nonsense. Scientific thinking was incapable ever of achieving comparable intuitive connection to the human spirit.[20]

Nietzsche, who had not yet discovered Wagner's horrible correspondence with his doctor, did not respond publicly. He merely noted privately that the article was vindictive, hurtful and badly argued. It made him feel as dislocated as a piece of luggage posted from an ideal world. He suffered a prolonged health crisis for the rest of the year. When he could manage it, he jotted down repudiatory material, which would appear in 'A Miscellany of Opinions and Maxims' and 'The Wanderer and His Shadow', becoming the second part of *Human, All Too Human*. The writing was a frustrating and distressing business:

'All of it – except for a few lines – was thought out on walks, and it was sketched in pencil in six small notebooks; the fair copy made me ill almost every time I set about writing it. I had to omit about twenty *longish* thought sequences, unfortunately quite essential ones, because I could not find the time to extract them from my frightful pencil scribblings . . . In the interim the connections between thought escape my memory; I have to steal the minutes and quarter-hours of "brain energy" as you call it, steal them away from a suffering brain.'[21]

Following his year of paid leave, he had returned to Basle to attempt teaching again. He felt that he could not carry on his life without feeling that he was doing something of practical use.

There was a new physician in Basle, Rudolf Massini. Consulting with Dr Eiser, he opined that *dementia paralytica* should not be discounted. He predicted probable blindness and he forbade all reading and writing for several years. Massini might as well have pronounced a death sentence.

It had been comparatively easy for Nietzsche to continue teaching while he had Johann Köselitz to read and write for him and Elisabeth to keep house, but Köselitz had moved on to pursue a career as a composer in Venice and Elisabeth was no longer prepared to fly to his side.

She had been affronted at the outright anti-Christianity of *Human, All Too Human*. The book brought shame on the family. Now her brother was talking of giving up his professorship, a step that would leave him poor and without status. It would quench the bright lustre reflected from the professorship onto his mother and herself. This would not improve her marriage prospects in Naumburg's repressive, patriarchal and, above all, conventional society.

It was time to change alliance. Borrowed radiance might be recovered from a different source, from Wagner and Cosima, whose star was at the zenith. Ever since Nietzsche had introduced Elisabeth to Cosima at Tribschen, she had been making herself useful in many little ways. Both women were intensely bourgeois and intensely religious. Both were equally repelled and wounded by *Human, All Too Human*. Cosima wrote to Elisabeth telling her frankly that she found the book intellectually insignificant and morally lamentable. The style was at once pretentious and slipshod. Cosima believed that on almost every page she could discover 'superficiality and childish sophistry'. Nietzsche's treachery was absolute. He had left them to fly into a 'well-fortified hostile camp', i.e. Jewry.

Elisabeth supported this view wholeheartedly. She had started a correspondence with a leading anti-Semite agitator whom she had met in Bayreuth, named Bernhard Förster. His nationalism and anti-Semitism appealed to her far more than her brother's Europeanism and Réealism. She had no intention of becoming a free spirit; on the contrary, she cherished every fetter that tied her to society and convention. Her brother's circle in Basle had been liberally scattered with bachelors but it had proved romantically fruitless. Time to settle back in Naumburg and concentrate on her marriage prospects.

Without Elisabeth to keep house, Nietzsche withdrew from visibility. He sold his furniture and moved to simple lodgings on the outskirts of town near the zoological gardens. Bachlettenstrasse 11 meant a long walk to the university, but he still valiantly continued to make his way there to fulfil his teaching obligations. Living alone, 'half-dead with pain and exhaustion', he kept careful notes of expenses, and drew up a Pforta-like timetable intended to keep him intellectually productive and financially within budget for the next two hundred weeks.

On 2 May 1879, he officially resigned his professorship, citing ill health. He placed his hopes in his doctors being right when they said his teaching and writing work were responsible for his abysmal health. He himself had also been blaming the siren song of Wagner. 'My very problematic thinking and writing till now have always made me ill; as long as I was really a scholar, I was healthy too; but then came music, to shatter my nerves, and metaphysical philosophy and worry about a thousand things which do not concern me at all . . .'[22] Once the two loads were lifted, he would surely regain physical health.

On 30 June, the university accepted his resignation, granting him a pension of three thousand Swiss francs for six years. He had not continuously been resident in Switzerland over a period of eight years, and so he did not qualify to become a Swiss citizen. He welcomed his statelessness. This was the position from which to comprehend a universal morality, to reshape good and evil based on a new evaluation of life, free of any merely receptive borrowing. Maybe at last he had become a truly free spirit.

Thinking to emulate his childhood hero Hölderlin, he identified an old tower in the walls of Naumburg where he would live cheaply, while working as a gardener. But it took only six weeks to realise that a gardener needed a stronger back and much, much better eyes. And so began the years of his wandering.

· THE WANDERER AND HIS SHADOW ·

In the Alps I am unassailable, especially when I am alone and have no
enemy but myself.

Letter to Malwida von Meysenbug, 3 September 1877

Nietzsche sold his possessions, apart from his books and a few pictures.
He entrusted management of his finances to his trusty friend Franz
Overbeck and he gave his notes and notebooks into Elisabeth's
safekeeping (a grave mistake and a hostage to fortune). He retained only
two trunk-loads of the books that he could not bear to be parted from.
They accompanied him as he made his rounds of the milk-and-air-cure
resorts of the Alps: Davos, Grindelwald, Interlaken, Rosenlauibad,
Champfèr and St Moritz. He ranged like Prometheus over the high
places, often walking for eight or ten hours a day, with his mind fixed
on the inscrutable purpose of the universe, discovering a wonderful
lucidity in contemplating the immense realm of the imperfectly
understood. He tramped the stony mountain paths as high as he dared,
but his ascent always had to stop short of the greatest heights, where
the bright light of the eternal snows pierced his eyes like bared swords,
as he noted down his thoughts towards the next book.

'In this book you will discover a "subterranean man" at work, one who
tunnels and mines and undermines. You will see him – presupposing
you have eyes capable of seeing this work in the depths – going forward
slowly, cautiously, gently inexorable, without betraying very much of
the distress which any protracted deprivation of light and air must
entail; you might even call him contented, working there in the dark.
Does it not seem as though some faith were leading him on, some
consolation offering him compensation? As though he perhaps desires
this prolonged obscurity, desires to be incomprehensible, concealed,

enigmatic, because he knows what he will thereby also acquire: his own morning, his own redemption, his own *daybreak*? . . . He will tell you himself of his own accord, this seeming Trophonius [son of Apollo, who was swallowed up by the earth and lived on, underground, as an oracular god], and subterranean, as soon as he has "become a man" again. Being silent is something one completely unlearns if, like him, one has been for so long a solitary mole.'

A passage from the preface to *Daybreak*, and a portrait of himself during the *Wanderjahre*, the wilderness years during which the purblind ex-philologist mole of yore wandered the mountains and shores of Europe transforming himself into the blind seer of vast, prophetic horizons.

The burrowing mole was at home below the tree line where the canopy softened the light to a green gloom. More importantly, it hid him from the clouds, which were full of electricity and persisted in a merciless persecution of him. Ever since Benjamin Franklin had apparently drawn down the electric energy from the clouds in his kite experiment of 1752, it was not altogether outrageous for the individual to imagine himself an electricity conductor, though today the notion of absorbing electricity from the atmosphere is considered a delusional symptom of mental illness, often associated with schizophrenia.

Nietzsche had always been peculiarly susceptible to electric storms. From his schooldays at Pforta onwards, his contemporaries had noticed that his most inspired and ecstatic outflows of creativity and musical improvisation were produced during thunderstorms. Dionysus' father, Zeus, had appeared as a thunderbolt, and with an increasing feeling of kinship to Dionysus, Nietzsche believed that he was probably more susceptible to the power of the electricity in the clouds than any other man on earth. He wondered about going to Paris, to display himself as a specimen at the exhibition of electricity that was taking place there, and he decided that electricity was even more deleterious to his health than Wagner's music.

'I am one of those machines which can explode,' he wrote; '. . . the electrical pattern in the cloud cover and the effects of the wind: I am convinced that 80% of my suffering results from *these* influences.'[2] The attacks now often involved three days of raging pain and vomiting, accompanied by the feeling of being half paralysed, sensations of seasickness and real difficulty speaking. And yet also, high in the thin mountain air, he found himself at times overwhelmed by sudden gushes of extreme happiness of an exquisite intensity that he had never before experienced. He felt himself so thinned, so deliciously etiolated, that he had the sensation of moving through the landscape like a zigzag doodle drawn on paper by a superior power wanting to try out a new pen. He began to rate the mountains by the capacity of their forests to hide him from the all-seeing sky.

The legendary Teutoburg forest, scene of the defeat of the Roman legions by the Germanic tribes, gave the darkest darkness and the greatest satisfaction. Threading gloomy shades, he filled twelve pocket-size notebooks in what he called his 'accursed telegram style' – the only way he was capable of recording the bursts of significant thought between headaches – though his publisher had already written to tell him that the market for telegraphic aphorisms was saturated and he really must change his prose style, should he wish to gain readers.

Despite this advice, he sent Schmeitzner 'A Miscellany of Opinions and Maxims' and 'The Wanderer and His Shadow', two collections of several hundred aphorisms each, which comprised the appendices to *Human, All Too Human*. He also sent an entire new book composed of 575 aphorisms called *Daybreak* (*Morgenröte*) subtitled *Thoughts on the Prejudices of Morality*. The thoughts it contained ranged from the morality of patting a dog to Nietzsche's more typical preoccupations: Wagner, free will, individual freedom, religion and the state.

Daybreak went further along the road of materialism. It was written during one of his periods of interest in contemporary scientific speculation, together with his delighted discovery of the seventeenth-century Jewish philosopher Spinoza. 'My solitude is now a solitude for two! I am really amazed, really delighted! I have a precursor!' He wrote a poem to Spinoza, in whom he saw mirrored his own 'denial of free will, purposes, evil, the moral world order and the non-egotistical . . . Of course the differences are enormous, but they are differences more of period, culture, field of knowledge.'[3] He read Robert Mayer's *Mechanics of Heat*, Boscovich's theory of non-material atoms, and *Force and Matter* (1855) by the materialist medical doctor Ludwig Büchner, whose bestselling book spread the gospel that 'the researches and discoveries of modern times can no longer allow us to doubt that man, with all he has and possesses, be it mental or corporeal, is a natural product like all other organic beings'. F. A. Lange's *History of Materialism* (1866) asserted that man was only a special case of universal physiology, and thought was only a special chain in the physical processes of life. When Nietzsche was looking back on this year and writing about it in *Ecce Homo*, the autobiography he wrote in 1888 when he was zigzagging between sanity and insanity, he described himself in thrall to a burning and exclusive fascination with physiology, medicine and natural science. This is what he set out to explore in *Daybreak*: the idea that man is merely a bodily organism whose spiritual, moral and religious beliefs and values can be explained by the physiological and medical. General interest at that time was growing in the idea that man might control the future by controlling his own evolutionary development through diet. It is an attitude famously summed up by the philosopher and anthropologist Feuerbach, who had died only a few years earlier: 'If you want to improve the people, give them better food instead of declamations against sin. Man is what he eats.'[4]

And yet, in direct contradiction to this, *Daybreak* also introduces speculation on the significance of the exaltation and ecstasy of madness on the history of ethics and morality. Nietzsche proposes that beneath the fearful pressure of millennia of custom, the only way to break out was 'by a dreadful attendant: almost everywhere it was madness which prepared the way for the new idea, which broke the spell of a venerated usage and superstition. Do you understand why it had to be madness which did this?' Madness was total freedom. It was the speaking trumpet of the divinity. If madness was not conferred, it must be assumed.

'All superior men who were irresistibly drawn to throw off the yoke of any kind of morality and to frame new laws had, *if they were not actually mad*, no alternative but to make themselves or pretend to be mad . . . How can one make oneself mad when one is not mad and does not dare to appear so? . . . Ah, give me madness, you heavenly powers! Madness, that I may only at last believe in myself! Give deliriums and convulsions, sudden lights and darkness, terrify me with frost and fire such as no mortal has ever felt, with deafening din and prowling figures, make me howl and whine and crawl like a beast: so that I may come to believe in myself! I am consumed by doubt, I have killed the law, the law anguishes me as a corpse does a living man: if I am not *more* than the law I am the vilest of all men.'[5]

The book ends with a clarion call to dare all:

'We aeronauts of the spirit . . . whither does this mighty longing draw us, this longing that is worth more to us than any pleasure? Why just in this direction, where all the suns of humanity have hitherto *gone down*. Will it perhaps be said of us one day that we too, *steering westward, hoped to reach an India* – but that it was our fate to be wrecked against infinity? Or, my brothers. Or? –'

Few authors are brave enough to end a book on 'Or? –'

His illness was his own Alexandrian journey to reach an India, his means of wrecking himself against infinity. Every painful seizure tested his ability not to be overcome, every recuperation was a rebirth confirming the value of suffering as the price of revelation. Recovery from the brink of death (imagined or real) inspired soaring creativity as day by day, alone, he inched towards the age at which his father had died, blind and insane, from 'softening of the brain', the age at which he had long expected the same for himself.

Looking back on the year 1879, he recorded 118 days of acute and disabling sickness. And, face to face with Thanatos, what had he achieved? A few minor writings, a failed professorship and some books that had failed to shake the world. The *Untimely Meditations* had petered out, *The Birth of Tragedy* had no meaningful impact beyond pleasing

Wagner, the father whom he had already outgrown, and *Human, All Too Human*, the book baring his Icarus aspirations that spirits should soar, whatever the cost in melting wax. The book had gained three admirers, no reviews, sold a mere hundred copies and goaded his publisher into warning him against producing more books in the only way that he was physically capable.

He determined that his spiritual isolation was to be reflected as completely as possible by his outer life. He wanted no human company, not even a scribe. Nothing must dilute the intensity of the subjective experience. Insanity must be risked, if it was the crucible of knowledge.

With the ghastly emotional occasion of Christmas looming, he returned to Naumburg, planning to take up his solitude in the tower in the town wall. But he was too ill. His mother and sister put him to bed in the old childhood home, the house on Weingarten. Round Nietzsche's bedbound free spirit flowed all the annoyingly petty rituals that ensured the continuation of the old order: church services, evergreens, cakes, ceremonial visits paid in best clothes, tepid emotion, wilful denial of rational analysis. Hardly a mind-renewing festival of wild Dionysian inebriation modified by sweet Apollonian reason, but he was in no position to denounce 'the falsified Protestant construction of history that we have been taught to believe in',[6] or, indeed, to take up any moral or ethical stance at all, for on 24 December he collapsed, and three days later he lost consciousness. His weeks of recovery were not helped by his mother nagging him to keep up his Greek. He was beginning to admit to his friends that he did not like his mother and his sister's voice grated on his nerves. He was *always* ill when he was with them. He avoided quarrels and conflict; he felt he knew how to handle them but it did not agree with him to have to do so.

On 10 February 1880, he was sufficiently recovered to flee. He jumped onto a train, summoning the useful and devoted Köselitz to meet him at Riva, on Lake Garda. Köselitz would make a fair copy of the stuttering notes that Nietzsche had jabbed into his notebooks. He would turn them into something that Schmeitzner was able to read and print.

Nietzsche took a curious form of possessive hold over the self-doubting composer, by the extraordinary step of renaming him. He gave him the name 'Peter Gast'. Köselitz immediately adopted it and retained it for the rest of his life. The genealogy of the name was riddlesome, a delicious mixture of the playful, the serious and the symbolic. 'Peter' for Christ's chief disciple, St Peter, whom Christ called 'the stone on which I build my church'.[7] Gast meaning 'guest'. The two words together combined into 'the Stone Guest', the name of the fateful character of the Commendatore in Mozart's opera *Don Giovanni*. The role of the Commendatore, or Stone Guest, is that of Nemesis. Identifying himself with the figure of Don Giovanni is one of Nietzsche's minor, but recurrent themes. He makes it clear that he is not the Don Giovanni of thousands of seductions but 'the Don Giovanni of knowledge', a reckless figure who chases up to the 'highest and remotest stars of knowledge' to explore forbidden realms, willing to sacrifice his immortal soul and forever endure the fires of Hell in order to gain occult revelation. In the opera, when finally Don Giovanni has overreached the bounds, it is the Stone Guest who forces him down to Hell to pay the price in everlasting torment. In giving Köselitz the name Peter Gast, Nietzsche was conferring on him the dual role of chief disciple and nemesis. The latter seems a singularly inappropriate role for the meek friend who ran around after Nietzsche for years, acting as unpaid secretary and amanuensis.

Peter Gast never failed rapturously to believe in Nietzsche's books and Nietzsche in his turn wholeheartedly supported Gast's musical compositions. Gast was the composer he might have been himself. He praised his genius to his friends and he hounded them for money to support Gast's comic opera *Il matrimonio segreto*, whose music was entirely free of Wagner's deadly and delicious metaphysical befogging. In March, the two of them left Riva for Venice, where Gast had made his home. Ostensibly Nietzsche was in Venice to speed on Gast's opera but in fact he was driving his friend to distraction with what Gast called 'Samaritan work'. This consisted of reading aloud to Nietzsche twice a day and taking dictation, as well as repeatedly rescuing his friend from a jumble of minor physical problems and mishaps.

Money stretched far in Venice. Nietzsche rented a very cold, vast room in the Palazzo Berlendis, reached by the most splendid marble staircase, and his window commanded an iconic view that was of enormous significance to his own generation and several to come. ·

'I have taken a room with a view to the Island of the Dead,'[8] he wrote.

There must have been something in the funerary view that compensated the rising generation for the collapse of traditional illusions. That same year that Nietzsche was there, the Symbolist Böcklin was painting *The Island of the Dead*,[9] a picture that would hang on the walls of Lenin, Strindberg, Freud and Hitler, and as a cultural badge on the walls of every Berlin intellectual from the 1880s to the 1930s, as Nabokov observed. Wagner was so struck by Böcklin's grasp of the mood of the moment that he invited him to design the sets for his new opera, *Parsifal*, in Bayreuth. Böcklin declined and so the commission went to Paul von Joukowsky instead.

Nietzsche's window commanded the Böcklin view of smooth, luminous water broken by funeral boats transporting the dead towards the enclosing walls of the cemetery island. Above the walls rose tall, dark cypress trees, pointing like fingers up to the heavens and the mystery that lies beyond the grave. The view would inspire Nietzsche to write 'The Tomb Song', one of his most beautiful poems, in which the graves on the island include the tombs of his youth, of the gentle, strange marvels of love and of the songbirds of his hopes.

Venice heated up; its mosquitos became active. Nietzsche abandoned the watery city without a backward look. Peter Gast got back to his own work, with relief.

For two years, Nietzsche wandered. In each new place, hope sprang that he had found his Arcadia. The beauty of the diverse prospects caused him to tremble and adore the earth, so profligate with its marvels, as though nothing could be more natural than to experience life as a transposed Greek hero, as both heroic and idyllic. '*Et in Arcadia ego* . . . And that is how individual men have actually *lived*, that is how they have enduringly *felt* they existed in the world and the world existed in them . . .'[10]

But in each new Arcadia he would eventually discover some intolerable imperfection: either it was too high, or too low, or too hot or too damp or too cold, or it was situated wrongly beneath the electric clouds and the all-seeing sky. There was always a good reason for the wanderer to move on.

In the summertime, he took up residence in the cool alpine regions but when the mountains became too cold and the brightness of the first snowfall threatened his eyes, he embarked on disastrous train journeys (lost luggage, lost spectacles, lost sense of direction) to the warmth of the French Riviera or Italy. And then, in July 1881, he discovered his Arcadia in Sils-Maria, one of the many pretty hamlets dotting the ravishing landscape of the Upper Engadine around St Moritz. Sils-Maria seized his soul as Venice never had. 'I would have to go to the high plateaus of Mexico overlooking the Pacific to find anything similar (for example, Oaxaca), and the vegetation there would of course be tropical,'[11] he wrote with crazy lack of reason to Peter Gast, going on in the same letter to reassure Gast that his secretarial duties might soon be coming to an end as he had heard of a new typewriter invented by a Dane. He had sent the inventor a letter of enquiry.

The Swiss tourist boom was just beginning. There were several modest hotels in Sils-Maria but even so they would have been too expensive and too sociable. Instead Nietzsche took a monastic upstairs room in the simple house belonging to Gian Durisch, the mayor of the village, who sold groceries downstairs and kept pigs and chickens in the garden. It cost him a franc a day.[12] A tall pine tree grew close to the east-facing window of his bedroom-cum-study, filtering the light that came in to a dim green. This was a kindness to his eyes.

He did not love Sils-Maria because it spared him illness. On the contrary, in July and again in September it brought him closer than ever to the brink; 'I am desperate. Pain is vanquishing my life and will . . . Five times I have called for Doctor Death.'[13] But the deeper

the descent, the higher the exaltation; 'thoughts have arisen the
like of which I have never seen before . . .' He compared himself
to a machine that might explode, and at the start of August he did
indeed experience his first combustible thought since proposing the
Dionysian/Apollonian dichotomy. Standing on the shore of Lake
Silvaplana beside a monumental pyramid-shaped boulder that later he
was to name 'Zarathustra's Rock', he conceived the thought of eternal
recurrence:

'What if some day or night a demon were to steal into your loneliest
loneliness and say to you: "This life as you now live it and have lived
it you will have to live once again and innumerable times again; and
there will be nothing new in it, but every pain and every joy and every
thought and sigh and everything unspeakably small or great in your life
must return to you, all in the same succession and sequence . . . The
eternal hourglass of existence is turned over and over again, and you
with it, speck of dust!"'[14]

A truly terrifying idea, and such an important one that he made a
note on a scrap of paper that it had come to him '6,000 feet above sea
level and much higher above human things'.

It probably related to a number of scientific books he had been
reading, on which he made notes:

'The world of forces does not suffer diminution, otherwise in
infinite time it would have grown weak and perished. The world of
forces suffers no cessation; otherwise this would have been reached
and the clock of existence would have stopped. Whatever state this
world *can* attain it must have attained it, and not once but countless
times. Take this moment: it had already been once and many times
and it will return as it is with all its forces distributed as now: and so
it stands with the moment that gave birth to it and the moment that is
its child. Man! Your whole life will be turned over like an hourglass
time and again, and time and again it will run out – one vast minute
of time between, until all the conditions which produced you, in the
world's circular course, come. Then you will find every pain and every
pleasure and every friend and enemy and every hope and every error

and every leaf of grass and every shaft of sunlight, the whole nexus of all things. This ring, in which you are a tiny grain, shines again and again. And in every ring of human existence altogether there is always an hour when – first for one, then for many, then for all – the most powerful thought surfaces, the thought of the eternal recurrence of all things: each time it is for humanity the hour of *midday*.'[15]

It can be no coincidence that he expressed the idea of the life of man as the ring of human existence. Wagner had not only composed his *Ring* but had meticulously structured it as a ring, an eternal recurrence, a circular tale whose hourglass turns and turns again and again.

Nietzsche also wrote down the name Zarathustra for the first time in his Sils-Maria notebook, but only the name. Both ideas would take some more years to ripen.

By October 1881, Sils-Maria was getting cold. 'I travelled with all the energy of a madman to Genoa', where he eventually settled in an attic. 'I have to climb a hundred and sixty-four steps inside the house, which is itself situated high up in a steep street of palaces. Being so steep, and ending in a great flight of steps, the street is very quiet, with grass growing between the stones. My health is in *terrible* disorder.'[16] He was husbanding his money. Often this meant that he lived for days on dried fruit. Sometimes his kind landlady would help him cook. He could not afford to heat his room. He would go and sit in cafés for warmth but the minute the sun came out he went to a lonely cliff by the sea to lie beneath his parasol, motionless as a lizard. It helped his head.

Generally Nietzsche was not concerned with the impression he was making on people. During these migrant years, people remembered his quietness, his passivity, his soft voice, his poor but neatly kept dress, the scrupulous good manners he showed towards all, particularly women, and the eerie absence of expression produced by the fact of his mouth being permanently invisible behind the moustache and his eyes behind blue- or green-lensed glasses, his whole face further deeply shaded by the green visor. But for all that, he was no shadow, he was never overlooked; his presence was all the more noticeable for the *noli me tangere* aura within which he moved. He made the discovery that 'The gentlest, and most reasonable of men can, if he wears a large moustache, sit as it were in its shade and feel safe there – he will usually be seen as no more than the *appurtenance* of a large moustache, that is to say a military type, easily angered and occasionally violent – and as such he will be treated.'[17]

Paul Rée came to Genoa in February 1882, bearing the typewriter. The Malling-Hansen Writing Ball was a hemispherical contraption resembling a brass hedgehog with each bristle ending in a letter. When depressed by a finger, the bristle printed that letter onto the page. The machine had attracted some notice when it was exhibited in Paris. Nietzsche's hopes were high that it might enable him to write by touch, thus sparing his eyes. It was not an immediate success. 'This machine is as delicate as a small dog and causes a lot of trouble.' It had been damaged in transit and was not working properly but even after it was repaired it was no easier for his eyes to peer at typewriter keys than at the nib of a pen inching along the page. Fortunately, for the moment, Paul Rée was at hand to help.

They went to the theatre to see Sarah Bernhardt play *La Dame aux camélias* but the divine Sarah was no greater success than the typewriter: at the end of the first act she collapsed. The audience waited an hour for her to come back and when she did, she burst a blood vessel. Nevertheless, her statuesque form and commanding manner roused in Nietzsche tender memories of Cosima.

In March, Rée moved on to Rome to rejoin Malwida von Meysenbug, who had transferred her 'Academy of Free Spirits' from Sorrento to Rome, where it was now called 'The Roman Club'. Rée burst in one evening, harassed and broke, having lost all his money on the way, gambling in Monte Carlo. Apparently a benevolent waiter had lent him the money to get this far. Malwida scuttled out to pay off the waiting cab while Rée joined the circle of assembled free spirits, and found himself immediately spellbound by the startling personality of Lou Salomé,[18] an elegant and cosmopolitan twenty-one-year-old half-

Russian girl of great magnetism, originality and intelligence. Lou was travelling with her mother, ostensibly for her health but in fact to take advantage of greater intellectual opportunities than Russia liked to offer its women. Lou's father, a Russian general ennobled for his part in the Napoleonic wars, was dead, whereupon Lou and her mother had travelled from St Petersburg to Zurich for Lou to pursue her intellectual ambitions. She attended lectures at Zurich University but she had started to spit blood, a signal to move south. A letter of introduction brought her to Malwida's Roman salon where, not for the first time or the last, Lou plunged into the role of intellectual femme fatale. Lou Salomé bewitched many eminent intellectuals during her long lifetime, including Rainer Maria Rilke and Sigmund Freud.

Nietzsche's name was pronounced as that of a god by Rée and Malwida at the Roman Club. Naturally, Lou expressed a strong wish to meet him. Nietzsche was still in Genoa, and Lou immediately started a close relationship with his friend Rée. When Malwida's literary salon closed its doors at midnight, Rée would escort Lou home. Soon they were strolling the streets around the Colosseum every night between the hours of midnight and two. Such behaviour naturally shocked Lou's mother. Even the progressive feminist Malwida protested. 'Thus I discovered', Lou wrote disingenuously, 'the extent to which idealism in such matters can interfere with the urge toward personal freedom.'[19] She was never averse to playing siren or Circe. By her own admission she had early determined that she would get her way at all times. She regarded truth-telling as 'enforced stinginess' that should never be allowed to interfere with a primary goal. 'I was mightily spoiled at home, so I felt omnipotent. Without my image in the mirror I would be homeless,' she wrote in her memoirs, which are devastatingly clear-eyed about her own personality while magnificently careless of other truths.

Rée wrote ecstatically to Nietzsche about the 'energetic, unbelievably clever being with girlish, even childish qualities . . .The Russian girl you must absolutely get to know.'[20]

Sniffing one of Malwida's marriage plans, Nietzsche replied jokily from Genoa that if this meant marriage, he'd put up with it for two years, but no longer. What Nietzsche did not know was that Lou was as averse to the idea of marriage as he was. All her life, she preferred to live with two men at a time. She did, in fact, marry five years later but only because her suitor stabbed himself in the chest and threatened to finish the job if she refused. They remained married for forty-five years, devoted to each other throughout, though the marriage was never consummated and she was perfectly happy for the housekeeper to be her husband's long-term mistress while Lou imported her own devoted admirers into the marriage, the first of whom was Rée.

In Genoa, Nietzsche saw the opera *Carmen* for the first time. As soon as he could, he saw it again. Before he died he would see it twenty times. *Carmen* replaced his obsession with *Tristan und Isolde*. With music by Bizet and a libretto based on a novella by Prosper Mérimée, the opera had no pretensions towards the sublime or even the extraordinary. Unlike Wagner, it offered no adventures of the soul and might even be called a materialist opera. *Carmen* requires no super-sized orchestra. Its tunes are tremendously hummable. It lasts a short time. It ignores the metaphysical. It is not about gods and legends, not even about kings and queens. It tells a tabloid tale of lust among the lower class. Don José is an undistinguished little corporal whose well-regimented, narrow life collides with the Dionysian in the shape of Carmen, a passionate and sexually voracious girl who works in a cigarette factory. Carmen is a femme fatale who (like Lou Salomé) takes and discards men on her own terms. The uncomprehending and uncontrollable uproar of lust, jealousy and possessiveness that Carmen rouses in Don José inevitably leads to him murdering her in a Dionysian frenzy.

Having expressed her wish to travel to Genoa to meet Nietzsche, Lou became angry on hearing that he would not wait there for her to come. He had decided to leave Genoa for Messina. In terms of Nietzsche's health, the decision made little sense. If Genoa was getting too hot for him in the month of March, Sicily was hotter still. But his recent summers in the mountains had now made him decide that summering at higher altitudes brought him closer to the electricity in the clouds, aggravating his condition. Instead, he would try a summer at the furthest distance achievable from heaven: sea level. Besides, *Carmen* had roused a hunger for the south.

'The vulgar element in everything that pleases in Southern Europe . . . does not escape me; but it does not offend me, just as little as does the vulgarity that one encounters on a walk through Pompeii [he was probably referring to the erotic art] and basically even when reading any ancient book. Why is this? Is it because there is no shame and everything vulgar acts as confidently and self-assuredly as anything noble, lovely, and passionate in the same kind of music or novel? "The animal" has its own right, just like the human being; let it run about freely – and you too, my dear fellow man, are still an animal, despite everything!'[21]

The other pull to Messina was Wagner, who was spending the winter there with Cosima. There had been no contact between Nietzsche and Wagner for three years, but Nietzsche had frequently dreamt of him and Cosima. His dreams were friendly, positive and ungrudging. He would like to see them again.

He wrote eight light-hearted little poems called *The Idylls of Messina*, mostly about boats and goats and maidens, and he boarded a boat for Messina with a high heart. He was horribly seasick. By the time he arrived in Sicily, he was physically wrecked and Wagner and Cosima had already left. Wagner had suffered chest spasms in Palermo and run home. The scorching sirocco was blowing from the Carthaginian coast, a wind well known for depressing the spirits and gritting every surface and crevice with tiny, unbearable particles of sand. The only redeeming feature of Nietzsche's uncomfortable trip to Sicily was the sight of the volcano of Stromboli, whose legends of flying ghosts would later enter his tale of Zarathustra.

Cards and letters from Rée continued to arrive hymning the intelligence of Lou Salomé. Nietzsche received a letter from Malwida that was almost a summons: 'A very remarkable girl (I believe Rée has written to you about her) . . . seems to me to have arrived at much the same results you have so far in philosophical thinking, i.e. at practical idealism with a discarding of every metaphysical assumption and concern for the explanation of metaphysical problems. Rée and I agree in the wish to see you together with this extraordinary being . . .'[22]

Another dreadful boat ride brought him back from Sicily. When he had recovered, he boarded a train for Rome.

· PHILOSOPHY AND EROS ·

Women, or the most exquisite of them, know this: a little fatter, a
little thinner – oh, how much destiny lies in so little!
            Thus Spoke Zarathustra, Part III, 'Of the Spirit of Gravity', Part 2

Before she had even met Nietzsche, Lou had determined to live with
him and Rée in a *ménage à trois.* She envisioned it an *Heilige Dreieinigkeit,*
a Holy Trinity of philosophising free spirits 'filled almost to bursting
with spirituality and keenness of mind'.

Her fantasy took shape during the time leading up to Nietzsche's
arrival in Rome, as she prowled miasmic midnights round the
Colosseum with Rée pontificating on philosophy and tantalising her
with endless talk of his brilliant friend.

'I will confess honestly', she wrote, 'that a simple dream first
convinced me of the feasibility of my plan, which flew directly in the
face of all social conventions. In it I saw a pleasant study filled with
books and flowers, flanked by two bedrooms, and us walking back
and forth between them, colleagues, working together in a joyful and
earnest bond.'[1] The disposition of the two bedrooms between the
three of them was not made clear.

Lou did not hide her unconventional plan from Malwida, who called
it a brazen fantasy and began to worry. Lou's ineffectual and permanently
outmanoeuvred mother talked of summoning her brothers against the
disreputable scheme. Everyone was against it. Even Rée, Lou said, was
'somewhat perplexed', though he was wholeheartedly in love. Within
the first three weeks of knowing her he had asked her to marry him,
including in the proposal the unusual condition that there would be no
sex, because it disgusted him. Lou was also disgusted by sex following
a traumatic episode in her late teens in St Petersburg when her trusted

intellectual mentor, a married elderly Dutch priest with daughters of her own age, had suddenly forced himself upon her. Rée's proposal of a *mariage blanc* would have been to her taste had she been fond of her reputation. It would certainly have conferred respectability. But Lou never gave a fig for her reputation. Throughout her long life, she loved nothing better than to *épater les bourgeois.*

On 20 April 1882, Nietzsche left Messina on a freighter, arriving in Rome on the 23rd or 24th. After a few days of being cosseted by Malwida in the luxurious Villa Mattei, he was deemed sufficiently recovered from the sea journey for the meeting with Lou. They had all decided that this should take place in the Basilica of St Peter's, a curious choice for an atheist circle of free spirits.

It was his first time in Rome. No Baedeker could prepare him for the journey from Malwida's villa near the Colosseum, to St Peter's where he would at last meet the mysterious girl. Like Theseus following Ariadne's clue through the Minotaur's labyrinth, he followed the thread of shade cast by Bernini's colossal Tuscan colonnade. Once inside the incense-dimmed gloom of the basilica, it was difficult for his eyes to discover her. Lou would later burgeon into a lush and abundant beauty, bursting, not unlike Judith Gautier, into silks and frills and furs, but at this stage her invariable uniform as philosopher's apprentice was of a nun-like purity: a high-necked, dark-coloured long-sleeved dress to the floor, underpinned by a tight corset silhouetting an hourglass figure. She wore her dark-blond hair rigorously drawn back from a face of classic Russian beauty, wide, with high cheekbones. Her eyes were blue; her gaze was often described as intelligent, intense and passionate. She was conscious of her beauty and she enjoyed its power.

She says that what first struck her about Nietzsche was the force of his eyes. They fascinated her. They seemed to look more inwards than outwards. Though half blind, they did not possess any spying or flinching quality. They did not have that peering, intruding quality of the near-sighted. 'Above all, his eyes appeared like guardians and protectors of his treasures – silent secrets – not to be glimpsed by the uninvited.'[2]

This must have been a later conclusion. In St Peter's he would have been wearing his tinted spectacles, without which he could see nothing. Lou surely could not have seen anything of his eyes through the thick lenses and the ecclesiastical gloom.

'Inwards, as it were, into the distance' is how Lou describes his gaze. It might just as well be a self-portrait, a depiction of her own glance. Others often described her eyes as possessing the oddly detached quality of gazing at far horizons. It made them long to snap their fingers, capture her whole glance, touch her remote inner core, force her to see the physical world in front of her. The contradiction between her headlong, passionate recklessness and these strangely remote eyes gave her an exceptional talent for extracting confession. She listened like a mirror, reflecting back the talker's thoughts. She said little but her passivity encouraged further revelations. She would be the person whom Sigmund Freud allowed to psychoanalyse his daughter Anna.

Nietzsche greeted her with words he had obviously rehearsed:

'From what stars have we fallen together here?'[3]

'From Zurich,' came her pedestrian reply.

Nietzsche at first found her Russian-accented voice harsh. She, too, was initially disappointed. She had expected to meet a whirlwind of a man, a person as flamboyant and as revolutionary as his thought, or at least a man of commanding presence. Here was a man so ordinary, so unnoticeable, so easily overlooked that it was laughable. Smallish in stature, tranquil in demeanour, with carefully combed, plain brown hair, and neatly arranged clothes; it seemed that he intended to be as unremarkable as possible. His speech was quiet, almost noiseless. His laughter was quiet, too. He gave the overall impression of careful thoughtfulness. He stooped his shoulders slightly as he spoke, almost as if to push out the words. He gave her the uncomfortable feeling that part of him was standing aside.

Could this really be the iconoclast who, Rée had told her, boasted that he had wasted a day if he had not lopped off at least one of his beliefs? This taciturn solitude was a challenge. She wanted to discover what lay behind the careful distance he put between his real self and the world. She felt somehow deceived by his 'studied, elegant posture'.

His studied and elegant posture was obviously as well rehearsed as his greeting, which immediately elevated the two of them to a higher realm of destiny and fate, placing their meeting on the wheel of eternal recurrence by referencing a passage from his second *Untimely Meditation*: '. . . when the constellation of the heavenly bodies is repeated the same things, down to the smallest event, must also be repeated on earth: whenever the stars stand in a certain relation to one another a Stoic again joins with an Epicurean to murder Caesar and when they stand in another relation Columbus will again discover America'.[4]

While Lou and Nietzsche conversed in St Peter's, Rée had arranged himself in the concealing gloom of a nearby confessional box, ostensibly with the pious intention of working on his notes but obviously to eavesdrop. Lou implies that she and Nietzsche plunged straight into discussing their future triune existence, and where it should take place, though later she backtracks, contradicting the story of her dream of the *Heilige Dreieinigkeit* by saying that Nietzsche intruded himself on a plan that she had already made with Rée that just the two of them should live together in intellectual partnership. Whatever actually took place during this first week of their acquaintanceship in Rome, there is no doubt that the three were making plans to live together. Nietzsche entered into the scheme with enthusiasm. He wished to become a student again. He wanted to attend lectures at the Sorbonne in his pursuit of scientific validation of his ideas on eternal recurrence. Lou and Rée were happy to go to Paris, where they might further their acquaintance with Ivan Turgenev.

The meeting in St Peter's so overpowered Nietzsche that he had to retire to his bed at Malwida's villa, where Rée and Lou visited him. He enjoyed reading and reciting to them from the book he was writing, *The Gay Science*, an effervescent outpouring of his irrepressibly jubilant mood as he stood on the brink of impending adventure. In the introduction he says that the book is nothing but an amusement after long privation and powerlessness, an outpouring of reawakened faith in tomorrow expressing his sudden sense of anticipation, of reopened seas. He had begun writing it in Genoa during the time when he was seduced by the uncomplicated physicality of *Carmen*, by the portrayal of the eternal feminine in Carmen herself and by the tantalising idea that in Rome there was a beautiful intellectual girl named Lou Salomé who was telling everybody that she was determined to meet him. And now they had met, and there was the prospect of Paris.

For all her professed devotion, Lou had not read any of Nietzsche's books but no matter: her intensity, her intelligence and her seriousness made a deep impression on him.

Nietzsche has a reputation for misogyny that is often well deserved. He wrote foul things about women during the many periods of his life when he felt overwhelmed by chain-sickness induced by his mother and Elisabeth. But during this period his sympathy for women and his insight into their psychology is remarkable for its time.

The aphorisms on women in *The Gay Science* are notably positive and sympathetic. More importantly, he expresses the revolutionary idea that there was something quite amazing and monstrous in the paradoxical upbringing of upper-class women. They were brought up as ignorant as possible about matters erotic, and told that such things were evil and a matter of the deepest shame. Then they were hurled as if by a gruesome lightning bolt into marriage – and subjected, precisely by the man they loved and esteemed most, to the terror and duty of sex. How could they cope with the unexpected and shocking proximity of god and beast? 'There', he concluded perspicaciously, 'one has tied a psychic knot that may have no equal.'[5]

It might be a description of the relationship between Lou and her revered older teacher, and the lasting traumatic effect upon her of his sudden god-turned-beast carnal attack.

In the week following the meeting in St Peter's, Lou became ever more fascinated by Nietzsche. She saw him as one who wore his mask awkwardly. It was obvious to her that he was playing a part so as to fit into the world. He was like some god who had come out of the wilderness and down from the high places, and put on a suit in order to pass among men. The visage of the god must be masked, lest men die faced with his dazzling glance. It allowed her to reflect that she herself had never worn a mask, never felt the need of one in order to be understood. She interpreted his mask as placatory, as springing from his goodness and pity towards other people. She quoted his aphorism, 'People who think deeply feel themselves to be comedians in their relationship with others because they first have to simulate a surface in order to be understood.'[6]

He suggested she consider living by the principles that he had decided to live by, *Mihi ipsi scripsi* ('I have written for myself') and Pindar's 'Become what you are, having learned what that is'. She took both for lifelong principles.

Lou developed her own interpretation of Nietzsche's psychology, and she wrote about it at length, in a great many articles and in a book.[7] She placed enormous importance on his illness as a creative source. He needed no flamboyance, no outward proof of genius, so long as he had his illness. It enabled him to live numberless lifetimes within the one. She noticed how his life fell into a general pattern. A regular recurrent decline into sickness always demarcated one period of his life from another. Every illness was a death, a dip down into Hades. Every recuperation was a joyful rebirth, a regeneration. This mode of existence refreshed him. *Neuschmecken* ('new-tasting') was his word for it. During each fleeting recuperation the world gleamed anew. And so each recuperation became not only his own rebirth, but also the birth of a whole new world, a new set of problems that demanded new answers. It was like the annual fertility cycle of the god being ploughed into the ground. Only through this excruciating process could new insights open up to him. Within this larger cycle of enormous upheavals, there was also the smaller daily cycle. His mental pattern was that of the waves breaking restlessly on the shore, ever advancing, ever retreating, caught in the ghastly impetus of perpetual motion from which there could be no rest. 'Falling ill through thoughts and recuperating through thoughts'; Lou had no doubt that 'he is the cause of his own self-induced illness'.[8]

From the start, Nietzsche took the triune cohabitation seriously. Impishly, he renamed it the *un*holy trinity, though at the same time he took social convention seriously enough to feel the need to defend Lou's reputation by extending a proposal of marriage; 'I would consider myself obligated to protect you from people's gossip, to offer to marry you . . .' He asked Rée to deliver the proposal.

It was a curious commission for Rée to fulfil as he himself had already proposed to Lou and was falling ever more deeply in love. On receipt of Nietzsche's proposal, Lou worried that rivalry for her hand would imperil the whole intellectual experiment. There was no doubt that the enterprise would, and must, be powered by the force of erotic energy but this was never to be translated into the physical. She instructed Rée to decline on her behalf, asking him to explain to Nietzsche that basically she was disinclined to marriage on principle. Anyway, she added on a practical note, if she married she would lose her pension as the daughter of a Russian nobleman, and this was her only source of income.

Rome was becoming humid and insalubrious. Nietzsche had been long enough in bed. If he was to recover, he needed cool, refreshing air. He decided to leave for the north Italian Alps with Rée. Frantic to join them, Lou pleaded with Rée to arrange things.

'Most Commanding Miss Lou,' Rée replied, 'Tomorrow morning at about eleven, Nietzsche will call on your mother, and I shall accompany him to pay my respects . . . Nietzsche cannot answer for how he will feel tomorrow, but would like to introduce himself to your mother before we meet again at the lakes.'

Lou's mother warned Nietzsche against her daughter in no uncertain terms. Lou was uncontrollable and dangerous; she was a wild fantasist. But the plan went forward. Lou and her mother left Rome on 3 May, Rée and Nietzsche a day later. On 5 May, they were all reunited in Orta where, the following day, Nietzsche and Lou slipped away from the other two to ascend the Monte Sacro, a peak as shrouded in myth and symbol as Mont Pilatus.

He was to describe his ascension of the mountain with Lou as the most exquisite experience of his life.

Orta's Monte Sacro rises quietly to middle height above Lake Orta, a modest sheet of water in the area that contains the larger, more spectacular, and far more famous lakes Maggiore and Lugano. But its beauty is undisputed and its grim historico-religious significance unrivalled. It was the site of the first recorded witch-burning in Italy in the Middle Ages. Local legend has the witch's ghost, like Pilate's, haunting the site of its dreadful death. In the wake of the Council of Trent (1545–63), when the Roman Catholic Church was combating both the Protestant Reformation and the seemingly unstoppable rise of Islam, Orta's Monte Sacro was consecrated one of the sacred sites within Europe. These new-made sacred places were dedicated alternative sites of veneration following the backlash from the crusades that had closed off the Holy Land to pious pilgrims.

In 1580 the Monte Sacro was declared 'a new Jerusalem', whose ascent gained the soul the same credit as a pilgrimage to the original. Its transformation was carried out with all the brio with which the Vatican was simultaneously raising Michelangelo's dome over St Peter's. The little mountain was transformed into a Baroque landscapist's idea of the journey to heaven. A fluidly winding path, a *via sacra* or *via dolorosa*, corkscrewed up the mountainside; it was cunningly planted with sacred groves, whose green billows alternately hid or revealed sublime views of the lake below or the snow-crowned Alp above. To progress up Monte Sacro was like an outdoor version of the Stations of the Cross, or a journey through the rosary. At every next bend of its spiralling itinerary, the leafy green clouds opened up to reveal a new object of contemplation. Twenty-one tiny, exquisite Mannerist stone chapels punctuated the pilgrimage path, each little chapel ornamented with spiritual signs and symbols: pretty fish and scallop shells, suns and moons, lilies and roses and stars. The chapels' interiors were fully frescoed and inhabited by groups of lifelike terracotta statues narrating the sacred stories of the life of St Francis.

In the three hundred years between its creation and Lou and Nietzsche's ascent, the Monte Sacro had become a place of forlorn, decaying beauty. Jungle verdure had knitted up the undergrowth, half-obliterating intended vistas. Ancient trees sinking back into the soil seemed to have kept pace with the decay of the Christian faith, which Lou and Nietzsche did not mourn, and the decay in spirituality, which they did.

While they climbed, their conversation concerned their youthful wrestling with God. She became convinced that he, like herself, was of a fundamentally religious nature. She too had lost her intense Christian faith at an early age. Both found themselves talking of a profoundly religious need which was unsatisfied. It drew them together against Rée, whom they agreed in finding almost offensive in his insistent de-souled materialism. Nietzsche subjected her to a sort of philosophical initiation test, a rigorous questioning of her knowledge and her beliefs, and he found the quality of her replies so sympathetic and so intelligent that, he tells us, he imparted something to her of his philosophy that he had not yet told anybody else. He does not tell us what this was. Maybe he expounded his theory of the eternal recurrence, which was much on his mind at the time. Maybe he mentioned the prophet Zarathustra, whom he was then glimpsing as his future mouthpiece. Maybe he talked through his other secret, the death of God, which he described in the book he was preparing for publication, *The Gay Science*.

Later he wrote to Lou, 'Back in Orta, I conceived a plan of leading you step by step to the final consequence of my philosophy – *you* as the first person I took to be fit for this.'[9]

The ascent of Monte Sacro had left him convinced that he had found in Lou the disciple he had long sought. She would be an indomitable priestess and perpetuator of his thought.

It left Lou foretelling that the world would live to see Nietzsche as the prophet of a new religion, one that recruited heroes as disciples.

Both of them described how similarly they thought and felt about things, and how words tumbled between them. They took words, like food, from each other's mouths. Individual command melted as they finished each other's thoughts and completed each other's sentences.

When they came down from Monte Sacro, he said to her, quietly, 'I thank you for the most exquisite dream of my life.'

The sight of the two of them descending, as radiant and transformed as if they had been making love up there, made Lou's mother furious. Rée was overwhelmed by jealousy. He pestered her with questions. Lou crushed his petty prying by responding impenetrably, 'His very laughter is a deed.'

Over the years that followed, and through all the events that came between them, neither of them ever denied the profound importance of their intellectual and spiritual communion on Monte Sacro, though neither explained it either.

Later in her long life, Lou often found herself asked whether she and Nietzsche had kissed on Monte Sacro. Then she would hood her faraway eyes and answer, 'Did we kiss on Monte Sacro? I can no longer remember.' Nobody dared ask Nietzsche the same question.

From Orta he went straight on to Basle to visit his dear friends Franz and Ida Overbeck, who reported he looked suntanned, vigorous and happy. He stayed with them for five days. Not once did he have a nervous attack, despite two long sessions at the dentist. His only suffering, Ida noted, was the thought that he was so little known and read. After every publication he hoped to receive enthusiastic approbation, to be greeted by the public as a new star in the heavens, and to find followers and disciples. It had not happened yet, but now he was convinced that it would. He told the Overbecks of his hopes that in Lou he had found his alter ego: the other half of a brother-and-sister brain. Now he would go more into the world, he told them. He would be less solitary, more open to contact with things and with human beings.

While he was staying with the Overbecks, between talking of bright futures, he would jump up and play something on the piano. In the evenings he astonished them by staying up uncharacteristically late. Franz and Ida Overbeck delighted in his very evident joy. They were his steadiest friends. He had entrusted his financial affairs to Franz, and Ida had taken it upon herself to smooth the waters around him as best she could, a service Nietzsche appreciated when it crossed his mind.

The same day he arrived with the Overbecks, 8 May, he dashed off a note to Rée: 'The future is completely sealed, but not *dark*. I must absolutely speak once again with Frl. L. [Fräulein Lou] in the Löwengarten, perhaps? In boundless gratitude your friend N.'

The Löwengarten in Lucerne contains a very beautiful sculpted relief of a dying lion carved into the rock face. It commemorates the heroism and fidelity of the Swiss guards who fell during the storming of the Tuileries Palace in the French Revolution. The monument's inscription, '*fidei ac virtuti*' ('for loyalty and bravery'), might contain some sort of subtext to the meeting with Lou.

When he arrived at Lucerne station on 13 May, Lou and Rée were there to meet him on the platform. They escaped Rée to reach the Löwengarten together, where Lou says that Nietzsche again proposed and she again refused. All we know from Nietzsche's side is a drawing that he made when he was in the asylum during the years of his insanity. It shows the very clearly identifiable lion monument and two figures beneath it, embracing.

When they rejoined Rée, all three went off to a photographer's shop, where they posed for the famous photograph that has, rightly or wrongly, become permanently associated with the saying that Nietzsche puts into the mouth of an old woman in *Thus Spoke Zarathustra*: 'You go to women? Do not forget the whip!' Maybe the light-hearted photograph was Lou's idea, maybe Nietzsche's. It certainly was not Rée's; he hated being photographed and he looks very awkward standing in his neat suit alongside Nietzsche. The two men are posed like a pair of carthorses between the shafts of a wooden farm cart. Lou crouches on the cart looking both playful and determined as she brandishes a whip over them. She had decorated the whip with blooms of lilac. Nietzsche looks rather pleased with himself, both owlish and impish, as if enjoying the joke.

From the photographer's studio it was but a short walk to Tribschen. Once more the two of them shed Rée, and Nietzsche conducted her round his Island of the Blessed, initiating her into its mysteries. She says he spoke of Wagner with deep emotion.

In some sort of attempt at directing the life of this marvellous girl whose fate, he had no doubt, was to be intimately connected with his own, he arranged for her and her mother to move on to Basle to stay with the Overbecks. Maybe the idea was that Franz and Ida would convince their guests of Nietzsche's exemplary character, fidelity and virtue, but Lou was not terribly interested in this domestic plan. Spending time with the homely theologian and his wife appealed far less to her than making the acquaintance of Basle's most famous scholar, Jacob Burckhardt. Her behaviour during the brief visit left Ida Overbeck concluding that, while Nietzsche had given himself over to the hope of having found his alter ego in Lou, she was not willing 'to be dissolved in Nietzsche'.

He sent Lou his book *Human, All Too Human,* and he sent a poem that Lou had written, called 'To Sorrow' (*'An den Schmerz'*), to Peter Gast in Venice, with the request that Gast set it to music.

'This poem', ran Nietzsche's accompanying letter to Gast, 'has such power over me that I have never been able to read it without tears coming to my eyes; it sounds like a voice for which I have been waiting and waiting since childhood. This poem is by my friend Lou, of whom you will not yet have heard. Lou is the daughter of a Russian general, and she is twenty [*sic*] years old; she is as shrewd as an eagle and as brave as a lion, and yet still a very girlish child, who perhaps will not live long . . . She is most amazingly well prepared for *my* way of thinking and my ideas. Dear friend, you will surely do us both the honour of keeping far from our relationship the idea of a love affair. We are *friends*, and I shall keep this girl, and this confidence in me sacrosanct.'[10]

13

· THE PHILOSOPHER'S APPRENTICE ·

Paris is still in the foreground but I somewhat dread the noise and
would like to know whether the sky is *serene* enough.

Letter to Franz Overbeck, October 1882

While Lou and her mother went to the Overbecks in Basle, Nietzsche
went straight from Lucerne to Naumburg to prepare *The Gay Science*
for his publisher. He hired the services of a bankrupt tradesman, who
took dictation while Elisabeth read from the manuscript in which he
announces for the first time the death of God. He tells it like this:

'Haven't you heard of that madman who in the bright morning
lit a lantern and ran around the marketplace crying incessantly, "I'm
looking for God! I'm looking for God!" Since many of those who did
not believe in God were standing around together just then, he caused
great laughter. Has he been lost, then? asked one. Did he lose his way
like a child? asked another. Or is he hiding? Is he afraid of us? Has he
gone to sea? Emigrated? . . . The madman jumped into their midst
and pierced them with his eyes. "Where is God?" he cried; "I'll tell
you! *We have killed him* — you and I! We are all his murderers. But
how did we do this? How were we able to drink up the sea? Who
gave us the sponge to wipe away the entire horizon? What were we
doing when we unchained this earth from its sun? Where is it moving
to now? Where are we moving to? Away from all suns? Are we not
continually falling . . . Is there still an up and a down? Aren't we
straying as though through an infinite nothing? Isn't empty space
breathing at us? Hasn't it got colder? . . . Do we still hear nothing
of the noise of the gravediggers who are burying God? Do we smell
nothing of the divine decomposition? — Gods, too, decompose! God
is dead! God remains dead! And we have killed him. How can we

console ourselves, the murderers of all murderers! The holiest and mightiest thing the world has ever possessed has bled to death under our knives: who will wipe this blood from us? . . . Is the magnitude of this deed not too great for us? Do we not ourselves have to become gods merely to appear worthy of it? There never was a greater deed — and whoever is born after us will on account of this belong to a higher history than up to now!"'

The crowd look at him disconcertedly and the madman observes, 'This deed is still more remote to them [the post-deists] than the remotest stars — *and yet they have done it themselves!*' He throws the lantern that gives the new light down onto the ground. Leaving the crowd in the market place, he forces his way into the churches that lie in his path. In each church he strikes up a requiem for the soul of God, using a form of words that is a blasphemous parody of the requiem for the dead. The people, though they no longer believe in God, are offended by his behaviour and they evict him forcibly from their churches.

'What then are these churches now,' he asks them, 'if not the tombs and sepulchres of God?'[1]

Later in the same book, Nietzsche rehearses another idea that he will enlarge on in his later philosophy: that following the death of a god, his statue will still be shown for centuries in a cave where it will continue to cast a tremendous and gruesome shadow on the wall. God is dead, yes. But, given the ways of men, Nietzsche prophesies, there will remain for thousands of years the shadow of the morality he imparted. It is the stern job of the Argonaut of the spirit to vanquish the shadow, as well as the god himself.[2]

Both stories placed a heavy burden on the shoulders of nineteenth-century rationalists (such as Rée) who, having killed God, did not seem to realise the consequence that you cannot keep the ethical content of Christianity without its theology. The rational materialist must also address the consequent switch in moral power. In this lurked the possibility of vast and catastrophic consequences for mankind. '*Incipit tragoedia,*' Nietzsche prophesied at the end of this passage, tragedy looms.

The looming event of the summer of 1882 was the Bayreuth Festival. It was to premiere *Parsifal*, the opera for which Judith Gautier had usurped Cosima's role as muse. As a founder member of Bayreuth's *Patronatsverein* (Patrons' Society), Nietzsche had a right to buy tickets. Lou very much wished to go. Bayreuth had become the contemporary Parnassus, the fashionable place for Europe's great and famous to assemble over the months of July and August.

Parsifal is a retelling of the Christian legend of the Holy Grail, the cup from which Christ drank at the Last Supper. King Amfortas is chosen to unveil the Grail despite his unworthiness for the sacred task. He has been grievously wounded by a spear in his side while sexually distracted by the witch Kundry. (In the first draft, Amfortas is wounded in the genitals but this was later amended to a more Christ-like positioning.) The wound bleeds unstoppably. Who amongst the Grail knights is worthy to staunch the sacred blood? Parsifal! a holy fool made wise through Christian pity (a plot line that Nietzsche, who despised both foolishness and pity, could not approve). Nietzsche was already familiar with the libretto and he knew he did not want to go to Bayreuth to hear the opera.

We must now go back five years, to Nietzsche staying with Malwida at the Villa Rubinacci in Sorrento and Wagner staying nearby. It was during this period that Nietzsche's health had given Wagner such concern that he had later written to Nietzsche's doctor to discover whether excessive masturbation might be the cause. Elisabeth had concocted the legend that the final breach between the two men occurred on their last walk together in Sorrento, but while there had been a cooling over intellectual differences, there had been no actual breach, and with the turn of the year, as 1877 gave way to 1878, Nietzsche sent Wagner his newly completed book *Human, All Too Human* and Wagner sent Nietzsche the newly completed libretto of *Parsifal*. The two works almost crossed in the post. Nietzsche likened this to rapiers clashing in the air.

He disliked the libretto on many grounds. 'More Liszt than Wagner, spirit of the Counter-Reformation . . . too Christian, time-bound

. . . No flesh and much too much blood. The language sounds like a translation from a foreign tongue.'³

Wagner's dislike of *Human, All Too Human* was equally strong. While Wagner was becoming more pious, Nietzsche had been freeing himself of 'those hidden priests the philosophers', notably Schopenhauer. Wagner remained a dedicated Schopenhauerian until he died. There could be no road to intellectual reconciliation.

During the weeks preceding the 1882 festival, in which *Parsifal* was to be premiered, Nietzsche studied the musical score. He found it bewitching. The sorcerer of Bayreuth had not lost his magic. Nietzsche longed to hear the music played but his pride would not let him attend Bayreuth without a personal invitation from Wagner. He would consent to come only if he was invited to ride in Wagner's carriage to the opera house, as they had ridden together at the ceremony of the laying of the foundation stone. He hoped and he waited but the longed-for invitation never came.

In preparation for the festival, Lou at last managed to shed her mother, who returned to St Petersburg with, one imagines, some relief. Before she left, she formally handed over the chaperonage of her wayward daughter to Rée's mother. Frau Rée proceeded with Lou to the family's luxurious country estate at Stibbe. Rée followed. Wishing to have Lou to himself, he firmly told Nietzsche that there was no room for him to join the two of them on the enormous property.

By now, Rée and Lou were talking baby-talk: she was his 'little snail' (*Schneckli*) and he was her 'little house' (*Hüsung*). Together they kept a 'nest book' (a joint diary) recording their stay in the Stibbe 'nest'. Rée's mother was talking of Lou as her adoptive daughter. One gets the impression of gritted teeth.

Nietzsche was not going to give his pair of Bayreuth tickets away to Lou and Rée to attend the festival together without him. Instead, he would give the tickets to Lou and his sister Elisabeth. The shared experience would surely knit the two women together in a spiritual sisterhood that might be deepened and consolidated. With this aim, he invited the two of them to join him after the festival for a little holiday in the picturesque village of Tautenburg, near Dornburg. Rée was not included in the invitation.

While he waited for the realisation of this delightful plan, Lou wrote him seductive letters from the Stibbe estate. Flatteringly, she described him and Rée as 'two prophets of the past and of the future . . . Rée discovers the verdict of the gods while you destroy the twilight of the gods.' Suggestively she wrote that the books he sent her entertained her better in bed than anything else. His letters to her gradually lost their rigidity. He admitted that when he was alone he often spoke her name out loud, just for the pleasure of hearing the sound of it.

She wrote, consenting to join him and Elisabeth for the holiday in Tautenburg and he poured out his joy.

'Tautenburg, July 2, 1882

Now the sky above me is bright! Yesterday at noon I felt as if it was my birthday. *You* sent your acceptance, the most lovely present that anyone could give me now; my sister sent cherries; Teubner sent the first three page proofs of *Die fröhliche Wissenschaft* [*The Gay Science*], and on top of it all, I had just finished the very last part of the manuscript and therewith the work of six years (1876–82), my entire *Freigeisterei* [freethinking] . . . Oh, dear friend, whenever I think of it, I am thrilled and touched and do not know how I could have *succeeded* in doing it – I am filled with self-compassion and the sense of victory. For it is a victory, a complete one – for even my physical health has reappeared . . . everyone tells me that I am looking younger than ever. Heaven preserve me from doing foolish things – but from now on! – whenever you advise me, I shall be *well* advised and do not need to be afraid . . .

Entirely *yours*, F.N.'

The news of his good health was more wish than fact. The report of youthful good looks was a vain boast from the thirty-seven-year-old to the twenty-one-year-old, in his triumph at having outmanoeuvred Rée in the struggle for dominance of the philosophico-erotic triangle.

Elisabeth and Lou rendezvoused in Leipzig. Each was eager to make a good impression on the other. By the time they reached Bayreuth they were addressing each other by the familiar *Du*. Elisabeth had arranged rooms in the same lodging house for the two of them. There was no escape from intimacy.

There were receptions at Wahnfried for two or three hundred people every night and parties in between. Elisabeth liked to think of herself as an intimate of Cosima's but she was made painfully aware that her domestic usefulness did not entitle her to Cosima's attention in this elevated social context. In fact, nobody here was much interested in Nietzsche's ageing sister.

'I have not yet met many people I know,' she wrote grimly to her mother, 'but it was very amusing at dinner, though really expensive. As a joke, we are all going to eat at the vegetarian table tomorrow.'[4]

By contrast, interest in Lou was voracious. Young, beautiful, aristocratic, vivacious, rich, cosmopolitan, self-confident and uninhibited, she was known to be one of Malwida's scholarly 'free spirits'. Lou was quick to reveal that this free spirit was not only paying lip-service to the dangerous doctrine, but proposing actually to live it. Bayreuth gasped as she spoke openly of spending the coming winter unchaperoned, studying and philosophising with Rée and Nietzsche. She showed people the photograph of her brandishing the whip over the backs of her two pet philosophers. It made for excellent festival tittle-tattle. But scandal did not end there. Further frisson was added by the subject matter of Wagner's now five-year-old correspondence with Nietzsche's doctor, which had somehow become known. Nietzsche the masturbator! The leak probably came about because Wagner, a busy man accustomed to delegating, had channelled some of his correspondence with Dr Eiser through Hans von Wolzogen, the editor of *Bayreuther Blätter*.[5] Von Wolzogen, a passionate Wagnerite and anti-Semite, had no time for Nietzsche whom he jealously perceived as betraying the Master by his apostatic abandonment of the house philosopher (Schopenhauer) and the sacred cause (Bayreuth), and who was now apparently welded to an unprincipled girl (Lou), and an 'Israelite' of doubtful sexuality (Rée). For his part, Nietzsche had never concealed that he considered von Wolzogen an intellectual mediocrity.

Spiritual sisterhood was not developing between Lou and Elisabeth. Lou was destroying her own good name as well as her brother's by displaying that ridiculous photograph. Lou was a brazen hussy. She coquetted with every man she met. Her sensational figure was undoubtedly due to 'false breasts'.

Who knows how puzzled Elisabeth must have been by former friends cold-shouldering her in disgust or embarrassment at the rumoured sexual habits of her brother. Lou, who was welcome to run in and out of Wahnfried, says that when Nietzsche was mentioned Wagner fell into great agitation and left the room, demanding the name should never be spoken in his presence. It is a reaction that might speak of a guilty conscience.

With her unerring instinct for the man of the moment, Lou entered into a lively flirtation with Paul von Joukowsky, the entertaining thirty-seven-year-old gay artist who had designed the sets for *Parsifal*. Like her, he was half German and half Russian. They had much in common including an interest in spiritualism that was made infinitely more interesting by Lou's conviction that her path through life was distinguished by poltergeists following her about and knocking out mysterious messages.

Von Joukowsky's position at Wahnfried rested upon the remarkably kitsch picture he had made of the Wagner children as the Holy Family the previous year. Siegfried took the part of Jesus, the girls were Mary and the angels, and the painter himself was Joseph. When Böcklin had refused Wagner's request to design the sets and 'decorations' for *Parsifal*, the appointment of von Joukowsky had followed hard on. His designs satisfied even Wagner's taste for silks, satins, thousands of flowers and pink lighting. In fact, they were such an enormous success that they were used at Bayreuth throughout two-hundred-and-some revivals of the opera, until they finally fell apart in 1934. Von Joukowsky knew the secret of the letters. Whether he told Lou or whether she heard it some other way, we do not know but given the circumstances it must be unlikely it escaped her ears.

Another of Lou's easy conquests was Heinrich von Stein. In the place of Nietzsche, von Stein had been awarded the position of young Siegfried's tutor. An ardent Schopenhauerian (it went with the post), he and Lou at first differed on questions of philosophy, only to come together so warmly over their differences that von Stein invited her to visit him in Halle.

Altogether the week in Bayreuth was proving a marvellous one for Lou and appalling for Elisabeth. She poured out her anger, frustration and jealousy of Lou in writing her only novella.[6] The characters are hardly even thinly disguised. Lou is the Polish 'Fräulein von Ramstein', whose figure has an impossibly thin waist and a deep bosom that is obviously due to a generosity of padding. She has staring eyes, frizzy hair and a yellow complexion. The plump red lips of her voracious sea-anemone mouth are permanently suggestively parted. Despite all this, she is dangerously attractive to men. Her highbrow ugliness ensnares Georg, the hero of the story – Nietzsche disguised very lightly indeed. As innocent as he is noble, Georg believes Fräulein von Ramstein's nice speeches of love, philosophy and *Freigeisterei*. Little does he know that the treacherous girl has already made exactly the same speeches and loving approaches to 'a grammar school teacher' (Rée). Luckily, Georg sees sense just in time. He settles down with Nora, a good girl of fair Saxon complexion and mild, delightful character: a triumphant self-portrait of the author.

It is not a great literary work but it must be conceded that the indignation that drove the story was not completely misplaced: all the time Lou was in Bayreuth she was keeping Rée informed of everything. He became frantic with jealousy of Nietzsche and von Joukowsky. He told her that he had no scruples in acting mendaciously and deceitfully against Nietzsche, or any other man who wanted her. 'You will find out that I am the most ridiculous jealous man that you've ever met.'[7]

Lou was not unduly susceptible to the influence of music, but Nietzsche was desperately keen she should share his passion. He insisted she stay for the second performance of *Parsifal*. This suited her well, but before even the second performance, Elisabeth had had enough of Lou's immodest behaviour. The final straw came when Lou commanded von Joukowsky to kneel at her feet to alter the hem of her dress while she was still wearing it. Outraged, Elisabeth sent Nietzsche a telegram, and left for Tautenburg. Nietzsche hurried to meet her at the station. Hoping for wonderful reports of Lou, he heard only a litany of complaints.

Von Joukowsky and Heinrich von Stein were against Lou joining Nietzsche and Elisabeth in Tautenburg. They urged her to stay on in Bayreuth. Malwida, too. She foresaw nothing but trouble from the projected threesome. Lou remained in Bayreuth, telling Nietzsche she was in bed with a cold. He sent his wishes for a speedy recovery. As he made no reference to Elisabeth or any other unpleasantness, Lou deemed it safe to throw off her pretended illness and she wrote him a charming letter expressing her sincere gratitude for Elisabeth's care during their time together in Bayreuth. Nothing was going to get in the way of her three weeks' philosophical discipleship.

For her part, Elisabeth had no choice but to stick to the plan. If she now withdrew her chaperonage she would be stripping away the last fig leaf of reputation from the Nietzsche family name, leaving it completely naked.

Caught in the middle, Nietzsche simply begged, 'Do come. I am suffering too much for having made you suffer. We will endure it better together.'[8]

When Lou arrived on 6 or 7 August, Elisabeth was there to meet her. It so happened that on the train journey from Bayreuth, Lou had shared a carriage with Bernhard Förster, the schoolmaster whom Elisabeth had been cultivating energetically and was hoping to marry. Elisabeth's jealousy now extended to Lou trying to steal her lover as well as her brother. There was a spectacular quarrel. How could Lou go about flirting with every man she met? How could she drag the respectable Nietzsche name through the mud in this way? Lou 'laughed wildly' at this and replied, 'Who first soiled our study plans with his low designs? Who started up the mental friendship when he could not get me for something else? Who thought of concubinage? Your noble, pure-minded brother! Men want only one thing and it is not mental friendship!'

Elisabeth retorted grandly that such things might be common enough among mere Russians but were ridiculous in connection with her pure-minded brother. She demanded that Lou stop this indecent talk. Lou told her she was accustomed to talking a lot more indecently to Rée, adding that Nietzsche had suggested that if he could not have her in marriage, it would be better to live together in a 'wild marriage' (*wilde Ehe*) but if Elisabeth thought she had designs on her brother she was much mistaken. Lou could sleep all night in the same room as him and not feel in the least bit aroused. The horror of this coarse remark made Elisabeth vomit. Compresses were applied.[9]

Nietzsche had arranged for the two women to be put up in the vicar's house in Tautenburg. He decorously took a room in a nearby farmer's house. The morning following the quarrel, the three of them met up. Nietzsche confronted Lou with Elisabeth's reports of her perfidies. She simply denied everything. None of it had taken place. Elisabeth's accusations had no basis in fact. Elisabeth says that Lou was then asked to leave but she pretended to be ill and retired to bed.

To demonstrate her superiority, Elisabeth set out on a programme of uplifting walks in the beautiful woods where the 'adorable, scampering squirrels' helped her to recover her equilibrium. Nietzsche meanwhile spent his time scuttling up and down the creaking wooden vicarage staircase, whose explosive detonations Lou put down to poltergeists. She would not let him into her room, so he slipped notes under her door. Eventually he was allowed in to console his 'naughty' Lou and kiss her hand. Soon she was sufficiently recovered to get up.

The following three weeks, Elisabeth lurked, sulked, admired squirrels and complained to her correspondents about being mocked for her sacrifices, ridiculed by her brother and displaced by Lou. The other two took long, exhilarating walks together in the quiet half-light of the Tautenburg forest, he twice shaded by his green eyeshade and his parasol and she by her hat and a red scarf. When they returned to his room in the farmer's house, she would wind her scarf round the lampshade to soften the lamplight and make it kinder to his poor eyes. They talked until midnight, and beyond. It drove Nietzsche's landlord mad because he had to stay up to escort her back to the vicarage. And still the cows would need milking at dawn.

Both describe talking for ten hours at a stretch. Nietzsche became increasingly convinced that he had found his alter ego, the other half of the brother-and-sister brain. Their only real inequality was in their writing style. Lou still wrote in the over-lush manner of a breathless schoolgirl, whereas Nietzsche's prose style combined precision and brevity with often shocking, bacchanalian vitality. Rightly, he thought himself one of the three greatest stylists in the German language, the other two being Luther and Goethe.

He drew up a style guide for her:

Style should be lively.

Know exactly what you want to say before you start writing.

Suit your style to the recipient.

Long sentences are an affectation. Only people who have long duration of breath are entitled to write in long sentences.

Finally, 'It is not good manners or clever to deprive one's reader of the most obvious objections. It is very good manners and *very clever* to leave it to one's reader alone to pronounce on the ultimate quintessence of our wisdom.'[10]

Lou's interpretation of their conversations during their three weeks in Tautenburg was that, fundamentally, they spoke of nothing but God. She concluded that Nietzsche was the more religious for being godless. It was the pain of this that drove his philosophy. His entire intellectual development derived from his loss of belief and from his emotions attending the death of God. The possibility of finding some substitution for the lost god obsessed him.

He spoke of Darwinism. In former times, he explained, one had ascribed the sense of grandeur in man to his godly origins. This path had now become closed 'because at its portal stands the ape, amid other horrible animals, and apprehendingly he bares his teeth as if to say, "no farther in this direction!"' And so mankind pushed tirelessly at opposite paths and directions by which to prove its grandeur.[11] Man valued human greatness as based upon a shedding of the animalistic. The aim was to be thought of as no longer an animal. Or at least a superior animal, a dialectical and reasonable being.[12]

It was possible that man's commanding intellectualism would spoil his capacity for happiness. It was even possible that mankind would perish of this passion for knowledge. But who would not prefer the fall of mankind to a decline in knowledge?[13]

He explained to her that he wished to examine, and probably shrug off, the anthropocentric fallacy. Natural phenomena should not be viewed from a short-sighted, narrowly human perspective. To this end he had decided that he would take a number of years — possibly ten — to study the natural sciences at university either in Vienna or Paris. From now on, philosophical conclusions would be based on empirical observation and experiment.

They also spoke of the eternal recurrence. He told her that he wanted to learn how to see what is necessary in things as beautiful. 'Thus I will be one of those who make things beautiful. *Amor fati* [love of fate]: let that be my love from now on! I do not want to wage war against ugliness. I do not want to accuse; I do not even want to accuse the accusers. Let *looking away* be my only negation! And, all in all and on the whole: some day I want only to be a Yes-sayer!'[14]

To love your fate, to accept it and embrace it, was to love and embrace the doctrine of eternal recurrence. This was not, he impishly insisted, to embrace a superstitious, astrological passivity or a recumbent oriental fatalism but if man had come to know himself and become himself, then fate must be embraced. If one had character, one had typical experience which also recurred. If life was a long line stretching from the past to the future and one was at a point on this line, one was there through one's own responsibility. This made the conscious soul duty bound to say yes to this moment and be prepared to be happy that, in the wheel of time, it might recur again and again.

One must be fleet of foot; one must dance. Life was not simple. If, one day, man would dare construct an architecture corresponding to the nature of the soul, that architect would have to take the labyrinth as the model. To give birth to a dancing star, one must first have chaos within. Inconsistency, changes of mind and urges to wander were a duty. A fixed opinion was a dead opinion, a made-up mind was a dead mind, worth less than an insect; it should be crushed underfoot and utterly destroyed.

Lou's observations on their three weeks together are of value, even though her reportage is shaped by twelve years of hindsight. No one else ever spent three weeks being indoctrinated by him in his philosophy.

After three weeks, Lou could stand no more of this intensity. On 26 August, Nietzsche accompanied her to the station. On leaving, Lou presented him with a poem, 'A Prayer to Life' ('*Gebet an das Leben*'). He set it to music, expressing to her the hope that it would be one small path by which the two of them might reach posterity together – other paths also remaining open.

With more excitement than sensitivity, Nietzsche commissioned Louise Ott, the woman with whom he had fallen in love during the first Bayreuth Festival, to look into accommodation for the Trinity in Paris. He fantasised that when they were all together in Paris, they would sit around the piano listening to Louise's nightingale voice sing Lou's 'Prayer to Life', set to his own music.

Lou fled Tautenburg straight to the Stibbe-nest and Rée. All along she had been keeping him informed with instalments of the 'nest book'. Her final conclusion was that she had looked into Nietzsche's subjective abyss, where she had found Christian religious mysticism renamed as Dionysianism and fundamentally a mask for bodily lust. 'Just as Christian (like every) mysticism attains crude religious sensuality at its highest ecstasy, so the most ideal form of love always returns to sensuality.' She wondered if this might be a sort of revenge conducted by the animality of human nature upon the spiritual, and whether it was this that was drawing her away from Nietzsche and towards Rée, who posed no sexual threat.

The Sunday following Lou's departure, Nietzsche took a train home to his mother in Naumburg. Elisabeth refused to accompany him. Her eyes, she said, were so swollen from tears that she could not inflict the shock of such a sight upon her mother.

He fell straight into playing the devoted son. All was calm until a letter arrived from Elisabeth, telling all. It ignited such a spectacular quarrel that Franziska accused him of being a liar and a coward. He was a disgrace to his father's name; he had dishonoured his father's grave. Her words contained the elemental horror of a mother's curse. He never forgot them.

He fled to Leipzig, reflecting bitterly that he still suffered from what he called 'chain-sickness': emotional attachment dragging you down on your way to becoming the being who you are.

'First, one has the difficulty of emancipating oneself from one's chains; and, ultimately one has to emancipate oneself from this emancipation, too! Each of us has to suffer, though in greatly differing ways, from the chain-sickness, even after he has broken the chain.'[15]

To welcome Lou and Rée to Leipzig, he organised attendance at a séance. They were both susceptible to such things. After the show, he planned to dazzle them by an impressive refutation of spiritualist nonsense. But the medium proved herself so incompetent that he had nothing against which to pit his well-rehearsed arguments.

The Trinity passed the next few weeks apathetically. They attended a few concerts but for the most part they sat around composing clever aphorisms. Nietzsche continued correcting and polishing Lou's prose, which had not lost, and never would lose, its tendency towards vague overreaching and over-colourfulness. His annotations in her margins now boldly addressed her by his pet name for her, 'Märchen', which means 'fairy tale' but also 'fabulist'.

The three wrote aphorisms to describe each other. The aphorism describing Lou read: 'Woman does not die of love, but wastes away for want of it.' Rée was described by 'The greatest pain is self-hate.' For Nietzsche, 'Nietzsche's weakness: supersubtlety.' For the Trinity itself: 'Two friends are most easily separated by a third.'[16]

Schopenhauer had spoken of a republic of genius forming a kind of bridge over the turbulent stream of becoming but they were none of them managing to cross that bridge. Nobody was acting honestly, or speaking openly. The 'becoming' of each was foundering on the rock of the two others as each drowned in ever-deepening pretence. The Holy Trinity had turned into a dishonest triangle in which none of them was acting as a free spirit.

Earlier that year, Nietzsche had ecstatically declared to the Overbecks that he would go more into the world and be more with people. It had turned out to be a course of action that had demonstrated that even such a small, idealistic human unit as a trinity of allegedly free spirits succeeded only in imprisoning the participants in new-forged chains of sentiment, resentment and obligation. Any attachment brought with it new-forged chain-sickness.

On 5 November, Lou and Rée simply disappeared. Nietzsche had no idea what had happened, or why. He hovered over the letterbox, uncertain of his immediate fate, but no letters came. After ten days of this he tore himself away from Leipzig to Basle, where he had promised to attend the forty-fifth birthday celebrations of his good friend Franz Overbeck. Here too, the letterbox was the centre of his world. Had any letters arrived? he kept asking Ida Overbeck. Might she have misplaced anything? Might anything have become lost? Was she keeping anything from him? When the time came for him to depart, she was terribly struck by the desolation of his parting words. 'So I really am going into utter solitude.'

A few weeks later, the devious Rée sent Nietzsche a postcard preposterously reproaching him for abandoning them. Ever forgiving, ever indulgent, Nietzsche responded with a message of forgiveness for Lou: the 'higher soul' always acted beyond blame and reproach. He wished her to continue on her task of 'sweeping the heavens clean', even though he felt that the entire dignity of his life's task had been called into doubt by her behaviour.

Between November and February he spent an enormous amount of time writing her letters. Some he posted, some remained in draft.

They were variously loving, loathing, belittling, accusatory, forgiving, reproachful or insulting. She had the 'predatory pleasure-lust of a cat'. She wrote vengeful schoolgirl letters. She was a monstrosity, a brain with only a rudiment of a soul. Given her energy, will and originality of mind, she was destined for something great; given her morality, she would probably end in a penitentiary or madhouse.

He never saw Lou or Rée again. They had not travelled to Paris, as he thought. They had hidden from him for a few days in Leipzig before going on to Berlin. Here they took up residence in an apartment configured exactly as she had envisaged for the Holy Trinity: two bedrooms separated by a salon. Lou set up a literary salon in imitation of Malwida. It was of no literary distinction but it thrummed with sexual tension. Rée continued to fight his addiction to gambling and to edgy encounters with young men in the streets after midnight. Lou was addressed in the salon as 'Your Excellency'. Rée was known as 'the Maid of Honour'.

Lou brought with her to Berlin her gift copy of *Human, All Too Human*, in which Nietzsche had inscribed a poem:

> Darling – quoth Columbus – never
> Trust another Genoese!
> Across the brine he stares forever,
> Over the distant deep blue seas!
>
> His loved ones lures he from afar
> Through space and time's immensity –
> Above us star shines next to star.
> Around us roars eternity.[17]

14

· MY FATHER WAGNER IS DEAD.
MY SON ZARATHUSTRA IS BORN ·

What would there be to create if gods – existed?
Ecce Homo, 'Thus Spoke Zarathustra', Section 9

In November 1882, Nietzsche left Basle for Genoa, the birthplace of Columbus who crossed unexplored oceans to discover a completely new world. One of the attractions of Columbus was that he had no idea whether he would find land. Nor, indeed, had Nietzsche, as he spoke grandly of voyaging to India like Alexander and Dionysus before him. Given his chronic seasickness, he was plainly speaking of a metaphorical voyage to the *terra incognita* of the human interior.

His general health was extremely bad over the winter of 1882–3. It cannot have helped that he was taking huge doses of opium in vain attempts to summon elusive sleep and dull the emotional pain of what he described as the last agonising death throes concerning Lou. In mid-December, he wrote an attention-seeking letter jointly to Lou and Rée, telling them that he had taken a huge dose of opium and '. . . even if I should happen one day to take my life because of some passion or other, there would not be much to grieve about . . .'[1] Letters mentioning overdoses of opium and suicide were also sent to Overbeck and Peter Gast; 'The barrel of a revolver is for me now a source of relatively pleasant thoughts,'[2] etc. His old friends had long known that suicide must always be a possibility and they also knew that no interference could, or would, affect the outcome.

On his arrival in Genoa, the new Columbus discovered that the boarding house he liked was full, so he moved down the coast, finding a tiny, cheap *albergo* in Rapallo. The substitution mattered not at all to his creative imagination. An Argonaut of the spirit could be Columbus departing for America, or he could be Dionysus or Alexander departing for India just as well from Rapallo, which could stand in his imagination for both Genoa and ancient Greece.

'Imagine an island of the Greek Archipelago, arbitrarily covered with woods and hills, which owing to some accident one day swam close up to the mainland and was unable to swim back again. To my left the Gulf of Genoa up to the lighthouse. There is certainly something Greek about it . . . something piratical, unexpected, buccaneering . . . I have never lived so long in genuine Robinson Crusoe insularity and oblivion.'[3] The *albergo* was clean but the cuisine was awful. He had yet to be served a decent piece of meat.

He had been two months in Rapallo when his mother sent him a Christmas letter so liberally sugared with Naumburg virtue that it gave him the courage to reply that he would return future letters unopened. Time to break free of chain-sickness. This must include Elisabeth. He instructed his friends not to let his family know his new address. 'I cannot stand them any longer. I wish I had broken with them earlier!'

He was alone on Christmas Day. Reinvigorated maybe by the symbolic day of birth and rebirth, he wrote his first forward-looking letter. It was addressed to Overbeck. 'My lack of confidence is now immense,' he confessed. 'Unless I can discover the alchemical trick of turning this – muck into gold, I am lost. Here I have the most splendid chance to prove that for me "all experiences are useful, all days holy and all people divine"!!!'[4]

The alchemical trick could only be achieved by the solitary Argonaut who was prepared to wreck himself against infinity. 'Solitude has seven skins; nothing can come through them any more . . .'[5] The result was the book *Thus Spoke Zarathustra (Also sprach Zarathustra)*, an ecstatic, poetic, prophetic spiritual odyssey through the modern moral world. Not unlike the travels of Gulliver or the voyages of Sinbad or Odysseus, the book is an extended parable that is preoccupied with the issues of its times. The ancient Persian prophet Zarathustra comes down from the mountain after the death of the concept of God in order to point out that if mankind can rise to it, morality may exist in a post-deist world so long as there is the honesty, consistency and courage to scrub clean the walls of the cave that still bear the shadow-writing of supernatural beliefs.

Thus Spoke Zarathustra was not the first appearance of the Persian prophet in Nietzsche's published writing. His previous book, *The Gay Science*, had ended with a long aphoristic paragraph headed *'Incipit tragoedia'* ('The tragedy begins')[6] in which, bewilderingly, he introduced a character called Zarathustra, who had not previously been mentioned in the book at all. 'When Zarathustra was thirty years old, he left his homeland and Lake Urmi and went into the mountains,' began the last section of *The Gay Science*. Where on earth was Lake Urmi? What mountains was he talking about? Who was Zarathustra?

'There', the passage in *The Gay Science* continues, 'he enjoyed his spirit and solitude, and did not tire of that for ten years. But at last his heart changed – and one morning he arose with rosy dawn, stepped before the sun, and spoke to it thus:

'"You great heavenly body! What would your happiness be if you did not have those for whom you shine! For ten years you have climbed up to my cave without me, my eagle, and my snake, you would have become tired of your light and of this road; but we awaited you every morning, relieved you of your overabundance, and blessed you for it. Behold, I am sick of my wisdom, like a bee that has collected too much honey; I need outstretched hands; I would like to give away and distribute until the wise among humans once again enjoy their folly and the poor once again their riches. For that I must step into the depths, as you do in the evening when you go behind the sea and bring light even to the underworld, you over-rich heavenly body! Like you I must *go under*, as it is called by the human beings to whom I want to descend."'

This 'going under' appears to refer to Nietzsche's own 'going under' at the time of writing *The Gay Science*, when he had joyfully descended from the heights of loneliness to share the overflowing abundance of his ideas with Lou, through whom his 'honey' (his wisdom) would be distributed. When he was writing this, he still believed that he had found his first disciple in her.

The passage continues, "'So bless me then, you calm eye that can look without envy upon all-too-great happiness! Bless the cup that wants to overflow in order that the water may flow golden from it and everywhere carry the reflection of your bliss! Behold, this cup wants to become empty again, and Zarathustra wants to become human again." Thus began Zarathustra's going under.'

Here ends *The Gay Science* as published in 1882.

The final book as we know it today contains his revisions of 1887 which include a new introduction, a fifth section containing thirty-nine additional aphorisms, and quite a few poems. But when, in 1883, he wrote the first part of *Thus Spoke Zarathustra*, the book takes up exactly where the original 1882 *Gay Science* left off. Between writing the two books he had lost Lou, and, in her, his chosen disciple. *Faute de mieux*, her role as the vehicle to ensure his mortal legacy was to be taken by Zarathustra. Often, outside the book, Nietzsche refers to Zarathustra as his son.

Why did Nietzsche choose Zarathustra? Zarathustra, also called Zoroaster, was a Persian prophet who probably lived some time between the twelfth and sixth centuries before Christ. Zarathustra's sacred text, the *Zend-Avesta*,[7] tells that the gods worshipped by the very ancient Persians were evil. Thus Zarathustra presented a key to the problem of evil that could never be answered by Judaism, Christianity or Islam, whose all-powerful gods were all-good. In Zoroastrianism the god of light and good is called Ahura Mazda (also known as Ormuzd). He is in constant conflict with the god of darkness and evil, Angra Mainyu (Ahriman), and his *daevas*. At the end of time, Ahura Mazda will score a final victory, but until then he is not in control of events. Consequently, Zoroastrianism, unlike the three great religions of the book, escapes the paradox of an all-powerful good God who is responsible for what many people take to be unnecessary evil.[8]

Zarathustra's ten years of solitude in the mountains between the ages of thirty and forty might stand for Nietzsche's post-Basle decade of independent thinking, which was often conducted on high mountains. Zarathustra is forty, the same age as the writer Nietzsche is, when he comes down 'to be among the people'. He carries down fire, as Prometheus had carried the fire that would transform cultures and civilisations and as the Holy Ghost had carried down tongues of fire at Pentecost. Fire bestows upon the chosen ones (the enlightened ones) the gift of 'speaking in tongues', i.e. in words that are universally comprehensible. It is a synonym for wisdom and for revelation. Zarathustra's fire has the specific ability to scorch meaning into the meaninglessness of life following upon the death of God. His mouth alone (through Nietzsche's) will be the first to address the nihilism, despair and devaluation of moral life that was reaching its crisis within the context of nineteenth-century materialism.

All gods are dead, Zarathustra preaches. Now we want the superman to live. I teach you the superman. 'Human being is something that must be overcome.'[9]

What is man? A hybrid between plant and ghost. What is the superman? He is the meaning of the earth who remains faithful to the earth. He does not believe those who offer extra-terrestrial hopes: they are despisers of life, who die self-poisoned.

The superman knows that whatever seems cruel, random or disastrous is not a punishment sent from the eternal reason-spider above to punish the sinner. There is no eternal reason-spider and no eternal reason-spider-web. Rather, life is a dance floor for divine accidents.[10] Meaning must be found through saying 'yes' to the divine accidents on the dance floor.

Zarathustra preaches to the villagers that man is a bridge, not a goal. This is man's glory. The human is between beast and superman, a rope fastened over an abyss.

On hearing this, Zarathustra's first disciple emerges from the crowd to attempt to cross the abyss by walking the tightrope. A buffoon jumps up and topples the tightrope walker, who falls to the ground and dies. Zarathustra takes the body of his first disciple, the tightrope walker, for burial. He is mocked by the common herd. Despite this, he resolves to show them the rainbow bridge that stretches – not to Valhalla the home of the gods, where Wagner's rainbow bridge led – but to the state of becoming the superman.

This he does by giving them his beatitudes (eighteen of them; Christ gave eight). They are not commandments and they are impenetrably mystical. The first reads: 'I love those who do not know how to live except by going under, for they are those who cross over.' The last: 'I love all those who are like heavy drops falling individually from the dark cloud that hangs over humanity: they herald the coming of the lightning, and as heralds they perish.'¹¹

The sun stands at mid-day and he enjoys time with his animals. The eagle is 'the proudest animal under the sun' and the serpent is coiled like a ring around the neck of the eagle. The serpent is 'the wisest animal under the sun'. Nietzsche often took the eagle as standing for himself and the serpent as standing for Lou (the serpent is female and he uses the same word, *klügste*, for the cleverness of Lou and the cleverness of the serpent). The two animals together hold an increasing significance for him. They recall many symbols, including the fatal omen that heralded the Fall of Troy (which may stand for the fall of any doctrine or civilisation) when Apollo through a serpent cursed Cassandra who, like Nietzsche, was blessed with the gift of foreseeing the future. Cassandra's curse, like Nietzsche's, was that nobody would believe her words or her predictions.

Narrative is now abandoned and Nietzsche gives us instead twenty-two aphoristic discourses on subjects ranging from individual virtue to what constitutes criminality, to how to make a good death. The full list comprises:

On the Three Metamorphoses
On the Teachers of Virtue
On the Hinterworldly
On the Despisers of the Body
On the Passions of Pleasure and Pain
On the Pale Criminal

On Reading and Writing
On the Tree on the Mountain
On the Preachers of Death
On War and Warriors
On the New Idol
On the Flies of the Market Place
On Chastity
On the Friend
On a Thousand and One Goals
On Love of the Neighbour
On the Way of the Creator
On Little Women Old and Young
On the Adder's Bite
On Child and Marriage
On Free Death
On the Bestowing Virtue

They give us Nietzsche's ideas on those subjects, couched in his alter ego Zarathustra's archaic, biblical language.

Unsurprisingly in view of his recent experience, women are now given very harsh treatment, in striking contrast to his gentle understanding of them in *The Gay Science*. Is it not better to fall into the hands of a murderer than into the dreams of a lustful woman? he asks. And the famous 'You go to women? Do not forget the whip!'[12]

'On Free Death' is probably the section most revolutionary for his time. Christian teaching on suicide considered the ending of one's own life an unforgivable sin. Suicides were buried in unhallowed ground outside the walls of the churchyard. This symbolised their soul's eternal exclusion from Heaven. But Nietzsche suggests the option of voluntary euthanasia for those in intolerable pain, those who realise that their quality of life has vanished, or those who simply feel that their time has come. He recommends that they should be allowed voluntarily to end their own lives without whiff of criminality or eternal damnation.

Each of the twenty-two discourses models how to live honourably and truthfully to the ideal of the superman who is non-religious, independent, self-disciplined and creative. Each ends with the words 'Thus spoke Zarathustra.' The book ends on an optimistic, ecstatic and characteristically opaque note:

"'And that is the great noon, where human beings stand at the midpoint of their course between animal and *Übermensch* and celebrate their way to evening as their highest hope: for it is the way to a new morning.

"'Then the one who goes under will bless himself, that he is one who crosses over; and the sun of his knowledge will stand at noon for him.

"'*Dead are all gods: now we want the Übermensch to live.* – Let this be our last will at the great noon!" –

'Thus spoke Zarathustra.'

The book is short, barely a hundred pages. Its cadences are poetic, repetitive, hypnotic, brief and dynamic. He said that he wrote it – or it wrote him – in ten days of ecstatic inspiration and revelation. In fact it probably took him a little longer, nearer a month.

On 14 February 1883, he sent it to his publisher Schmeitzner, describing it in his covering letter as 'a fifth gospel'. He went from Rapallo to Genoa to post it, maybe for the joy of launching it from the proper place on its symbolic voyage, or maybe for the advantage of the swifter postal service from Genoa. While he was there, he learned from a newspaper of Wagner's death the previous day. He took it as an omen, a supernatural connection: another pair of rapiers clashing in mid-air. Bending the truth a little, he observed that the finishing section was accomplished precisely at that sacred hour when Richard Wagner died in Venice.

Wagner's soul was voyaging to join the other Argonauts of the spirit. Wagner, too, had once been wrapped in the seven skins of solitude of the visionary prophet. Now that he was dead, Wagner's earlier and purer self could be reclaimed. Nietzsche was therefore entitled to refer to *Thus Spoke Zarathustra* as a new *Ring*. His father Wagner was dead; his son Zarathustra was born.

It was a mark of Nietzsche's discretion and spiritual generosity that, as he revealed in a letter to Franz Overbeck a week after Wagner's death, he had known for some time the import of Wagner's wretched correspondence with his doctors. 'Wagner was by far the *fullest* human being I have known, and in *this* respect I have had to forgo a great deal for six years. But something like a deadly offence came between us; and something terrible could have happened if he had lived longer.'[13] On 21 April he wrote more openly to the musician Peter Gast, 'Wagner is rich in malicious ideas, but what do you say to his having exchanged letters on the subject (even with my doctors) to voice his *belief* that my altered way of thinking was a consequence of unnatural excesses, with hints of pederasty?' A few months later, in July, he also mentioned to Ida Overbeck an 'abysmal treachery of revenge' that had come to his ears the preceding year.

There had indeed been abysmal treachery and public humiliation, not only by Wagner, but by Lou and Rée as well.

On receipt of *Zarathustra*, his publisher did not hail it as a fifth gospel. In fact he showed no signs at all of producing the book. When Nietzsche enquired, Schmeitzner vaguely blamed printers' delays. Nietzsche replied with a sarcastic note saying that Schmeitzner might have had the money to pay the printer if he had not squandered it on anti-Semitic pamphlets. This did not produce the desired result.

Nietzsche was disappointed, exhausted and isolated. In addition he was probably malnourished as he sought out the cheapest meals in town, and he was certainly over-medicated. He was dosing himself with dangerous drugs, writing out prescriptions and signing them 'Dr Nietzsche'. The Italian pharmacists gave him whatever he requested.

He felt acute self-disgust; 'Not for a moment have I been able to forget, for instance, that my mother called me a disgrace to my dead father . . . My whole life has crumbled under my gaze: this whole eerie, deliberately secluded secret life, which takes a step, every six years, and actually wants nothing but the taking of this step while everything else, all my human relationships, have to do with a mask of me and I must perpetually be the victim of living a completely hidden life. I have always been exposed to the cruellest coincidences – or, rather, it is I who have always turned coincidence into cruelty . . . I am in a bad way. It is night all around me again. I feel as if the lightning had flashed . . . I shall inevitably go to pieces, unless something happens – I have no idea *what*.'[14]

He saw no point in living but felt compelled to rise to the incarnate wrestling match that demands of old Laocoön that he set about it and vanquish his serpents. But if he was to live, he wanted nothing to do with people. Even lodging in a little *albergo* or a farmer's cottage was too much company for him. 'There is no limit to the quiet, the altitude, the solitude I need around me in order to hear my inner voices. I would like to have enough money to build a sort of ideal dog kennel around me – I mean, a timber house with two rooms, and it would be on a peninsula which runs out into the Sils lake and on which there used to be a Roman fort.'[15]

Alternately chilled and sweating through the night, feverish and subject to constant chronic exhaustion, he had no appetite and a dull palate. The 'old headache' worked on him between seven in the morning and eleven in the evening. Failing to find a heater to warm his room in Rapallo, Nietzsche moved back to Genoa. Vaguely he was hoping that someone would drag him out of Europe, whose geography and climate he blamed for his physical and mental maladies. Regarding himself, as usual, as a 'victim of a disturbance in *nature*', he now blamed Mount Etna for the problems he had previously attributed to the electricity in the clouds. The energy flow of the volcano, which was busy grumbling and threatening to erupt, was responsible for his fluctuating symptoms.[16] There was comfort in this thought. It saved him from accusing individuals of causing his misery.

In this weakened mental and physical state, he yielded to a clumsy conciliatory approach from Elisabeth. Soon she had him ensnared in her flattering version of the recent past. He was the utterly blameless victim of the Russian viper and 'the Jew Rée'. He told her that he was ready to 'put my human relations, somewhat jumbled just now, back in order, beginning with you. As for the typewriter, it is on the blink like everything weak men take in hand for a while, be it machines or problems or Lous.'[17]

He was still waiting for Schmeitzner to publish *Zarathustra* and he asked Elisabeth to intervene. She succeeded where he had failed, possibly because Schmeitzner knew her to be a fellow anti-Semite. In her turn, Elisabeth persuaded Nietzsche to join her in a very unpleasant campaign of letter writing to the authorities to get Lou expelled from Germany and sent back to Russia as an immoral personage. In fact, the campaign had the unforeseen consequence of turning Lou into a writer. She realised that if she was branded an immoral personage it might result in the withdrawal of her Russian pension. This was her only source of income, so she set to making money by writing. She produced an autobiographical *roman-à-clef* called *Im Kampf um Gott* (*Struggling for God*). The Nietzsche character is an ascetic with a passion for chastity and whores. Lou herself is a high-class courtesan and 'a slave of her unrestrained lower nature'. Rée is her protector, 'the Count'. The book ends with her killing herself by taking poison. The racy seduction narrative is punctuated by all the characters' philosophical struggles to find some sort of religious or non-religious meaning in the world. When Nietzsche read it a couple of years later, he recognised 'a hundred echoes of our Tautenburg conversations in it'.[18] She had even called the girl Märchen, his special name for her.

Elisabeth failed in her scheme to get Lou deported. Undaunted, she launched herself into a campaign to separate her brother from 'the *Israelite* Rée'. Nietzsche had long been cured of Réealism in his philosophy. He had learned the art of aphoristic writing from Rée but he had moved on from Rée's materialism. These days Rée looked to him like a man with no ideals, no goals, no obligations and no instincts, content to be Lou's companion, if not her servant.

Elisabeth egged on the separation, telling him that it was Rée who had told Lou that the plans for the Trinity had always been founded on Nietzsche's lustful, low aim of 'a wild marriage'. Nietzsche believed her and he became tormented by the thought that Rée had betrayed their friendship by ridiculing his philosophy to Lou and turning her against him. Self-pity and suspicion spiralled. He wrote to Rée, accusing him of being a sneaking, insidious, low mendacious fellow, and Lou the mouthpiece, the terrible mouthpiece, of his ideas. Lou was a calamity, a sterile, dirty, evil-smelling she-ape with false breasts. (We recognise Elisabeth's hand in the reference to false breasts.) Nietzsche's wild accusations produced a threat of libel action from Rée's brother Georg, who challenged him to a duel with pistols. Fortunately, the challenge was never followed up.

'I never hated anyone till then,' he wrote to Elisabeth, 'not even Wagner, whose perfidies went far beyond anything achieved by Lou. It is only now that I feel truly humiliated.'[19]

Nietzsche's father, Karl Ludwig
Nietzsche (1813–49), priest.

Nietzsche's mother, Franziska,
née Oehler (1826–97).

Friedrich Nietzsche aged seventeen.
His confirmation portrait:
the start of doubt.

Nietzsche's sister Elisabeth aged
seventeen. Her confirmation
portrait: no doubt at all.

Richard and Cosima Wagner, 1875, when Nietzsche was worship-struck by both.

Cosima Wagner, *c.*1870, at the start of Nietzsche's relationship with her.

Tribschen, Wagner's home. Mont Pilatus in the background.

The chapel on Mont Pilatus.

Nietzsche's beloved Sils-Maria: 'Philosophy is living in high mountains.'

Sils-Maria: the author at the rock where Nietzsche experienced the Zarathustra revelation.

Gian Durisch's house in Sils-Maria. Nietzsche's room is at the top right.

Lou Salomé, the *femme fatale* who fascinated Nietzsche, Rilke and Freud.

'When you go to women, do not forget the whip.' Lou Salomé wields the whip over Nietzsche and Paul Rée.

The Försterhof, Paraguay, from which Elisabeth Nietzsche ruled her anti-Semitic colony.

Nietzsche in 1882 at the height
of his powers.

The typewriter, which Nietzsche
never managed to make behave.

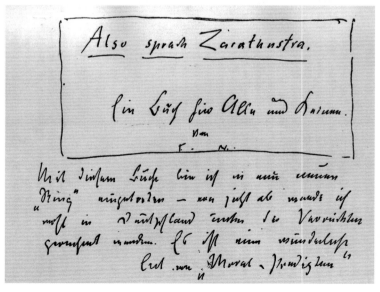

Nietzsche announces the book *Thus Spoke Zarathustra*, February 1883.

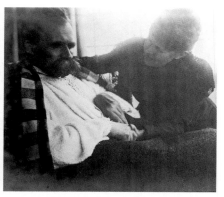

The insane Nietzsche in his
mother's care, 1890.

Elisabeth poses lovingly over the brother
in her power.

Hitler looking sad at Elisabeth's funeral.

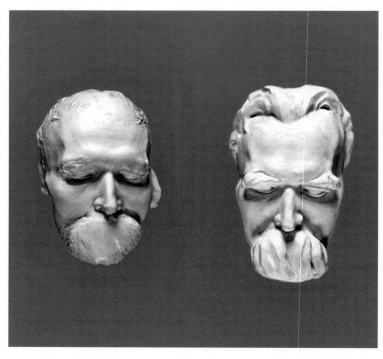

Nietzsche's death masks. On the left, the original. On the right, as 'improved' by sister Elisabeth.

15

· ONLY WHERE THERE ARE GRAVES ARE THERE RESURRECTIONS ·

> In the second part [of *Zarathustra*] I have cavorted like a clowning acrobat almost. The detail contains an incredible amount of personal experience and suffering which is intelligible only to me – there were some pages which seemed to me to drip with blood.
>
> Letter to Peter Gast from Sils-Maria, end of August 1883

Promoter of free spirits though she was, Malwida could not excuse Lou's bad behaviour. Taking Nietzsche's side against her former protégée, she invited him to recuperate by visiting her in Rome. He packed up his heavy trunk of books, now weighing 104 kilos and christened 'the club foot'. He arrived on 4 May 1883 to meet up with Elisabeth, who had been continuing to work on closer relations with her brother.

Elisabeth and Malwida never saw themselves as rivals. Throughout the following month their cooperative care was sufficiently soothing for Nietzsche to cease taking chloral hydrate drops for his insomnia. Malwida's money paid for healthful trips into the springtime landscape of the *campagna* around Rome with its wildflowers, rough farmhouses and skimpy remnants of ruins. When their carriage clattered them back to the museums of Rome, of all the artefacts he saw, Nietzsche was most moved by two virile busts of Brutus and Epicurus and three landscape paintings by Claude Lorrain[1] nostalgically evoking the Golden Age. The canvases had been inspired by the artist's own trips into the *campagna*.

The absurdity of the author who had declared God dead finding spiritual nourishment in the stronghold of the Roman Church was not lost on Nietzsche. He upset the two women by occasionally referring to himself as the Anti-Christ. He was gripped by revulsion at the sight of people climbing the steps of St Peter's on their knees, and he used it as a symbol of religious idiocy when he wrote the next part of *Zarathustra*.[2]

June came. Rome fell into its settled monotony of oppressive heat. He thought of summering in Ischia, like an ancient Roman; but instead he and Elisabeth travelled to Milan where they parted company, for him to travel on to Sils-Maria. It was a fortunate change of plan. In a month, Ischia was shaken by an earthquake that killed more than two thousand people.

Nietzsche did his best thinking in the open air. Place was vitally important to him. On the day he arrived back in his beloved alpine hamlet he greeted the place; 'Here my muses live . . . this region is blood and kin to me and even more than that.'[3] It led him to describe the process of inspiration that, for him, was inextricable from sense of place:

'Does anyone at the end of the nineteenth century have a clear idea of what poets in strong ages called *inspiration*? If not, I will describe it. – If you have even the slightest residue of superstition, you will hardly reject the idea of someone being just an incarnation, mouthpiece, or medium of overpowering forces. The idea of revelation in the sense of something suddenly becoming *visible* and audible with unspeakable assurance and subtlety, something that throws you down and leaves you deeply shaken – this simply describes the facts of the case. You listen, you do not look for anything, you take, you do not ask who is there; a thought lights up in a flash, with necessity, without hesitation as to its form, – I never had any choice. A delight whose incredible tension sometimes triggers a burst of tears, sometimes automatically hurries your pace and sometimes slows it down; a perfect state of being outside yourself . . . All of this is involuntary to the highest degree, but takes place as if in a storm of feelings of freedom, of unrestricted activity, of power, of divinity . . . This is *my* experience of inspiration; I do not doubt that you would need to go back thousands of years to find anyone who would say: "it is mine as well". –'[4]

The second part of *Zarathustra* came to him during the ten days between 28 June and 8 July 1883. 'All parts conceived on strenuous marches; absolute certainty, as if every thought were being called out to me.'[5]

Like the first part, it is divided into the small, intensely compressed sections that he could manage to organise while on his four- or six-hour walks and transfer into his notebooks without any practical help. The landscape of his inspiration took the path round the two little lakes of Silvaplana and Silsersee whose intensely turquoise water formed the shimmering floor to the luminous overhang of steep-sided mountains capped with eternal snows. It was a completely self-contained world from which Nietzsche continued to tell the story of Zarathustra, whose home was by Lake Urmi and who went into solitude in the mountains, and who referred to his aphoristic pronouncements as summits, or mountain peaks.

Nietzsche hardly emerges from the pages of *Zarathustra* Part II as an example of his own ideal: the 'Yea-sayer' who has managed to repudiate jealousy and revenge by turning 'It was thus' into 'I wished it so.' *Zarathustra* II is full of allusions to Lou and Rée. It is peppered with sudden, furious outbursts accusing his enemies of murdering him. They make no sense within the narrative of the book.

In the section called 'Of the Tarantulas', Lou and Rée are clearly identified as the tarantulas by the symbol of the trinity on their backs. 'Divinely sure and beautiful', when the tarantula bites him she takes his soul and makes it giddy for revenge.[6]

The text is interrupted by three poems. He had written the first, 'The Night Song', earlier when he was in Rome and the carriage rides through the arcadian landscape of the *campagna* had roused his regret at his distance from the age of heroes, his yearning for the past, and his yearning for love.

In the second poem, 'The Dance Song', Zarathustra sees young girls dancing in a meadow. He awakens sleeping Cupid, who dances with the girls. Life speaks to him through words that Lou had used to him, telling him she is merely a woman and no virtuous one at that. Woman by nature is fickle, wild and changeable, she tells him, and woman rejoices in this. But men yearn for profundity, fidelity and mystery in women and so they endow the female sex with these virtues and covet what they have imagined.

He reproaches her that when he gave her his greatest secret she valued it at naught. 'Thus matters stand between the three of us . . . She is fickle and stubborn; often I saw her bite her lip and comb her hair against the grain. Perhaps she is evil and false and in all things a female; but when she speaks ill of herself, precisely then she seduces the most.'

The third and final poem, 'The Tomb Song', opens with the view from his window in Venice across to the Island of the Dead. In its tombs have been buried his youth, together with 'the gentle marvels of love' and 'the songbird of my hopes'.

He curses his enemies who have cut short his eternity and stolen his nights, condemning him to sleepless torment.

When the book was finished, he found himself astonished at how autobiographical the text was. It took him by surprise to see how his own blood dripped from the pages, but he felt certain that only he would be able to see it.[7] In his next book he was to pursue the idea that all philosophy (not only his own) was autobiography.

Lou wished to engineer a meeting but she dared not do it directly. Knowing that Nietzsche was in Sils-Maria, she and Rée took up residence in the little village of Celerina, close by. They were travelling with a comparatively new acquaintance, a young man named Ferdinand Tönnies who was dazzled to have been taken up as the third member of the Trinity. Tönnies would eventually become a founding father of German sociology but for now all his books and his glories were before him and he was simply an emotional greenhorn who felt excited and privileged to occupy the third room in the hotel.

Nietzsche had never set eyes on Tönnies, so Lou and Rée sent him out to Sils-Maria to extend the olive branch. But when he caught sight of Nietzsche taking the air, swathed in his customary heavy defences against the light of the sun and the electricity in the clouds, and further wrapped in 'my azure solitude with which I draw circles around myself and sacred boundaries', Tönnies did not dare approach. And so the summer passed without rapprochement.

Time was already softening Nietzsche's hatred of Lou. He had opened the door to her. He had shown her the tightrope. She had almost had the courage to mount it. Although she had not risen to the ultimate challenge, she had been the closest to understanding, and she remained the cleverest animal he knew. If he were to be faithful to his own idea of the eternal recurrence, which demanded that one should, on looking back on the past, turn every 'It was' into 'I wanted it thus', he must say 'yes' to Lou's almost-commitment and continue to cherish it.

If he was to live up to his own ideal of the Yea-sayer who accepts his fate he must also acknowledge his own part in the actions of the war between Elisabeth and Lou. The rancour and resentment that he had felt against Lou now switched to hatred of Elisabeth, as he further realised how she had manipulated him. Her malice, lies and concoctions had drawn him into an extended and dishonourable campaign of vengeance against Lou and Rée. Worse even than the stupid letters she had incited him to write and the fabrications she had caused him to believe was the fact that Elisabeth had succeeded in making him untrue to himself. Once more he had succumbed to chain-sickness, to sentiment and resentment and misplaced loyalty to a dishonest past.

He loathed how Elisabeth had managed to stir up in him a steady resentment precisely at the time when his deepest conviction was to denounce all envy, jealousy, vengeance and punishment and instead to affirm, to be one who wants nothing other than as it is. Elisabeth's own resentment, her squid-ink jealousy had clouded his brain with 'evil, black feelings; among them there was a real hatred of my sister, who has cheated me of my best acts of self-conquest for a whole year . . . so that I have finally become the victim of a relentless desire for vengeance, precisely when my inmost thinking has renounced all schemes of vengeance and punishment. This conflict is bringing me step by step closer to *madness* – I feel this in the most frightening way

. . . Perhaps my reconciliation with her was the most fatal step in the whole affair – I *now* see that this made her believe she was entitled to take revenge on Fräulein Salomé. Excuse me!'[8]

Elisabeth sent him a gleefully triumphant letter telling him how much she was enjoying this 'brisk and jolly war'. It led him to observe wearily that he was not made to be anyone's enemy, not even Elisabeth's.

Previously he had cut all communication with his mother and Elisabeth. If he did so again, this would be another negative act, a nay-saying. Instead, he would keep contact in a neutral way, send letters reporting on his laundry needs and requesting small items, like sausages. This would be a yea-saying. He would retain his integrity, while sustaining the illusion of a connection.

But this convenient compromise was soon upset. In September he received an urgent call from Franziska, summoning him to return home to Naumburg. Elisabeth, the stubborn Llama, was talking of going to Paraguay to throw in her lot with the anti-Semitic agitator Bernhard Förster.

Franziska did not want to lose her housekeeper-daughter. And Nietzsche was appalled by the idea of Elisabeth joining her future to a ranting demagogue whose moral and political views he abhorred. Besides, it lent a whole new layer of dishonesty to Elisabeth's rapprochement with him over the past year: all the time of the supposed reconciliation in Rome and afterwards, she had been hiding from him that she was corresponding with the tin-pot racist whom she knew he despised. 'I do not have his enthusiasm for "things German", and even less for keeping this "glorious" race *pure*. On the contrary, on the contrary –'[9]

Bernhard Förster was a year older than Nietzsche, a handsome, upstanding blood-and-soil patriot of military carriage and correct tailoring. He was notably hirsute: exceptionally thick combed-back brown hair sprang from a high V-shaped forehead. His eyebrows jutted, his fine moustaches maintained a perfect horizontal. From his chin flowed the long, wavy brown beard of an Old Testament prophet, though he would not have enjoyed the Semitic comparison. His eyes were unsettling, their irises almost transparent; the colour of glacier ice. The eyes of an idealist fixed on far horizons. He was a fanatical proselytiser for open-air hiking, vegetarianism, the health-giving properties of gymnastics, and the abolition of alcohol and vivisection. A man of strongly held convictions rather than a man of intellect, he dreamed, like Nietzsche and Wagner, of remaking Germany, but while they both envisaged accomplishing this through cultural means, Förster's approach was racial. The Jewish race constituted a parasite on the body of the German people. Purity of blood must be restored.

Förster and Elisabeth had known each other vaguely for some years through their mothers, both Naumburg widows and pillars of the church. Elisabeth had no reason to pursue the acquaintanceship until the failure of her stint as housekeeper for her brother in Basle brought it home to her that she could neither count on a future with him, nor on marriage to any of his immediate circle. A dreary future caring for her elderly mother stretched before her. Ageing spinsters, however virtuous, commanded neither power nor social status in Naumburg. She must find a husband without delay.

She had met Förster at the Bayreuth Festival of 1876. Afterwards in Naumburg she took the trouble to dazzle him. She initiated a correspondence based on her fervent support of his cause. 'All my knowledge is but a weak reflection of your own tremendous mind . . . My talents are practical. That is why all your plans and magnificent ideas excite me: they can be translated into actions.'[10]

Once she started on the correspondence, it is comical to trace how quickly she infuses her letters with the personality of a jolly, gallant, madcap girl, ever more warmly devoted to Förster and to his politics. He remained correct, formal and myopically unaware of what was going on. Eventually she had to catch his attention by sending him money for the anti-Semitic cause and talking up her own fortune. Even so, it took him a long time to understand that he was being offered a bride whose dowry was sufficient for the realisation of his dream.

In May 1880, Förster sent her a copy of the anti-Semitic petition he was planning to present to Bismarck. He asked her to collect signatures.

She collected with a will. The petition begged that the Jews who were 'destroying Germany' be deprived of their vote, excluded from the legal and medical professions, and that further Jewish immigration be halted and those un-naturalised be expelled in the name of the purification and rebirth of the human race and the preservation of human culture. A total of 267,000 signatures were collected. The petition was ostentatiously transported through the streets of Berlin by horse and carriage, to be presented to Bismarck, who refused it. A year later, a furious and frustrated Förster launched into an anti-Semitic tirade on a Berlin tram that led to a bloody fist fight, causing him to lose his teaching job at the *Gymnasium*, whereupon he co-founded the Deutscher Volksverein (German People's Party), a thuggish, racist party spouting nationalism and misapplied evolutionary theory. German soil had been forever polluted by the sons of Abraham and worshippers of the Golden Calf. The Volksverein party would set up a New Germany, a colony of pure-blooded Aryans on soil that had never previously been racially contaminated. He spent two years wandering South America, searching for the ideal spot.

Elisabeth corresponded with him regularly. When he told her that five thousand marks might purchase a handsome piece of land in Paraguay, she offered to send him the sum, coyly apologising lest a gift of money insult him. Upset by the hardness of his life in Paraguay, she offered him eight hundred marks so that he could hire a servant. 'In the Middle Ages people gave the tenth of their possessions to the Church as a mark of their respect for the highest ideals. Why should you refuse to accept my offering?' She went on to inform him that her fortune comprised twenty-eight thousand marks. In case he had missed the point, she described herself as a very practical woman and an excellent housewife, just the sort of helpmeet, in fact, desperately needed by a brave pioneer. She judged him well. Her money was not sufficient to finance the entire venture but it was far more than any other believers had yet offered.

Förster returned to Germany. He recruited colonists. He wrote pamphlets. He undertook tours of the country. He gave speeches whose scripts, like the scripts of all good rabble-rousers, included 'Applause!' or 'Lively applause!' at appropriate points.

Wagner had refused to sign Förster's 1880 petition. Though Wagner had his own anti-Semitic prejudices, he had nothing but contempt for the man, considering him tiresome, uncultured and not very intelligent. But this was not the general view in Bayreuth, where Nietzsche's old enemy Hans von Wolzogen, the editor of *Bayreuther Blätter*, was delighted to give Förster a platform to publish his ridiculous articles (the one on education proposed that all existing girls' schools should be shut down by the police on the first day his party came to power). The newspaper opened up useful access to the Bayreuth Patrons' Societies up and down Germany. This became Förster's main network, providing the audiences for his applause-prompted speeches.

September 1883 was an unhappy month in Naumburg. While Nietzsche and his mother were united in trying to dissuade Elisabeth from throwing in her lot with Förster, his mother and Elisabeth joined against Nietzsche in a campaign to get him to cease his blasphemous philosophising, take up a respectable life and return to university teaching. Might he not also cease to associate with people who were 'not nice'?

Franziska and Elisabeth were hounding him, he was having no effect on the obstinate Llama's decision to marry the appalling Förster and he had spent a whole month enduring her insufferable racism and blinkered self-righteousness. It was time to leave.

On 5 October, he left for Basle, where he could always count on sound advice concerning Elisabeth and his finances from the Overbecks.

Somewhat restored, he departed to winter by the sea. Though still spellbound by the idea of Columbus's discovery of new worlds, he returned to Genoa only perfunctorily before moving on. He gave as his reason (which was patently untrue) that he was too well-known in the city to enjoy the 'azure solitude' necessary to creativity.

He settled in Nice, where he took a little room in the modest Pension de Genève on the petite rue St Etienne. He loved the hills behind Nice for their stern wind. He praised the wind as a redeemer from earthly gravity. Sometimes he took the train or tram along the coastline through St Jean Cap Ferrat and Villefranche, clambering up the rugged heights from which he could see, or imagined he could see, the dark blue smudge of Corsica interrupting the glossy horizon of the sea. He placed great significance on the fact that his pulse beat at the same rate as Napoleon's: a slow, inexorable sixty to the minute. In this brisk landscape, with Napoleon taking Columbus's place as the Argonaut of the spirit, he was again visited by whirlwind inspiration. It gave him the third part of *Zarathustra* over another period of roughly ten days.

Zarathustra travels by ship from the Isles of the Blessed across the sea. Eventually he reaches the original town that he visited in the first book, but it is no more receptive or fruitful than it was the first time around. He returns to his cave, where he enlarges on the idea of the eternal recurrence as the great affirmation of life that is sufficient to generate huge joy in the present, thus conquering nihilism. He ends the book – which he thought would be the final book of Zarathustra – with a blasphemous parody of the last book of the New Testament, the Revelation of St John the Divine. He calls it 'The Seven Seals' and it consists of an ecstatic and mystical poem of seven verses celebrating his marriage to Eternity in a nuptial ring of recurrence. Each of the seven verses ends with the same words;

'Never yet have I found the woman from whom I wanted children, unless it were this woman whom I love: for I love you, O Eternity!

'*For I love you, Oh Eternity!*'

He finished the book on 18 January. A fortnight previously he had been visited in his *pension* by Dr Julius Paneth, a young Viennese-Jewish zoologist. Paneth knew Nietzsche's books and he came to pay homage to the author. Paneth expected a prophet, a seer, an orator *fortissimo furioso*. Like Lou, he was astonished to find an unusually mild man, ostensibly uncomplicated and friendly. There wasn't a trace of the prophet about him. They spent six hours in conversation, during which Nietzsche was natural, quiet, innocuous and unselfconscious. Though he was serious and dignified, he was humorous too, and responsive to humour. Their talk began with some perfectly banal conversation about the weather and the boarding house. When the conversation turned to the subject of his thoughts and his books, Nietzsche's manner did not alter, but remained at a steady and courteous *pianissimo*. He told Paneth that he had always felt he had a mission, and that he had the capacity for seeing images when he closed his eyes, very vivid ones, which were always changing. There was an inspirational quality to them but physical discomfort, such as illness, turned them ugly, frightening and unpleasant.[11]

Nietzsche made another new acquaintance just a couple of months after he had finished the third part of *Zarathustra*. She confirms that he was as unassuming and self-effacing as Julius Paneth had discovered. Resa von Schirnhofer[12] was a wealthy twenty-nine-year-old feminist who had travelled to Nice having just finished her first semester of study at the University of Zurich, one of the first universities to admit women students. In due course, Resa would write a doctoral thesis comparing the philosophical systems of Schelling and Spinoza. She came to Nice at the suggestion of Malwida von Meysenbug, who had not entirely given up on finding Nietzsche a bride.

Resa took up Malwida's introduction with mixed feelings. She admired *The Birth of Tragedy* but she had seen the notorious photograph of Nietzsche and Rée harnessed to Lou's cart. She was among the many to whom Lou had shown it at the Bayreuth Festival of 1882, and her reservations concerning the photograph led to a certain embarrassment on meeting Nietzsche, but her doubts were dispelled almost immediately by 'his serious professorial appearance' and his guileless sincerity. During the ten days she spent on the Riviera between 3 and 13 April 1884, they were together most of the time.

By now, Part III of *Zarathustra* had been finished and sent off to the printer. Nietzsche might be expected to speak only of himself and his work but instead, he took great interest in her reading programme. He recommended many French authors: the brothers Goncourt, Saint-Simon on history, Taine on the French Revolution and Stendhal's *Le Rouge et le Noir*. He told her that Stendhal had announced 'with astounding certainty' that he would become famous forty years later and Nietzsche fully expected the same to happen to him.

However great the mental distance was between the philosopher and the student, she found him above all kind, natural, humorous and very human. He was a person of exquisite sensitivity, tenderness and courtesy. He was scrupulously well mannered towards everybody he met, but even more so to ladies old and young. It made him a popular guest at the Pension de Genève, where they referred to him as 'the dear, half-blind professor' and performed small kindnesses for him that might make his life easier. Resa soon felt so free with him that she chattered about anything. When she told him that she sometimes had interesting dreams, he solemnly advised her to keep paper and pencil on hand at night, as he did himself. He placed importance on dreams and the significance of nocturnal thoughts, 'since at night we are often visited by rare thoughts, which we should record immediately on awakening in the night, for by morning we can usually not find them again, they have fluttered away with the nocturnal darkness'.[13]

While it was an affectionate relationship, it was no more than that. Nietzsche's passions were not ignited as they had been by Lou. Resa and Nietzsche did not argue as equals. There was a communion but not a kindred intelligence. She brought out in him the teacher who had so enjoyed instructing young minds at the *Pädagogium*. He spoke to her seriously but carefully so as not to overextend her. In a conversation on objectivity, he warned her that it was impossible to be free of prejudices. She must always be aware of that. One discards prejudices only to fall into new ones.

He gave her a present of the three parts of *Zarathustra* inscribed '*In nova fert animus*' ('The spirit carries one to new things'). He took her on the walk up Mont Boron that had been one of his inspirational walks during the composition of *Zarathustra* III. Even here, he did not play the mystic or the didact. Clouds of butterflies rose from the fragrant thyme at their passing. Below them, the green curl of Nice's Baie des Anges scintillated with white-painted ships. He talked of them taking the boat to Corsica.

When they had nearly reached the top, French sentries blocked their steps and turned them back. They had strayed onto forbidden ground, trespassed on Fort du Mont Alban, the ancient fortification that had kept lookout over the territorial squabbles between France and Italy throughout the previous three hundred years. Nietzsche was delighted by this toy-soldier encounter. His excited mood was further heightened by the sudden rise of a mistral wind that dispelled the clouds and their electricity, leaving the blue sky clear and free. He led her down to a little café, where he introduced her to vermouth. He accompanied her nose-wrinkling sips with a whimsical commentary in rhyming couplets on their adventure in the ridiculous world around them, starting with the subject of the *bewachte Berg*, the well-guarded mountain.

He invited her to accompany him to a bullfight in Nice. She had her reservations, but he assured her that here the *corrida* was governed by an official regulation that prohibited the use of horses, or the killing of bulls. The six bulls that succeeded each other in the ring seemed to know the rules just as well as the matadors. Soon the tame skirmishes seemed so absurd that both were seized by uncontrollable laughter. When the primitive orchestra struck up the music from *Carmen,* it had an electrifying effect on Nietzsche. In an instant, he travelled from hysterical laughter to ecstasy. He called her attention to the pulsating rhythms and she understood the power the music exercised over him. It stirred her blood as well, and she wrote that she was surprised it raised, even in her animal-loving soul, a strong desire to see a real *corrida de toros* with its stylised cruelty and wild, Dionysian glorification of heroic death.

He recited 'The Tomb Song' to her and he asked her to read him 'The Dance Song', which Zarathustra sings while Cupid and the girl are dancing in the meadow. She saw in it 'A transparent web woven from threads of melancholy, it hovers tremblingly over the dark abyss of the longing for death.'

Afterwards, he remained silent and sad for a long time.

They had spent ten days together. A week after Resa left Nice, Nietzsche travelled to Venice. Here Heinrich Köselitz (alias Peter

Gast) was continuing, with Nietzsche's ill-judged encouragement, to whip his small musical talent into writing an opera. On reading the score, Nietzsche criticised it almost as harshly as von Bülow had once criticised his own musical efforts, but Peter Gast took Nietzsche's pronouncements in a humbler spirit. He even changed the title and the language of the libretto at Nietzsche's suggestion. The Italian *Il matrimonio segreto* (*The Secret Wedding*) became the German *Der Löwe von Venedig* (*The Lion of Venice*). This unnecessary wielding of power over the hapless Gast was maybe a manifestation of Nietzsche's own collapse of confidence following the printing of the first three books of *Zarathustra*.

His publisher was unenthusiastic about all three. Even Jacob Burckhardt, who had understood and greatly valued the first two parts, was sufficiently embarrassed on being asked his opinion on the third to respond evasively by wondering whether Nietzsche was thinking of trying his hand at play-writing?

Nietzsche's health took a sharp decline over the summer. His eyes pained him greatly and there were bouts of vomiting that lasted for days on end. The doctors had no new answers for his eyes, or for his ruined stomach, or for any prospects of sleep. And so he resorted again to self-medication, relying heavily on powders of chloral hydrate, a powerful hypnotic drug and sedative used to relieve insomnia and to reduce anxiety. Incorrect doses of this drug produce nausea, vomiting, hallucinations, confusion, convulsions, breathing and heart irregularities: all the symptoms, in fact, that Nietzsche was taking it to relieve.

Desperation led him back to his beloved Sils-Maria, where he had made his room in Gian Durisch's house his own by paying for it to be decorated in a wallpaper he had taken a fancy to, a floral patterned paper in soothing tones of green, brown and blue.[14] The room is as small and as simple as one could possibly imagine. A low ceiling, a tiny window, a narrow bed, a small rustic table in front of the window, a bootjack that in his day often had a boot jammed in it.

There was barely room to cram in the 'club foot', the 104 kilos of books.

Resa von Schirnhofer called on him in Sils-Maria in mid-August. Her summer semester at university had finished and she was walking with a fellow-student back from Zurich to her native Austria. Resa was shocked to see a dramatic change in Nietzsche, both physically and in his conversation, from their days together in Nice.

He was ill for much of her visit but there came a moment when he was fit enough to take her on the walk to the Zarathustra rock, some forty-five minutes from Gian Durisch's house. The matter-of-fact Nietzsche was gone. Speaking fierily and urgently, he poured out 'an abundance of ideas and images in dithyrambic pronouncements'; Resa is careful to stress that although his conversation was both changed and startling, Nietzsche spoke without either megalomania or boastfulness. He spoke with naïve and boundless astonishment, as if the flow was something puzzling to him, an influence beyond his control. He told her that it set his entire being in vibrant unrest.

When they left the Zarathustra rock and turned to go home through the woods, a herd of cows came charging down the hillside towards them. Resa was frightened of cows and she began to run. Nietzsche simply pointed his famous constant companion, the umbrella, at them, waving it back and forth. It put the cows to flight. He laughed, making Resa ashamed of her cowardice. She explained that when she was five years old, she and her mother had been charged by a bull and barely managed to escape. At this, Nietzsche grew solemn and expounded on the wave-effect, often through an entire life, of a nervous shock experienced in early childhood.

Resa did not see him the following day. He was confined to bed again. A day and a half later, she called in on Gian Durisch's house to enquire after his health. She was led into the little low-ceilinged, pine-panelled dining room to wait.

Suddenly the door opened and Nietzsche appeared, looking weary, pale and distraught. Leaning against the doorjamb for support, he immediately began to talk of his intolerable condition. He complained that he got no peace. When he closed his eyes he saw only a ghastly growing jungle of ever-changing forms, a revoltingly luxuriant abundance of fantastic flowers constantly winding and twining in a speeded-up cycle of growth and disgusting decay. Resa had read Baudelaire. She wondered if he were taking opium or hashish.

Still leaning against the door, he asked her in a weak voice, with disquieting urgency, 'Don't you believe that this condition is a symptom of incipient madness? My father died of a brain disease.'

She was too confused and frightened to answer right away. In a state of almost uncontrollable anxiety, he urgently repeated the question. Paralysed by fright, she found nothing to say.

16

· HE AMBUSHED ME! ·

> By the way, the whole of *Zarathustra* is an explosion of forces that have
> been building up over decades. And the originator of such explosions
> can easily blow himself up. I have often wanted to.
>
> Letter to Franz Overbeck, 8 February 1884

Nietzsche had supreme confidence in *Zarathustra*, even though sales
were dismal and his most uncritical supporters, Overbeck and Peter
Gast, echoed his publisher's advice. All agreed that he had written
enough Zarathustra books and he had written enough in the aphoristic
style. There was no appetite for it. But Zarathustra would not leave
him alone. He kept making more notes. It seemed to have become a
pattern that he would be visited by Zarathustra-inspiration over the
period of Christmas and the New Year. He produced a fourth volume
between December 1884 and April 1885, exactly a year after Part III.

It was a great shock to him when Schmeitzner simply refused to
publish it. Political and ideological differences between Nietzsche
and Schmeitzner had widened considerably during the writing and
publication of the earlier parts. A slow crescendo of mistrust had
been building up between author and publisher, making the process of
getting each part to publication increasingly difficult.

Nietzsche had been mildly amused when Part I had been held up in
a queue behind a printing of half a million church hymnals, but it was
a different matter when he learned that Schmeitzner was publishing
the journal *Antisemitische Blätter* (*The Anti-Semitic Times*), and that this
reflected the publisher's own political views.

Zarathustra III was the eleventh book Schmeitzner had published for
Nietzsche. None of them had made any money. Schmeitzner printed
in editions of one thousand, and the *Zarathustra* books had sold fewer

than a hundred copies each. No wonder he was reluctant to continue.

From the moment he resigned from Basle, Nietzsche had maintained an almost total lack of attention to, and knowledge of, his personal finances. His wilful naïveté made his publishing affairs confusing. His main source of income was his pension from the University of Basle, which gave him three thousand Swiss francs (2,400 German marks) a year. In 1879, in a rush of enthusiasm, Nietzsche had entrusted his publisher with the investment of his savings from his salary and pension, amounting then to some 1,600 marks. He had also inherited small family legacies from Grandmother Erdmuthe, Aunt Rosalie and his father's stepbrother. These had been placed in careful, long-term investments watched over by his mother. Franz Overbeck also kept some money for him in Switzerland. When he had overspent, he sometimes applied to Overbeck for Swiss francs, sometimes to Schmeitzner for marks. Sometimes he instructed Overbeck to send money to Schmeitzner. Only as a last resort did he apply to his mother, whence money came accompanied by homilies on extravagance and dire warnings of financial Armageddon.

Schmeitzner was honourable in paying Nietzsche the royalties owed him, but just as *Zarathustra* III was being printed, Nietzsche found himself in need of five hundred Swiss francs to repay money that he owed, mostly to a second-hand bookshop. Schmeitzner promised to pay him by 1 April 1884. The date came and went. Nietzsche became anxious. Schmeitzner by now held either 5,000 or 5,600 marks, a sum of great importance for Nietzsche's future security. The pension from the university had been granted for only six years and was due to end in June 1885. Nietzsche had a very real fear for how he would live when it ceased. Schmeitzner wrote, 'As sorry as I am about the money complications, there is a great difference between someone who is impoverished and someone who has a fortune but is forced to hold on to houses and a publishing business for a few years – meaning that these assets are not liquid . . .'[1]

He suggested that if Nietzsche needed money quickly, he remainder the stock of Nietzsche's unsold book for twenty thousand marks, out of which sum Nietzsche would be repaid. This was thoroughly alarming. No author likes his books to be remaindered.

In the event, nobody was prepared to purchase the 9,723 remaindered books. New Year's Day 1885 passed, and Schmeitzner had not honoured his promise to pay the money. Nietzsche engaged 'a very clever lawyer', a distant relative of his mother named Bernhard Daechsel, to act for him. Daechsel was not optimistic. Schmeitzner promised the money in June but again failed to produce it. In August, Nietzsche took it into his head that he should force an auction of the books and bid for the ones he wanted, so that he could republish them in a new format. He wanted only *Human, All Too Human* and its supplement 'A Miscellany of Opinions and Maxims', as well as 'The Wanderer and His Shadow' and the first three parts of *Zarathustra*.

Later in August, he instructed his lawyer to demand a forced auction of Schmeitzner's entire publishing house. Finding himself locked out of his own premises was sufficiently frightening for Schmeitzner to repay Nietzsche 5,600 marks in October. This meant that Schmeitzner did not have to sell either his publishing house or his stock of Nietzsche's books. A good outcome for Schmeitzner but a bad one for Nietzsche, who viewed his books as now buried forever in 'this anti-Semitic pit'.[2]

He paid off his debt to the second-hand bookstore in Leipzig and he indulged himself as a music patron by arranging a special private performance of the overture to *The Lion of Venice* by his protégé Peter Gast. He also pleased his mother by paying for a fine new marble stone for his father's grave. As far as we know, Nietzsche was responsible for the wording on the stone. It follows Christian convention undeviatingly: 'Here reposeth in God, Carl Ludwig Nietzsche, Pastor of Röcken, Michlitz and Bothfeld, born 11 October 1813, died 30 July 1849 Whereupon followed him into Eternity his younger son Ludwig Joseph, born 27 February 1848, died 4 January 1850. Charity never faileth. 1 Cor. 13.8'.

He wrote to Carl von Gersdorff, asking him to finance a small private printing of some twenty copies of *Zarathustra* Part IV.[3] Von Gersdorff did not even reply. Fortunately, the University of Basle decided it would renew payment of his pension for another year and he decided to print the book privately.

Zarathustra IV reads like an extended revenge fantasy on all who had perturbed him throughout his life, from God to the leeches that were fastened by doctors onto his head to suck out his blood.

Zarathustra is living in his cave with his animals, who encourage him to go up to the top of the mountain. Here he has conversations with 'the higher men' who until now have spearheaded culture. They include kings, the Pope, Schopenhauer, Darwin, Wagner and even Nietzsche himself.

One by one, Zarathustra sends them all to his cave, where they will discover wisdom. When Zarathustra reaches his cave, he discovers them worshipping an ass. In the absence of a god, mankind will worship anything. Zarathustra gives them a Last Supper at which he preaches to them (at length) on the higher man, the superman. He warns them not to will beyond their powers, not to trust in him to put right what they have done badly. He refuses to conduct the lightning away from them. He conducts a *Dies Irae*, a wrathful Day of Judgement.. He triumphs over all.

Wagner, 'the Sorcerer whose music voices most sweetly the danger, the ruination of instinct and good faith, of good conscience', seizes a harp and tries to win Zarathustra's disciples away from him with a song. The Wanderer's shadow snatches the harp away from him and counters with a long, very bizarre song bursting with overblown images. There are girl-kittens full of misgivings and blond-maned lion monsters and other weird hybrids and phantasmagoria that conjure, in literature, nothing so much as Samuel Taylor Coleridge at his most baroque under the influence of laudanum. How much this passage owed to Nietzsche's sleeping powders and how much to a desire to parody the Revelation of St John the Divine can endlessly be argued. Some see it as referring back to his experience in the Cologne brothel.

The narrator of the poem is identified as the first European voice under the palm trees. He roars like a moral lion before the daughters of the desert. Displaying the usual complexity of the occidental reacting to the orient, he loses himself in admiration for the palm trees swaying at the hips in the wind. Longing to do likewise, he does so, losing a leg in the process. Undismayed, and walking on one leg while drinking in the fairest air with nostrils swollen like goblets, he roars. Eventually Zarathustra leaves his cave glowing and strong, 'like a morning sun that emerges from dark mountains', and with this ends what he called 'the terrific exuberant daring of this whole mariner's tale'.

Nietzsche himself believed *Thus Spoke Zarathustra* was his most important work and despite, or perhaps because of, its mystical complexity, it became his most popular work, not that it brought him any recognition in his own lifetime. *Zarathustra* develops the key themes of his mature philosophy: eternal recurrence, self-overcoming and becoming the *Übermensch* through blazing if baffling visions that challenge us to think for ourselves.

It is one of Nietzsche's most frustrating, teasing traits that, true to his aversion to interfering with our freedom of thought, he refuses to show us the path leading to becoming the *Übermensch*; nor, indeed does he tell us what the *Übermensch* is. We know that Nietzsche envisions the *Übermensch* as the strong man of the future, the antidote to the moral and cultural pygmyhood spawned by centuries of European decadence and Church domination. He is the figure who, despite the death of God, does not succumb to scepticism and nihilism; his freedom from belief enhances his life. His freedom from religious belief is equal to his resistance to transferring that belief to science. The *Übermensch* does not need beliefs for a feeling of a stable world.

How does the *Übermensch* attain this state? Nietzsche never tells us. The nearest he comes to description is invariably broad and infuriatingly abstract. In *Ecce Homo*, the *Übermensch* is described as being cut from wood that is simultaneously hard, gentle and fragrant. He works out how to repair damage, he uses mishaps to advantage and he knows how to forget. He is strong enough that everything turns out for the best for him and whatever doesn't kill him makes him stronger.[4] In *Human, All Too Human* he is described as knowing himself a traveller to a destination that does not exist. But this does not blight his life; on the contrary, his liberation lies in taking pleasure in uncertainty and in transience. He welcomes every new dawn for the evolution of thought that it will bring. His existential anguish can be assuaged despite the absence of the ideal, or the divine.[5]

Typically Nietzsche inspires us to higher things in these passages, without laying down laws. Nietzsche, who liked to describe himself as the Argonaut of the spirit, as well as the philosopher of 'perhaps', identifies no specific problem of the human condition to solve, but his broad description of the *Übermensch* encourages us each towards our own independent solution.

The private printing of some forty copies by Constantin Naumann in Leipzig cost him 284 marks and 40 pfennigs. When it was eventually ready in May 1885, he hugged it to himself, keeping it concealed from anybody who might review or publicise it. His excuse was that the words 'publicity' and 'public' sounded identical in his ears to the words 'whorehouse' and 'strumpet'.[6] He sent out only seven complimentary copies: to von Gersdorff, Overbeck, Peter Gast, and Paul Widemann, the friend who had accompanied Gast to Basle at the start of the friendship; a comparatively new admirer called Paul Lansky also received a copy. Lansky was proposing to write a book about Nietzsche but he irritated Nietzsche because he looked like a cobbler and had a habit of sighing. No copy was sent to Burckhardt. One went to Elisabeth and, oddly, one to Bernhard Förster.

Nietzsche was keeping away from Naumburg. Elisabeth was approaching her thirty-ninth birthday and she had suggested to Förster that he return to Germany in March 1885 so they could be married on 22 May, the anniversary of Wagner's birth. The compliment did not go unnoticed in Bayreuth, where Cosima had taken over the running of the festival and all its affairs. Cosima's anti-Semitism had always been more visceral than Wagner's. Her widowhood gave it ample room to flourish and the network of the Wagner Societies acted as echo chamber for racial prejudice across the whole of Germany.

Nietzsche received news of Elisabeth's preparations for her wedding with calm and detached interest. He made it plain that he would not attend the ceremony and he had no intention of meeting his future brother-in-law. Elisabeth requested that he give her Dürer's 1513 engraving of *The Knight, Death and the Devil* as a wedding present. He loved the picture. He had given a copy of it to Wagner in the Tribschen days, when they had thought of the knight as symbolising the two of them riding to the rescue of German culture. His own copy of the engraving was one of the few possessions he had not sold when he left Basle. He had entrusted it to Overbeck throughout his wandering years. It was too fragile and precious to rattle about among his books in the club foot. He asked Overbeck to send it to Elisabeth in Naumburg, where it arrived in time for the wedding. The couple thanked him so profusely that he assumed he had passed the normal bounds of generosity for a present on such an occasion. He expressed his wish that the future of the young couple might be more cheerful than that depicted in the picture.

His letters home were tactful and uncritical but he could not resist teasing the Llama over little things. Förster's love-name for Elisabeth was 'Eli'. Did the two of them realise that this was the Hebrew for 'my God'? Could, Nietzsche wondered, a rabid vegetarian such as Förster successfully found a colony? The English had been the best at such things and their success seemed to have been founded almost exclusively on phlegm and roast beef. He had observed that a teetotal, vegetarian diet gave rise to irritation and gloom, the opposite to what was needed in such ventures. His own latest diet was based almost exclusively on meat, egg yolks, rice, rhubarb, tea, cognac and grog. He recommended it as the most efficient means of gaining the greatest substance from the least material.

But for all his teasing frivolity, when the occasion came, he wrote Elisabeth the most serious letter he had written to her since his schoolboy letter on the question of belief. Calling it 'a sort of account of my life', he told her that his life seemed to him a series of wearisome attempts to fit into false milieux. 'Almost all my human relationships have resulted from attacks of a feeling of isolation . . . My mind is burdened with a thousand shaming memories of such weak moments, in which I absolutely could not endure solitude any more . . . there is about me something very remote and alien so that my words have other colours than the same words from other people . . . everything I have written hitherto is foreground; for me the real thing begins only with the dashes . . . these things are for me recreation but, above all, hiding places, behind which I can sit down again for a while.

'Do not therefore think me mad, my dear Llama, and especially forgive me for not coming to your wedding – such a "sick" philosopher would be a bad person to give away a bride! With a thousand affectionate good wishes, Your F.'[7]

He spent the wedding day itself on the Venice Lido, sea-bathing with a family from Basle. His thoughtful, introverted letter, together with his evident emotional calm surrounding the wedding, does seem to give the final *coup de grâce* to the persistent legend of his inappropriate fondness for his sister.

Of significance was his request, 'Do not think me mad.' In Sils-Maria, he had appeared to Resa von Schirnhofer in terror of heredity insanity. In conversations with Resa he had brought to her attention the book *Inquiries into Human Faculty and Its Development* (1883) by Francis Galton, Darwin's cousin and the founder of eugenics.

The 1850s, the early years of Nietzsche's life, had seen the dawning of the understanding of the transmission of hereditary diseases. This had given rise to the idea of inheritable 'degenerate' or 'bad' blood. With his father and various outlying members of his family suffering from varying degrees of insanity, Nietzsche could hardly shrug himself free of the idea which, in contemporary quasi-scientific thought, carried with it the tendency to moral degeneration. The theory waxed throughout Nietzsche's lifetime, culminating in the 1892 publication of Max Nordau's bestselling, hugely influential and appallingly racist book *Degeneration*, which pandered to mankind's desire for certainty by preaching an inescapable fate determined by blood. Nietzsche had addressed this in *Zarathustra* by suggesting that we must confront not only the ghosts of dead ideas and dead beliefs, but also what we have inherited from our parents that runs through our blood. Only by this action can each fulfil his own potential, becoming what he is.

In the same conversation with Resa von Schirnhofer, Nietzsche had emphasised that heredity did not necessarily spell inescapable fate. Empathy with foreign cultures and understanding of the 'other' might play a part in the outcome of a life. Resa had remarked how neither by his external appearance nor his spiritual nature did he strike her as typically German. The shape of his head reminded her of a portrait she had seen in a gallery in Vienna by Jan Matejko, a Polish painter best known for heroic historical portraits of members of his race.

Nietzsche adopted the idea with gusto. From now on he would freely tell people that he was not in fact a German but a Pole. He was descended from Polish aristocrats whose family name was Nietzky. As a one-time philologist, he was excessively delighted by the supposed etymology of the name, which, he said, meant 'nihilist' in Polish.

This made for an excellent mask to don. He was at once transposed into a good European by blood as well as by cultural inclination. It distanced him from Naumburg virtue and the German nationalism being preached up and down the land by his new brother-in-law.

The newlyweds did not immediately take up their mission to Paraguay. Franziska proposed that, until things settle down, Förster should become tutor-by-descent to the grandchildren of one of the three Altenburg princesses who had briefly been tutored by Elisabeth's father. Franziska's greatest hope resided in Princess Alexandra, who was now Grand Duchess Constantin of Russia. Her daughter was the Queen of Greece and she had seven sons obviously in need of tutoring. Eager to make this happen, Franziska offered to pull the right strings, though she admitted there might be language difficulties, not to mention, Förster added darkly, the growing power of the Jews.

Elisabeth's more practical suggestion was that it would be far more advantageous for her beloved to drum up finance and get on with recruiting colonists in Germany rather than from a forward position in Paraguay. This was undoubtedly true and Förster spent the nine months between their wedding and their embarkation for Paraguay travelling up and down the land addressing not only the Wagner Societies, whose members were too refined to see themselves as the first wave of colonising stone-breakers, but also lowlier organisations of farmers, carpenters and other skilled artisans who were not too proud to be in the useful vanguard.

He aimed to recruit twenty families. Each family must put up between one thousand and ten thousand marks. When a capital sum of a hundred thousand marks had been achieved, the suitable tract of land would be 'secured' and each family would receive their plot. They might cultivate their bit of land as they wished, and pass it on to their heirs, but they might never trade or sell it. Little wonder recruits were slow in coming. Most skilled artisans in such a position emigrated much more easily, cheaply and with fewer conditions to America, a fact Förster deplored; 'Whenever a German becomes a Yankee, mankind suffers a loss.'

While Förster was tub-thumping, Elisabeth was enjoying making her mother's house in Naumburg the centre of propaganda for her husband's venture. At last she had a job for her considerable mind and organisational talents. Every contact was bombarded with letters packed with information concerning the marvellous opportunity to invest in Paraguay. She helped prepare for publication her husband's book: *Deutsche Colonien im oberen Laplata-Gebiete mit besonderer Berücksichtigung von Paraguay: Ergebnisse eingehender Prüfungen, praktischer Arbeiten und Reisen 1883–1885* (*German Colonies in the Upper La Plata Regions with Particular Regard to Paraguay: Results of Thorough Research, Practical Work and Travels 1883–1885*). It gave a completely misleading picture of Paraguay as Demeter's garden, a place where the deep, red, ridiculously fertile loam hardly needed to be scratched to burgeon into bursting cornucopian abundance. It was, in short, a place as fecund physically and spiritually as Germany had been in the fine old days before the arrival of foreigners had infected the fatherland with their degeneracy, making Germany not a fatherland but a stepfatherland. Ur-Germany could, and would, rise again on Paraguayan soil. One hundred racially pure colonists, uncorrupted by foreign blood and ideas, were to be given the opportunity to hand down German values and German virtue to posterity.

While preparing the book for publication, Elisabeth overstepped the bounds of wifely subordination. She improved her husband's plodding prose and she rewrote his introduction. He did not like this. He liked it less when she called in her brother as editorial consultant. As a frontispiece to the book, Förster had chosen a fine photograph of himself looking craggy and bemedalled over the stirring motto, 'In defiance of all obstacles stand your ground!' Nietzsche told Elisabeth that this was a ridiculous act of vanity. Förster was furious. The photograph was a necessary tool to illustrate his manly suitability to lead people halfway across the world. There was an angry exchange of letters. Elisabeth reproached Förster for belittling her judgement. He accused her of betraying him by siding with her brother against him. It was their first quarrel. The book went out complete with photograph and motto.

It was important to Elisabeth that her husband and her brother should meet before she left for Paraguay. Nietzsche chose the occasion of his forty-first birthday, 15 October 1885, because he felt it would bring pleasure to his mother and his sister to see him on that day. He spent two days in Naumburg, and the two men met for the first and only time in their lives. They shook hands, drank to each other's health and wished each other good luck. Nietzsche was relieved that Förster was less appalling than he had expected. He found him not unpleasant in person. For the Llama's sake, it was reassuring that Förster plainly had the physical strength to see the venture through.

Two days after the meeting with Förster, he wrote to Franz Overbeck, telling him that all the time he had been in Naumburg he had felt ill, but he was puzzled as to whether this feeling came from inside outwards or outside inwards. He expressed the hope that the ghastly birthday celebration had marked his very last visit to

Naumburg but he knew, even as he put pen to paper, that this could not possibly be. Once the Llama had travelled abroad, the Naumburg chain-sickness would rest on him exclusively and this would make the chains weigh even heavier. As for the meeting with Förster, Nietzsche told Overbeck that the description of his brother-in-law that had been published in *The Times* of London hit the mark. The newspaper had reported that 'he is a man, like too many of his countrymen, of one idea, and that idea is Germany for the Germans, and not for the Jews'.[8] Nietzsche confirmed that he had found Förster monomaniacal in his focus on anti-Semitism. But that was something he knew already; he wasn't going to change anything by challenging him on that score, and so he had decided that he might as well try to get something useful out of the meeting: an evaluation of the capacities of Förster's mind. It was hardly one to respect, Nietzsche concluded, being not only as prejudiced as advertised, but also precipitate and narrow. For his part, Förster found Nietzsche pretty contemptible: a typical head-in-the-clouds professor, physically a weak specimen and far from the type he needed for his colony. He was relieved that Nietzsche had refused Elisabeth's invitation to join them on their journey to Paraguay.

17

· DECLAIMING INTO THE VOID ·

> Philosophy as I have understood and lived it, is voluntary living in
> ice and high mountains — a seeking after everything strange and
> questionable in existence, all that has hitherto been excommunicated
> by morality.
>
> *Ecce Homo*, Foreword, Section 2

The following two years, Nietzsche descended ever deeper into himself as he wandered Europe's most beautiful landscapes, living in cheap boarding houses and hotels. His was the quiet, courteous, stoop-shouldered and increasingly shabby presence that was easily ignored by his fellow-guests. Once they had wished him 'Good morning, Professor,' or '*Bon appétit*,' further conversation could easily be avoided. In the communal dining rooms he distanced himself further from the feasting gannets by adhering to small portions of meagre and idiosyncratic diets usually based around weak tea, eggs and meat; sometimes he just ate fruit and drank milk. He hoped such self-denial would spare him the intestinal blitzkriegs waged on him by his body, but nothing defended him from relentless episodes of vomiting, cramps, searing pain in the temples and diarrhoea that might last for seven days on end. Bedbound and agonised in rented beds, he was completely dependent on the kindness of strangers.

Notwithstanding his appalling health, throughout the summer months he strode the high Alps for hours on end, jabbing at his notebooks. During the winter he took trains between the resorts along the scalloped coasts of France and Italy, endlessly questing for the dry air and sunshine that would warm his bones without blinding him by its brilliance. Florence pleased him briefly with its 'subtle, dry air, redolent of Machiavelli' but soon he was objecting to the coffee-grinder rumble of traffic on cobbles.

Nice promised well until 23 February 1887, when his ink bottle assumed a life of its own and started jumping about on his desk like a performing flea. The house rattled and trembled. Other houses round about collapsed and fell. Half-dressed people poured into the shattered streets. Never before had he witnessed panic prevail. The only soul impervious to the general terror was an old and very pious lady who was convinced that the good Lord was not entitled to do her any harm. The earthquake destroyed the room in the Pension de Genève where he had written the third and fourth parts of *Zarathustra*. This left him badly disturbed by the transience of things, which now demonstrably included his own recent history.[1]

He made an inventory of his worldly possessions. They amounted to some shirts, trousers, two coats, slippers and shoes, shaving and writing paraphernalia, the club foot and a saucepan that Elisabeth had sent him that he had never managed to get to grips with. He had published fifteen books. The last had sold a hundred copies. His existence was dependent on a pension from a Christian university. Following the increasingly anti-religious tenor of his books, he expected it to be withdrawn at any time.

By his own estimation, he was now seven-eighths blind. Bright lights had always caused excruciating pain. A new general blurring, together with spots dancing about his field of vision, was providing him with daily ocular justification for pondering the nature of what we take for reality.

Seen from the outside, Nietzsche's life during 1886 and 1887 looks quiet and harmless but it was during this time that, with all the fury of the neglected prophet, he was examining the foundations of our moral and intellectual traditions and taking a hammer to them in the books of his mature philosophy.

The affirmative part of his philosophy was done. *Zarathustra* had set fingerposts on the path of life pointing the way for the Yea-sayer, the post-religious man prepared to take on for himself the doubts, inconsistencies and horrors of the world. But Zarathustra's cry had not been heard. The task of the new books was 'as clear as it could be': Zarathustra would be made plain.

This time Nietzsche would not present his thoughts in Biblical parody or dressed up as the epic legend of a hero. Nor would he bury this new book. As no publisher had the slightest interest in publishing his work, he would publish it himself. He would have it printed privately at his own expense in an edition of six hundred copies. If he sold three hundred he would get his money back. Surely that was not impossible?

Beyond Good and Evil (1886) was subtitled *Prelude to a Philosophy of the Future*. Unlike *Zarathustra*, it is a thick book of nearly two hundred pages but even so, he felt the need to write a further book, to clarify this book that he had written to clarify *Zarathustra*. And so the next book that followed on *Beyond Good and Evil* was called *On the Genealogy of Morality* (1887) and subtitled *By Way of a Clarification and Supplement to my Last Book*.

Taking up the role of the philosopher of perhaps and the cave minotaur of conscience, he set himself up in angry opposition to society's indolent, good-natured, moral apathy in clinging to the Judeo-Christian code of morality while no longer believing in the religion itself. This was to live by hypocrisy and untruth! To live like three-quarter Christians!

A hundred years following God's death, Nietzsche predicted, his shadow would still be cast on the walls of the cave. The cave minotaur would explore the dangerous perhaps in order to scrub the walls clean, to redefine ideas of good and evil – if indeed such things as good and evil exist. Such an examination required a critique of civilisation itself, a critique of the foundations of modernity, of the modern sciences, the modern arts and modern politics. As such, it was to be a 'nay-saying' to what he described as the degeneration of modernity. Such a nay-saying could only be valid if it began with an examination of truth.[2]

'Supposing that truth is a woman,' the first sentence of the introduction to *Beyond Good and Evil* begins arrestingly, 'and why not?

Aren't there reasons for suspecting that all philosophers, to the extent that they have been dogmatists, have not really understood women?'

What do we take for truth? The lofty edifices of European thinking. But they rest on the cornerstones of dogmatists who from time immemorial based their theories on a mixture of folk superstition – such as the superstition about souls – and some daring generalisations from very limited human, all-too-human, experiences.

Man cannot live without such untruths. He cannot bear life without measuring reality by purely invented fictional systems such as philosophy, astrology and religion. These three monsters have roamed the earth through the ages, and we have shaped the architecture of our superstitious beliefs in their image. Man had originally been free, but he had bricked himself into beliefs, madly constructing Zoroastrian observatories, Greek and Roman temples, Egyptian tomb pyramids and Christian cathedrals. He chose to erect an architecture of fear and awe, whose very foundation is the terror that death might lead to nothing more than oblivion. We have enslaved ourselves to priests, astrologers and philosophers. Their influence is grievous, and dangerous to man's psychology.

We must call into question our notions of good and evil as eternal absolutes rather than fleeting conventions. The place to start is with the man who inculcated his hocus-pocus idea that absolute truth exists: Plato.

The most protracted of all errors throughout the last two thousand years has been Plato's invention of pure spirit. With this invention, Plato cast a drab, cold, grey net of concepts over the rainbow whirlwind of the senses – the rabble of the senses, as he called them.[3]

Was the nature of truth really to be found in Plato's famous cave where people, chained to a wall, were unable to turn their heads and realise that the things they saw on the walls of the cave were merely the shadows of real objects held up against the fire blazing behind them? Deluded, they took the shadow show for reality or 'truth'. Thus Plato burdened us with the idea of the difference between appearance and reality. His theory of form assumed that there existed the ideal form of every thing. From the form of the colour red to the form of justice, apparently there existed the ultimate, and ultimately unknowable, benchmark for every object and quality. Schopenhauer called on Plato's theory of forms in his own theory of will and representation, a theory of a purely invented world that Nietzsche had already refuted in *Human, All Too Human* by grasping Voltaire's bright torch of reason and casting its dazzling light onto the shadowy walls of the cave.[4]

Philosophers are no better than cunning pleaders for their prejudices, sly spokesmen for their ideas which they baptise 'truths'.[5] Philosophers are snake oil salesmen of the soul. Their doctrines amount to edicts imposing self-tyranny upon human nature. Philosophy always creates the world in its own image; it cannot do otherwise. Philosophy is glorification of universalisation. It is imposition. It seeks to make all existence exist only after its own image. Philosophy is a 'tyrannical drive, the most spiritual will to power, to the "creation of the world", to the *causa prima*'.[6]

As for science, it is no better. The conclusions of the knowledge-microscopists provide no more truth than do the philosophers. The meaning of science is not religion. Yet science, somehow, is becoming substituted for religion. The modern world is mistaking scientific theory for moral dogma.

'Now it is beginning to dawn on maybe five or six brains that physics too is only an interpretation and arrangement of the world (according to ourselves! if I may say so) and *not* an explanation of the world. But to the extent that physics rests on belief in the senses, it passes for more, and will continue to pass for more, namely for an explanation, for a long time to come. It has our eyes and our fingers as its allies, it has visual evidence and tangibility as its allies. This helped it to enchant, persuade, *convince* an age with a basically plebeian taste.' But what has been explained? Only that which can be seen and felt.[7]

Interpretation of the world by 'Darwinians and anti-teleologists' leads Nietzsche to step back from his earlier outright condemnation of Plato's theory of the ideal. It at least offered us 'a type of enjoyment', in contrast to scientists who labour with the 'greatest possible stupidity' and the 'smallest possible force' to appeal to 'a sturdy industrious race of machinists and bridge-builders of the future'.[8]

While humans rapturously hail natural laws, what they really want is to reverse the theory of the natural. 'Living – isn't that wanting specifically to be something other than this nature? Isn't living assessing, preferring, being unfair, being limited, wanting to be different?'[9]

Having sown alarming doubt in every direction, he proposes that the philosopher of the dangerous perhaps finds the idea of untruth just as interesting as the idea of truth. Why not inspect truth from multiple perspectives? From, for example, frog perspective?[10] Given that truth, as he has already told us, is as mysterious as the nature of a woman, he goes back to the point that the eternal feminine is incapable of truth because 'what does truth matter for a woman! Nothing is so utterly foreign, unfavourable, hostile for women from the very start than truth, – their great art is in lying, their highest concern is appearance and beauty.'[11]

All truths are only personal interpretations. We are nothing but our memory and our mental states existing in the society in which we belong – a statement that the last sentence in the above paragraph certainly confirms. His late philosophy was vengefully misogynistic. Lou, having turned down his marriage proposals on the grounds that as a free spirit she would never marry, had recently dealt him another hammer blow by the announcement of her engagement to Fred Andreas. Nietzsche never replied to her letter. Apart from an unrevealing letter to Malwida commenting contemptuously that 'nobody knows who this Andreas is', he kept his thoughts and emotions to himself.[12]

Having examined the nature of truth, *Beyond Good and Evil* goes on to examine the nature of self. This Nietzsche does through examining the consequences of saying 'I think', in a bravura passage that wobbles the very foundations of western thinking by deconstructing Descartes's famous 'I think therefore I am'.

'People said that "I" was a condition and "think" was a predicate and conditioned – thinking is an activity and a subject *must* be thought of as its cause.' What if the reverse were true? What if 'think' were the condition and 'I' the conditioned? In that case, '"I" would be a synthesis that only gets *produced* through thought itself.'[13] It is impossible to be sure that there is an 'I' who thinks, impossible to know that it has to be something at all which thinks, that thinking is an activity and operation on the part of an entity thought of as a cause. It is impossible to know that what is designated as 'thinking' has already been determined – that I *know* what thinking is. Might 'I' not be merely a synthesis produced by thinking?

'Whoever dares to answer these metaphysical questions right away with an appeal to a sort of *intuitive* knowledge, like the person who says: "I think and know that at least this is true, real, certain" – he will find the philosopher of today ready with a smile and two question-marks. "My dear sir," the philosopher will perhaps give him to understand, "it is improbable that you are not mistaken: but why insist on the truth?"'[14]

That which we experience in dreams becomes just as much a part of the total economy of our souls as anything we have 'really' experienced. Psychology rather than dogma is the key to making sense of the world.[15]

Having called into question the nature of self and declared objective truth to be an impossible fiction, he mischievously goes on to point out that to assert that objective truth is a fiction is to make a statement of objective truth which must itself be a fiction.

This leaves us gazing into an endless succession of looking-glasses dizzyingly reflecting – what? – truth? – or the vertiginous perspective of endless perhaps? We are left to solve that problem for ourselves. Distrusting all system-builders, Nietzsche steadfastly refuses to build a system for us. He loves to contradict himself in the realm of ideas, and to force us into the position of the free spirit who is independent of him.

To establish whether one is ready for independence one must not cling to anything, not even a sense of one's own detachment. Few are made for such independence. It is the privilege of the tightrope walkers, those who are daring to the point of recklessness.

Leaving the meditation on the free spirit, Nietzsche turns to address religion with a typically robust and attention-getting opening, asserting pugnaciously that the past almost-two-thousand years had overseen the protracted suicide of reason by means of the imposition of religious doctrine upon the individual. Through his own personal experience of the conflict between self-realisation and self-abnegation to religious doctrine, Nietzsche feels entitled to conclude that the first human sacrifice to religion is the sacrifice of one's own true nature.

How did we willingly adopt the Judeo-Christian values that turned us into obedient cattle? Why did we adopt what Nietzsche calls the slave morality? He takes the term from the fact that historically Jews and Christians were slaves, first in Babylon, then under the Roman Empire. Powerless to impose their will upon the world but lusting after power, the slaves were eaten up with resentment against their masters. Asserting their only possible revenge, they inverted values by incorporating their grievances into a religion that imposed glorification on their own miserable and suffering condition.[16]

Sensuality and lust for power were demonised. The words 'riches' and 'power' became synonyms for evil. Christianity was a denial of the will to life made into a religion. Christianity hated life and hated human nature; it poisoned the world by denying the realities of human nature, turning everything into a conflict between 'ought' and 'is'. The morality born in slavery perpetuated slavery, giving continuing meaning to the nihilism of the downtrodden.

Nietzsche specifically chooses the French word *ressentiment* to describe the foundation of slave morality. *Ressentiment* is a word with a fuller meaning than mere resentment and jealousy. It is a neurosis, a need to inflict pain upon the self as well as upon the other. *Ressentiment* encompasses the position of the resentful powerless who lack (or enjoy the lack of) the means to purge their resentment by taking revenge. And so, *ressentiment* led the slaves to lie their weakness into strength, to 'take revenge on Rome and its noble and frivolous tolerance' by over-turning the previous morality of power and superiority, and replacing it with the moral superiority of victimhood and the glorification of the downtrodden.

As St Augustine observed, resentment is like taking poison and hoping the other man will die.

How did this bizarre reversal of values come about? How did asceticism come to triumph over the life-affirming values?

While Nietzsche both raised and partially answered this in *Beyond Good and Evil*, he had by no means finished with it. In June 1887, he began *On the Genealogy of Morality, A Polemic*, giving it a title that noticeably attests to the contemporary post-Darwinian preoccupation with the question of descent. As usual, he wrote it very quickly, in about four weeks. The book contains three long essays whose intention is to excavate the very roots of the family tree of morality, proposing to dig even further back in time than Judeo-Christianity. It would investigate the time when man left the sea to walk on two feet.

At some moment in prehistory, he conjectures, there arose some specific practice that was bad for the community. It led to the imposition of punishment. This was the moment of the construction of morality; this was when our instincts were first reined in by a punitive society. Over time, the imposition of punishment led to introspection. Introspection led to conscience.

Conscience, then, is the price of social structure and it is the toll taken on the soul when the Judeo-Christian ascetic tradition with its 'thou shalt not' buries our most natural instincts beneath the deadly burden of guilt. Instincts that are not discharged outwardly become internalised. Burdened with bad conscience, we turn against ourselves in misery and self-loathing that is stoked by the legend of original sin and by the asceticism imposed by priests. The concept of existential neurosis would come later, but this is undoubtedly what Nietzsche was describing as he drew a picture of modern man who has 'no external enemies or obstacles but rips himself apart, persecutes himself, gnaws at himself, gives himself no peace, he is like an animal who batters himself raw on the bars of his cage'.[17] How can we be liberated from our imprisoning bars of bad conscience and self-disgust in the cage constructed by the ascetic priest? The antidote to the slave morality is the morality of the *Übermensch*; the free, affirmative, independent spirit. The moral quality of this higher man is driven by his life force, his will to power. Though Nietzsche saw evolutionary theory as describing merely a moral-free means of preserving life, his 'will to power' obviously owes a great deal to Darwin's survival of the fittest, but Nietzsche takes it further. Nietzsche's will to power is both a symbol of man's potential and a parable of the importance of self-overcoming.

No part of organic life is static. From infancy onwards we are after power. All organic life is constantly in a dynamic and chaotic condition of creation and decay: of overpowering and being overpowered. The tree root pulverising the bedrock is the will to power. The expanding ice cracking the cliff and redrawing the shoreline is the will to power. It is in the microscopic moss-spore in a roof-tile of the palace, whose burgeoning into a green sponge will cause a flurry of footmen to rush around with buckets – or even result in the collapse of the roof and the regime. The will to power is never still. It is the ever-shifting dynamic of every personal relationship and all relationships between groups and between countries.

He says the will to power is an emotion, the emotion of command. What is called freedom of the will is essentially superiority with respect to something that must obey. But this something need not be outside ourselves. Nietzsche is also talking about self-mastery. 'The one who wills takes his feeling of pleasure as the commander, and adds to it the feelings of pleasure from the successful instruments that carry out the task, as well as from the useful "under-wills" or under-souls – our body is, after all, only a society constructed out of many souls.'[18]

The man who has mastered himself is able to withstand the uncertainty sown by the multiple perspectives of 'perhaps'. With the courage to desert certainties, any idea of a 'result' or a 'conclusion' is obsolete. And so the 'higher man' or 'superman' or 'free spirit' or *Übermensch* or 'philosopher of the future' or 'philosopher of perhaps' or

'Argonaut of the spirit' – call him what you will – is playful. Life is no longer a table of laws. It is a dance to the music of 'what if?' Awareness of ourselves and awareness of the world around us both depend on the conception that we ultimately do not understand either ourselves or the world. He who gazes into the void finds the void gazing back into him. It is hardly a comfortable position. But woe betide you if you do not have the courage to live by the principle of 'what if?', because then you are one of the 'last men', the three-quarter Christians who enjoy the religion of comfortableness by clinging to outdated certainties.

It is true that there is no such thing as truth – perhaps.

On the Genealogy of Morality is the book in which the blond beast (*'die blonde Bestie'*) prowls onto the stage. Nietzsche probably owes his tainted reputation as much to those words as to any others. The blond beast has become understood as a racial classification and a creature of political purpose: Nietzsche's Aryan superman prefiguring Hitler's 1935 racial laws of German Honour and German Blood. But this is a grotesque misrepresentation. There are five mentions of the blond beast and three 'blond beast' passages in Nietzsche's writing and none of them have anything to do with racial classification, let alone the idea of a master race.

In the first passage, Nietzsche is exploring how the concepts of good, bad and evil first arose in the early civilisations. He is describing how the oldest form of state emerged from the mists of prehistory. He does not say what period of history he is talking about, or even what part of the world, but he leaves us in no doubt that the blond beast who takes command and builds the first states is the savage ancestor common to all races:

'At the centre of all these noble races we cannot fail to see the beast of prey, the magnificent *blond beast* avidly prowling round for spoil and victory; this hidden centre needs release, from time to time the beast must out again, must return to the wild: – Roman, Arabian, Germanic, Japanese nobility, Homeric heroes, Scandinavian Vikings – in this requirement they are all alike. It was the noble races which left the concept of the "barbarian" in their traces wherever they went; even their highest culture betrays the fact that they were conscious of this and indeed proud of it.'[19]

The inclusion of Arabs, Greeks and Japanese here surely argues that Nietzsche was more excited by the euphony of putting the two words 'blond' and 'beast' together than by accurate portrayal of racial types. More dangerously, the passage continues, 'In the aftermath of that inextinguishable horror with which Europe viewed the raging of the blond Germanic beast for centuries . . . we may be quite justified in retaining our fear of the blond beast at the centre of every noble race and remain on our guard: but who would not, a hundred times over, prefer to fear if he can admire at the same time, rather than *not* fear, but thereby permanently retain the disgusting spectacle of the failed, the stunted, the wasted away and the poisoned . . . sickly, tired and exhausted people of whom today's Europe is beginning to reek . . .'[20]

The second mention of the blond beast comes in the second essay of *On the Genealogy of Morality*. Again, he is speculating on the formation of the earliest states on earth. 'I used the word "state"; it is obvious who is meant by this – some pack of blond beasts of prey, a conqueror and master race, which, organised on a war footing, and with the power to organise, unscrupulously lays its dreadful paws on a populace which, though it might be vastly greater in number, is still shapeless and shifting. In this way, the "state" began on earth.'[21]

This predatory horde of conquerors and masters had no sense of morality or responsibility. Guilt towards the subject population, together with responsibility and consideration for its subjects, was as meaningless to them as the idea of abiding by contracts.

Unconsciously perhaps, Nietzsche's description of the psychology of the early world ruled over by the lion-like blond beast goes back to the mythic world that Wagner portrays in the *Ring* cycle, and the morality and psychology of its gods and heroes. Wagner's gods and heroes roamed their primeval forests exactly like Nietzsche's blond beasts: disregarding law and contracts, raping and pillaging. Wagner's gods ruled without moral boundaries and without either social or individual conscience. But over the cycle of the four operas, Wagner demonstrates that even within their framework of pure self-interest, his all-powerful menagerie of blond beasts discover the inescapability of the fact that actions lead to consequences, consequences to codes of law, and codes of law to punishment – though neither Wagner nor the gods and heroes in his *Ring* ever progressed so far as to abide by contracts, or develop much of a conscience.

The third and final mention of the blond beast occurs in one of Nietzsche's last books, *Twilight of the Idols* (1889). In a furious essay entitled 'Improving Humanity', he once again rages against priests and philosophers for preaching realities that do not exist. Their morality is anti-nature and their doctrines are merely instruments for taming and domesticating man the primitive, blond beast, whose civilising is achieved at a staggering cost to himself.

'To call the domestication of an animal an "improvement" almost sounds like a joke to us. Anyone who knows what goes on in a zoo will have doubts whether beasts are "improved" there. They become weak, they become less harmful, they are *made ill* through the use of pain, injury, hunger, and the depressive affect of fear. – The same thing happens with domesticated people who have been "improved" by priests. In the early Middle Ages, when the Church was basically a zoo, the choicest specimens of the "blond beast" were hunted down everywhere, – people like the Teuton nobles were subjected to "improvement". But what did an "improved" Teuton look like after being seduced into a cloister? He looked like a caricature of a human being, like a miscarriage: he had turned into a "sinner", he was stuck in a cage, locked up inside all sorts of horrible ideas . . . There he lay, sick, miserable, full of malice against himself, hating the drive for life, suspicious of everything that was still strong and happy. In short, a "Christian" . . . The church understood this: it has ruined people, it has weakened them, – but it claims to have "improved" them.'[22]

These are the mentions of the blond beast in Nietzsche's own published writing. They are far from a call for the blond beast as representative of the German master race fuelled by the will to power, to grind humanity beneath its jackboot. However, there is no doubt they contain ugly elements which could be developed further into incitements to racism and totalitarianism. It would be naïve simply to ignore them as a starting point for the connective power of thought to spread infection.

This was a point that was picked up at the time by the literary critic and editor of *Der Bund*, J. V. Widmann,[23] who wrote a prescient review of *Beyond Good and Evil* headed 'Nietzsche's Dangerous Book':

'The stocks of dynamite used in the building of the Gotthard Tunnel were marked by a black flag, indicating mortal danger. Exclusively in this sense do we speak of the new book by the philosopher Nietzsche as a dangerous book. This designation entails no trace of reproach against the author and his work, as that black flag likewise was not meant to reproach the explosives. Even less could we think of delivering the lonely thinker up to the crows of the lecture room and the rooks of the pulpit by pointing to the dangerousness of his book. Intellectual explosives, like the material sort, can serve very useful purposes; it is not necessary for them to be used for criminal ends. Only one does well to say clearly, where such explosive is stored, "There is dynamite here!" Nietzsche is the first man to find a way out but it is such a terrifying way that one is really frightened . . .'[24]

It was thrilling at last to be noticed as a powerful and dangerous thinker. Within the week, Nietzsche had copied out the review (a laborious process, given his eyes) and sent it to Malwida. This was the first review of his work for a long time and it mitigated the fact that the book had sold only 114 copies.

18

· LLAMALAND ·

> My sister is a vengeful, anti-Semitic goose!
> Letter to Malwida von Meysenbug, 1884

In February 1886, Elisabeth and Bernhard Förster and their little band of pure-blooded anti-Semitic patriots set sail from Hamburg on the *Uruguay* bound for Paraguay. Nietzsche had still only seen his brother-in-law the once to shake his hand. He did not go down to the quay to see them off. Before leaving, Elisabeth gave Nietzsche a ring engraved with her own and her husband's initials and she urged him to invest in the colonial venture. If he did, she would name a plot of land after him. Rather call it Llamaland, he replied drily.[1]

He saw the principles on which Nueva Germania was founded as contemporary expressions of the slave mentality. Fatherland-ism, super-patriotism and anti-Semitism simply masked the jealous, vengeful *ressentiment* of the impotent. Considering their content, it was odd that Nietzsche sent his latest books to Elisabeth.

15 October 1887, his forty-third birthday, found him on one of his intermittent visits to Venice for a month of music and recuperation with the ever-devoted Peter Gast. As Nietzsche's eyesight deteriorated, his handwriting morphed into hieroglyphics. Gast was now the only person who could decipher them for the printer. In the city where Wagner had died following a row with Cosima over the composer's latest infatuation for a young English soprano, Nietzsche was making notes on Dionysus and Ariadne, harking back to the Tribschen idyll when he had been composing *The Birth of Tragedy*. In echo, he was roughing out a satyr play.

With his mind more on the present, he was also making notes on psychology. He made a list of the transfigural states that confirm our lust for life. It was headed by the sexual drive, after which came intoxication, meals and springtime. He admitted to his notebook that nihilism was a normal default position when a goal (such as Heaven) has been removed and the highest values are devalued.[2] He also noted strong misgivings concerning the master morality; 'To greatness belongs dreadfulness: let no one be deceived about that.'[3]

The only greeting he received on his birthday was from his mother. He wrote back with news that he knew would delight Franziska: her birthday letter had reached him just as he was writing 'a little letter to the South American Llama'. Elisabeth's letters home painted a picture of her colony flourishing, and he rejoiced in his sister's success even though he could not support the ideals behind it.[4]

Before they had set off to Paraguay, Förster's recruitment drive had yielded only fourteen families willing to sign up. Most of them were from Saxony, the province that had spawned both Richard Wagner and Elisabeth Nietzsche. Among the grim-eyed recruits, blood-and-soil nostalgia for the ancient fatherland sprang so strong that they exemplified everything that Nietzsche had written about *ressentiment* driving the slave morality. The little band of angry nationalists was composed of peasants, artisans and small tradesmen who felt left behind, their lives devalued by relentless industrial, economic, social and political progress. None was an artist or an intellectual.

The month-long sea voyage on the cheapest possible boat to South America was rough and squalid. It was followed by a frightening river journey up the Rio Paraguay at the mercy of an indifferent brown-skinned crew. The simple, country-bred German colonists could not understand the language in their ears or the pattern of the stars in the sky, or the unfamiliar growth of leaves on the trees and grass on the ground. Strange creatures flashed through the incomprehensible vegetation, further disrupting their peace of mind. Unknown fevers took hold of them. They hallucinated. They became blistered with sunburn and swollen with insect bites. One of their children, a little girl, died. They buried her in a hasty grave on the riverbank and steamed quickly on.

At last they arrived at Asunción, the capital city of Paraguay. To the Germans, the words 'capital city' meant a stone-built hub of order and government. But here the streets were of mud, houses of the same material and the swarming, opportunistic and unfriendly population of the same hue. Long years of war had blown great holes and chasms in the few stone buildings. The president's palace and the customs house had taken on the contours and convexities of delirium. Tall trees sprang from ballroom floors. Tentacular vines ate ornamental plasterwork.

In 1886, Paraguay was a country still wrecked from the long War of the Triple Alliance (1864–70) in which it had fought heroically, and finally unavailingly, against the united powers of Brazil, Argentina and Uruguay. According to a contemporary source, the population before the war had been 1,337,439. Afterwards, it stood at 221,079.[5]

Bernardino Caballero, a hero of the war, had taken power six years before Elisabeth arrived. With an international debt equivalent to nearly £5 million at the time,[6] colonists were a vital source of money for his country, as well as a means of repopulating the empty land.

On 15 March 1886, thirty-nine-year-old Elisabeth descended from the boat like Naumburg virtue embarking on a church picnic. In greenhouse heat, she wore a long black gown, a bonnet over a high hair-do and spectacles on her nose. (Elisabeth's squint was always more pronounced than her brother's, though her eyes never gave her comparable pain.) Sweating peons followed, wrestling her piano down the narrow crocodile-back gangplank. In the wake of his wife came the conquering hero: high starched collar, black frock coat, beard jutting, decorations glinting on his chest. Förster's whole appearance spoke of leadership, much as the frontispiece photograph of his book which Nietzsche had scorned as a piece of authorial vanity. Following the splendid couple and their piano draggled the small and exhausted band of cultural warriors, perspiring, pasty and skinny, their intestines scoured by months of shipboard hygiene.

Nobody knew exactly where Nueva Germania was. The Försters had brought their countrymen out to populate a concept, a fiction, a nowhere.

Neither Förster nor Elisabeth had ever done a business deal in their lives when they came across an enterprising character named Cirilio Solalinde who said he owned Campo Cassacia, an area of about 600 square kilometres (about 231 square miles), some 150 miles north of Asuncíon. According to Solalinde, it comprised useful forest and much excellent, fertile farming land. It could easily be reached by a further boat journey up the Rio Paraguay. He offered to sell it to them for 175,000 marks. This was far beyond their means. Solalinde brokered a deal. He sold the land cheap to the government for eighty thousand marks, whereupon the government granted Förster the right to colonise it for a down payment of two thousand marks. Should Förster succeed in settling 140 families by the end of August 1889, he would gain title to the land. Failure to do so would result in forfeiture. These terms were not publicly broadcast. Elisabeth and Förster never spoke of themselves as other than owners, or rulers, of Nueva Germania.

Elisabeth waited two years in Asuncíon while the colonists constructed a home fit for her to inhabit. Finally, on 5 March 1888, it was ready.

'We arrived at our new homeland and made our entry like kings,' she reported in a long, triumphant letter to her mother, going on to describe how she rode like an ancient Norse goddess in a cart drawn by six oxen. Along her triumphal route, 'shouts of joy' rose from the festively dressed colonists assembled in front of their mud-brick huts. The very sight of her aroused a frenzy of patriotic semi-religious fervour. They presented her with flowers and cigars. They held out their babies for her to bless. Suddenly, out of nowhere, there appeared eight splendid horsemen leading Förster's favourite horse decorated with rosettes in the nationalist colours of red, white and black. Nimbly, Förster sprang into the saddle. A procession formed behind the royal couple, Elisabeth in her ox cart and Förster on his patriotically caparisoned steed. Behind them trotted riders on horseback and behind them came 'a long train of people'. Amid all this glorification, Elisabeth informs her mother honestly but regretfully that no cannon salute marked their passing but many 'cheerful gunshots' rang out.

'A charming small wagon' now materialised. It was lavishly decorated with palm fronds and contained a red throne, which she ascended. It sounds like a Bayreuth production of a Wagner opera designed by von Joukowsky.

The procession made its way to Försterröde. This was the name they had given to what was intended to become the capital city. Here the chief colonist, a certain Herr Erck, made a solemn speech of welcome, after which they moved on to the projected town square where a triumphal arch had been erected. Beautiful maidens presented Elisabeth with flowers. Speeches of grateful submission were made. The people cried, 'Long live the mother of the colony!' It pleased her that the colonists were so gallant that they toasted her first – before Förster. After a rousing chorus of *'Deutschland, Deutschland über Alles'*, they passed beneath a second triumphal arch that had been erected in front of the Försterhof, the magnificent mansion that she and Förster would make their home. More speeches. More flower maidens. Elisabeth admitted that the mansion's exterior was rather ugly (the photograph bears this out) but she reported no end of magnificence indoors: high ceilings, wide doors draped with curtains, soft chairs, comfortable couches and of course her piano. She also, she said, owned 'five small ranchos and three medium-sized ones', hundreds of head of cattle, eight horses, a store with thousands of marks' worth of goods and twenty servants to whom they could afford to pay good salaries. Piously she lamented that she had too many worldly possessions.

Franziska basked. Cosima Wagner might be queen of Bayreuth but Elisabeth was queen of an entire colony! How Elisabeth's fine position in the world contrasted with the personal insignificance of her brother! How her list of worldly goods outshone his! Naumburg chatter decided that Förster would almost certainly become the next President of Paraguay.

Elisabeth was still hounding Nietzsche to invest in the venture. Why hold on to dull, safe, old-world securities when he could get a fabulous return from her new world? Overbeck advised against. This made for another grudge that, like Overbeck's position on Lou, Elisabeth would hold forever against him and his wife. Nietzsche tried to temper his refusal through humour by saying that he could not support 'the llama [who] has jumped away from me and gone among the anti-Semites'. This probably did not amuse her. She did manage to wring money from Franziska's faithful old servant Alwine, money that the old lady would never see again and could ill afford to lose.

By July 1888, only forty families had come out and some of them had already packed up and returned home. The overdraft was growing. Interest rates were alarming. Elisabeth's dowry and the colonists' down payments had been spent. There was nothing for basic construction and development of roads and sanitation, or even clean water for the settlers to drink.

Elisabeth knew the terms of the lease. From the day she moved into the Försterhof, she had eighteen months to bring the number of colonists up to 140 families. She wrote to everybody she knew and many she did not. Letters and appeals went out to the various colonial societies in Germany that had been founded to organise and support such ventures. But her great work was a newspaper campaign in *Bayreuther Blätter*. Through this, she discovered her capacity as a populist. It opened her eyes to the enormous influence that popular writing could exercise, and how easily misinformation can build a legend. The legend of Nueva Germania proved a fine rehearsal for the legend she would later build around her brother.

Elisabeth's siren-song articles painted the place as a jolly El Dorado, festooned with brightly coloured hammocks suspended in the trees. She admits that the hammocks are covered with mosquito nets but these are more necessary against the heavy night dew than against the few, the very few, biting insects. The natives are called 'peons'. Racists need not fear them. 'Peons' make delightful servants, happy, obedient and energetic. When the master appears at the door, they rush to be first to obey his orders. Like children, they love presents. A few cigars or some freshly baked bread will propel them competitively to fulfil their masters' every wish. Nueva Germanians lead the life of lotus-eaters. At breakfast they have their fill of delicious coffee, bread and syrup, after which they oversee the cultivation of fruit and vegetables that practically spring from the ground of their own accord, so fertile is the blessed soil. Elisabeth's 'hundreds of head of cattle' were the remnants of pre-war herds that had run wild following their owners' death in the War of the Triple Alliance. When tamed, the cows were useful to the vegetarian colony for milk, butter and cheese, but roaming feral bulls presented a continuing problem.

Elisabeth's nemesis arrived in March 1888, in the person of a tailor of peasant stock named Julius Klingbeil. A true believer, he had paid five thousand marks to follow his hero, Bernhard Förster.

On arrival, Klingbeil discovered that things were very different from the stories Elisabeth told in her articles. The climate was cruel, the mosquitos ruthless. Tropical insects conferred nameless, ghastly fevers. The much-praised soil was infertile and backbreaking to cultivate. The Paraguayan servants were idle, sullen, resentful, insubordinate, given to lounging about and addicted to yerba maté tea. Each colonist had paid for a patch about a mile from the next. They were prey to loneliness, boredom, depression, sickness and malnutrition. Meaning had vanished from their lives. Many were unmanned by inertia and terror as they tried to make a new life to a horror-movie soundtrack of roars, growls and screams of jaguars, pumas, tapirs, wild boar, wild bulls, howler monkeys and unidentifiable others. Boa constrictors dangled from the trees. Spiteful mosquitos followed them in clouds, attracted by their sweat. The river harboured alligators, nameless toothed fish, even denser veils of mosquitos, and a water snake that reputedly attained a length of eight yards.[7] Wells must be dug for clean water, often only to be found at great depth. Tropical rains turned jungle tracks to mudslides, and newly cleared fields to chocolate lakes.

Everything was controlled by the Försters. Each colonist must sign an agreement not to do business outside the colony. Any small enterprise, such as selling butter or cheese or little woodcarvings, must go through the Försters' store. This was also the only place they could buy necessary provisions and medicine. They had emigrated on the understanding that their stake would be reimbursed if they should wish to return to Germany but this was a condition Förster could not possibly afford to honour. Powerless and unable to obtain justice, their plight was ignored by the domineering couple who ruled over the colony in corrupt cahoots.

Like all new colonists, Klingbeil was summoned to the over-furnished Försterhof to meet his admired leader and to be persuaded into actually buying the plot to which his five thousand marks had secured him the right. Klingbeil expected to meet the hard-faced, noble-browed Aryan hero of the frontispiece. Instead he discovered a haunted, trembling husk of a man. Förster could not sit still. He fidgeted. He was the personification of a bad conscience who could not look you in the eye.[8] He was rambling, evasive, unable to concentrate or to sustain a line of thought. Klingbeil's disillusion was immediate and complete. He realised that what the other colonists had told him was true. Elisabeth was the master of the colony.

Elegantly dressed, voluble and assertive, Elisabeth skittered round the table and thrust a map at Klingbeil. It showed the whole of Nueva Germania divided up into plots. A name was written on every plot but one. She fraudulently informed him that all the plots except his own had been sold. If straight away he came up with the purchase price, he might secure it. But Klingbeil was thorough. It did not take him long to discover that the Försters lacked legal title to the land they were selling.

Quickly Klingbeil returned to Germany to puncture the reputation of the mendacious couple. Eventually he published a two-hundred-page book, *Revelations Concerning Dr Bernhard Förster's Colony New Germany in Paraguay*.[9] It unmasked the Försters as fraudsters, liars, charlatans and tyrants. In no uncertain terms he named Elisabeth as the moving spirit behind the spineless husband whom she bent to her will. The colonists were worse off than even the poorest day-labourers back in the homeland. They toiled and suffered while the haughty couple sat on European furniture, drinking alcohol and even, despite the colony's vegetarian principles, feasting on meat at their well-polished dining table.

Elisabeth was never frightened of conflict. In fact, she relished it. She flew straight into print. Klingbeil was a traitor and a liar. He had been planted by the Jesuits to bring down the colony. Her husband was a glorious leader, an idealistic genius who tirelessly pursued his selfless dream in the cause of the greater happiness of mankind. She and Förster were sacrificing their all for their loyal and indefatigable workers.

Von Wolzogen continued to publish her fresh fairy tales in *Bayreuther Blätter*, but they were too much for everybody else. Elisabeth was discredited. Even the Chemnitz Colonial Society ceased to publish her refutations.

Back in Paraguay, Förster had more or less collapsed. He spent most of his time in a San Bernardino hotel, nursing a bottle and leaving the future of the colony in his wife's supremely capable hands.

'In Paraguay things are as bad as they could be,' Nietzsche wrote to Franz Overbeck in his Christmas letter of 1888. 'The Germans who were lured over there are in rebellion, demanding their money back – there is none. Acts of violence have already occurred; I fear the worst.'[10] But Elisabeth's talent for self-delusion was bottomless. Her letters home continued to taunt her brother with her glory and her fame, and to compare it to his own miserable obscurity.

He understood that she was behaving over Nueva Germania exactly as she had behaved over Lou.

Franziska still believed in Elisabeth. Nietzsche counted the overcoming of compassion as one of the noble virtues, along with the overcoming of chain-sickness. He named pity as his inner enemy. But despite himself, he could not bear to be the instrument of his mother's disillusion. His letter to Overbeck continues, 'My mother still has no notion of this – that is *my* masterpiece.'[11]

19

· I AM DYNAMITE! ·

My ambition is to say in ten sentences what other people say in a book
– what other people do *not* say in a book.

Twilight of the Idols, Section 51

In the winter of 1887–8 Nietzsche returned to Nice, where the
Pension de Genève had been redecorated after the earthquake. He was
childishly delighted that they allowed him to choose the wallpaper for
what was now 'his' room. He chose a reddish-brown paper, striped
and speckled. They had given him a chaise longue, as well as the bed.
He knew that they were charging their 'dear, half-blind professor' five
and a half francs a day, while the other guests paid between eight and
ten. It was 'a torture for my pride', but what was to be done? He was
already struggling to pay the rent. He was financing the publication
of his own books and he found himself applying alarmingly often to
Overbeck for advances on his pension and his investments.

The weather in Nice was disappointing that winter. It rained
torrentially for ten days on end, and it was cold. A south-facing
room would have been warmer, but he could not afford it. Life
was a blue-fingered shiver and he worried that his handwriting was
decipherable only to those who could decipher his thoughts. Gast and
Franziska came to his rescue. Gast sent him a warm dressing gown
and Franziska transformed the colour of his fingers by sending him a
little stove. He named it his fire-idol and capered around it in pagan
leaps and dances to restore his circulation. From now, the little stove
with its hundredweight of fuel would join him and the club foot on
his travels.

He had written music to accompany Lou's poem, the 'Prayer to
Life', which he had renamed 'Hymn to Life',[1] and Peter Gast had

arranged it for chorus and orchestra. It would be his only published musical score and he paid Fritzsch to print it up handsomely, with curly lettering and other pretty flourishes. He and Gast sent it out to all the conductors they knew, including, bravely, Hans von Bülow. Nobody wanted to perform it. Nevertheless, Nietzsche was delighted with the fact that it was in print. He expressed the hope that it should be played in his memory at some future time, by which he presumably meant his funeral, and he reiterated the idea that, at least in this small way, he and Lou had now been joined together for posterity.

Following the review by J. V. Widmann describing *Beyond Good and Evil* as dynamite, he was now at last optimistic that his own books might also achieve posterity. Much encouraged, Nietzsche sent out about sixty-six complimentary copies. This was an enormous number compared to the seven he had sent of his previous book, *Zarathustra* IV, and those seven had been accompanied by paranoid notes instructing the recipients to keep secret the wisdom contained in the book because it was too precious to be spread. Now he wished above all for his words to be heard.

Widmann further gratified him with the information that the composer Johannes Brahms had been most interested by *Beyond Good and Evil* and was now turning his attention to *The Gay Science*. Seeing a crack in the door, Nietzsche sent him the score of the 'Hymn to Life'. He hoped, too, to interest him in Peter Gast's struggling opera *The Lion of Venice*, but Brahms was far too experienced in such approaches. He simply sent a formal acknowledgement of receipt.

Jacob Burckhardt received *Beyond Good and Evil* with trepidation. He had been embarrassed by the final part of *Zarathustra*. What on earth would Nietzsche come up with next? The quiet man who lived above the baker's shop was always inclined towards cautious disengagement; it was entirely predictable that he should begin his response to the book by saying that he had little knowledge of philosophy. That established, he went on to praise Nietzsche's arguments and his vision of the degeneration of contemporary society through the herd that had been corralled into the slave mentality by the ascetic priest.

Burckhardt had little time for democracy. Nietzsche's description of the strong man who must forge the future tallied well with the picture that Burckhardt had drawn of the egoism, avarice, violence and cruelty of the Italian princes, whose will to power had replaced the Middle Ages with the Renaissance, thus, ironically, enabling the next five hundred years or so of liberal humanism.

Nietzsche had also sent the recent books to Hippolyte Taine, the French literary critic and historian who was interested in the interpretation of history through environmental factors. Like Nietzsche and Burckhardt, Taine bitterly condemned the French Revolution. Taine wrote back encouragingly, saying he kept *Zarathustra* on his nightstand and read from it last thing at night.[2]

The second volume of the *Journal des Goncourt* had just come out, an account of the boulevardier Parisian life of the urbane Goncourt brothers and the regular theatre parties and dinners at which, in Nietzsche's envious words, 'the most intelligent and sceptical minds' in Paris met. Taine was among these brilliant-minded diners, along with the literary critic Sainte-Beuve, the novelist Flaubert and Théophile Gautier. Sometimes they were joined by Turgenev. Nietzsche was jealous of the sophisticated gatherings where 'exasperated pessimism, cynicism and nihilism alternated with a lot of joviality and good humour'.[3] He would have been quite at home there himself, he commented. If only something like it had existed for him.

Lacking a congenial dining circle, he went to visit Erwin Rohde, his old friend from student days at Leipzig. Rohde was now a professor of philosophy; soon he would become Vice-chancellor of the University of Heidelberg. Their meeting was thoroughly unsatisfactory on both sides. Nietzsche complained that Rohde provided not a single word of intelligent conversation. Rohde described sensing in Nietzsche an indescribable strangeness, something uncanny, as if he came from a country where no one else lived. Rohde was the first to detect that something was seriously wrong. He was unsympathetic to Nietzsche's new, lofty claims that a great destiny lay upon him, that he was the first philosopher of the age, 'something decisive and doom-laden standing between two millennia'.[4] In Rohde's ears, this sounded like megalomania. His reaction was to withdraw. He ceased to reply to Nietzsche's letters and he did not acknowledge the new books that Nietzsche continued to send to him as they came out. Rohde found them increasingly frivolous and unrealistic. The two men never met again.

A happy surprise came in the shape of a letter from Denmark, from the author and critic Georg Brandes.[5] Nietzsche had sent him *Human, All Too Human* and *Beyond Good and Evil*. Finally, on receipt of *The Genealogy of Morality* in November 1887, Brandes responded quickly and enthusiastically.

Georg Brandes was the foremost literary critic in northern Europe. A political and religious radical, he coined the term *indignationslitteratur* ('indignation literature' or 'protest literature') for the books that in the 1880s respectable husbands concealed from their wives and daughters, books that bishops preached against from their thrones, and that often were censored or banned. Brandes championed 'dangerous' free spirits such as Kierkegaard, Ibsen, Strindberg, Knut Hamsun, Balzac, Baudelaire, Zola, Dostoevsky and Tolstoy. He was seen as an idol of perversity by the politico-clerical establishment, who were given to referring to him as the Anti-Christ.

In England, Brandes was a friend of George Bernard Shaw and John Stuart Mill. His 1869 translation of Mill's essay on 'The Subjection of Women'[6] into Danish had a great effect on the feminist movement in Scandinavia, reflected in Ibsen's plays (Ibsen's wife Suzannah was an ardent feminist). In Russia, Brandes was a friend of the revolutionary Kropotkin,[7] and he pushed to get Pushkin, Dostoevsky and Tolstoy better known outside their own country. His book *The Main Currents in Nineteenth-Century Literature* eventually ran to nine volumes and earned him wide international adulation. He lectured in the Balkans, in Poland and in Finland. When he came to talk in Greece, he was lodged at the Prime Minister's apartment. During his triumphant lecture tour of the United States, he was repeatedly crowned with laurel wreaths. Writers deluged him with their work. Sometimes he received thirty or forty letters a day. To be noticed by Brandes was a megaphone for a dissident or an obscure author.

Brandes had met Paul Rée and Lou Salomé while he was living in Berlin between 1877 and 1883. They must have discussed Nietzsche but Brandes had written nothing on him at that time. The direction that Nietzsche's writing had taken with *Zarathustra* did not appeal. With its archaic psalmist's language and its weird religio-mysticism it was not a book that fitted with his principle of loosening up and modernising literature. However, *Human, All Too Human* and *On the Genealogy of Morality* were another matter. He wrote to Nietzsche on 26 November to tell him that he had found in him 'the breath of a new and original spirit. I do not yet fully understand what I have read; I do not always know towards what issue you are headed. But there is much that accords with my own thoughts and sympathies – the contempt for ascetic ideals and the deep indignation against democratic mediocrity, your aristocratic radicalism . . .'

Aristocratic radicalism! On 2 December, Nietzsche replied in an excited and rather chaotic letter that this was the shrewdest remark he had ever read about himself. He told Brandes of his isolation and he quoted the words of Ovid that were engraved on Descartes's tomb, '*Bene vixit qui bene latuit*' ('He lived well who hid well'). Immediately he contradicted this sentiment by going on to say that he would welcome the idea of meeting Brandes one day. Beneath his signature, he added, uncertainly, 'N.B. I am three-quarters blind.'[8]

Brandes must have access to his cave! He instructed Fritzsch to send him the latest editions of all his writings, which now included the new prefaces. He even instructed Peter Gast to send him a copy from the small printing of *Zarathustra* IV.

Brandes proposed lecturing on Nietzsche at the University of Copenhagen in the spring. This provoked a splutter of letters acquainting Brandes with the facts behind each book, some helpful, some supremely irrelevant. *Human, All Too Human*: 'all conceived on strenuous marches, perfect example of a man inspired'. *The Birth of Tragedy*: 'finished in Lugano, where I was living with Field Marshal Moltke's family'.

He enclosed a curriculum vitae of rare eccentricity.

'I was born on October 15, 1844, on the battlefield of Lützen. The first name I heard was that of Gustavus Adolfus.[9] My ancestors were Polish noblemen (Niëzky) . . . Abroad I am usually taken for a Pole; this very winter the visitors' list at Nice entered me *comme Polonais* [as Polish]. I am told my head occurs in Matejko's pictures . . . In the winter of 1868–1869 the University of Basel offered me a professorship; I was as yet not even a Doctor . . . From Easter 1869 to 1879 I was at Basel; I was obliged to give up my rights as a German subject, since as an officer (Horse Artillery) I should have been called up too frequently and my academic duties would have been interfered with. I am none the less master of two weapons, the sabre and the cannon . . . from the earliest days of my Basel existence an indescribably close intimacy sprang up between me and Richard and Cosima Wagner, who were then living on their estate of Tribschen, near Lucerne, as though on an island, and were cut off from all former ties. For some years we had everything, great and small, in common, a confidence without bounds . . . As a result of these relations I came to know a large circle of persons (and "personesses"), in fact pretty nearly everything that grows between Paris and Petersburg. By about 1876 my health became worse . . . till it reached such a climax of habitual suffering, that at that time, I had 200 days of torment in the year. The trouble must have been due entirely to local causes, there is no neuropathic basis for it of any sort. I have never had a symptom of mental disturbance; not even of fever, nor of fainting. My pulse was at that time as slow as that of the first Napoleon (= 60) . . . The report has been put about that I was in a madhouse (and indeed that I died there). Nothing is further from the truth . . . After all, my illness has been of the greatest use to me. It has released me; it has restored to me the courage to be myself . . . I am a brave animal, a military one even. Am I a philosopher, do you ask? – But what does that matter!'[10]

Brandes used this account to introduce Nietzsche at the start of two lectures he gave in April 1888 at Copenhagen University on '*Friedrich Nietzsche, En Afhandling om aristokratisk Radikalisme*' ('Friedrich

Nietzsche, A Discussion of Aristocratic Radicalism'). The lectures were open to the general public. Such was Brandes's authority and reputation that over three hundred people came to hear him talk about the unknown philosopher.

'My principal reason for calling attention to him is that Scandinavian literature seems to have been living quite long enough on the ideas that were put forward and discussed in the last decade,' the final lecture concluded. 'A little Darwinism, a little emancipation of woman, a little morality of happiness, a little freethought, a little worship of democracy etc. Great art demands intellects that stand on a level with the most individual personalities of contemporary thought, in exceptionality, in independence, in defiance and in aristocratic self-supremacy.'

The theatre erupted. The applause was certainly not for himself, Brandes told Nietzsche. This was extremely gratifying. It led Nietzsche to ponder whether the Danes' understanding of the idea of the master morality was due to their familiarity with the Icelandic sagas.

He wrote to all his friends, telling them the wonderful news of this great success. He also told Elisabeth, who wrote back from Paraguay with the utmost scorn, saying that she supposed her brother wanted to become famous too, like her. It was a nice state of affairs, to be sure, to achieve fame through Jewish scum like Georg Brandes, who went round 'licking all the plates'.[11]

With her unerring nose for such things, she had sniffed out that Georg Brandes was Jewish. The family, like many in Denmark, had changed their name, which had originally been Cohen, to the more Danish-sounding Brandes. It made it a little easier to get on.

Nietzsche wrote, telling Elisabeth that after reading her letter several times, he felt compelled to part with her for ever. It was a painful and torturous letter but not bitter. In it, he tried to explain the heavy task, the monstrous destiny that he felt hung upon him, the mighty metallic music that played in his ears, separating him fatefully from the vulgarity and mediocrity of equality. It was not his personal choice but his fate to challenge humanity as a whole with his terrible accusations. 'There attaches to my name a quantity of doom that is beyond telling.' Finally he begged Elisabeth to keep on loving him. He signed the letter, 'Your brother'. He never posted it. The letter remained in draft.[12]

The attention paid to the books by Widmann, Taine, Burckhardt and Brandes encouraged him in the struggle that he had referred to in the letter to Elisabeth. Rohde was right: he did feel as if he came from a country in which no one else lived. That summer, he felt strange. His body clock went wild. Normally a creature of iron discipline concerning diet and timetable – strict systems that he used to exert control over his wayward sickness – he found himself waking and dressing and working in the middle of the night. He wrote of an epochal change coming over him as he readied himself for the monumental task to come: no less than the completion of the relentless underground struggle against everything that human beings till now had revered and loved. He would write a number of books, probably four. Together, they would finish the transvaluation of all values that he had begun with *Human, All Too Human* and *On the Genealogy of Morality*. He was thinking of the title: *The Will to Power. Attempt at a Revaluation of All Values.* This time he would demolish the whole edifice, not just part of it. Philosopher after philosopher would be toppled, teacher after teacher, religion after religion.

First he must find the place. Once more he found himself confronted by the annual problem of where to go in the springtime, when the sun shone unbearably bright on the French and Italian Riviera but his beloved mountains were still frozen. He consulted Peter Gast, who was still in Venice. Maybe with a sense of self-preservation, Gast suggested Turin.

It would be a relatively simple train journey from Nice to Turin. He would have to change trains in Savona but there would be porters to help him with his luggage. This he accomplished, and once his luggage was safely stowed away on the new train he felt safe to wander off and look around. He climbed back onto a train but it was not the right train. It was not the train that contained his luggage. It steamed off in the wrong direction, towards Genoa, the opposite direction to Turin. To recover from this catastrophe, he had to retire to bed for two days in an hotel, firing off a volley of telegrams. Eventually the situation was sorted out. On 5 April, he was at last in Turin, and reunited with his luggage.

Georg Brandes's words 'aristocratic radicalism' were much on his mind. The city of Turin fitted the description. His first impression was of elegance, worthiness and seriousness. Turin was the seat of the ruling House of Savoy. It was slow and courteous and thoroughly 'European'. There was none of the flash-and-dash characteristic of Italian cities. It was a stage set for him to inhabit, an 'untimely' place in his sense of the word: outside time. He saw in it a unity of nobility, impersonality and tranquillity. He praised the city's courtliness and its integrity, which even extended to the colour of its architecture in harmonising tones of primrose yellow, shading through terracotta to his favourite reddish brown. Each solemn, scrupulously clean piazza was overseen by a laughing fountain or a noble bronze hero gravely immortalised in the classical style.

To the northwest of the city, the horizon was closed by the white peaks of his beloved, snow-topped mountains. He was convinced that their far influence gave the air the same dry quality that he had found in Sils-Maria. It suited his constitution and stimulated his brain. Where Sils-Maria had forests, shady and quiet, to give subdued light to his eyes, Turin had arcades – 10,020 metres of them, so he believed. They provided the ideal degree of light for the purblind mole to take his exercise on a sunny day, while cultivating his thoughts and scrawling them in his notebooks. On a rainy day, he could walk their length for hours, without the paper getting wet. Turin satisfied his longing for an inter-season place to belong. He made up his mind that it would become the third home on his annual round on earth: Nice and Sils-Maria being the other two.

During this year he was periodically overtaken by periods of euphoria. His initial meeting with Turin triggered just such an excessive rush of enthusiasm. His letters repeatedly describe Turin as possessing everything of the best: from the *gelati* to the quality of the air. The cafés were the most beautiful he had ever seen, the ice creams the most delicious he had ever eaten. The food was wonderfully digestible. Without exception, Turin's little *trattorie* provided the cheapest and best nourishment in the world! His intestines could cope with anything in this place.

He found lodgings in the centre of town, perched high on the third floor of number 6, Piazza Via Carlo Alberto. The splendid view from his window looked out over the magnificent piazza to the rippling pink-and-white Baroque facade of Palazzo Carignano, where King Victor Emmanuel II had been born. Nietzsche enjoyed informing his many correspondents of this fact.

Adjacent to Nietzsche's apartment was the Galleria Subalpina, a glass-and-wrought-iron behemoth built some ten years previously in the heyday of the international passion for erecting Crystal Palaces. The Subalpina's long gallery was on the scale of a railway station without all the tiresome bother of trains. Fifty metres long and three storeys high, the Subalpina was Turin's bid to rival Venice's St Mark's Square to become one of the great public drawing rooms of Europe. Beneath its vaulting panes, the place housed everything the idling bourgeois could desire. There were potted palms, and orchestras, and cafés where a *gelato* and a glass of water could be nursed for as long as one dared, and antiquarian bookshops that could be browsed for as long again. Most gratifying to Nietzsche was the concert hall. He had only to open the window of his room to hear *The Barber of Seville* wafting up to him without having to pay for a ticket. He wished they were putting on *Carmen*.

The ready-made public theatre that was Turin permitted him to exist in uncluttered isolation. He was without the benevolent presence of Peter Gast, who hovered over him in Venice. He was without the discreet benevolence of the summer crowd that nannied him in Sils-Maria. There were no kind people to make considerate allowances for his eyesight and his finances, as there were in Nice. In Turin he could be a free spirit untrammelled by the burden of other people's compassion.

Nietzsche was disturbed by the contradictions in his life. To both Franz Overbeck and Peter Gast he confided his worries that he was becoming too harsh in his judgement, too severe; that his state of chronic vulnerability was breeding in him an excess of hardness. He worried that this attitude was dragging him down into the pit of *ressentiment*. Nevertheless, there was no going back from the necessary severity of his revaluation of all values. Just as with his earlier, if less ambitious conception of the same idea of moral revaluation – his *Untimely Meditations* – his outline for the new work went back and forth with his ideas but fundamentally the revaluation would expand on the themes already expounded in *Beyond Good and Evil* and *On the Genealogy of Morality*. The Entry into the Tragic Age of Europe was an idea that merited several underlinings in his notebook. It was to be linked to the idea of the eternal recurrence.

First, however, he must write another piece on Wagner. The composer had been dead five years but Nietzsche could not yet put him to rest. He spent weeks writing *The Case of Wagner: A Musician's Problem* (*Der Fall Wagner. Ein Musikanten-Problem*).

The slim volume, around thirty pages long, reads as a continuing and finally hopeless struggle to free himself of the enchantment Wagner cast over his senses. It is hardly a coherent argument. The whole book speaks of his resentment of the capacity of Wagner's music to manipulate his emotions, and of his struggle against being robbed of his free will by its powerful pull.

The Case of Wagner opens by praising *Carmen* as Bizet's masterpiece. Nietzsche declares it perfect. He swears that every time he hears it, it makes him a better philosopher. This leads straight into an attack on German Romanticism as a whole and Wagner in particular.

Wagner's appallingly delicious capacity for manipulating his audience into heightened emotional states is far from healthy. It is decadent. Sometimes quasi-religious decadent (*Parsifal*), sometimes nationalistic-decadent (*Meistersinger*). Wagner is the artist of decadence. Is Wagner a human being at all? Isn't he rather a sickness? Has his music not made mankind sick? One pays heavily for being Wagner's disciple. One must acknowledge that all modern music is sick. Decadence goes deep.[13]

Finally, he does admit that all other modern musicians count as nothing compared to him,[14] though Bayreuth is a complete misunderstanding of its founder: it is an idiocy.

There is a curious structure to the book. Nietzsche attaches two postscripts and it is in these that he at last admits to his admiration of *Parsifal*. It is Wagner's greatest masterpiece. 'I admire this work, I would like to have written it myself.'[15]

On 5 June, he left Turin to spend the summer months in Sils-Maria, where he took up his old room in Gian Durisch's house. Switzerland was having a stormy summer, rainy and cold. The weather changed every three hours, and his mood with it. There were even some flurries of snow but the usual crowd had arrived, with its smattering of bluestocking women among the alpine tourists. This year, there were also a couple of excellent musicians. Nietzsche took his meals at the Hotel Alpenrose, just over the bridge from his lodgings. On mornings when the weather was impossible, he would go into the 'conversation room' in the hotel, to listen to and to talk about music.

Resa von Schirnhofer was not there this year but he enjoyed the stimulating female company of Meta von Salis-Marschlins,[16] whom he had met four years earlier in Zurich. A handsome, aristocratic brunette, Meta was the last member of the wealthy and noble Swiss family of Marschlins. Her brains and determination outran even her lofty pedigree. Ten years younger than Nietzsche, she was one of the New Women, feminists encouraged to an independent intellectual life by the example of Malwida von Meysenbug. She had studied law and philosophy at Zurich University, and during the previous year she had become the first Swiss woman to obtain a doctorate. Meta wrote poems and books and she campaigned for equal opportunities for women, though not for all women. Her selective brand of feminism truly qualified as aristocratic radicalism. She was not interested in

Herdenglück, the happiness of the herd, but in extending civic rights to women of innate nobility and intelligence whatever their origins. This would make the world more aristocratic rather than more democratic. She applied the principle to men as well as women. In her memoir on Nietzsche, she placed him in the category of *Élitemensch*: those whose noble thought outweighed their humble blood.

They talked of Dostoevsky, whom Meta had discovered on the recommendation of Natalie Herzen (the same Natalie Herzen whom Nietzsche had thought might do as a bride, if only she'd had money). Nietzsche had discovered Dostoevsky by chance, on picking up a French translation of *Notes from Underground* in a bookshop. Like his chance discovery of Schopenhauer when he was twenty-one and, later, Stendhal when he was thirty-five, Dostoevsky made a lightning-strike connection. Dostoevsky's words were 'really a piece of music, *very* foreign, very un-German music' and his psychological insight had the power of genius.[17] The first book led Nietzsche on to seek out more. He went on to read *The House of the Dead*, again in French translation. Dostoevsky's moving and unsparing description of his years of exile and imprisonment in Siberia had a powerful effect on him. 'Build your homes by Vesuvius,' Nietzsche had cried, and Dostoevsky had done just this. He was a demon of truth, a demon of lucidity, a feral savage, an Argonaut of the spirit, a man whose suffering had equalled Nietzsche's own. Dostoevsky's supreme humiliation through long years of imprisonment equalled Nietzsche's enduring humiliation through his long years of illness and literary neglect.

Dostoevsky had all this in common with Nietzsche, together with a thorough knowledge of the gospels that was equal to Nietzsche's own. He was capable of presenting raw Christianity, Ur-Christianity, the sacred religious state before it had been robbed of its innocence by later interference and interpretation. Dostoevsky was a holy anarchist. He understood that the true psychology of the Redeemer had nothing to do with priests, with state religion or with orderliness. It had nothing to do with the vindictiveness of the slave morality. Attempts to justify it 'scientifically' were supremely irrelevant. Christianity had been perverted by such things. Nietzsche felt they shared the opinion that Christianity had been polluted by its legacy, which was called 'religion'. It had been compromised by the necessity to live in the world, a necessity that could not but turn a Redeemer into a holy fool.

As Nietzsche and Meta von Salis-Marschlins took their evening walk alongside the lake towards the Zarathustra rock, she reported that tears filled Nietzsche's eyes as he spoke of *The House of the Dead*. He told her that it had made him condemn a whole series of intense feelings in himself, not because he did not have them but because he felt them all too strongly, and he knew their danger. Meta does not tell us what these feelings were but presumably he was talking about the dangerous and weakening effect of pity, and its uselessness in practical terms. He wrote about it soon after. Pity is decadent. It is the practice of nihilism. Pity negates life. It wins people over to nothingness, though it is not called nothingness. It is called 'the beyond', or God, or 'the true life', or nirvana, or salvation. Aristotle understood. Famously he saw pity as a dangerous pathology that needed to be purged from the system every once in a while. Greek tragedy was the purgative.[18]

The previous summer, Meta had taught Nietzsche to row on the lake and they went out on boating expeditions, during which he talked a great deal of his childhood, his schooldays and his mother. He described himself as a strange child. His mother had very beautiful eyes. Meta detected an air of sadness and weariness in him that had not been there before.

But the old impishness was not entirely extinguished. A mountain resort of great beauty will always have its quota of amateur artists who set up their easels *en plein air* to immortalise their talents. When he came across a young Irish girl making studies of wild flowers, he advised her to put something ugly into the picture. The beauty of the flowers would be emphasised by the contrast. A few days later he captured a toad, and put it in his trouser pocket. He brought it to the artist, very pleased with himself. She retaliated by catching some grasshoppers and putting them in a bonbon jar. She knew that he was very fond of sweets. When he unscrewed the lid, out they jumped. The intimate circle of summer tourists deemed this an excellent exchange of practical jokes.[19]

In mid-July, he had finished writing *The Case of Wagner*. On the 17th, he mailed the manuscript to the printer Naumann, who would publish it for him. Naumann found it completely illegible and mailed it back. Nietzsche sent it to the ever-patient Peter Gast, who, as usual, put his own work aside to solve Nietzsche's problem. The book was printed and published in September.

He estimated that every book cost him one thousand francs to produce. His pension from Basle was three thousand. Meta understood. Tactfully she gave him a thousand francs to help with printing expenses. In July, he received a further gift of two thousand for the same purpose from Paul Deussen, with a note saying that he was passing on an anonymous gift from 'a few people who would like to make up for Mankind's sins against you'. Nietzsche suspected that the gift was from Deussen himself or from Rée, who was also in Berlin at the time. He calculated his annual publishing expenses at 285 marks in 1885, 881 marks in 1886 and 1,235 marks in 1887. His friends' gifts gave him the freedom to continue, even escalate, the printing of his works without fear of ruin.

He was writing *Twilight of the Idols* (*Götzen-Dämmerung*). The title was an obvious challenge to Wagner, whose fourth and final opera in the *Ring* cycle was titled *Götterdämmerung* (*Twilight of the Gods*). The book was to be the first in the great revaluation. Its subtitle, *How to Philosophise with a Hammer*, signalled his intention to take a hammer to all existing values, to see if they rang true or hollow. If they rang true, they might stand.

The opening of the book has nothing to do with this agenda. It plunges straight into 'Epigrams and Maxims', forty-four aphorisms, among them some of his best known:

Is man God's mistake? Or is God man's mistake?

What doesn't kill me makes me stronger.

If you have your why? in life, you can get along with almost any how? People *don't* strive for happiness, only the English do.

The perfect woman commits literature the way she commits a small sin: as an experiment, in passing, looking around to see whether anyone noticed and to make certain someone *has* noticed.

Evil men have no songs. – So why do the Russians have songs?

When you look for beginnings, you become a crab. Historians look backwards; and they end up *believing* backwards too.

Contentment protects you, even from colds. Has a woman who knew she was well dressed ever caught a cold?

How little is required for happiness! The sound of a bagpipe. Without music, life would be a mistake. Germans even imagine God singing songs.

I distrust all systematisers and avoid them. The will to a system is a lack of integrity.

Ostensibly random, simple, even frivolous; the clever 'epigrams and arrows' lull the reader before Nietzsche picks up the hammer to crash it against the idols that are the targets of the book. Socrates, Plato, Germany, free will and 'improving' humanity are all attacked ferociously, with the heaviest hammer blows being reserved for the 'sick cobweb weavers', the priests and philosophers.

In *Twilight of the Idols* Nietzsche feels he has closed the ring. He has come full circle, as he acknowledges in the last sentence of the book:

'And with this I come back to the place that once served as my point of departure – the *Birth of Tragedy* was my first revaluation of all values: and now I am back on that soil where my wants, my *abilities* grow – I, the last disciple of the philosopher Dionysus, – I, the teacher of eternal return . . .'[20]

20

· TWILIGHT IN TURIN ·

Whoever fights with monsters should see to it that he does not
become one himself. And when you stare for a long time into an
abyss, the abyss stares back into you.

Beyond Good and Evil, Part IV, Section 146

On 2 September 1888, Nietzsche finished *Twilight of the Idols*. It was
already the second book he had written that year. The following day
he began on yet another.

As recently as August he had been thinking that the big work
would be *The Will to Power*. Over the previous months he had made an
enormous number of notes towards it but on 4 September, the very
same day he started writing the new book, he changed his mind and
jotted down what he called the final plan for the revaluation of all
values. Intended to shake the very foundations of thought, it would
now consist of four books.

The first book would be: 'The Anti-Christ. Attempt at a Critique
of Christianity'.

The second: 'The Free Spirit. Critique of Philosophy as a Nihilistic
Movement'.

The third: 'The Immoralist. Critique of the Most Deadly Form of
Ignorance, Morality'.

The fourth: 'Dionysus. Philosophy of Eternal Recurrence'.

Nietzsche now was in a steady state of unsteadiness, of exhilaration,
of delight with himself and imperviousness to the world. He even
ignored the atmospheric conditions, which previously had hovered
over him like an aerial dictator governing his moods and capabilities.

The weather in Sils-Maria in the late summer of 1888 was a
meteorological scandal. An astonishing quantity of water fell from the

sky. When he snatched time from the main task of writing the first book to keep in touch with his habitual correspondents, he included, with almost parental pride and with millimetric precision, statistics on the amount of rainfall. The lakes that had defined the landscape all the seven years he had been coming here now shifted their shapes, gliding like amoebas. They absorbed space, altering the quality of light that was so important to him. His customary walks became unnavigable. Streaming leaves clattered raindrops on his head. Paths underfoot clotted with clogged bunches of fallen vegetation, treacherous to the progress of a semi-blind man. The Zarathustra rock that had formed a symbolic transition between two elements as it rose on one side from the shore, on the other from the lake, was now completely ringed by water. The Chastè peninsula, on which he dreamed of building his hermit's hut, was no longer a peninsula but an island.

He too.

Meta von Salis-Marschlins had concluded her summer visit to Sils-Maria. His musical friend the Abbé von Holten had also left. This meant an end to conversations about Wagner with the kindly Abbé, who had taken the trouble to learn Peter Gast's musical compositions so as to give Nietzsche the pleasure of listening to his friend's work. For a few short weeks Nietzsche turned his mind obsessively to nailing down the difference between the ancient metric rhythm of verse, which he called 'time rhythm', and later metric rhythm, which had its roots in the 'barbaric' world and which he called 'emotion rhythm'. He put forward the idea that the 'time rhythm' of the ancient classical world was used as 'a kind of oil upon the waters', a means of mastering emotion, putting a rein on passion and to a certain extent, eliminating it. 'Emotion rhythm' had its roots in the primitive. It had been tamed by Church music to become the Germanic barbarous rhythm, which was used as a means of heightening emotion.[1]

On 20 September he left Sils-Maria for Turin. The journey was not without incident. The land for miles around Como was flooded. At one point the train had to be conducted over a wooden bridge by torchlight. Normally this would have been enough to drive the chronic invalid into agonised illness for days on end, but his spirit felt liberated by the force of the water. The liquid element had released its will to power.

During his previous stay in Turin, the city had conferred on him feelings of amplitude, freedom and pride; it had wrought a miraculous improvement in his health and abundant creativity. Now, on his return, he discovered that the place called up something even greater. Pacing the shadow-streaked arcades and glistening riverbank he was overwhelmed by the intoxicating sensation that here he had at last reached the affirmative spiritual state of the *Übermensch*. If all his life had found its moment in the now, he was content to say yes to the entire ring, to everything that had gone before and everything that would come after. The present moment contained all, and it was glorious. 'I am now the most grateful man in the world . . . it is my great harvest time . . . everything has become easy for me . . .'[2]

His letters to his correspondents from this time describe, as before, how everything in Turin is the best of its kind that he has ever experienced but now the city's noble character has been even further exalted by the celebration of the marriage between the Prince Amadeo, Duke of Aosta and ex-king of Spain, and his twenty-one-years-younger niece, the Princess Maria Laetitia, daughter of Napoleon Jerome Bonaparte and great-niece of the Emperor Napoleon. Turin's everyday reality had become Bayreuthian. Members of the royal houses of Bonaparte and Savoy processed between the city's great palaces. The pavements swarmed with gold-laced, chocolate-soldier dignitaries and their ladies in boudoir shades of silk and satin reminiscent of Wagner's more intimate tastes. The city had transformed itself into a grand theatre incomparably suited to the solitary whose illusory sense of self was tipping into megalomania.

Directly beneath a fulsome report of the royal wedding, a newspaper of the time[3] published, without irony, an article headed 'The Sanitary Marriage', which related that in the United States of America there was 'developing from the amalgamation of many strains, a race wholly new to the world. Our immigrants, as they intermarry with those who have preceded them, produce descendants of a quicker, more aggressive mental type than their own, and it is noted by Darwin that the limbs and bodies of these descendants are very noticeably longer than those of their ancestors . . . Soon we shall apply the laws of proper selection in marriage . . . there exist also . . . young men and women who, by reason of their infirmities never ought to marry.' Eugenics was in the air. In seven years' time Alfred Ploetz would publish his pioneering work on 'racial hygiene', scrambling together his own corrupt interpretation of Nietzsche's concept of the *Übermensch* and Darwin's survival of the fittest to give spurious validation to his biological theories of selection.[4]

Nietzsche had returned to his previous lodging in Turin, on the third floor of Via Carlo Alberto 6, opposite the mighty Palazzo Carignano, which was still bustling importantly in the wake of the noble nuptials. In the sunlit uplands of Nietzsche's permanently joyful mood, he noted how tenderly his landlord, Davide Fino, welcomed him back, as did his wife and children. Fino ran a little newspaper shop downstairs, where he sold stationery and postcards. He only charged twenty-five francs a month for the room, with boot and shoe cleaning thrown in. This was far cheaper than in Nice, where Nietzsche had to pay five and a half francs a day with meals thrown in, but the meals in the little Turin *trattorie* only cost him one franc fifteen centimes. A mere twenty centimes bought him a cup of coffee and it was the most excellent coffee in the world! The dear, affectionate proprietors of the little eating-houses were nothing like the venal strip-wallets of Nice and Venice. They called his attention to the best things they had to offer, and he was graciously pleased to accept their benign suggestions. Nobody here expected a tip, so he gave one. A tip of ten centimes and he was treated like a king.

The Turin landscape was superb. The glorious trees along the noble banks of the River Po glowed rich gold against a lapis lazuli sky. His loyalty to Nice had been pure foolery! How could he have extolled that chalky, treeless, stupid bit of landscape around the Riviera? Here one lived timelessly, an untimely figure moving through a landscape of classical antiquity, an eternal inhabitant of an arcadian painting by Claude Lorrain. And the air! There could be no other air of such exquisite purity. Day after day dawned with the same boundless perfection and plenitude of sun. (In fact Turin has rather a poor climate with a yearly average of 117 days of rain, highest in the months of October and November, the months during which Nietzsche was painting this picture of perfection to his correspondents.) Via Carlo Alberto has been described as a melancholy street, having the dark monotony of a car tyre. But perception is all and he did perceive, and report, a pluperfect place, and also that an extraordinary change was coming over him. The headaches and nausea were suddenly gone. His appetite was gigantic. He could digest anything. Never had he slept better. Some sort of apotheosis was taking place.

To complete his satisfaction, Davide Fino's house contained a piano. He played it for hours in the evenings. Fino's daughter, who knew about such things, said the music she heard through the walls sounded Wagnerian.

He had no companions during his time in Turin. Not even any visitors. The days were spent working furiously, *tempo fortissimo*, on the book he had begun in Sils-Maria.

The Anti-Christ, subtitled *A Curse on Christianity*, is a short, vitriolic work that hurls abuse at Christianity. The word *Antichrist* in German may mean 'Anti-Christ' or 'anti-Christian'. Nietzsche preserves his respect for the person of Jesus Christ throughout, while damning the religion that subsequently grew up in His name.

A great deal of the book revisits what he has already said in *Twilight of the Idols* and *On the Genealogy of Morality*.

He reiterates his thoughts concerning Christianity's dishonesty in devaluing life on earth against the hypothetical life to come. This erroneous favouring of cotton-wool-cloud eternity over trash-heap everyday reality powered *ressentiment*, the vengeful, jealous, morally superior mindset used by priests to subdue whole populations whom they managed to reduce to slave mentality.

The whole fictitious world of religion was rooted in hatred of nature and profound unease concerning reality. And so the entire realm of subsequent morality throughout the Christian world was invalidated, because everything fell under this concept of imaginary cause and effect. Christianity's hostility to reality was unsurpassed. Once the concept of 'nature' had been branded as counter to the idea of God, the whole natural world had been branded reprehensible, including man's nature, which, unimproved, was condemned as damnable.

Nietzsche makes it clear that his condemnations are reserved for the Church and priests rather than for Jesus Christ, the founder of the religion, whom he admires and reveres.

In an unspoken reference to Dostoevsky, he suggests that Christ, the holy anarchist who roused up the lowly, the outcast and the sinners to oppose the ruling order, would be banished to Siberia today. Christ had died for political rather than religious reasons. The proof for this was the inscription on the Cross. The words 'King of the Jews' were dynamite. It would always be a threatening title so long as the Jews had no physical territory to call their own.

Christ, 'the bringer of glad tidings', died as He lived and as He taught – not to redeem mankind but to demonstrate how one ought to live. What He bequeathed to mankind was His practice. It was demonstrated in His bearing before the judges, before the guards, before every kind of mockery and calumny and finally in His bearing on the Cross. Not to resist the evil man, the unjust situation, even to love it; this was supreme absence of *ressentiment*. This was *amor fati*, eternal affirmation.

The subsequent Christian Church had been moulded by the second-rate interpreter St Paul. It was he who turned Christ's exemplary life into a legend of guilt sacrifice in its most repulsive and barbaric form. The blood sacrifice of the innocent man for the sins of the guilty – what atrocious paganism! It was Paul who focused hatred against the world and hatred against flesh. It was he who gathered up every opportunity to spread *ressentiment*. Paul had guessed how you can use a small, sectarian movement to kindle a worldwide fire, how you can use the symbol of God on the Cross to take everything lying below, everything filled with secret rebellion, the whole inheritance of hidden anarchistic activities in the Roman Empire, and unite them into the mighty power that became the Christian Church.[5]

It is a translation of Christianity into politics that would hold up better without the last section in the book, where Nietzsche takes on the role of God by delivering a final judgement. As with much of his writing at this time, it is impossible to judge whether he is exercising extreme Swiftian satire or extreme seriousness, or if it simply represents a temporary spike in a graph tracking a mind that is growing unstable.

It is headed:

Law against Christianity

Given on the Day of Salvation, on the first day of the year one

(– 30 September 1888, according to the false calculation of time)

War to the death against vice: the vice is Christianity.

All priests should be locked up.

Participation in church services is an attack on public morality.

The execrable location where Christianity brooded over its basilisk eggs [Israel? Jerusalem?] should be razed to the ground. Being the most *depraved* spot on earth, it should be the horror of all posterity. Poisonous snakes should be bred on top of it.

The preacher of chastity is the real sinner.

Priests should be ostracised, starved and driven into every kind of desert.

The words 'God', 'saviour' and 'redeemer' should be used as terms of abuse to signify criminals.

The rest follows from this.

This is the last page in the book and he signed it 'The Anti-Christ'.

The day he finished *The Anti-Christ*, 30 September, was noted as a day of great victory, the seventh day (a Biblical reference: God made the world in six days and rested on the seventh). He spent the day 'like a leisured God', wandering beneath the sun-gilded poplars along the banks of the mighty River Po.

Printed copies of *The Case of Wagner* arrived. He mailed them out far and wide. Ever since Georg Brandes had given his series of lectures in Copenhagen, Nietzsche pictured himself as an international figure. He boasted of interest in America. The world had become his audience. He had lost inhibitions concerning the question of whom he would mail the new book to, and what he would ask of them.

He sent it to Bizet's widow, who was reputed to read German. He sent it to Paraguay, where it greatly offended his brother-in-law, who had based his entire travelling salesmanship of Nueva Germania on working the Wagner circuit and the Wagner cult. Elisabeth was equally offended. She would have got nowhere without Cosima's patronage.

Georg Brandes responded enthusiastically, enclosing the addresses of certain high-born radicals in St Petersburg. Several of Nietzsche's books had been banned in Russia, including *Human, All Too Human*, 'A Miscellany of Opinions and Maxims' and 'The Wanderer and His Shadow', mostly because of their attacks on Christianity (it was only in 1906 that the bans were lifted). Brandes recommended Prince Urussov and Princess Anna Dmitrievna Tenichev as 'superior connoisseurs' who would make his works widely known among Russia's radical intelligentsia. His advice was certainly astute. From now through the 1890s there was livelier interest in Nietzsche in Russia than in any other European country, judging from the number of publications on his work that appeared during that time.[6]

Nietzsche sent the book to Jacob Burckhardt with the heartfelt request that 'a single word from you would make me happy'. Burckhardt's opinion had always counted more for Nietzsche than Nietzsche's opinion had counted for Burckhardt. Secure in his well-constructed solitude within the structure of Basle University, Burckhardt could not even find one single word, and so he remained silent.

Nietzsche sent the book to Hippolyte Taine, in the hope that he might be able to 'open the great Panama Canal to France'. The key to this was translation into French. Nietzsche could not possibly afford to pay. While requesting Taine to translate it, he also sent three copies of the book to Malwida von Meysenbug, with the same purpose in mind.

Malwida's apartment in Rome was dominated by a formidable bust of Wagner gazing down on all comers from a high plinth. It had never been a problem for her to support Nietzsche while remaining loyal to the composer. Malwida was a lifelong expert in the art of the tightrope walk. She managed to live for decades in ostentatiously privileged comfort as a member of the establishment, while maintaining her reputation as an anarchist. Her life might be symbolised by her ascension to Garibaldi's yacht in the well-cushioned armchair that was the prop and symbol of the bourgeois drawing room. On the Nietzsche/Wagner battlefield Malwida had always managed to keep a foot in both camps but the arrival of *The Case of Wagner* made demands beyond even her tactful neutrality. Her letter to Nietzsche pointing out the infelicities of the attack is now lost but she herself described it as 'considerate as possible'. One can believe it, given her customary emollience.

Nietzsche responded explosively: 'These are not things on which I allow anyone to contradict me. I am . . . the supreme court of appeal on earth . . .'[7]

A new note had entered his letters. They were increasingly aggressive, combative and peremptory. References to his divinity crept in here and there. He started to make peculiar claims for his status and his power. He judged that there had never been a more important moment in the history of the world. Humanity was terminally irresponsible, terminally distracted; it had no idea that the great questions of value were being asked, and settled, by him alone.

His revaluation would put the world back on course for the first time in centuries. His physical state gave him the irrefutable proof of his capacity to do so. When he looked at himself in the mirror, he saw a young man in exemplary condition. He had never looked so healthy, so well nourished. He looked like a man ten years younger than his real age, and at the height of vigour.

The only other time his looking-glass reflection had told him the same story was when he had been at the zenith of his love for Lou and confident in hopes of their future together.

It was the month of October 1888, and he was looking forward to his birthday. He felt beautifully attuned to this very moment, attuned to the season of autumn in his own self and in the world that surrounded him. The generous grapes in the vineyards round about Turin had turned that brown that bursts sweetness in the mouth. So it was with the words in his mouth. He was the ripe man of plenitude. All was in order.

Cheerfully, fatefully, on 15 October, he met his forty-fourth birthday.

Surely a day to begin another book! For the world's sake, this birthday deserved an autobiography. Again he was postponing the great revaluation. But he gave it no thought. Time was plentiful. He wished to set out the whole story: his books, his views, the incidents in his life, and his psychology. The world would be allowed to witness his transformation of every 'It was thus' into 'I wished it so'. Mankind, who had paid him no attention, would at last see its luck as he revealed the light and fright of himself.[8]

Setting himself up as the successor to the dead god, he called his autobiography *Ecce Homo*. He took the title from the Bible, choosing the fateful words used in St John's gospel at the very moment when Pontius Pilate, the Roman governor of Judea, condemned Christ to death,[9] after which he allegedly fled to drown himself out of remorse in that little black lake on Mont Pilatus above Tribschen. '*Ecce homo* [Behold the man],' Pilate had proclaimed when he produced his prisoner Jesus Christ, scourged and bleeding, bound and crowned with thorns, for the judgement of the people, who then condemned the living God to death by crucifixion.

Throughout *Ecce Homo*, Nietzsche continues to set himself up in competition with Christ – or as a second Christ, another living god who has been condemned to death. In Nietzsche's case, condemned to death by obscurity, by neglect, by lack of interest in his thought. *Ecce Homo* contains an enormous number of Biblical references and parodies, beginning with the very first sentence: 'In the expectation that soon I will have to confront humanity with the most difficult demand it has ever faced, it seems imperative for me to say *who I am*.'[10]

Everything in the book is gossamer, conundrum, riddle, dance, above all provocation. 'When I have, literally, to carry the destiny of man, it is part of my trial of strength to be a clown, a satyr . . . That the profoundest mind must also be the most frivolous one is almost a formula for my philosophy.'[11]

The trickster follows the overreaching title of the book with ludicrous chapter headings: 'Why I am so Wise', 'Why I am so Clever', 'Why I write such Good Books', 'Why I am a Destiny'. The chapters do their job of telling us exactly why he is so wise, clever and so on. They also mock the whole genre of autobiography itself. They acknowledge the fact that, however authors dress it up, autobiography is probably the most monstrous act of conceit that exists. In *Ecce Homo*, he explodes the convention of concealing authorial vanity behind the mask of modesty, self-deprecation and the blameless excuse of historical record keeping. Why not revaluate autobiography together with the revaluation of everything else? Why should autobiography not be used for bombast and trickery, for exaggeration and manic self-celebration mixed in with some things that did happen and some that did not and a lot of multi-perspectivism? Facts do not exist, only interpretations.

He begins the first chapter, 'Why I am so Wise', presenting us with a riddle. 'As my father I am already dead and as my mother I am still alive and growing old.' He has a foot in both worlds. Who is he? Not a saint, not a bogeyman but merely a disciple of Dionysus. He would rather be a satyr than a saint. He would rather knock over idols than set them up. The last thing he would claim would be to be an 'improver' of humanity. He invites us to take a look at his legs, and he points out that they are made of clay.

He goes on to establish his impeccable health. Taken literally this is total fiction, medical fantasy. We, who now know a little about his life, may read this self-description as specifically designed to refute the catastrophic shape that loomed, in that syphilomanic age, over every man who suffered from unexplained health problems and whose father had died of 'liquefaction of the brain'. He goes to great pains to tell us how sound he is physically. Yes, he has had his health troubles, but they are simply the result of a 'kind of local degeneration'. This little local degeneration is responsible for the general exhaustion and the profound weakness of the gastric system that, he admits, have tested his physical and his mental system to the limit. As a result, he has grown the skill and the knowledge to invert perspectives. He compares himself to the wounded surgeon who translates his own sickness into useful concern for the health of society. He alone, the wounded cultural physician, is capable of the revaluation of all values.

We suspect he must be serious when he tells us, yet again, that his formula for human greatness is *amor fati*, not wanting anything to be different, not forwards or backwards, not for all eternity.[12] He goes on to say that when he looks at his mother and his sister, they alone cause him the profoundest reluctance towards *amor fati* and eternal recurrence. 'When I look for my diametric opposite, an immeasurably shabby instinct, I always think of my mother and sister, – it would blaspheme my divinity to think that I am related to this sort of *canaille* [rabble, riff-raff]. The way my mother and sister treat me to this very day is a source of unspeakable horror: a real time bomb is at work . . . I do not have the strength to resist poison worms . . . I will admit that the greatest objection to 'eternal return', my truly abysmal thought, is always my mother and sister . . . People are *least* related to their parents: it would be the most extreme sign of vulgarity to be related to your parents.'[13]

He goes on to tell the whopping untruth that he is a pure-blooded nobleman of Polish ancestry with not a drop of 'bad' German blood in him. Nietzsche does not suggest that Franziska and Elisabeth share his Polish blood. And yet he still refers to them as 'my mother' and 'my sister'. What are we to believe, when he assures us solemnly that he is more truthful than any other thinker?

The essay that follows, 'Why I am so Clever', plays on an obsession with his lungs and his stomach as central to the whole philosophical exercise. He becomes a diet-and-exercise guru. If you avoid coffee and live in dry air, you will attain health equal to his own. Odd that he bans coffee while delighting in the world-beating coffee of Turin. He advises living in Paris, Provence, Florence, Jerusalem or Athens. Above all, do not live in Germany, where the climate discourages intestines, however heroically they may be disposed. Strong intestines are most helpful to the philosopher.[14]

Never believe an idea that occurs to you indoors. Keep the surface of your mind free of all great imperatives and do not try to know yourself. Contrary to everything he has advised hitherto, he earnestly recommends that the precondition for becoming what one is, is not to have the least notion of what one is.

'Those of us who were children during the quagmire of the fifties' are necessarily pessimists regarding German 'culture', for how can civilised thought exist when the bigot stands at the helm of the state? Nietzsche believes only in French culture. Once he is on the subject of culture, he cannot help himself but must again come round to the subject of Wagner, the first deep breath he took in his life. He admits that since first hearing *Tristan und Isolde*, he has always sought a work of art of the same sweet, shuddering infinity. Cosima Wagner has by far the most noble nature, as well as the best taste in Germany. At no price would he relinquish his days in Tribschen.

'Why I write such Good Books' gives a book-by-book account of all his published works. As he commented to his publisher, he might as well write his own reviews. Nobody else had done so.

The section 'Why I am a Destiny' opens:

'I know my fate. One day there will be associated with my name the recollection of something frightful – of a crisis like no other before on earth, of the profoundest collision of conscience, of a decision evoked *against* everything that until then had been believed in, demanded, sanctified. I am not a man, I am dynamite.'

These words have often been taken as weird prophecy or premonition of the Third Reich, sometimes even as pre-approval for such things to happen. But the rest of 'Why I am a Destiny', which is not a short chapter, makes it perfectly plain he is not referring to some future apocalyptic event but to the task he has set himself of challenging all previous morality.

The final sentence in the book reads, 'Have I been understood? Dionysus versus the crucified . . .' and the book ends with an ellipsis, as do so many of his writings.

He finished *Ecce Homo* on 4 November. It had taken three weeks to write. During that time he had been completely alone in the city of strangers. They hardly noticed his small figure walking the streets in a light overcoat with a blue lining and immense English gloves on his hands. His head was now perpetually held at an angle as he paced the stroboscopic light and shade of Turin's long stone arcades. Winter was on the way when he finished the book, and the mountains behind the long urban vistas had donned white wigs against a bleached sky.

Turin was yet again playing stage set to a great state occasion. Royal wedding had given way to state funeral, white satin to black ribbons, festive pomp to grave melancholia. The same royal enclave of power and privilege flooded Turin, this time for the solemn obsequies of Count Robilant. Nietzsche's love of *grandezza* promoted Robilant to son of King Carlo Alberto, though in fact he was merely his aide-de-camp.

He mailed the manuscript of *Ecce Homo* to his printer Naumann on 6 November. The accompanying letter serenely assured Naumann that it had been inspired by an unbelievable sense of wellbeing unique in Nietzsche's life. Naumann must typeset it immediately.

Naumann had not yet turned himself into a publisher, as he would in time. His job was not to edit but to print the book for the author who was paying the bill. Nietzsche was now urging him to print *Ecce Homo* before *The Anti-Christ* which Naumann must put on hold. *Ecce Homo* was the annunciatory book. Its job, like John the Baptist's, was to pave the way. There must be no border round the text. The lines of type must be made wider. Naumann suggested using cheaper paper. Nietzsche was horrified.

Having issued his instructions to Naumann, now the changes began. Nietzsche added sections, requested the manuscript back, mailed it back in December 1888, 'ready to be printed', added poems, changed his mind, changed it back again. There were so many things to occupy him. None of them was the next book in the great revaluation. He collected nine poems that he had composed between 1883 and 1888 and made fair copies of them for publication. After some false starts, he settled on the title *The Dithyrambs of Dionysus* (*Dionysos-Dithyramben*). The original meaning of the word dithyramb was a Greek choric hymn to Dionysus but over time it had come to be extended to any Dionysian or Bacchanalian hymn or poem.

In *The Birth of Tragedy*, Nietzsche had taken the Dionysian to signify ecstatic abandonment, as opposed to the lucid and controlled creativity of the Apollonian. As his thinking had progressed, the Dionysian mysteries had come to signify the fundamental will to life. 'What did the Hellenes guarantee for themselves with these mysteries? *Eternal* life, the eternal return of life; the future promised by the past and the past consecrated to the future; the triumphal yes to life over and above all death and change; the *true* life as the overall continuation of life through procreation, through the mysteries of sexuality.'[5]

The poem with the most obvious connection to Dionysus is 'Ariadne's Complaint'. It describes how Ariadne, deserted by Theseus on the island of Naxos, laments her fate and is visited by the god Dionysus. Nietzsche had first printed the poem in Part IV of *Thus Spoke Zarathustra*, in the chapter called 'The Magician', in which Zarathustra vanquishes the old sorcerer Wagner.

In Tribschen days, the accepted mythology had been that Wagner was Dionysus to Cosima's Ariadne, with Nietzsche and von Bülow playing Theseus, but now Nietzsche was consistently and openly taking the name of Dionysus, and Cosima/Ariadne was featuring in his writings with increasing frequency.

. The self-avowed Dionysus was no longer prisoner of the inhibitions that had restrained him in his early twenties. Eroticism overflows. 'Ariadne's Complaint' is an uninhibited fantasy which opens with the despairing Ariadne spread-eagled, shuddering and pleading with the god. Dionysus 'the huntsman behind the clouds' strikes her down by his lightning bolt. She acknowledges him as god. Trembling under his icy-sharp arrows, she bends herself, twists herself, tortured as she submits and is smitten by the eternal huntsman, the unknown god. He presses her too close; he climbs into her thought. She surrenders, rolling with rapture. Her hangman-god torments her. 'Come back,' she cries, 'my pain, my last happiness.' He appears in a flash of lightning. The poem ends with the line 'I am thy labyrinth'. Up till then it has been made very clear which of the lovers, Dionysus or Ariadne, is saying which line but there is no indication which of them says, 'I am thy labyrinth'. The conclusion must be both.

While he seldom dedicated his books to anybody, he dedicated the *Dithyrambs* to 'the poet of Isoline'. Decoded, this was Catulle Mendès, the 'lily in urine' writer who had accompanied Judith Gautier to Tribschen.

Mendès had written the libretto to Messager's opera *Isoline*, a Titania-and-Oberon fairy story with dragons, which was to be premiered in Paris the following month, December 1888. Since Tribschen, there does not appear to have been much connection, even in Nietzsche's mind, between himself and Mendès. Was Nietzsche, with this flattering dedication, planning to approach Mendès to translate his books into French? Malwida von Meysenbug had declined. Hippolyte Taine had declared his German not good enough and passed it on to Jean Bourdeau, who pleaded lack of time. The Panama Canal to France was not opening up.

On the strength of his relationship with Georg Brandes, Nietzsche wrote to the Swedish playwright August Strindberg, asking him to undertake the translation of *Ecce Homo* into French. Nietzsche introduced himself to Strindberg through the by-now-customary letter telling of his Polish ancestry, his impeccable physical health, his world fame and the perfection to which he had brought the German language; 'I speak the language of the rulers of the world.' He further tempted Strindberg with the promise that Prince Bismarck and the young Kaiser were to receive advance copies of the book 'together with a written declaration of war – military men will then be unable to retaliate by taking police measures'.[16] Strindberg himself was not at the greatest moment of mental stability in his life. He had no money, his first marriage to the wife he worshipped was crashing to disaster and they were living in a wing of a dilapidated castle overrun with peacocks and feral dogs and ruled over by a self-styled countess and her companion, a blackmailer, alchemist, magician and thief. It was an overheated concatenation of circumstances that gave rise to Strindberg's greatest play, *Miss Julie*, but even in this chaotic context, Strindberg realised that something was very wrong with Nietzsche. Was Nietzsche mad? he asked Brandes.

It was a question Strindberg was to ask again as Nietzsche's letters to him expressed an obsession with a couple of criminals whose horrible misdemeanours took up many column inches in Europe's more prurient newspapers, including those that Nietzsche read in Turin and Strindberg in Sweden. The first criminal was the mysterious 'Prado', a Spaniard who went by the name 'Linska de Castilon'. After exhausting his first wife's fortune of, reputedly, 1.2 million francs in Peru, he ran to France, where he committed robberies and murdered a prostitute. Then there was Henri Chambige, a law student who murdered the English wife of a Frenchman living in Algeria. The criminal genius was fascinating, Nietzsche insisted. He was 'a superior type to his judges, even to his lawyers, in self-control and wit, in exuberance of spirit', etc. Strindberg, who was living at the mercy of just such a criminal type, did not see Nietzsche's point. A month later, when Nietzsche came to write a letter to Jacob Burckhardt, both criminals had taken up their place in his increasing number of identities. He was not only Dionysus and the Anti-Christ but also Henri Chambige and Prado, and even Prado's father.[17]

He was starting to lose control of his features. He wrote jubilantly telling Peter Gast about it. It was of no account! Nothing to worry about!

He pulled so many silly stunts with himself! At concerts, the music affected him so much that he could not control his facial grimaces. He wept uncontrollably. He grinned. There were times when all he could do was stand in the public thoroughfare for half an hour grinning. For four whole days, between 21 and 25 November, he had found himself unable to give his face a serious expression. He concluded that anyone who had achieved such a state must be ripe to become saviour of the world. In two months' time, his would be the foremost name on earth. The most remarkable thing in Turin was the complete fascination he exerted over all classes and conditions of people. All faces changed when he entered a large shop or public space. He needed neither name nor rank nor money for them to place him always and unconditionally first.[18] With every glance he was treated like a prince. There was an extremely distinguished air about the manner in which people opened doors for him. Waiters, radiant and elegant to a man, served his food as though they were serving a king. He was making a mental note of all the individuals who had discovered him in this, his undiscovered period. It was not altogether impossible that his future cook was already attending on him. Nobody took him for a German.[19]

The four books of the great revaluation would soon appear, he told Overbeck. He was bringing out his big guns. As befitting an old artillery soldier, he was going to shoot the history of humanity in two, separating it into two halves. It was a somewhat *frosty* plan, he noted with a touch of wit that pleased him mightily, being appropriate to the season of winter that was setting in. But first, he would just take one more little pot shot at Wagner before 20 November, the date on which he had decided to leave Turin for Nice, or Corsica.[20]

The plan for Nice – or Corsica – was cancelled as soon as it was made. There was no point in Corsica now. The bandits had all been done away with, and the kings too.[21]

Thoughts, like travel plans, were gone in the instant of becoming. In his room the white mountain ranges of paper grew ever higher. His writings past and present floated like snowflakes from desk to floor as he wrote an enormous number of letters and cobbled together passages from his previous books to make *Nietzsche contra Wagner*, the fourth book he had written that year, the fifth if you included the *Dithyrambs*, and the second book with Wagner in its title.

The club foot had at last arrived from Nice. Now he could read his own books. They were magnificent. He was overcome by admiration for his own brilliance. It was uncanny how his thoughts had power over physical events. There were no coincidences any more. He only had to think of a person for a letter from them to arrive politely through the door. When he considered the tremendous things he had perpetrated between 3 September and 4 November, he thought it very probable there would soon be an earthquake in Turin.

On 15 December, he mailed the slim manuscript of *Nietzsche contra Wagner* to Naumann, together with the *Dithyrambs of Dionysus*. The printing of the other books must wait. Naumann must drop everything to print *Nietzsche contra Wagner*. Two days later the order was cancelled. Naumann received a telegram, '*Ecce vorwärts*' ('Proceed with *Ecce Homo*'). *Ecce Homo* 'transcends the concept of literature . . . There is no parallel to it even in nature herself; it blasts, literally, the history of mankind in two – the highest superlative of *dynamite*.'

Christmas time was upon the world. It was time to write Christmas letters:

To his mother,

'All in all, your old creature is now an immensely famous person: not exactly in Germany, for the Germans are too stupid and too vulgar for the loftiness of my mind, and have always cast aspersions on me, but everywhere else. My admirers are all very *exclusive* natures, all prominent and influential people . . . the most charming women, not excluding by any means a Mme la Princesse Tenichev! I have real geniuses among my admirers – today no other name is treated with so much distinction and reverence as mine . . . Luckily I am now ripe for everything that my task may require of me . . .

Your old creature'[22]

To Elisabeth,

'My sister . . . I am compelled to part company with you for ever. Now that my destiny is certain, I feel every word of yours with tenfold sharpness; you have not the remotest conception of what it means to be most closely related to the man and to the destiny in whom the question of millennia has been decided – I hold, quite literally, the future of mankind in the palm of my hand . . .'[23]

To Peter Gast,

'Dear friend, I want to recover all copies of the *fourth* part of *Zarathustra* . . . against all the chances of life and death. (I read it these last few days and almost died of emotion.) If I publish it later, after a few decades of world crises – wars! – then that will be the proper time.

Signs and wonders! Greetings from the Phoenix'[24]

To Peter Gast,

'Prince von Carignano has just died; we shall have a great funeral.'[25]

To Carl Fuchs,

'. . . The world will be standing on its head for the next few years: since the old God has abdicated, *I* shall rule the world from now on . . .'[26]

To Franz Overbeck,

'Dear friend . . . In two months I shall be the foremost name on earth . . .

I myself am working on a memorandum for the courts of Europe . . . I mean to sew up the Reich in an iron shirt and to provoke it to a war of desperation. I shall not have my hands free until I have the young emperor, and all his appurtenances, in my hands. Between ourselves! *Very much* between ourselves! Complete calm of soul! Ten hours of uninterrupted sleep.

N.'[27]

To Meta von Salis-Marschlins,

'*Verehrtes Fräulein* . . . I think no mortal has ever received such letters as I have . . . From the highest St Petersburg society. And the French! . . . The most remarkable thing here in Turin is the complete fascination I exert over all classes of people . . . My writings are printed with fiery zeal. Mme Kovaleska in Stockholm (she is descended from the old Hungarian King Matthias Corvin) . . . is regarded as the only living mathematical genius.

 Your N.'[28]

To Peter Gast,

'. . . When your card came, *what* was I doing? . . . it was the famous Rubicon. I no longer know my address: let us suppose that it will soon be the Palazzo del Quirinale.

 N.'[29]

To August Strindberg,

'I have ordered a convocation of princes in Rome – I mean to have the young emperor shot . . . Une seule condition: *Divorçons* . . .

 Nietzsche Caesar'[30]

To August Strindberg,

'*Eheu?* . . . not *Divorçons* after all?

 The Crucified'[31]

To Peter Gast,

'Sing me a new song: the world is transfigured and all the heavens rejoice.

 The Crucified'[32]

To Georg Brandes,

'Once you discovered me, it was no great feat to find me: the difficulty now is to lose me . . .

 The Crucified'[33]

To Jacob Burckhardt,

'I condone my boredom at having created a world. You are our great greatest teacher; for I, with Ariadne have only to be the golden balance of all things.

Dionysus'[34]

To Cosima Wagner,
'Ariadne, I love you.
Dionysus'[35]

To Jacob Burckhardt,
'Dear Professor:

Actually I would much rather be a Basel professor than God; but I have not ventured to carry my private egoism so far as to omit creating the world on his account. You see, one must make sacrifices, however and wherever one may be living. Yet I have kept a small student room for myself, which is situated opposite the Palazzo Carignano (in which I was born as Vittorio Emanuele) and which moreover allows me to hear from its desk the splendid music below in the Galleria Subalpina. I pay twenty-five francs, with service, make my own tea, and do my own shopping, suffer from torn boots . . . Since I am condemned to entertain the next eternity with bad jokes, I have a writing business here, which really leaves nothing to be desired – very nice and not in the least strenuous . . .

Do not take the Prado case seriously. I am Prado. I am also Prado's father, I venture to say that I am also Lesseps [the French diplomat who had a hand in the building of the Panama Canal] . . . I wanted to give my Parisians, whom I love, a new idea – that of a decent criminal. I am also Chambige – also a decent criminal . . .

As regards the children I have brought into the world, it is a case of my considering with some distrust whether all of those who enter the 'Kingdom of God' do not also come *out of* God. This autumn, as lightly clad as possible, I twice attended my funeral, first as Count Robilant (no, he is my son, insofar as I am Carlo Alberto, my nature below) but I was Antonelli myself. Dear Professor, you should see this construction; since I have no experience of the things I create, you may be as critical as you wish . . . I go everywhere in my student overcoat; slap someone or other on the shoulder and say: *Siamo contenti? Son dio, ha fatto questa caricature* [Are we happy? I am God, I have created this parody] . . . Tomorrow my son Umberto is coming with the charming Margherita whom I receive, however, here too in my shirt sleeves.

The *rest* is for Frau Cosima . . . Ariadne . . . From time to time we practise magic . . .

I have had Caiaphas [the Jewish High Priest who condoned the execution of Jesus] put in chains; I too was crucified at great length last year by the German doctors. Wilhelm Bismarck and all anti-Semites done away with.

You can make any use of this letter which does not make the people of Basel think less highly of me.

> With fond love
> Your Nietzsche'[36]

The letter was postmarked 5 January. Burckhardt received it the following day. He took it to Overbeck that same afternoon. Overbeck immediately wrote to Nietzsche insisting he should come to Basle. The following day, Overbeck received a letter signed 'Dionysus', informing him, 'I am just having all anti-Semites shot . . .'

Overbeck hurried over to the Basle psychiatric clinic to show the letters to the director, Professor Wille, asking him what he should do.

· THE CAVE MINOTAUR ·

> Can an *ass* be tragic? — Can someone be destroyed by a weight he
> cannot carry or throw off? . . . The case of the philosopher.
>
> *Twilight of the Idols*, 'Epigrams and Maxims', 11

It is not clear what exactly happened on the morning of 3 January 1889.
The story is they saw him as usual leaving Davide Fino's corner house
on the Piazza Carlo Alberto. They were used to the sad and solitary
figure wrapped in thought, often on his way to the bookshop, where
he was known to sit for hours with the book pressed very close to his
face, reading but never making a purchase. The piazza was full of tired
old horses drooping between the traces of carts and cabs waiting for
fares: miserable jut-ribbed nags being tormented into some semblance
of work by their masters. On seeing a cabbie mercilessly beating his
horse, Nietzsche broke down. Overwhelmed by compassion, sobbing
at the sight of it, he threw his arms protectively around the horse's
neck, and collapsed. Or so they said. Crises are so quickly come and
gone. Eyewitnesses see so many different truths.

Somebody must have known which house he lived in, for Davide
Fino was summoned. The police, too. Had it not been for Fino,
Nietzsche would have been taken off straight away and quite possibly
lost forever in the dark labyrinth of Italian institutions for the insane,
but Davide Fino brought him home.

Once in his third-floor room, Nietzsche let nobody in. For several
days, he shouted, sang at the top of his voice, raved and babbled to
himself. Day and night it went on. The Fino family climbed the stairs
and listened. He handed them letters to post to the King and Queen of
Italy, as well as the last delusional letters to Burckhardt and Overbeck.
He grew inordinately excited at the piano, playing his Wagnerian

music loudly and violently. He banged; he crashed. They turned their eyes apprehensively to the ceiling above, where his footfalls crept and jumped and stamped above their heads. He was dancing. Naked and capering, he was taking part in holy sexual frenzies, the orgiastic rites of Dionysus.

Fino contacted the German consul; he visited the police station; he consulted a doctor: Overbeck arrived on the afternoon of 8 January.

'A uniquely terrible moment' was how Overbeck described it. Even so, he caught Nietzsche during one of his comparatively calm periods. Over the next few days he would see far worse.

On entering Nietzsche's room, he discovered his friend cowering on the corner of a sofa. Ostensibly he was proofreading the pages of *Nietzsche contra Wagner*. He was holding the printed sheets up close to his bewildered face, like a child pretending to read. He knew the actions expected for the task. The paper must be *this* far from his nose; he must scan from left to right and back again. The words on the page obviously meant nothing to him.

At Overbeck's entrance, he rushed at him, embraced him violently and broke into sobbing. Then he sank back on the sofa, twitching, moaning and quivering. Overbeck was a quiet, steady man who was not given to emotional display but on seeing his old friend in this state his legs gave way; he staggered and almost collapsed.

The Fino family remained in the room with Overbeck and Nietzsche. The Turin psychiatrist Professor Carlo Turina, whom Davide Fino had consulted, had advised that when the patient was overexcited, bromide drops would calm him down.[1] A glass of water stood on the table ready. Without fuss, they gave him some. It tamed the wild creature. Loftily, he began to describe the grand reception that was planned for him that evening. This happy interlude did not last long. Soon he was speaking in chopped-up scraps of words and bursts of sentences punctuated by sudden convulsive starts of buffoonery, obscenities, outbursts on the piano and leaping and dancing. Being so familiar with the world of Nietzsche's ideas, Overbeck was more or less able to follow the references as they came and went. Nietzsche spoke of himself as the successor to the dead God, the clown of all eternities, the Dionysus torn to pieces. He twitched and jerked his body in orgiastic re-enactment of holy frenzy. And yet, all the while, there was an innocence about him. He did not arouse fear or horror in them, or even repulsion. Only immense pity. He, who had so often said that he considered the overcoming of pity a noble virtue.

When Overbeck had hastened over with Nietzsche's letters to the Basle psychiatric clinic, Dr Wille had been in no doubt that Nietzsche must be brought to his asylum immediately. This would not be easy, he warned Overbeck. He would not be able to accomplish it alone. He must travel with a man experienced in the coaxing and calming of the delusional. A German dentist, cunning in such things, was hired.

During the short time in Turin before they left for Basle, Overbeck set to organising Nietzsche's books and papers, so that they could be sent on by Davide Fino. Nietzsche lay in bed, refusing to get up. The only way the dentist could persuade him out of bed was by humouring his delusion of grandeur. Royalty was waiting! Receptions, pageants and musical entertainments were being prepared for him in the town! Nietzsche snatched up Davide Fino's nightcap, put it on his head like some sort of royal crown, and fought when they wanted to part him from it.

The bustling streets of Turin and the milling concourse of the railway station produced a sufficient number of people to sustain the illusion of a royal reception. He was coaxed onto the train.

Problems arose on reaching Novara, where they had to change trains and wait three hours for the connection. Nietzsche wished to address the crowds and embrace his loyal subjects but the well-practised dentist persuaded him that it was more fitting for a great personage such as himself to preserve his incognito.

So long as they colluded with his delusion he was docile as a child, but then suddenly his mind would take him to another place and another jagged fragment would burst through. When they had little chance of following his line of thought, he became furious. They gave him chloral to sedate him through the night. As the train rushed through the dark St Gotthard tunnel running beneath the Alps, Overbeck heard Nietzsche's voice clear and coherent singing the 'Gondola Song', one of his own poems that he had inserted into both his last books, *Ecce Homo* and *Nietzsche contra Wagner*.

> My soul, a stringed instrument,
> Invisibly touched,
> Sang secretly to itself,
> A Gondola song,
> Tremulous, rich with joy.
> Was anyone listening?[2]

At Basle a taxi was waiting. In his better days Nietzsche had known both Friedmatt, the Basle University Psychiatric Clinic, and its director Professor Wille, but he showed no signs of this as he entered. Dreading that recognition of the professor and the asylum would mean the discovery of his betrayal, Overbeck did not introduce the two men. Nietzsche enquired regally why this man had not been presented to him. It was not seemly to behave thus. On being told Professor Wille's name, he greeted him with great courtesy and fell seamlessly out of the royal charade into a perfectly lucid and astonishingly accurate recollection of a conversation the two men had held seven years previously on the subject of Adolf Vischer, a religious maniac.

Overbeck was then dismissed by the professionals. There was no place for him while they went through the business of the medical examination and psychiatric evaluation.

'For you, good people, I shall prepare the loveliest weather tomorrow,' Nietzsche said as he was led off.

He ate his breakfast ravenously. They noted how much he enjoyed his bath. He remained eight days in the clinic while they tested him and prepared a report.

'Body healthy and well developed. Muscular. Deep-chested. Heart sounds low-pitched, normal. Pulse regular 70. Pupillar disparity, right larger than the left, reaction to light sluggish. Tongue heavily furred.

Exaggerated patellar reflex. Urine clear, acid, containing neither sugar nor albumen.

'The patient asks often for women. Says that he has been ill for the past week and often suffers from severe headaches. Says he has had a few attacks. He felt exceptionally well and exalted during the attacks. He would have liked to embrace and kiss everybody in the street. He would have liked to climb up the walls. It is difficult to tie the patient's attention down to anything definite; he only gives fragmentary and imperfect answers, or none at all.

'No tremor and no speech disorder. The flow of speech constant, confused and without logical connection. Continues throughout the night. Often a high state of manic excitement. Considerable priapic content. Delusions of whores in his room.

'At times he will converse quite normally but then lapse into jokes, dances, confusion and delusion. Occasionally breaks into singing, yodelling and screaming.

'11 January 1889. The patient did not sleep at all during the night, talked without intermission, got up several times to clean his teeth, wash himself, etc. Over-tired in the morning . . . In the afternoon, out-of-doors, he is in a continual state of motor-excitement; throws his hat on the ground and occasionally lies down on the ground himself. – Talks confusedly and occasionally reproaches himself with having been the cause of several people's ruin.

'12 January 1889. After sulfonal, four or five hours' sleep with several interruptions. When asked how he feels replies that he feels so incredibly well that he could only express it in music.'

After eight days, a pattern of sorts emerged. He was quieter when he was in bed. The manic, loud, disruptive behaviour was worse when he was up. Indoors the rages were vocal: *aggravato fortissimo*. Out of doors it was more physical, with a tendency to take off pieces of clothing and lie down on the ground.

Professor Wille was an authority on syphilis. Many of his patients in the clinic were suffering from the syphilis of the brain that may come in the later stages of the disease. The diagnosis appeared to be confirmed by a small scar on his penis and by Nietzsche telling them that he had 'infected himself twice'. It was assumed he was referring to syphilis. They did not then have access to his medical records, which would have told them that earlier in his life, when he was in his right mind and examined by Dr Eiser, he had admitted that he had twice been infected with gonorrhoea.

By the end of eight days, Wille was confident in the diagnosis of *paralysis progressiva*, progressive paralysis and general paresis, the psychotic breakdown occurring in the last stages of syphilis. Overbeck now had the difficult task of informing Nietzsche's mother that her son was in an asylum.

On receiving the news, Franziska immediately left Naumburg for Basle, arriving on 13 January. She stayed the night with the Overbecks and on the following morning she went to the clinic. Before she could see her son, she must be interviewed by the doctors. She had to give them Nietzsche's familial and medical history.

'Mother gives the impression of a limited intelligence,' reads the report. 'Father, a country parson, suffered from brain disease after falling downstairs . . . One of the mother's brothers died in a nerve sanatorium. The father's sisters were hysterical and somewhat eccentric. – Pregnancy and confinement quite normal . . .'[3]

Franziska was in no doubt of her duty and her desire. She wished to look after her son. They would not let her. Franziska Nietzsche was a small, slight woman in her sixties whose genteelly inactive life had not endowed her with much physical strength. Her taller son was forty-four, skeletally strong, well muscled, irrational, physically unpredictable and intermittently violent.

There was no question he required more than a mother's care. Far be it from Franziska to disobey professional advice coming from a member of the male sex but she did manage a small victory in getting Nietzsche transferred to the psychiatric institution that was closest to her in Naumburg, the clinic in Jena.

Once again, it was decided that a professional escort was needed.

A young doctor named Ernst Mähly was selected. As it was too much for one man alone, he would be accompanied by an attendant. Mähly had been one of Nietzsche's students at Basle. He was 'a secret and silent adept, filled with suppressed reverence for the daemonic herald of the Transvaluation of all Values, the creator of *Beyond Good and Evil*'.[4] He also knew Otto Binswanger, the Principal of the Jena Clinic for the Care and Cure of the Insane. Mähly was surely the perfect link on this connecting journey. His mind must have the greatest chance of understanding the jigsaw fragments of speech and piecing them together into some sort of pattern that might provide clues to assist Professor Binswanger. A footnote to this episode is that when Ernst Mähly's life eventually ended in suicide, his father placed the blame on Nietzsche's influence.

On the evening of 17 January 1889, Nietzsche was for the second time organised into a journey to a railway station that would take him to an asylum. This time Overbeck was not to travel with him but he desperately wished to bid farewell to his friend. Overbeck experienced his second 'horrible, unforgettable' moment as he stood watching the little group walk across the station concourse in the wooden silence of a funeral procession. Nietzsche's gait was unnaturally stiff, like an automaton. It was nine o'clock in the evening and the harsh, artificial station lighting lent their faces the gruesome, mask-like hollows of phantoms.

When the curiously rigid figure had managed the steps from the platform up to the carriage, Overbeck boarded the train and entered the reserved compartment to bid him farewell. Catching sight of him, Nietzsche uttered a roaring groan, and leapt up to embrace him convulsively. He told him he was the man he had loved most of all. Then Overbeck had to leave.

Three days later, Overbeck wrote to Peter Gast that he was tormented by feelings that he had done his friend wrong. He had known in Turin that it was all over. He ought not to have practised such underhanded tricks and deception upon his dear friend. Now, he must labour for the rest of his life under the terrible burden of having delivered Nietzsche to a future of asylums. He should rather have taken Nietzsche's life, then and there, in Turin.

This was an extraordinary statement from a mild-mannered professor of theology, to whom murder was a very grave sin indeed. But his moral dilemma was further complicated as it crossed both friends' minds that Nietzsche might be feigning madness. Both Gast and Overbeck knew his willingness to dispense with the conventional interpretations of reality, his lifelong interest in madness and madmen, and how he was drawn to the sacred tumult of the orgiastic god. From Empedocles to Hölderlin, to the madman seeking God with a lantern in *Zarathustra*, he had so often come up with the thought that only the fragile bark of madness could carry the human mind over the Rubicon that must be crossed to reach revelation. It was the price that must be paid. Madness was the only engine strong enough to drive change through the morality of custom. The 'dreadful attendant', it was the mask and speaking-trumpet of divinity. Plato had said that it was only through madness that the greatest good things had come to Greece. But Nietzsche went further. All superior men who were irresistibly drawn to throw off the yoke of ready-made moralities, if they were not actually mad, had no alternative but to feign madness.

'I, too have been in the underworld, like Odysseus, and will often be there again; and I have not sacrificed only rams to be able to talk with the dead, but have not spared my own blood as well,' he had written. 'May the living forgive me if they sometimes appear to me as shades . . .'[5]

Struck as they were by the idea that their friend might be dipping into the underworld and donning the mask of madness to get to the other side, their suspicions could not hold out against the reality they observed over the next fourteen months when Nietzsche was confined in the Jena clinic. This was no mask, no Dionysian deception, no exaltation of the muses, no powerful mystery of thought. They had no doubt that they were observing the last wisps of an evaporating mind.

Nietzsche had already encountered the Jena clinic once before, when he was fifteen years old. He had seen and noted the vast institution on a summer holiday trip in 1859 when its sharp, grim outline had caused him to write melancholy and gruesome thoughts in his diary. Whereas the Basle clinic was a solid-looking bourgeois villa, not unlike Wahnfried in architectural style and scale, the Jena clinic was an enormous and forbidding pile, a towered and turreted institution of glaring orange and black brickwork. Inside, it bristled with prominent security features such as locks and bolts, padding in unusual places and heavily barred windows.

He was admitted as a 'second class' fee-paying patient. The decision was nominally made by Franziska but doubtless she turned for guidance to Overbeck, and he would have advised financial caution. The pension from Basle University had been drastically reduced from three thousand to two thousand francs. They had no idea how long he would be incarcerated. Second-class accommodation was certainly a prudent measure.

The institution's director, Professor Otto Binswanger, had studied neuropathology in Vienna and Göttingen. At an unusually young age – he was not yet thirty – he had been appointed director of the Jena institution; he also held the post of Professor of Psychiatry at the University of Jena. He wrote numerous papers on brain syphilis and *dementia paralytica*. He was steeped in psychiatry and neuropathology; his father had held a similar position before him. There was no question that Nietzsche was in one of the leading institutions for his condition. Unfortunately, Binswanger did not examine Nietzsche on arrival. The diagnosis sent over with the patient from the Basle clinic was adopted: *paresis* and *dementia paralytica*, dementia and progressive paralysis as a result of tertiary syphilis.

Syphilis was no longer regarded as sent directly from God as a punishment for sinful sexual liaisons. Mental illness was no longer a matter of the brutal, overcrowded madhouses where inmates were treated like a cabaret of amusing zoo animals. Cures had not arrived but humane treatment had. Calm, calm and always more calm was Binswanger's fundamental remedy. During the fourteen months Nietzsche spent in the Jena asylum, he was sedated and he was massaged with mercury ointment, the centuries-old remedy. There was no question of a cure or recovery. The condition was incurable. It was only a matter of waiting for the patient to die. This was expected to happen relatively quickly, in a year or two.

The fact that Nietzsche survived for eleven years, taken together with the absence of some of the expected symptoms of tertiary syphilis such as hair loss and nasal depression, make it a pity that Binswanger did not examine Nietzsche himself to confirm the diagnosis.[6]

Over the long months, Nietzsche continued psychotic, delusional, agitated and incoherent. He grimaced. There was unarticulated screaming with no external motive. Delusions of grandeur continued: he talked of councillors of legations, ministers and servants. There were also delusions of persecution. He saw a rifle aimed at him behind a windowpane and he cut his hand smashing the glass trying to get at it. 'They' cursed him in the night and used terrible contrivances against him. Fearful machinery was sometimes turned on him. Erotic delusions continued. One morning he reported that twenty-four whores had been with him in the night. He persisted in calling the chief warden 'Prince Bismarck'. He sometimes called himself the Duke of Cumberland, sometimes the Kaiser. He said he had been Frederick William IV 'the last time'. He told them that his wife, Frau Cosima Wagner, had brought him here. He often begged for help against nightly torture. He did not sleep on his bed but on the floor beside it. He twitched. He carried his head to one side. He ate enormously. By October, he had put on thirteen pounds. He broke a tumbler so as to protect his approaches with splinters of glass. He was incontinent. He urinated into his water glass. He smeared his faeces. He sometimes got away with drinking his urine. He chattered, screamed and groaned unnervingly. He could be heard from a long way away throughout the night. White hairs began to grow on the right side of his moustache.

During Binswanger's classes, Nietzsche took his turn in being one of the patients exhibited as a teaching aid. He did not perceive this as any sort of humiliation. While he did not know what he was doing there, he obviously felt his importance as a personage. He behaved courteously to the medical attendants, repeatedly expressing gratitude, comporting himself towards them as a gracious master to his servants. He thanked them for his splendid reception. He tried to shake the doctor's hand over and over again. Somewhere in his mind he knew that the doctor was of superior social standing, as he was himself.

When Binswanger wished to show off some disturbances in the patient's walk, Nietzsche moved so slowly and lethargically that the symptoms could not be seen. 'Now, Herr Professor,' Binswanger scolded, 'an old soldier like you surely can still march!' Upon which Nietzsche began to pace along the lecture hall with a firm gait.[7]

There were calm intervals of pathetic charm. He asked the doctor with a smile, 'Give me a little health.'

He had no idea where he was. Sometimes he was in Naumburg, sometimes in Turin. He conversed very little with the other patients. He stole books. He had his name written down on crumpled slips of paper. He would produce them and read his name aloud, 'Professor Friedrich Nietzsche', many times a day.

Just as, on leaving Turin, he had become attached to one of Davide Fino's caps, now he became intensely possessive of one of the clinic's caps. He wore it day and night and they dared not take it away from him. They assumed it was his royal headdress. He became irritated and agitated when they checked his pockets after a walk; he liked to fill them up with stones and all sorts of other small treasures.

After six months of sedation, his behaviour was sufficiently under control for his mother to be permitted to see him. She arrived on 29 July. It was judged best they should not meet in his room; nor should they meet in the ward for the insane, where he usually sat in the daytime. The meeting took place in the visitors' room. He told her that this was where he gave lectures before a select public. A pencil and some paper were lying about. He shoved them into his pocket, whispering to her mysteriously but quite merrily, 'Now I shall have something to do when I creep into my cave.'[8]

Six further months passed with little change. In December a noisy charlatan named Julius Langbehn got in touch with Franziska.

Langbehn was convinced that he was able to cure her son. He needed complete control to implement his cure and so he must be allowed legally to adopt Nietzsche. Langbehn was the bestselling author of the latest book to proffer a cure for the collapsing state of German culture. *Rembrandt as Educator* (*Rembrandt als Erzieher*) leant heavily for its title on Nietzsche's 'Schopenhauer as Educator'. Langbehn's solution to Germany's crisis was back-to-the-soil Christianity as portrayed by the good, uncorrupted German peasant souls depicted in Rembrandt's paintings. The fact that Rembrandt was Dutch did not appear to trouble him.

Langbehn had analysed Germany. Its problem was that it was over-educated. The professor and the expert, with their scholarship and their so-called 'expertise', must cease to be venerated. It would then follow, as night follows day, that the spiritual rebirth of Germany would be accomplished from within the fundamentally good German soul. Wisdom was to be found in the soil, in open air and in simple German hearts. The expulsion of foreign influences went without saying, particularly Jews. His book was the literary sensation of 1890. It was reprinted twenty-nine times during the first year of publication. Later he added two more extensive sections hymning two of Nietzsche's bêtes noires: anti-Semitism and Roman Catholicism. Langbehn also wrote poems; he considered himself a better poet than Goethe. He looked upon himself as a 'secret Emperor' whose healing powers would spiritually renew the German empire. Bismarck received him several times.

To 'cure' Nietzsche, the self-confessed Anti-Christ, would be a fine feather in Langbehn's cap. His considered view was that '"Atheists" like Shelley and "Anti-Christs" like Nietzsche are simply truant schoolboys who must be brought back into the fold.'[9] He prepared a legal document for Franziska to sign: 'I, the undersigned hereby pledge the legal guardianship of my son Friedrich Nietzsche . . .', etc. His plan was to take Nietzsche to Dresden, where the patient's royal fantasies would be indulged. Surrounded by a court and a retinue, Nietzsche would be treated as a king and as a child. Langbehn believed he could raise sufficient money to pay for the suitably grand mansion, elaborate furnishings, clothes, regalia and costumed courtiers (medical and domestic staff) to sustain the royal charade. Franziska's attendance as a nurse was grudgingly to be allowed, but only on Langbehn's strict conditions and permission.

Binswanger seemed to be as dazzled by the celebrity nationalist populist as the rest of the country. He permitted Langbehn to take daily walks with Nietzsche. His endless proselytising and attempts at exorcism eventually so maddened the patient that he upset a table over him and threatened him with his fists. Sinews stiffened by Overbeck, Franziska summoned up her courage and refused to sign the adoption agreement. This was the obvious moment for Langbehn's discretion to overcome his valour. He retired from the fray, to Dresden, to write pornographic poems, for which he would be prosecuted for obscenity. But the bestselling *Rembrandt as Educator* lived on as one of the early building blocks for the ideological foundations of the Third Reich. Hitler had a copy in his private library.[10]

In February 1890, Nietzsche's lethargy and tractability had improved to the extent that he was allowed to spend some hours with his mother on his good days. She took an apartment in Jena. Every morning, she called for him at the clinic at nine o'clock. Franziska was convinced that if only she might have custody of her dear, good boy, he might be returned to his right mind. The apartment had a second downstairs bedroom where Franz Overbeck and Peter Gast took it in turns to stay and be of assistance to her.

Walking for four or five hours a day had always been an important part of Nietzsche's routine. Indeed, it accounted for the skeletal and muscular strength remarked upon in both clinics' reports. Franziska had never been much of a walker but if this was the price, it was not too steep to pay. She would take his arm, or he would walk a little behind her, following her about, sometimes stopping to draw figures on the ground with his stick, or to stuff things into his pockets. While Franziska was delighted by his obedience, his two friends were horrified by his childish docility. There were always one or two oddities on the walks. He would break out into his noises. He tried to hit dogs, or strangers. He tried to shake hands with other people who obviously appealed to him in some unfathomable way. This frightened ladies.

Often they walked to the home of a family named Gelzer-Thurneysen. When they arrived, Franziska would tell Nietzsche to remove his hat and come indoors. He would remain shyly at the door of the drawing room while she went over to the piano and began to play. Slowly, he would approach, drawn by the music. Eventually he would place his fingers on the keys. He would begin to play standing up, then she would push him down onto the piano stool, and he would continue. She would know that she could safely leave him, lost in music. So long as she heard music, there was no need for her to be in the same room to supervise him.

On 24 March 1890, Franziska was granted custody of her son. They remained in the flat in Jena for six weeks but then one day Nietzsche gave her the slip. He undressed in the street, possibly intending to go for a swim, and was discovered by a policeman, who returned him to his mother. This made her terrified that he would be sent back to the asylum. She persuaded one of the young Gelzers to help her 'smuggle' him to the railway station, where they caught the train for Naumburg. Alwine, the faithful servant, greeted 'the professor' with joy. He was back in Weingarten 18, his childhood home.

The little two-storey house was ideally situated for looking after a disinhibited patient: the garden was small, fenced and gated. The ground-floor windows had stout shutters. One side of the house gave onto a vineyard; the other faced the wall of St Jacob's Church.

Franziska continued optimistically with the walking cure. Usually he followed her around quietly. If she saw a stranger approaching, she simply turned him round by taking his arm and distracting him, pointing to a view. The threat safely passed, she could turn him around again. If they met an acquaintance and she stopped to talk, she would instruct him to remove his hat. While she exchanged pleasantries, he would stand dully with the hat in his hand. If addressed, he would look uncomprehending. When the encounter was over, she would tell him to put on his hat and they would resume their walk.

As a boy, he had prided himself on swimming in the River Saale 'like a whale'. It was a recreation that had always brought him great pleasure. Franziska thought that the physical memory might aid recuperation but after a few attempts she had to desist. The excitement was too much; it rendered him uncontrollable.

If the 'dear child' was having an unusually noisy or obstructive day, he might easily be contained indoors. There were not many neighbours to be disturbed by shouts and screams. When he became unbearably loud and obstreperous, she simply put something sweet in his mouth, like a little piece of cut-up fruit. By the time he had chewed and swallowed, his attention had been distracted and the violent vocalising had subsided into more acceptable growls. He ate enormously. She said she gave him no chloral or sedatives. If that was so, it was a shutting down, a regression while the mother regained complete control of her beloved, incontinent, obedient boy child.

2 2

· THE EMPTY OCCUPANT OF
FURNISHED ROOMS ·

> I have a terrible fear that one day I shall be pronounced 'holy'. I do not
> want to be a saint, rather a buffoon . . . perhaps I am a buffoon.
>
> *Ecce Homo*, 'Why I am a Destiny'

In Paraguay, Elisabeth received the news of her brother's breakdown
early in 1889, just as the disgruntled colonist Klingbeil was publishing
his book denouncing the fraudulent couple and their Potemkin colony.[1]
There was no question of her going home to Germany. She was fighting
for the colony's life as she refuted Klingbeil's accusations in her articles
for *Bayreuther Blätter*, and she was fighting alone.

The marriage had become a battleground. Förster was spending his
time chasing money from one end of Paraguay to another, from San
Pedro to San Bernardino to Asunción, attempting to raise loans against
previous loans, at hair-raising interest rates, to ward off inevitable
bankruptcy. While he further entangled their finances, she remained
in Nueva Germania full of resentment at her husband's inadequacies,
while expending her considerable abilities on recruiting more colonists
from Germany. The quota agreed with the Paraguayan government
must be filled by August that year, or the colony would be lost.

On receiving the news of Nietzsche's breakdown, Elisabeth expressed
more pity for herself than for him. Yes, she had neglected her duty to
her brother. The poor lamb! He would have done so much better had
she stayed in Germany. But she would like to tell her mother that –
without boasting – the whole founding of the colony would have been a
shady and uncertain affair without her. She had never been anything but
an excellent wife, while Bernhard was a terrible egotist who had left all
the work up to her and shown no sympathy for her suffering.[2]

Klingbeil's accusations lay heavily on Förster's mind. Daily wandering the rim of the financial abyss, he was drinking heavily. Finally, on 3 June, he gave up the struggle and killed himself in an hotel room in San Bernardino, by swallowing a mixture of strychnine and morphine.

Newspapers had already reported his death as suicide by strychnine poisoning when Elisabeth arrived in San Bernardino. Her one purpose was to repudiate the suicide. She had no idea that Förster had posted what amounted to a suicide note to Max Schubert, the director of the Chemnitz Colonial Society: '. . . This is my last request: Please continue to put your considerable talents, your strength and your youthful enthusiasm in the service of the worthy enterprise that I have started. Perhaps it will prosper better without me than with me.'[3]

Just as Elisabeth had fabricated the story that her father's death was the result of bucket-passing heroics fighting a village fire, so now she used her great powers of persuasion on the local doctor to alter the cause of death to heart failure, due to the stresses of false accusations and the intrigues of enemies.

Within the month she was writing to her mother that it was a pity that she had not been with her beloved husband at the time, 'or I could have warded off the heart attack, using compresses and foot baths as we used to do'.[4] It is difficult to imagine that even Elisabeth believed one could ward off a heart attack by such means.

Swiftly, she constructed a legend to account for her brother's insanity: he had suffered a stroke brought on by a nameless, mysterious Javanese drug.

'In 1884 so far as I remember, he [Nietzsche] got to know a Dutchman, who recommended him a Javanese narcotic, and presented him with a fairly large bottle of this specific. The stuff tasted like rather strong alcohol and had an outlandish smell – and also an outlandish name, which I can no longer remember since we always called it "the Javanese narcotic". The Dutchman impressed us with the fact that only a few drops should be taken at a time in a glass of water . . . Later, in the autumn of 1885, he [Nietzsche] confessed that on one occasion he had taken a few drops too much, with the result that he suddenly threw himself to the ground in a fit of convulsive laughter . . . In one letter to Gast he speaks of his "grins", which must apply to the artificial laughter brought on by the Javanese narcotic. Finally, my brother himself gave a hint that supports this theory. During the early days of his insanity he used often to say in confidence to our mother that he "had taken twenty drops" (he did not mention of *what*) and that his brain had then "gone off the track". Perhaps his short-sightedness led him to pour in too much, and this may account for that terrible stroke.'[5]

Elisabeth settled her late husband's San Bernardino hotel bill with a deed to land she did not own, and set about organising a funeral that would do justice to a warrior-hero on his way to Valhalla. Her letter to her mother describing Förster's burial recalls the earlier letter describing her own triumphant entry into the colony. 'Sixty horsemen followed the coffin and fired a salute over his grave.'[6] The untrue report of his suicide had been put out by the Jewish press.

Elisabeth remained in Paraguay, trying hard to raise money to keep control of the colony until finally, in August 1890, she lost her battle. Ownership passed to the *Sociedad Colonizadora Nueva Germania en el Paraguay*. In December she returned to Naumburg to drum up support to regain German control of the colony. Franziska believed she was returning to look after her brother.

Elisabeth arrived a few days before Christmas. Her mother brought her brother to meet her at the station. Franziska was leading Nietzsche by the arm, like a child. He walked stiffly, like a Prussian soldier on parade, and he clasped a bunch of red roses. Franziska had to remind him to give them to Elisabeth. When he did so, he remembered who she was, and called her 'Llama'. That night, after he had been put to bed, mother and daughter sat up to talk. Elisabeth was shocked to hear loud animal howling coming from his room above.

Elisabeth remained in the family home, writing innumerable letters, petitioning colonial societies and government officials and scolding anti-Semitic organisations for their lack of support. She now changed the name she used to sign her articles: 'Eli Förster' became 'Frau Doktor Förster'. She published her first book, *Dr Bernhard Förster's Kolonie Neu-Germania in Paraguay.*[7] It rebutted Klingbeil's accusations and it appealed to her fellow-countrymen to support a weak, broken-hearted widow by setting up a corporation to buy back the shares from the foul foreigner. When the book was published, in late spring 1891, the existing colonists of Nueva Germania were particularly indignant that she repeated her husband's original and notoriously untrue claims concerning the unimaginable fertility of the soil and the marvellous abundance of clean water.

During the six months it took her to write the book, the question arose of her brother's unpublished books, the last works hastily written in Turin. By the end of March the printer/publisher Naumann had *Zarathustra* IV bound, printed and ready to send to the bookshops. A copy was sent to Franziska. She and her brother Edmund Oehler, an undistinguished cleric, had assumed the legal guardianship of Nietzsche but Franziska had no literary pretensions and she left Gast and Overbeck to manage publishing matters on an informal basis.

Gast and Overbeck were convinced of the importance of the unpublished manuscripts, and they encouraged Naumann to go to print. But when *Zarathustra* IV was sent to Franziska, both she and Elisabeth were shocked and horrified by the plainly blasphemous passages. Elisabeth frightened Franziska by telling her that she would be open to criminal charges if the book were published. Franziska and Oehler refused permission. This infuriated Naumann: a new spirit was abroad, a new avant-garde was stirring, and it was intensely interested in Nietzsche's writings.

In 1888, Kaiser Wilhelm I had died at last, at the age of ninety. Seventeen years previously, he had accepted the German crown in the Hall of Mirrors in Versailles, to Nietzsche's great distress and fear for the imbalance of Europe. In the intervening years, the Kaiser and his Iron Chancellor Bismarck had famously forged the arch-conservative and repressive Second Reich on industrialisation, capitalism, unscrupulous expansionism, the Protestant Church, artistic conservatism and censorship. All this had coagulated into one massive, congested, sclerotic, nationalist, repressive and authoritarian world power – as Nietzsche had feared would happen. Even while the edges of Nietzsche's mind were fraying, he had not let go of his horror of the Second Reich. His final megalomaniac ravings in Turin had dwelled on his imagined power to have the Kaiser, Bismarck and all anti-Semites shot.

The last decade of the century ought to have been a time of optimism, an era of artistic innovation, as it was in France. But the dawn of the new emperor, Wilhelm II, failed to illumine the German horizon. Even his own army officers, who in 1914 would follow him into the First World War, were confidentially describing the new Kaiser in 1891 as 'too changeable, too capricious, particularly in small things, too many incautious remarks . . . Does not seem to know himself what he wants. Rumours about psychological disturbance.'[8]

Political uncertainty was coinciding with the jumpy spirituality that always goes with the looming close of a century. Where was the revolutionary iconoclast, asked Count Harry Kessler, a student at the University of Leipzig at the time: 'A secret Messianism developed in us. The desert which every Messiah needs was in our hearts, and suddenly there appeared above it, like a meteor, Nietzsche.'[9] It was to the student Kessler that the disillusioned old military men had disclosed their lack of confidence in the new Kaiser's mental qualities and temperament.

Harry Kessler moved in the highest social, political and military circles throughout Europe. His family was rich, his mother stupendously beautiful: he was widely supposed to have been fathered by Kaiser Wilhelm I, an untrue supposition (the timing doesn't work) that did him no harm. Both Bismarck and the Kaiser treated him as a favourite young hope of the side. Harry Kessler would become a secret agent and an officer in the First World War, Germany's ambassador to Warsaw in 1918, an art activist, art patron and museum curator. He would ride in a cab with Nijinsky on the first night of *The Rite of Spring* and he would close Nietzsche's eyes when they had opened again in his coffin. He was the complete cosmopolitan. Had Nietzsche been capable of comprehending, he would have approved of Harry Kessler becoming a founding trustee of the Nietzsche archive.

Slim and elegant as a greyhound, multilingual, erudite, supremely well connected but never the grand seigneur, in 1891 the twenty-three-year-old student Kessler sniffed the air and found the future Nietzschean. Throughout the next forty years he promoted the new vision through the theatres, publishing houses, artists' studios and duchesses' drawing rooms of Europe until 1933, when he fled Germany on the Nazi assumption of power, and another story took over the pages of the history books.

As a university student in the late 1880s and early 90s, Harry Kessler was part of 'the Raskolnikov generation': those on whom Dostoevsky's novel *Crime and Punishment* had a profound effect. Kessler served as witness at the trial of a high-born fellow student who shot and killed his working-class girlfriend, after which the murderer failed to kill himself because his shot into his own chest was not well aimed.[10] It was a nihilist act inspired by Dostoyevsky's book, which made an unquantifiable impression on the first post-Christian despairing generation. A rash of such murders among students overcome by 'the great disgust', the will to nothingness, became known as 'the Raskolnikov effect' after the anti-hero in Dostoevsky's book.[11]

Into this end-of-the-century mood of nihilism, of Schopenhauerian pessimism, moral despair and wondering what, if anything, was worth striving for, Kessler describes Nietzsche as making an impact as profound and as widespread as Byron had made upon a previous generation.

Shipwrecked souls desperately seeking resolution between scepticism and a longing for peace, the generation clung to Nietzsche's removal of meaning from its illusory position outside of life, replacing it back into life itself. They venerated Nietzsche as a truly free spirit, a solitary voice extolling individualism, offering an alternative both to the decline of faith and to the steady assault of science upon the anthropomorphic assumption of the human ego. Nietzsche had created for them the possibility of meaning as something completely personal rather than, as Johann Fichte put it, 'a lifeless household item one can put aside or pick up as one wishes'. If faith was dead, philosophy remained worthwhile in its ability to justify the very soul of the person who adopted, and adapted, it.

The book that most affected Kessler was *Beyond Good and Evil*, with its Argonaut of the spirit who sailed uncharted seas in search of a new way to interpret the world, and new moral values to suit modern circumstances. Kill God, yes, but put the *Übermensch* in His place. The *Übermensch* as the outcome of a personal metaphysical struggle through the will to power existing in everyone and everything – though the struggle it depicts is not necessarily against others but against the petty emotions in oneself, such as envy and resentment.

The *Übermensch*, rather than the will to power, was the concept that made *Zarathustra* such a cult text at the end of the century. A path-breaking book for the avant-garde, it provided a way out of impasse and decadence. It sanctified the earth without the need for justification through Heaven and Hell. Nietzsche set the joyful dance of the Hellenic gods against the Church-dependency that had accounted for the degeneration and diminution of Christian-European man into the perfect herd animal. *Amor fati* flung the rope over the nihilist abyss, over the centuries of envy and *ressentiment* which had dragged the individual down to the level of the *Untermensch*.

Harry Kessler wrote, 'We must strive not for fellow-pity, but for fellow-joy, the greatest possible elevation of the quantity of joy and therefore of life force in the world . . . The thought is fundamentally the kernel of Nietzschean philosophy.'[12] Three years after leaving university, Kessler felt able to write, 'There is probably no twenty-to-thirty-year-old tolerably educated man in Germany today who does not owe to Nietzsche a part of his worldview, or has not been more or less influenced by him.'[13]

Determined to take advantage of this tide of attention and turn it into book sales, in 1891 Naumann brought out second editions of *Beyond Good and Evil*, *The Case of Wagner* and *On the Genealogy of Morality*.

Elisabeth reached for the law. She was still in Naumburg, helping her mother to look after Nietzsche at home, and she put off her return to Paraguay until Naumann agreed a very satisfactory contract to pay her 3,500 marks to publish the remaining works. Realising that Peter Gast was the only person actually capable of reading the manuscripts that were to be turned into books, Elisabeth appointed him editor and made preliminary arrangements for a cheap edition of the collected works before departing for Paraguay in July 1892 to settle her affairs.

Her return to the colony, together with the outrageous claims she had made in her new book, so incensed the colonists that they wrote to Max Schubert, the director of the Chemnitz Colonial Society and the man to whom Förster had written what amounted to his suicide note on the eve of his death. The colonists stiffly informed Schubert that Elisabeth's stint back in the fatherland had done nothing to cure her of her megalomania. On the contrary, they found her even more conceited and domineering than ever.

Stalemate settled over Nueva Germania. Elisabeth remained in the Försterhof with her cooks and her servants, trading acrimonious letters with the colonists through third parties and newspaper columns until the following April, when she succeeded in selling the mansion to a Baron von Frankenberg-Lüttwitz. Thus she managed to regain some of her dowry that she had sunk into the Paraguayan venture. Money secured, she briefed Franziska to send her a telegram saying that she was urgently needed at home to look after her sick brother.

The *Colonial News* printed what amounted to an expulsion notice: 'The first requirement for any effective improvement in the affairs of Nueva Germania is the removal of Frau Doktor Förster.' By the time it was published, thanks to her mother's telegram, Elisabeth had already left the colony on her sisterly errand of mercy.

In September 1893, she returned from Paraguay to Naumburg, and Dr Elisabeth Förster became Elisabeth Förster-Nietzsche.

This was an important year, during which Nietzsche's work blazed through the artistic avant-garde of both Berlin and Paris to wide effect through painting, playwriting, poetry and music. Scandinavians set the Nietzschean fire: the Danish literary critic Georg Brandes had lit the spark with his lectures alerting the world, and connecting the Swedish playwright August Strindberg with Nietzsche in 1888. As a direct result, before the year was out, Strindberg wrote the play *Miss Julie*, which took over from Henrik Ibsen's earlier play *Ghosts* as the most banned play in Europe and the USA, condemned by the censor to be produced only on experimental stages and in private theatre clubs. While *Ghosts* had brought the subject of syphilis onto the stage, *Miss Julie*, the story of an aristocrat and her father's valet, was infinitely more disturbing. It introduced no physical crisis, such as syphilis, but was a Nietzschean psychodrama, forensically tracking the force fields of submission and control thrown up by the mutual *ressentiment* and the conflicting will to power between the *Übermensch* and the *Untermensch*, played out through the Dionysian impulse of sex.

In 1892–3, Strindberg was living in Berlin and spreading Nietzsche's fame through a rackety cosmopolitan bohemian circle known as *Zum Schwarzen Ferkel* ('The Black Piglet'), named after their favourite drinking hole. The Norwegian artist Edvard Munch was part of the circle and Strindberg introduced him to Nietzsche's writings with such profound effect that Munch painted *The Scream*. It captured the zeitgeist as nothing else: Munch had produced the definitive icon of existential terror on contemplating the consequences of the death of God, and the subsequent responsibility of man to find meaning and significance to life. Rapidly reproduced through lithographs and prints, it swept the galleries and magazines of Germany and Paris.

The fourth individual contributing to Nietzsche's increasing fame was Lou Salomé. In 1889, Otto Brahm opened his experimental theatre, the Freie Bühne, in Berlin, and a year later he started the paper *Die freie Bühne für modernes Leben* (*The Free Stage for Modern Life*).[14] Lou, by now a celebrity in her own right, was living next door to Brahm and wrote copious articles on Nietzsche that often first appeared in his paper. Her articles widened interest in Nietzsche and in 1894 she published one of the first major studies on his life and work, *Friedrich Nietzsche in seinen Werken.*

The form of Nietzsche's work was having a great and immediate impact on the arts of the 1890s also. What in fact had been imposed on Nietzsche by his illness – his short, aphoristic, often non-sequential bursts that at first sight appeared disorganised and unfinished – was seized upon as a direct and arrestingly modern way of communication. Strindberg's plays are notorious for jettisoning the classical theatrical unities of time, space and action and for being incomprehensible on the page because they do not follow a logical progression, while being electrifying on stage for the same reason. Munch didn't clear up dribbles and splashes of paint; he left whole areas of canvas naked and unpainted. It was the painterly equivalent of the powerful effect of the half-glimpsed, the suggestive quality of the aphorism that Nietzsche had first seized upon in Sorrento, and upon which he built the powerful and extraordinarily modern strategy of 'the philosopher of perhaps', a position which gave him the power to end an aphorism, a train of thought or even an entire book with an ellipsis, putting the reader in charge of the conclusion while, at the same time, acknowledging that objective truth is not even conceivable for humans, the striving for it mere illusion.

In 1893, Elisabeth arrived in provincial Naumburg to the extraordinary cacophony of international interest in her brother's work.

Her first task was to organise a vast amount of paper. Franziska had faithfully preserved her son's letters and writings. In addition, there was all the material that Overbeck had very properly arranged to be delivered to Franziska when he brought Nietzsche back from Turin. The mother's lifelong sentimental archive had grown gigantic with papers that had been part of Nietzsche's luggage for years: notebooks, loose notes, long-superseded rough drafts, letters received, drafts of letters sent, and drafts of letters never sent.

Elisabeth had a ground-floor wall knocked down in her mother's house. She ornamented the subsequently enlarged room with carvings of Zarathustra's animals: the serpent, the lion and the eagle. The latter looked pleasingly like the German imperial eagle. She called it the Nietzsche archive and began to throw herself behind building a new legend, for which her elevation of Förster as a prophet of heroic manliness had been a mere rehearsal cut short.

She wrote to Nietzsche's correspondents demanding all the letters and other material they possessed, warning them that copyright belonged to the archive. Only Cosima Wagner and Franz Overbeck failed to comply. Cosima had a fair idea of Elisabeth's talents and inclinations. Elisabeth's version of the truth concerning the interaction between Nietzsche and Wagner was unlikely to be the same as her own. The Nietzsche archive would receive no help from her. Elisabeth interpreted this reaction as female vengeance and archive-rivalry by Cosima, who was continuing to build her own extremely successful Wagner archive at Bayreuth.

As for Overbeck's refusal to surrender his papers: he had no reason to cooperate, having long been the recipient of Nietzsche's confidences concerning his chain-sickness and his hatred and contempt for his sister. Overbeck's refusal deepened Elisabeth's long-standing grudge against him that had originated in his failure to support her over the Lou affair and had been aggravated by his advising Nietzsche against investing in Nueva Germania. Overbeck became an arch-enemy. He was 'probably Jewish'. He and Franziska were responsible for Nietzsche's current state. Elisabeth had nothing but criticism for their course of action when Nietzsche had first fallen ill. They should have taken him to a hospital rather than to an asylum. The dentist whom Overbeck had found to escort Nietzsche from Turin to Basle was a Jew and a fraud (he was indeed half Jewish). Elisabeth corresponded with Julius Langbehn and she sided with him against her mother. Overbeck and Franziska should have paid for 'first class' treatment and the outcome would have been completely different.

Peter Gast was another with too deep and thorough a knowledge of the past. Foolishly, he confided to Elisabeth that he was proposing to write a biography of Nietzsche. She told him roundly that nobody was qualified to do that but herself and she sacked him as editor of the archive. In his place she appointed Fritz Kögel,[15] a philologist and musician fourteen years her junior, with whom she had spent a flirtatious evening. Kögel was a handsome salon-charmer of romantic appeal with a wildly dishevelled haircut. He was not able to read Nietzsche's handwriting, but no matter. For the first couple of years, the archive was to all effects a salon where Elisabeth entertained, while Chief Editor Kögel flattered her, flirted with her and sang delightfully at the piano to entertain guests. Above the piano hung three pictures: a photograph of Nietzsche, a Van Dyck cavalier and Dürer's *The Knight, Death and the Devil*. From time to time, animal roars from upstairs disturbed the atmosphere of civilised refinement.

As the progressive paralysis spread through both brain and body the outbursts had become too violent and too unpredictable for Franziska to continue the programme of therapeutic walks in the open air. Nietzsche, who had loved to roam the high mountains, was now confined to two rooms on the second floor of the house and a small, enclosed veranda. Often he had to be led the few steps from his room to the veranda; he could not always find it on his own. His daily exercise was that of a caged animal. He paced backwards and forwards the length of the veranda, which was deliberately overgrown with plants so that he would be invisible to the outside world. Franziska dreaded that her beloved, insane son would be discovered by the authorities and snatched away from her.

He slept most of the morning. When he had been washed and dressed he would spend the rest of the day in the other room, sitting for hours brooding dully. Sometimes he would play with dolls and other toys. His mother read aloud to him for as long as her voice held out. He did not understand the words but he liked to hear their sound. He did not like visitors. When the barber came to trim his strongly growing beard and moustache, and the masseur to rub some circulation through his atrophying muscles, he objected violently. Even though they were regular visitors, he was convinced they had come to do him harm.

In order to get the job done, Franziska would caress him soothingly and put sweet-tasting morsels into his mouth. Sometimes she would recite nursery rhymes. Occasionally he would remember odd scraps of them and join in. Franziska and her faithful housekeeper Alwine became afraid of him when he was loud and violent but the fear that he would be taken away from them outweighed the distress caused by their physical struggle to subdue him.

Franziska periodically wrote down the 'sayings of my good sick son'. In 1891, he still remembered the orchard in his childhood home in Röcken. He could name the different sorts of fruit trees. He also remembered the library at the end of the hallway and a powder-explosion that had blown out all the windows. At the recollection of this, he laughed very much, after which he said seriously, 'Well little Lisa, your bathing boy, your darling, is saved. I have him in my pants-pocket.' But after this, Franziska's sporadic record demonstrates the thin skein of memory fraying and unwinding with every passing year. In 1895, four years after being able to name the fruit trees, he was no longer capable of feats of shared recollection of the days of his childhood. Responsive thought had broken down. His mother records a typical incident when she asked if he wanted a meal, and he replied, 'Do I have a mouth for it? Should I eat that? my mouth I say, I want to eat . . . What is that here? an ear What is that here? a nose What is that here? hands I do not love.' But somewhere in the labyrinthine brain there remained, if not some sort of recollection, then at least a dim shadow of what he had once been: if something pleased him or he found it beautiful, he called it 'a book', and he dwelled on the question of whether he was stupid. '"No, my dear son," I say to him, "you are not stupid, your books are now world-shaking." "No, I am stupid."'

Mercifully, it seems as if this was as near as he ever got to glimpsing that once he had possessed greatness, which now was lost.

15 October 1894 was his fiftieth birthday. Naumann paid fourteen thousand marks into his account. Finally his books were selling. Nietzsche had no idea.

His old friends came to wish him happy birthday but he did not know who they were. These days he only recognised his mother, his sister and the good Alwine. Overbeck described him as neither happy nor unhappy, and seeming, in some fearful way, beyond everything. Paul Deussen brought a birthday bouquet. For a moment the flowers caught his attention but then he forgot them. Deussen told him he was fifty years old and it meant nothing to him. Only the arrival of the cake engaged him.

The next year was characterised by dreadful excitability, roaring and shouting, alternating with periods of complete prostration. A visit by Overbeck coincided with the latter. He found Nietzsche in the same physical position he had found him in Turin, half-crouching on the corner of a sofa. His eyes were lifeless. Overbeck was reminded of a mortally wounded animal, cornered and longing for death.

Overbeck never saw Nietzsche again. Elisabeth publicly accused Overbeck of stealing part of the unpublished works. The real cause was his refusal to surrender the letters, which she knew contained unflattering references to herself and would not necessarily uphold her version of events. The letters were eventually published in 1907–8 but only after Elisabeth had taken the case to court and won a judgement that stipulated that the disputed passages be replaced by blank spaces, a censorship that won her reputation no credibility.

Things had grown impossible between mother and daughter. The contrast within the house between Franziska and Alwine ministering to the inert Nietzsche upstairs and Elisabeth's lively musical salon downstairs was intolerable.

Elisabeth wrote a ten-page letter denouncing Franziska as unfit to care for Nietzsche. She wished to become his custodian and transfer him to a new archive along with his works, but the family doctor refused to support Elisabeth's claim against her mother.

Franziska was understandably upset. She was further upset by Elisabeth producing the first volume of biography of her brother in 1895, *The Life of Nietzsche* (*Das Leben Friedrich Nietzsches*). Franziska was bewildered by the book. She complained that she hardly recognised

THE EMPTY OCCUPANT OF FURNISHED ROOMS

any truth in the account. But as Franziska was barely literate (as Binswanger had noted at the Jena clinic), she had no recourse in print to refute her daughter's story. Franziska had never cultivated influential contacts that might spring to her defence. Overbeck supported her but he had altogether retired from the distasteful fray by donating the letters that Elisabeth coveted to Basle University. Characteristically, Overbeck was leaving it to posterity to judge.

In December 1895, Elisabeth drew up a contract to give her sole copyright of Nietzsche's manuscripts and papers. She offered her mother thirty thousand marks for all the rights and royalties from his works. Franziska conceded reluctantly. She did not want to give her daughter complete power over the literary estate but on the other hand, the money ought to be sufficient to guarantee a secure future for herself and her son. It was not a large sum in terms of the income from his books, considering that they had brought in almost half that amount the previous year. Admiration for Nietzsche's work was now so widespread that Elisabeth had no trouble raising the money. Three of her brother's wealthy admirers provided her with the sum: Nietzsche's old friend Meta von Salis-Marschlins, a banker named Robert von Mendelssohn, who was Jewish (Elisabeth's anti-Semitism did not extend to financial squeamishness), and Count Harry Kessler.

From then until Elisabeth's death in 1935, she controlled access to and publication, editing and copyright of all Nietzsche's work, as well as letters written to and by him. She had put herself in the position to exercise whatever censorship she desired, to shape her brother's writing and his life story, and to receive the royalties for whatever she permitted to be published.

In April 1897, the *Sturm und Drang* between mother and daughter finally blew itself out. Worn out and unhappy, Franziska died at the age of seventy-one, probably of cancer of the womb. Elisabeth gained full control of Nietzsche the man, as well as his works.

The first thing to do was to move him and the archive to a more suitable location. Naumburg was a backwater. It seemed to her that Weimar presented the solution; here he could take his place in the pantheon of German culture.

Weimar had become Germany's seat of the Muses on the arrival of Goethe in 1775. The transformation into 'our German Athens' had been completed by the great men of letters of the golden age: Fichte, Herder, von Humboldt, Schelling, Schiller and Wieland. In 1848, Liszt had taken on the cultural mantle, instituting a silver age by forming a cultural association, the *Neu-Weimar-Verein*, and directing early productions of Wagner's operas at the court theatre.

The archives of both Goethe and Schiller were housed in Weimar, and Elisabeth calculated that sharing in this glory would further the chance of the Nietzsche archive attaining equality with Cosima's Wagner archive in Bayreuth, which she viewed with piqued admiration.

To sell a small house in Naumburg and buy a big one in Weimar required money. Meta von Salis-Marschlins was happy to pay. How better to repay Nietzsche for the summers they had spent together in Sils-Maria? While Meta had merely taught him to row a boat on Lake Silvaplana, he in exchange had taught her that a woman, too, can become an *Übermensch*.

Meta discovered the newly built Villa Silberblick,[16] a rather ugly foursquare brick mansion on the southern outskirts of Weimar. It was smaller than Wahnfried, but as there was no need to accommodate a concert hall it was perfectly large enough. The Villa Silberblick's glory was its position; it was named for its silver view. It was, and is, situated at the top of the gently rising Humboltstrasse, commanding the finest view over the town and thus the finest over one of Europe's great neo-classical landscapes, created by Goethe on his return from his Italian journey. Goethe, like Nietzsche, had fallen in love with the *campagna*, the countryside around Rome, and with its representations on the canvases of Claude Lorrain. When he came home, Goethe set about remodelling the undulating contours of the Weimar plain into a miniature version of Arcadia. Meadows were transformed into Elysian fields. Temples and grottoes were tucked into bends of the winding River Ilm. The view from the windows of the Villa Silberblick stretched for at least ten miles over this recreation of the beloved landscape that had inspired Nietzsche, lovesick for Lou, to compose 'The Night Song'.

The Villa Silberblick's two-storey veranda was the place where Nietzsche would sit almost every day for the three years that comprised the rest of his life. If his eyes were capable of seeing it, which was far from certain, he would have been reminded of the *campagna* and the landscape of the life-changing walk with Lou up the Monte Sacro, flattened out onto the Thuringian plain and shading away at its edges into the black billowing bulges of the Ettersberg forest.

To Meta, it seemed a most suitable location for her dear friend. She purchased the villa and its grounds for thirty-nine thousand marks. Without informing her, Elisabeth embarked on an extravagant building programme, throwing out a bathroom here, a balcony there, and sending the bill to Meta, who was outraged to be charged for unnecessary cosmetic improvements. But what she found worse was Elisabeth's mania for publicity. Meta read an article by a journalist describing how Nietzsche had been put on display for his benefit: first sleeping, then awake, then crouched in a chair and fed pieces of cake. It was too much for her. She broke off the connection.[17]

In July 1897, with the alterations completed, Elisabeth organised a well-publicised secret nighttime journey. The philosopher was transported in a wheelchair by train from Naumburg to Weimar, arriving at the station's private entrance, which had been opened specially. Normally it was reserved for the exclusive use of the Grand Duke of Saxe-Weimar. From the moment of her arrival, Elisabeth was never seen around town on her own two feet. She travelled only by carriage, accompanied by a coachman and a footman sitting on the box.[18]

One of the earliest visitors was Count Harry Kessler. Arriving in August, he was astonished to be met at the station by a liveried servant sporting the five-pointed coronet of the nobility on his gilded buttons.[19] Kessler had come to talk about *Thus Spoke Zarathustra*. Richard Strauss's musical piece of the same name had been premiered the previous year, causing a sensation. Kessler proposed a deluxe bibliophile edition of

Zarathustra. Kessler also wanted to hasten publication of the late poems, as well as *Ecce Homo*, which had still not been published. Elisabeth was not responsive. Besides suppressing the uncomplimentary passages about herself in *Ecce Homo*, it suited her better to release parsimonious little snippets of it in her biographical articles on her brother. This preserved her privileged position as the gatekeeper, the only one with access to the valuable autobiography: a very strong weapon to use in silencing anyone who might question (shades of the Klingbeil affair) the authenticity of what the archive put out. She clung onto the text of *Ecce Homo* for another eleven years before allowing publication. Even then, she only allowed Kessler to publish it in what is known as 'the bank director's edition', a luxurious limited edition designed by van de Velde, printed in black and gold ink, which netted her 29,500 marks.

On this, Harry Kessler's first visit to the Villa Silberblick, Elisabeth was more interested in discussing suitable funeral arrangements for Nietzsche, who was far from dead upstairs. She had already determined that her brother should be buried in the grounds of the Villa Silberblick, as Wagner had been buried at Wahnfried, but the city authorities were being difficult. Harry Kessler felt that the Chastè peninsula in Sils-Maria would be a more suitable place but this met with no enthusiasm from Elisabeth. She did, however, offer him editorship of the archive. He did not accept, despite the winsome charm with which fifty-one-year-old Elisabeth made the proposal to twenty-nine-year-old Kessler.

Elisabeth was positively Viennese in her love of flirtation with handsome young men half her age. The archive's first editor, Fritz Kögel, had been sacked when he fell in love with a girl closer to his own age and became engaged to her. Elisabeth then hired young Rudolf Steiner, who later would attach himself to Madame Blavatsky's religious cult of theosophy before founding his own mishmash 'spiritual science' called anthroposophy, based on visions he had experienced in his youth. Together with Steiner's editorial work at the Nietzsche archive, Elisabeth employed him to instruct her in her brother's philosophy but it was a case of the crank visionary failing to instruct the obstinate llama. Steiner gave up, saying she was incapable either of taking instruction or of comprehending Nietzsche's philosophy. Both were probably true.

Kessler's refusal left the archive in need of an editor. An avalanche of paper had recently arrived from Sils-Maria. When Nietzsche had left Sils for what turned out to be the last time, his room in Gian Durisch's house had contained all sorts of notes and jottings. He told Durisch that it was rubbish, and that he should burn it. Durisch got as far as putting it in a cupboard but before he could get around to bonfiring, pilgrims arrived to walk Zarathustra's mountains and touch his rock. They seized upon any sacred relic, whether the writing on it read 'I have forgotten my umbrella'[20] or speculated on the differing meanings of the crucified Christ and Dionysus torn to pieces. When Elisabeth got to hear, she demanded everything be sent to Weimar, where it joined the ever-deepening snowdrift of the literary estate, the *Nachlass*.

Finally Elisabeth had to swallow her pride and bring back Peter Gast as editor. He really was the only one who could read the late handwriting, and this was vital to Elisabeth's ambition to shape the chaotic *Nachlass* into a book of her own making and publish it in Nietzsche's name. She planned to give it the title *The Will to Power* and to present it as his magnum opus, his revaluation of all values. She had no doubt that from the *Nachlass* scraps she could create the book that, occasionally during his last sane year, Nietzsche had mentioned that he was thinking of writing, or that he had written, or that he no longer needed to write following completion of *The Anti-Christ*.

Nietzsche was never rich. He had the poor man's parsimonious habit of using the same notebooks over and over again until they were full up. Unless there is marked deterioration in the handwriting, there is often no clue to chronology or thought sequence. Sometimes he wrote from the front to the back, sometimes from the back to the front. Pages and passages were crossed out or written over. Profundities shared the page with scribbled shopping lists.

While Gast worked away at the *Nachlass*, the Villa Silberblick became a place of pilgrimage where Nietzsche's texts, photographs and incunabula were displayed alongside framed lace veils, folkloric Paraguayan artefacts and a bust of the pioneering Dr Förster, hero of the noble causes of Aryanism and anti-Semitic colonisation. Elisabeth held a salon on Saturdays and a lot of parties in between. Visitors were excitedly conscious that above them, 'separated only by a layer of beams' as one remarked, lay the Nietzsche-Zarathustra idol. Special visitors were allowed a distant glimpse of the figure upstairs, now always dressed in the long-sleeved floor-length robe of white linen borrowed from sacred iconography.

The susceptible visitor found it easy to imagine Nietzsche apotheosised, and semi-religious accounts began to appear in print. They often focused on his eyes. The sublime prince of the intellect had eyes with the mystical capacity to gaze deeper into the abyss of the human heart and higher to the icy peaks than those of any other living person. Nietzsche's poor, semi-blind eyes were compared to twin stars, celestial orbs and even galaxies. 'Whoever saw Nietzsche at this time,' wrote Rudolf Steiner, 'as he reclined in his white, pleated robe, with the nobility of his enigmatic, questioning face and the leonine, majestic carriage of his thinker's head – had the feeling that this man could not die, but that his eye would rest for all eternity upon mankind and the whole world of appearance in this unfathomable exultation.'[21] The architect Fritz Schumacher, whom Elisabeth called in to design a monument to her brother, said that 'No one who saw [him] could have believed that he was looking at a body from which the mind had fled. One had to believe one was looking at a man who had risen above small, everyday things.'[22]

Elisabeth liked to display him after dinner. Often she arranged for him to be half-glimpsed through a misty curtain, like a spirit at a séance.[23] Few were as clear-eyed as Harry Kessler, who probably saw him most often as he used to spend the night in the Villa Silberblick when he had business to discuss with Elisabeth. He would find himself starting up in bed when Nietzsche gave voice to the 'long, raw moaning sounds, which he screamed into the night with all his might; then all was still again'.[24]

Kessler did not see a sick man or a prophet or even a lunatic in Nietzsche, rather an empty envelope, a living corpse. The exposed hands with their tributary veins of green and violet were waxy and swollen, as on a dead body. The permitted overgrowth of the moustache that covered the entire mouth and chin was a deliberate concealment of the lapse into vacant idiocy that an uncontrolled mouth cannot fail to reveal. Unlike the pilgrims, Kessler saw nothing in Nietzsche's eyes. Nothing mad, nothing frightening, nothing spiritual. 'I would prefer to describe the look as loyal and, at the same time, of not quite understanding, of a fruitless intellectual searching, such as you often see in a large, noble dog.'[25]

Nietzsche suffered his first stroke in the summer of 1898. The next came the following year. In August 1900, he caught a cold and developed breathing difficulties. A witness who preferred to remain anonymous, maybe fearing Elisabeth's long and vengeful reach, reported on Nietzsche's end. The description sounds as if it was written by a nurse who had looked after the patient for some years.

He or she noted that following his transfer to Weimar, Nietzsche was incapable of reading, of comprehension or indeed of lucid speech, although there had been no lack of interviews with the poor unfortunate. The interviewers seldom saw Nietzsche face to face. All contact went through Elisabeth, all reports flowed through her while Nietzsche lay paralysed down one side, helpless in what the witness called his 'mattress grave', hemmed in by pushed-up furniture to prevent his escape. Physical functions were performed with difficulty, not least because whenever Nietzsche saw a shiny object, he tried to stuff it into his mouth. Apart from this, he was on the whole a good and obedient patient. His condition was desolate and hopeless but he was rarely in physical pain.

Harry Kessler bears out this description but Elisabeth's bulletins told a different story. Nietzsche was taking great pleasure in his favourite author – apparently Guy de Maupassant. According to her, Nietzsche retained his power of speech till the last. 'How often he praised me for what I did. How often he comforted me when I looked sad. His gratitude was touching. "Why do you cry, Lisbeth?" he would say. "We're quite happy."[26]

The two accounts of his death also vary. His death struggle was hard, but not very long, writes the anonymous witness, who was obviously experienced in observing deathbeds, and who went on to comment that Nietzsche's impressive constitution, 'which was imposing even in the coffin', might perhaps have struggled longer, had the will been there.[27]

Elisabeth recounted the death differently. One day, as she was sitting opposite him, a terrible storm was brewing. His whole expression changed and he fell over, unconscious, from a stroke. (Elisabeth was fond of strokes.) 'It looked like this great mind was to perish amid thunder and lightning but he recovered in the evening and tried to speak . . . When I handed him a glass of refreshment it was towards two o'clock in the morning and he pushed aside the lampshade so that he could see me . . . Opening his magnificent eyes, he gazed into [my] eyes for the last time and cried out joyfully: "Elisabeth!" Then all at once he shook his head, closed his eyes voluntarily and died . . . So it happened that Zarathustra perished.'[28]

He died on 25 August 1900.

Elisabeth summoned Harry Kessler. He cut short his visit to the *Exposition Universelle* in Paris where the world was greeting the arrival of the new century by lighting up the Eiffel Tower in celebration of the wonder of electricity. Kessler arrived in Weimar to the vision of Nietzsche laid out in his coffin in the archive room, crowded in by potted palms and flowers.

The making of a death mask was commonly carried out by sculptors. Elisabeth had asked Max Klinger and Ernst Geyger to come and do it but both were too busy, and so the task fell to Harry Kessler. He set to, pulling in a young apprentice who was there to help with the funeral decorations. The head had fallen to one side and they had to raise it a little, to straighten it. They were relieved when the task was completed. Elisabeth made copies of the death mask and gave them away as *memento mori*. But it was not long before she decided that the death mask was not sufficiently impressive. A second, improved version was made and also given away to the specially favoured. The forehead had been heightened to rival Socrates' and the hair of the fifty-five-year-old Nietzsche augmented to resemble the luxuriant locks of a young Apollo.

Nietzsche had let it be known that he wished to descend into his tomb like an honest pagan. For music, he wanted only his setting of Lou's 'Hymn to Life'. No Christian ritual. Above all, no priests.

A long, Christian service was held round the coffin in the archive room. Music was by Brahms and Palestrina. An interminable eulogy of Polonius-like pedantry was delivered by an art historian named Kurt Breysig. Some said that if Nietzsche had heard it, he would have thrown Breysig out of the window and the congregation after him.[29]

The following day everything moved to Röcken, where the coffin, decorated with a shiny silver cross, was interred in the middle of the row of family graves that contained his father and his mother and his baby brother Joseph. Elisabeth later had second thoughts about this, as she did about the death mask. She had his coffin moved from the centre to the end of the row. When the time came, she wished to spend eternity in the middle of things.

Elisabeth inherited thirty-six thousand marks from Nietzsche when he died. The Nietzsche archive was formalised, with Harry Kessler appointed as one of its trustees. He took up the directorship of Weimar's Grand Ducal Museum of Arts and Crafts and set about organising Weimar's next cultural age as a *Gesamtkunstwerk* centred around Nietzsche, just as its first golden age had centred round Goethe. It was another attempt at achieving the dream that Nietzsche and Wagner had once shared: the creation of a coherent new German cultural identity embracing all the arts in one unified vision.

Kessler brought in Henry van de Velde to head the School of Arts and Crafts in Weimar, and to transform the interior of the Villa Silberblick, which was now known as *Das Nietzsche-Archiv*. Van de Velde was the bright Belgian proponent of the latest style, called *Jugendstil* in

Germany and art nouveau in France. Before Kessler brought van de Velde to Weimar, he had designed the interior of *La Maison de l'Art Nouveau* for the famous Paris art dealer Samuel Siegfried Bing, who made the market in the style.

Jugendstil's emphasis on natural forms and hand-crafting chimed with Nietzsche's ideas of the strength of the sub-logical and irrational force of the natural world over the force of machines. The Kaiser said that the wave-like curves of van de Velde's interiors made him feel seasick, but Elisabeth delighted in the transformation of the archive into a much-visited modernist style icon. The letter 'N' for Nietzsche in *Jugendstil* sinewy lines ornamented everything from wood panelling to door handles.

The very heart of the *Gesamtkunstwerk* must be Nietzsche's published texts. Kessler commissioned van de Velde to design a clean, new typeface to free Nietzsche's soaring words from the archaic Gothic tangle of traditional German Blackletter script.

While van de Velde took care of the decorative arts, Kessler took on the fine arts. He was well acquainted with the legendary Paris art dealers Ambroise Vollard and Paul Durand-Ruel. His Weimar gallery became an outpost of avant-garde Paris, showing Impressionists, post-Impressionists and Expressionists. He knew many of the artists personally, including Monet, Renoir, Degas, Bonnard, Redon and Vuillard, as well as the sculptor Maillol, whom he wished to commission to make a giant nude statue symbolising the *Übermensch* as part of a 1911 plan for a large Nietzsche monument. The proposed committee for this monument demonstrates the wide spread of interest in Nietzsche at the start of the twentieth century. As well as Maillol it included George Bernard Shaw, George Moore, W. B. Yeats, Gilbert Murray, William Rothenstein, Harley Granville-Barker, Eric Gill, Auguste Rodin, Maurice Denis, Anatole France, Henri Bergson, Charles Maurras and Maurice Barrès. The plan foundered on the outbreak of the First World War.

Edvard Munch was summoned to Weimar to paint a posthumous 'ideas portrait' of Nietzsche in 1906. Size of canvas often reflected

Munch's opinion of his subject matter and his 'ideas portrait' of Nietzsche is one of his largest. Like the *Scream* figure, Nietzsche stands against a railing that runs diagonally across the canvas into infinity.[30] While the *Scream*'s railing runs from bottom right to top left, Nietzsche's railing runs from bottom left to top right, an interesting statement on how Munch viewed the different mental journey of each figure. The gigantic figure of Nietzsche dwarfs a small church that is placed in the landscape: Munch, like Nietzsche, had originally been destined for the priesthood by his own hyper-religious family and, like Nietzsche, he had taken a very different path.

Elisabeth and Munch did not get on. Nevertheless she wanted him to paint her portrait. Choosing an awkwardly proportioned canvas, he made a great fuss of her flounced dress and gave her the hard, implacable face of an executioner.[31]

Up on her own green hill, Elisabeth felt she had at last attained equal status with Cosima. Cosima died in 1930 and Elisabeth in 1935, by which time her period in charge of Nietzsche's output was more than twice as long as the sixteen years between him publishing his first book, *The Birth of Tragedy*, and writing his last, *Ecce Homo*. During those years Elisabeth was the spider at the centre of the Nietzsche archive, weaving her brother's words into her own web and inflating her own reputation through presenting her brother as the mystic prophet of her own convictions.

Elisabeth had never understood the concept-quake that lay at the base of her brother's thought. She had never understood his rejection of all systems and of all philosophies that reduced the world to a single system. The revolutionary opposition to certainty that led him to describe himself as the philosopher of 'perhaps' was beyond her comprehension. She ignored his idea of himself as a practical joker, the philosopher who would rather be seen as a buffoon than a saint. She ignored his idea that truth had no single definition but might fruitfully be examined as a question of perspectives. She ignored his idea that there existed no eternal reason-spider but merely accidents on the dance floor of life, and that existence was no less meaningful for that. In complete control of his works, she did not even understand the purpose behind his chief intellectual exploration: how to find value and meaning in an uncertain universe in which neither the ideal nor the divine existed.

In 1901, a year after Nietzsche's death and twelve years after he lost his reason, Elisabeth published a new book in his name, *The Will to Power* (*Der Wille zur Macht*), as Volume XV of the collected works. It consisted of a collection of 483 aphorisms selected from the *Nachlass*, the notes and drafts that Nietzsche never intended to be read by anybody else, let alone published. Nietzsche was always neurotically scrupulous concerning what was eventually published, as one sees from his correspondence with Gast and with his publishers. What Elisabeth published in *The Will to Power* did not represent his final views on anything. By the time of its 1906 reprinting, Elisabeth had tripled the book in size: 483 aphorisms had swelled to 1,067. Elisabeth was revelling in her posthumous editorial control.

Image was an important component of the Nietzsche legend, and Elisabeth commissioned brawny sculptures, radiant paintings and effectively lit photographs. Nietzsche was even depicted as Christ wearing a crown of thorns. Managing the literary output, she turned out books and articles and selected snippets of his writing. With no one to gainsay her version of events, she wrote an imaginative second volume of biography, *The Lonely Nietzsche*, produced an unreliable account of the *Nietzsche–Wagner Correspondence*, and a book on *Nietzsche and Women* that pursued her grudge against Lou. Following her expanded version of *The Will to Power*, Elisabeth was nominated for the 1908 Nobel Prize in literature. She would be nominated a further three times for her writings on her brother.[32] The University of Jena awarded her an honorary doctorate, after which her signature found its final form: 'Frau Dr. Phil. H. C. Elisabeth Förster-Nietzsche.'

In the years building up to the First World War, while Harry Kessler still exerted a degree of power, interest in the archive was cosmopolitan and intellectual. It attracted more critics, creative writers and artists than philosophers. Confirmed Nietzscheans included Hugo von Hofmannsthal, Stefan George, Richard Dehmel, Richard Strauss, Thomas Mann, Heinrich Mann, Martin Buber, Carl Gustav Jung, Hermann Hesse, Paul Heyse, Rainer Maria Rilke, Max Brod, Albert Schweitzer, André Gide, the dancers Vaslav Nijinsky and Isadora Duncan and the aviator Graf Zeppelin. Other early devotees included George Bernard Shaw and W. B. Yeats, H. G. Wells, James Joyce, Wyndham Lewis, Herbert Read and T. S. Eliot. H. L. Mencken was probably the earliest of the American enthusiasts, followed by Theodore Dreiser, Eugene O'Neill, Ezra Pound and Jack London. In France, Hippolyte Taine, Jean Bourdeau, André Gide, Paul Valéry, Alfred Jarry and Eugène de Roberty. In Italy, Gabriele D'Annunzio and Benito Mussolini.

This would have been astonishing enough to Nietzsche, who had so often expressed his horror at the idea of having disciples, but the political tenor of the Nietzsche cult would have horrified him further still. The approach of the First World War gave impetus to a bellicose form of Nietzscheism that took the will to power as a moral teaching sanctioning violence and ruthlessness, the *Übermensch* as the greatest brute, and the blond beast as an incentive towards a racial breeding programme. Elisabeth's newspaper articles encouraged these twisted interpretations, enthusiastically describing her brother as a friend of war.

One hundred and fifty thousand copies of *Zarathustra* were printed in a special pocket edition for German soldiers in the First World War, to be taken into battle alongside Goethe's *Faust* and the New Testament. One wonders what on earth they used them for, just as one wonders what Nietzsche, who was so hostile to pan-German militarism, would have made of this development.

'If we could dissuade from wars, so much the better,' he had written in one of his late notebooks. 'I would know how to find better use for the twelve billion that it costs Europe each year to preserve its armed peace; there are other means of honouring physiology than through army hospitals . . . To take such a select crop of youth and energy and power and then to put it in front of cannons – that is *madness*.'[33]

The first major political figure to realise how Nietzsche's philosophy could be adapted to his own ideas of nationalism and the use of violence was Mussolini. As a young man, well before his ascent to power, he had been of the generation to find hope in Nietzsche.[34] In 1931, when the archive had become thick with Nazis and Mussolini had become Italy's fascist dictator and very thick with Hitler, he sent Elisabeth a telegram congratulating her on her eighty-fifth birthday. She admired Mussolini greatly, and set about persuading the Weimar National Theatre to put on a play co-authored by him called *Campo di Maggio*.[35] When it was performed in February 1932, Hitler showed up in the theatre with stormtroopers and presented Elisabeth with a large bunch of red roses. They met again a year later, at a performance of *Tristan* in honour of the fiftieth anniversary of Wagner's death. By this time Hitler was Chancellor of Germany.

'We are drunk with enthusiasm because at the head of our government stands such a wonderful, indeed phenomenal, personality like our magnificent Chancellor Adolf Hitler,' gushed Elisabeth. '*Ein Volk, Ein Reich, Ein Führer.*'[36]

The long descent of the Nietzsche archive into the Nazi camp had begun in the inter-war period of the Weimar Republic (1918–33), when Germany was roiling with resentment at its humiliating defeat in the First World War and suffering the appalling crises of the Great Depression, hyperinflation and six million unemployed, with the consequent rise of the political extremes of communism and National Socialism.

During the Weimar Republic, the archive was right at the centre of politics as Elisabeth welcomed the National Socialists (Nazis), whose aggressive nationalism and anti-Semitism chimed with her own. She appointed her cousin Max Oehler as chief archivist. Oehler was a career soldier who had come back from the First World War smarting at Germany's defeat and had joined the National Socialist party. He would occupy this position in the archive until Hitler fell.

Elisabeth and Oehler packed the archive with National Socialists who would write the philosophy of their party in Nietzsche's name. The Villa Silberblick became the den of vengeful tarantulas that Nietzsche had foreseen and warned against:

'My friends, I do not want to be mixed in with and mistaken for others. There are those who preach my doctrine of life, and at the same time they are . . . tarantulas . . . "That the world become full of thunderstorms of our revenge, precisely that we would regard as justice," – thus they speak with one another . . . They resemble the inspired, but it is not the heart that inspires them – but revenge. And when they are refined and cold, it is not the spirit but envy that makes them refined and cold. Their jealousy even leads them along the thinkers' path; and this is the mark of their jealousy . . . From each of their laments revenge sounds, in each of their praisings there is harm, and being the judge is bliss to them. But thus I counsel you my friends: mistrust all in whom the drive to punish is strong! Those are people of bad kind and kin; in their faces the hangman and the bloodhound are visible . . .'[37]

The tarantulas, all men of high standing, were appointed as editors or members of the archive committee. Among them were Carl August Emge, Professor of Legal Philosophy at Jena University, prospective Nazi minister for the Thuringian government and an important signatory to the declaration of three hundred university lecturers supporting Hitler in March 1933. Another editor was the philosopher Oswald Spengler, whose most poisonous influence on the manipulation of Nietzsche's ideas was his belief in Social Darwinism: the corruption of Darwin's theory of evolutionary selection through conflict and survival of the fittest translated into German racial supremacy, justifying eugenics and, eventually, the Final Solution. The terms *Übermensch* and 'master morality' were gifts to Spengler. Harry Kessler seethed with fury and contempt at Spengler's utterly mediocre presence in the archive and his endless spouting of trite and trivial slogans.

Alfred Bäumler, Professor of Philosophy at the Universities of Dresden and Berlin, prepared Nietzsche's texts for new editions, including yet another edition of *The Will to Power* that again gave the impression the text had been authored by Nietzsche himself. Bäumler headed the science and scholarship division of Alfred Rosenberg's department for Supervision of All Intellectual and Ideological Education,[38] which produced textbooks for schoolchildren that taught theories of race and blood as fact. Bäumler has been described as the single person most responsible for establishing the link between Nietzsche and Hitler.[39]

Bäumler oversaw the notorious book burning in Berlin. Just a few days earlier the philosopher Martin Heidegger had joined the Nazi party in a public ceremony replete with swastikas. He appeared on podiums in support of the Nazification of the universities and he appealed for more book burnings across the country.[40] Heidegger joined Bäumler as an editor in the archive, where they took the extraordinary view that Nietzsche's published works hardly counted because the real philosophy resided in the *Nachlass*, the literary estate that Elisabeth had already manipulated to her own ends. The elevation of the *Nachlass* to the status of Holy Writ was the key to allowing the philosophers and editors in the archive to cut and paste the dislocated fragments and reassemble them to convey their own ideas.

Harry Kessler watched in dismay: 'Inside the Archive, everyone from the doorkeeper to the head, is a Nazi . . . It is enough to make one weep . . . through the open door I had a view of the sofa where Nietzsche sat, looking like an ailing eagle, the last time I saw him . . . Mysterious, incomprehensible Germany.'[41]

Kessler fled into exile, leaving his beloved Germany and his beloved philosopher, whose affirmative Dionysian dance of life was being turned into a *danse macabre* by Germany's new masters.

Hitler followed up his first meeting with Elisabeth by calling on her in the archive on 2 November 1933. Chancellor of Germany, he arrived with full escort, carrying his customary whip. He remained in the archive for an hour and a half. When he emerged the whip had gone. In its place he grasped Nietzsche's walking stick, presented to him by Elisabeth.[42] She had also given him a copy of the 1880 petition against the Jews that Bernhard Förster had presented to Bismarck. Hitler sent a parcel of native German soil to Paraguay, to be scattered on Förster's grave.

Hitler was infatuated with the idea of himself as the philosopher-leader. He loved to drop the great names. It is impossible to prove whether Hitler ever studied Nietzsche. It is widely believed he did not. The surviving books known to have comprised his library during his time in prison in 1924, when he wrote *Mein Kampf*, do not include any works by Nietzsche.[43] It is of course possible that they were part of his book collection at the time and have since been lost but his later library preserves no well-thumbed copies. The notorious film of the 1934 Nuremberg Rally was given the deliberately Nietzschean title *Triumph of the Will*, but when the director Leni Riefenstahl asked him whether he liked to read Nietzsche, he answered, 'No, I can't really do much with Nietzsche . . . he is not my guide.'[44]

The complicated ideas contained in the books were of no use to him but simple slogans and titles such as the *Übermensch*, the 'will to power', 'master morality', 'the blond beast' and 'beyond good and evil' could be put to infinite misuse. Hitler's pianist Ernst Hanfstaengl, who accompanied him on at least one visit to the Nietzsche archive, grimly but aptly described his Führer as a bartender of genius who took whatever might go into the mixing of his poisonous genocidal cocktail.[45] Nietzsche was far from the only philosopher selectively misused in this way. Cherry-picked quotations from Kant and others supported anti-Semitism, nationalism and German master-race exceptionalism. As Hanfstaengl observed, 'the guillotine twist which Robespierre had given the teachings of Jean-Jacques Rousseau was repeated by Hitler and the Gestapo in their political simplification of the contradictory theories of Nietzsche.'[46]

But even as the archive's propagandists and phrasemongers usurped Nietzsche's words and meaning, there were among the Nazis themselves those who realised the absurdity of their party's appropriation of Nietzsche. Ernst Krieck, a prominent Nazi ideologue, sarcastically remarked that apart from the fact that Nietzsche was not a socialist, not a nationalist and opposed to racial thinking, he could have been a leading National Socialist thinker.[47]

In 1934, Hitler visited the Villa Silberblick, bringing Albert Speer, the architect whom he favoured to design the world-bestridingly triumphalist architecture of the Third Reich. To Elisabeth's delight, Speer was to design a Nietzsche Memorial. Mussolini contributed by sending a monstrous oversized Greek statue of Dionysus.

Elisabeth was now approaching her ninetieth year. She spent much of it in bed, having *Mein Kampf* read aloud to her. Nine days before she died, she wrote of Hitler, 'One cannot but love this great, magnificent man if one knows him as well as I do.'[48]

Death was kind to Elisabeth. She caught influenza and died a few days later, painlessly and peacefully, on 8 November 1935.

Elisabeth died as she had lived, untroubled by self-doubt. She had never had problems convincing herself of what she wanted to believe and she died happily certain that she was the person her brother had loved the best. She also sincerely believed that it was through her own greatness that his immortality had been assured. It was she, not her brother, who had built the archive. It was she, not her brother, who had been nominated for the Nobel Prize. It was she, not her brother, who had been awarded an honorary doctorate from the ancient University of Jena. It was she, not her brother, who had presided over the vast sales of his books. It was she, not her brother, who rejoiced in the friendship of the highest in the land, the Chancellor of Germany himself.

Hitler sat in the front row of the archive room at Elisabeth's lying in state. He laid an ostentatiously enormous wreath and he listened solemnly to the extravagant eulogies praising Elisabeth as the co-priestess of Eternal Germany – the other priestess being Cosima Wagner. How pleased Elisabeth would have been at that. Hitler did not often allow himself to be photographed looking sad, but on this occasion he did.

'I am frightened', Nietzsche had written, 'by the thought of what unqualified and unsuitable people may invoke my authority one day.

Yet that is the torment of every great teacher of mankind: he knows that, given the circumstances and the accidents, he *can* become a disaster as well as a blessing to mankind.'[49]

To be a source of political theories had never been Nietzsche's aim. The irony of his appropriation is that he was only ever interested in man as an individual, rather than man as a herd animal – be the herd political or religious.

Nietzsche described man as 'the sick animal' because he is provided with everything and yet is infected with an insatiable need for the metaphysical that can never be assuaged. In an attempt to satisfy this eternal and indestructible need, many of his contemporaries turned to science and Darwinism but, as Nietzsche pointed out, the meaning of science is not religion, and evolution is far from a moral road. Evolutionary 'good' and 'bad' only equal 'more useful' and 'less useful', and this has nothing to do with morals or ethics.

Nietzsche's statement 'God is dead' had said the unsayable to an age unwilling to go so far as to acknowledge the obvious: that without belief in the divine there was no longer any moral authority for the laws that had persisted throughout the civilisation built over the last two thousand years.

What happens when man cancels the moral code on which he has built the edifice of his civilisation? What does it mean to be human unchained from a central metaphysical purpose? Does a vacuum of meaning occur? If so, what is to fill that vacuum? If the life to come is abolished, ultimate meaning rests in the here and now. Given the power to live without religion, man must take responsibility for his own actions. And yet Nietzsche saw his contemporaries remaining content to live in lazy compromise, refusing to examine their own inauthenticity: refusing to swing the hammer at the idols to see if they ring true.

It remains a thoroughly modern challenge. Perhaps part of Nietzsche's enduring appeal lies in his unwillingness to provide us with an answer. We are meant to find the meaning and the answer, if there is one, for ourselves: this is the true accomplishment of the *Übermensch*.

One might reject science as faith; one might reject religious faith itself but still retain moral values. First, man must become himself. Secondly, *amor fati*; he must accept what life brings, avoiding the blind alleys of self-hatred and *ressentiment*. Then finally man can overcome himself to find true fulfilment as the *Übermensch*, the man at peace with himself, finding joy in his earthly purpose, rejoicing in the sheer magnificence of existence and content with the finitude of his mortality.

Tragically for Nietzsche, the need to overcome ourselves became so blatantly distorted into the need to overcome others that it has tended to overshadow his ability to ask the eternal questions in such a gloriously provocative way. Similarly, his devotion to examining every facet of the truth and never recommending an answer beyond 'perhaps . . .' has afforded infinite potential for interpretation.

If you visit the Villa Silberblick today, you will find that trees have grown up in the garden, hiding the magnificent view for which the villa was named. But if you walk beyond the trees into the field beside the garden, you can enjoy the view that was once visible from Nietzsche's balcony. As your eye roves over Goethe's ravishing Enlightenment recreation of classical perfection, you are overtaken by delight, marvelling at man's capacity to use nature's simple materials of soil and stone, water and plants, and shape them into a symbolic vision of the earth's perfectibility through his own high ideals. We are offered a vision of transcendence stretching for ten glorious miles before finally the pretty rills and sheep-dotted meadows disappear into the inky billows of the Ettersberg forest, and here a new landmark rises up against the trees on the horizon: the tall, smoke-blackened crematorium chimney of the Buchenwald concentration camp.

Just as that terrible chimney looms over the landscape whose purpose was to illustrate man's highest cultural aspirations, so Nietzsche's prophetic utterances also remain overshadowed by dreadful connotations.

'I know my fate,' he had written. 'One day there will be associated with my name the recollection of something frightful – of a crisis like no other before on earth, of the profoundest collision of conscience, of a decision evoked *against* everything that until then had been believed in, demanded, sanctified. I am not a man, I am dynamite.'[50]

Hearts shaped by history sink at the prophecy. But only in our imagination, darkened by the long shadow of hindsight, is this the cry of a man wanting to unleash evil upon the world. Rather, it sounds the triumphant call of the man who blasted a tunnel through his own age's heavy indifference to the consequences of the death of God, opening the way for audacious Argonauts of the spirit to reach new worlds.

· APHORISMS ·

The worst readers are those who behave like plundering troops:
they take away a few things they can use, dirty and confound the
remainder, and revile the whole.

Human, All Too Human, Book II, Section 137

People have been recognising themselves in Nietzsche's aphorisms for
over a hundred years. Below is a personal selection of some that seem
to have strong contemporary resonance. Often they contradict each
other, reminding us how Nietzsche loved to provoke, calling himself
the philosopher of 'perhaps'. Their pithiness combined with the ability
to mean what the reader happens to see in them (rather like Bob
Dylan's lyrics) means that many of his sayings have been disseminated
into popular culture. Given that his ideas pass into the zeitgeist through
a variety of different translations, the source in his writings is given in
the section below, but the text is drawn eclectically from the most
popular versions.

THE ABYSS

Man is a rope fastened between animal and superman – a rope over
an abyss.

Thus Spoke Zarathustra, 'Zarathustra's Prologue', Part I, Section 4

He who fights with monsters should look to it that he does not
become a monster himself. And if you gaze long into the abyss, the
abyss gazes back into you.

Beyond Good and Evil, 'Epigrams and Entr'actes', 146

ART

Art is the supreme task, the truly metaphysical activity in this life.
The Birth of Tragedy, Foreword to 'Richard Wagner'

BOREDOM

Even gods can't escape boredom.
The Anti-Christ, Section 48

Isn't life a hundred times too short to be bored?
Beyond Good and Evil, 'Our Virtues', Section 227

The objective of all human arrangements is through distracting one's thoughts to cease to be aware of life.
Untimely Meditations, 'Schopenhauer as Educator', Section 4

Haste is universal because everyone is in flight from himself.
Untimely Meditations, 'Schopenhauer as Educator', Section 5

CHRISTIANITY

Christianity is a romantic hypochondria for those unsteady on their feet.
Notebook 10, Autumn 1887, 127

The Kingdom of Heaven is a condition of the heart – not something that comes 'upon the earth' or 'after death'.
The Anti-Christ, Section 34

The very word 'Christianity' is a misunderstanding – in truth, there was only one Christian, and he died on the cross.
The Anti-Christ, Section 39

St Luke 18 verse 14 improved – He that humbleth himself wishes to be exalted.
Human, All Too Human, 'On the History of Moral Sensations', Section 87

EXASPERATED BY HIS FAMILY

People are *least* related to their parents; it would be the greatest
vulgarity to be related to your parents.
Ecce Homo, 'Why I am so Wise', Section 3

FAME

One must pay dearly for immortality; one has to die several times
while one is still alive.
Ecce Homo, 'Thus Spoke Zarathustra', Section 5

I am not a man, I am dynamite.
Ecce Homo, 'Why I am a Destiny', Section 1

FORMULA FOR GREATNESS

My formula for human greatness: *amor fati*, love your fate. Want
nothing different, neither backwards or forwards for all eternity.
Not just to tolerate necessity – but to love it . . .
Ecce Homo, 'Why I am so Clever', Section 10

GOD

God is dead; but given the way of men, there may still be caves for
thousands of years in which his shadow will be shown. – And we –
we still have to vanquish his shadow, too.
The Gay Science, Book III, Section 108

God is dead! God remains dead! And we have killed him. How shall
we comfort ourselves, the murderers of all murderers? What was
holiest and mightiest of all that the world has yet owned has bled to
death under our knives: who will wipe this blood off us? What water
is there for us to clean ourselves? What festivals of atonement, what
sacred games shall we have to invent? Is not the greatness of this deed
too great for us? Must we ourselves not become gods simply to appear
worthy of it?
The Gay Science, Book III, Section 125

Is man God's mistake, or is God man's mistake?
Twilight of the Idols, 'Epigrams and Maxims', Section 7

LIFE
Become what you are.
The Gay Science, Book III, Section 270

Man is a bridge, not a goal.
Thus Spoke Zarathustra, 'Zarathustra's Prologue', Part I, Section 4

No one can construct for you the bridge on which you must cross the stream of life, no one but you alone.
Untimely Meditations, 'Schopenhauer as Educator', Section 1

Life itself is will to power.
Beyond Good and Evil, 'On the Prejudices of Philosophers', Section 13

Live dangerously! Build your cities on the slopes of Vesuvius!
The Gay Science, Book IV, Section 283

To give birth to a dancing star one must first have chaos within.
Thus Spoke Zarathustra, 'Zarathustra's Prologue', Part I, Section 5

We want to be poets of our life – first of all in the smallest most everyday matters.
The Gay Science, Book IV, Section 299

What doesn't kill me makes me stronger.
Twilight of the Idols, 'Epigrams and Maxims', Section 8

He who has a *why?* in life can tolerate almost any *how?*
Twilight of the Idols, 'Epigrams and Maxims', Section 12

Man does not strive for happiness; only the Englishman does that.
Twilight of the Idols, 'Epigrams and Maxims', Section 12

One should take a bold and dangerous line with existence: whatever happens, we're bound to lose it.
Untimely Meditations, 'Schopenhauer as Educator', Section 1

How can a man know himself? He is a thing dark and veiled; and if the hare has seven skins, man can slough off seventy times seven and still not be able to say: 'This is really you, this is no longer outer shell.'
Untimely Meditations, 'Schopenhauer as Educator', Section 1

No victor believes in chance.
The Gay Science, Book III, Section 258

The advantage of a bad memory is that one can enjoy the same good things for the first time *several* times.
Human, All Too Human, 'Man Alone with Himself', Section 580

Virtue no longer meets with any belief; its attraction has disappeared. Someone would have to think of a way of marketing it afresh, perhaps as an unusual form of adventure and excess.
Notebook 9, Autumn 1887, 155

MARRIAGE
Some men have sighed over the abduction of their wives, but more over the fact that nobody wished to abduct them.
Human, All Too Human, 'Woman and Child', Section 388

MATHEMATICS
The laws of numbers assume there are identical things, but in fact nothing is identical with anything else.
Human, All Too Human, 'Of First and Last Things', Section 19

Mathematics would certainly not have come into existence if one had known from the beginning that there was in nature no such thing as a straight line, no perfect circle or absolute magnitude.
Human, All Too Human, 'Of First and Last Things', Section 11

THE METAPHYSICAL WORLD

Even if the existence of a metaphysical world were demonstrated, it is certain that knowledge of it would be as useless as knowledge of the chemical composition of water to a shipwrecked sailor.
Human, All Too Human, 'Of First and Last Things', Section 9

MONSTERS

To greatness belongs dreadfulness, let no one be deceived about that.
Notebook 9, Autumn 1887, Section 94

MOUSTACHES

The gentlest, most reasonable man may, if he wears a large moustache, sit as it were in its shade and feel safe. As the accessory of a large moustache he will give the impression of being military, irascible and sometimes violent – and will be treated accordingly.
Daybreak, Book IV, Section 381

MUSIC

Without music, life would be a mistake. Germans even imagine God singing songs.
Twilight of the Idols, 'Epigrams and Maxims', 33

Is Wagner a human being at all? Is he not rather a disease? He contaminates everything he touches – he has made music sick.
The Case of Wagner, Section 5

MUSIC AND DRUGS

You need hashish to get rid of unbearable pressure. Well then, I need Wagner. He is the antidote to all things German.

Ecce Homo, 'Why I am So Clever', Section 6

NATIONALISM

'*Deutschland, Deutschland über Alles*', I'm afraid that was the end of German philosophy.

Twilight of the Idols, 'What the Germans Lack', Section 1

For even if I am a bad German, I am at all events a very good European.

Letter to his mother, August 1886

PHILOSOPHY

To live alone one must be an animal or a god, says Aristotle. But you can be both – a philosopher.

Twilight of the Idols, 'Epigrams and Maxims', Section 3

Plato is boring.

Twilight of the Idols, 'What I Owe to the Ancients', Section 2

There could never have been a Platonic philosophy without such beautiful young men in Athens. Plato's philosophy is more accurately defined as an erotic contest.

Twilight of the Idols, 'Skirmishes of an Untimely Man', Section 23

Today's philosophers want to enjoy the divine principle of incomprehensibility.

Daybreak, Book V, Section 544

Mystical explanations are considered deep; the truth is they are not even shallow.

The Gay Science, Book III, Section 126

To find everything profound – that is an inconvenient trait. It makes one strain one's eyes all the time, and in the end one finds more than one might have wished.
The Gay Science, Book III, Section 158

Philosophy offers an asylum to a man into which no tyranny can force its way, the inward cave, the labyrinth of the heart – and that annoys the tyrants.
Untimely Meditations, 'Schopenhauer as Educator', Section 3

Thoughts are the shadows of our feelings – always darker, emptier, simpler.
The Gay Science, Book III, Section 179

The Socratic equation: reason = virtue = happiness was opposed to all the instincts of the earlier Greeks.
Twilight of the Idols, 'The Problem of Socrates', Section 4

PHILOSOPHY/TEACHING
You repay a teacher badly by becoming merely a pupil.
Ecce Homo, Foreword, Section 4

How to ruin a youth: instruct him to hold in high esteem only those who think like him.
Daybreak, Book IV, Section 297

PHOTOGRAPHY
Being photographically executed by the one-eyed Cyclops I try each time to prevent disaster but I come out every time eternalised anew as a pirate or a prominent tenor or a Boyar.
Letter to Malwida von Meysenbug, 20 December 1872

POLITICS

Morality is herd instinct in the individual.
The Gay Science, Book III, Section 116

Every one who has ever built a 'new heaven' only mustered the power
he needed through his own hell.
On the Genealogy of Morality, Essay 3, Section 10

He who thinks a great deal is not suited to be a party man: he thinks
his way through the party and out the other side too soon.
Human, All Too Human, 'Man Alone with Himself', Section 579

No one talks more passionately about his rights than he who in the
depths of his soul doubts whether he has any.
Human, All Too Human, 'Man Alone with Himself', Section 597

POSSESSIONS

Possession usually diminishes the possession.
The Gay Science, Book I, Section 14

One possesses one's opinions the way one possesses fish – insofar,
that is, that one possesses a fishpond. One has to go fishing and
be lucky – then one has one's own fish, one's own opinions. I am
speaking here of living fish. Others are content to possess a cabinet of
stuffed fish – and in their heads, convictions.
Human, All Too Human, Book IV, 'The Wanderer and His Shadow',
Section 317

POST-TRUTH

Convictions are more dangerous enemies of truth than lies.
Human, All Too Human, 'Man Alone with Himself', Section 483

People who live in an age of corruption are witty and slanderous; they know that there are other kinds of murder than by dagger or assault; they also know that whatever is *well said* is believed.
The Gay Science, Book I, Section 23

The most perfidious way of harming a cause consists of defending it deliberately with faulty arguments.
The Gay Science, Book III, Section 191

REALITY TV
Without cruelty there is no festival: thus the longest and most ancient part of human history teaches – and in punishment there is so much that is festive!
On the Genealogy of Morality, Essay 2, Section 6

To see others suffer does one good, to make others suffer even more.
On the Genealogy of Morality, Essay 2, Section 6

THE ROMANTIC HERO
The distinction that lies in being unhappy (as if to feel happy were a sign of shallowness, lack of ambition, ordinariness) is so great that when someone says, 'But how happy you must be!' we usually protest.
Human, All Too Human, 'Man Alone with Himself', Section 534

For those who need consolation no means of consolation is so effective as the assertion that in their case no consolation is possible: it implies so great a degree of distinction that they at once hold up their heads again.
Daybreak, Book IV, Section 380

TRUTH?

There are no moral phenomena, only moral interpretations of phenomena.

Beyond Good and Evil, 'Epigrams and Entr'actes', Section 108

The fact that something happens regularly and predictably does not mean that it happens necessarily.

Notebook 9, Autumn 1887, 91

The irrationality of a thing is no argument against it – rather a condition of it.

Human, All Too Human, 'Man Alone with Himself', Section 515

There are no facts, only interpretations.

Notebooks, Summer 1886–Autumn 1887, Section 91

SEX

Sex: the thorn and stake of all body-despisers for it mocks and makes fools of all teachers . . .

Sex: the slow fire on which the rabble are stewed in lust . . .

Sex: innocent and free for free hearts . . .

Sex: I shall fence my thoughts and my heart so pigs and pilferers do not break in . . .

Thus Spoke Zarathustra, Part III, 'On the Three Evils', Section 2

THE STATE

The state wants men to render it the same idolatry they used to render the church.

Untimely Meditations, 'Schopenhauer as Educator', Section 4

Everything the state says is a lie, and everything it has it has stolen.

Thus Spoke Zarathustra, Part I, 'On the New Idol'

State is the name of the coldest of all cold monsters. Coldly it lies; and this lie slips from its mouth: 'I, the state, am the people.'
Thus Spoke Zarathustra, Part I, 'On the New Idol'

TRAVEL SUPPLEMENT
Philosophy, so far as I have understood it and lived it so far, is living freely in ice and high mountains.
Ecce Homo, Preface, Section 3

Even the most beautiful scenery is no longer assured of our love after we have lived in it for three months, and some distant coast attracts our avarice.
The Gay Science, Book I, Section 14

Never trust a thought that occurs to you indoors.
Ecce Homo, 'Why I am so Clever', Section 1

WAGE SLAVES
Overwork, inquisitiveness and compassion – our modern vices.
Notebook 9, Autumn 1887, Section 141

It is the misfortune of active men that their activity is almost always a bit irrational. For example, one must not enquire of the cash-amassing banker what the purpose for his restless activity is: it is irrational. Active people roll like a stone, conforming to the stupidity of mechanics.
Human, All Too Human, 'Tokens of Higher and Lower Culture', Section 283

Today as always, men fall into two groups: slaves and free men. Whoever does not have two-thirds of his day for himself is a slave, whatever he may be: a statesman, a businessman, an official, or a scholar.
Human, All Too Human, 'Tokens of Higher and Lower Culture', Section 283

WARFARE
Whoever lives for the sake of combat has an interest in the enemy staying alive.
Human, All Too Human, 'Man Alone with Himself', Section 531

The waters of religion are ebbing away, leaving swamps and stagnant pools; the nations are drawing away from each other in the most hostile fashion, longing to tear each other to pieces.
Untimely Meditations, 'Schopenhauer as Educator', Section 4

WOMEN
God created woman. And boredom did indeed cease from that moment – but many other things ceased as well! Woman was God's *second* mistake.
The Anti-Christ, Section 48

Two things a real man wants: danger and play. That's why he wants woman – the most dangerous plaything.
Thus Spoke Zarathustra, Part I, 'On Little Women Old and Young'

Women know this: a bit fatter, a bit thinner – oh! How much destiny lies in so little!
Thus Spoke Zarathustra, Part III, 'Of the Spirit of Gravity', Section 2

You go to women? Do not forget the whip!
Thus Spoke Zarathustra, Part I, 'On Little Women Old and Young'

WRITERS

There is something comical in the sight of authors who enjoy the rustling folds of long and involved sentences: they are trying to cover up their feet.
The Gay Science, Book IV, Section 282

Only those with very large lungs have the right to write long sentences.
Rules of Writing set out for Lou Salomé

Thoughts in a poem. The poet presents his thoughts festively, on the carriage of rhythm: usually because they could not walk.
Human, All Too Human, 'From the Souls of Artists and Writers', Section 189

If it is true that the forests are going to get thinner, might the time come when libraries should be used for firewood? Since most books are born out of smoke and vapour of the brain, maybe they should return to that state. If they have no fire in them, fire should punish them for it.
Untimely Meditations, 'Schopenhauer as Educator', Section 4

I am the first German to have mastered the aphorism, and aphorisms are a form of eternity. It is my ambition to say in ten sentences what everyone else says in a whole book – what everyone else does *not* say in a whole book.
Twilight of the Idols, 'Skirmishes of an Untimely Man', Section 51

· CHRONOLOGY ·

1844 Friedrich Wilhelm Nietzsche born on 15 October. First child of Karl Ludwig Nietzsche, priest, and Franziska (née Oehler) at Röcken in Saxony.

1846 Sister Elisabeth Nietzsche born on 10 July.

1848 Brother Ludwig Joseph Nietzsche born on 27 February.

1849 Death of Karl Ludwig Nietzsche on 30 July from 'brain softening'.

1850 Death of Ludwig Joseph on 4 January. Family moves to Naumburg. Nietzsche attends the public elementary school.

1851 Nietzsche attends the private institute of Professor Weber.

1854 Nietzsche attends Naumburg Cathedral School.

1858 Franziska, Friedrich and Elisabeth move within Naumburg to Weingarten 18. In the autumn, Nietzsche begins school at Schulpforta.

1860 Founds *Germania*, a literary and musical club with his friends Gustav Krug and Wilhelm Pinder. Beginning of lifelong friendship with Erwin Rohde.

1864 Graduates from Schulpforta in September. Enrols at Bonn University in October, studying theology and classical philology. Joins the Franconia fraternity.

1865 Leaves Bonn for Leipzig University. Drops theology. Studies classical philology under Professor Friedrich Ritschl. Discovers Schopenhauer. Visits a Cologne brothel.

1867 Military service. Begins training in the 2nd Cavalry Battalion, 4th Field Army Regiment.

1868 Wounded in riding accident. Is enchanted on hearing Richard Wagner's *Tristan und Isolde* and *Meistersinger* overtures. Increasingly disaffected with philology. Meets Wagner in November.

1869 Appointed Extraordinary Professor of Classical Philology at Basle University. Renounces Prussian citizenship. Visits Wagner and his mistress Cosima von Bülow at their villa, Tribschen, in Lucerne. First ascent of Mont Pilatus. Makes notes for *The Birth of Tragedy from the Spirit of Music*. Is present at Tribschen when Cosima gives birth to Wagner's son, Siegfried. Spends Christmas at Tribschen.

1870 Promoted to full professor. Public lectures on 'Ancient Music Drama', 'Socrates and Tragedy' and *Oedipus Rex*. War is declared between Germany and France in July. Enrols as medical orderly in Franco-Prussian War. Treating the wounded, he becomes infected with diphtheria and dysentery and is hospitalised. Returns to Basle. Beginning of friendship with Franz Overbeck, professor of theology and critic of Protestantism. Wagner marries Cosima.

1871 Applies unsuccessfully for Chair of Philosophy at Basle. Writes *The Birth of Tragedy from the Spirit of Music*. End of Franco-Prussian War. Second German Reich declared. Wilhelm I crowned Emperor.

1872 Rides in carriage with Wagner at the laying of the foundation stone of the Festival Theatre in Bayreuth. *The Birth of Tragedy* is published. It is harshly criticised by Ulrich von Wilamowitz-Möllendorf and stoutly defended by Erwin Rohde. No students of Classics enrol for his winter lectures on Greek and Latin rhetoric. Richard and Cosima Wagner leave Tribschen for Bayreuth.

1873 Begins 'Philosophy in the Tragic Age of the Greeks', which remains unfinished. Meets Paul Rée. First *Untimely Meditation*, 'David Strauss, the Confessor and the Writer', published in August. Writes hectoring 'Exhortation to the Germans' to raise money for Bayreuth. It is rejected.

1874 Publishes two *Untimely Meditations*: 'On the Uses and Disadvantages of History for Life' and 'Schopenhauer as Educator'. Wagner finishes the *Ring* cycle and invites Nietzsche to spend summer in Bayreuth. Nietzsche takes health cure in Black Forest.

1875 Begins writing fourth *Untimely Meditation*, 'Richard Wagner in Bayreuth'. Health very poor but continues teaching. Elisabeth comes to Basle to look after him. Meets lifelong supporter Heinrich Köselitz (later known as Peter Gast). Severely ill over the winter.

1876 Publishes 'Richard Wagner in Bayreuth' in time for the opening of the first Bayreuth Festival. Flirts with Louise Ott. Leaves Bayreuth suddenly. Begins work on *Human, All Too Human*. Proposes to Mathilde Trampedach, who declines. In October, obtains sick leave from Basle. To Genoa; first sighting of the sea. To Sorrento with Malwida von Meysenbug and Paul Rée. Reads Voltaire and Montaigne. Last meeting with Wagner.

1877 In Sorrento until early May. Visits Capri, Pompeii and Herculaneum. Medical examination by Dr Otto Eiser. Eyes very bad. Resumes lecturing in the autumn, dependent upon Peter Gast as amanuensis and Elisabeth as housekeeper.

1878 Publishes *Human, All Too Human*. Sends it to Wagner. Wagner sends Nietzche the libretto of *Parsifal*. Neither enjoys the other's work. Wagner attacks Nietzsche in *Bayreuther Blätter*. Elisabeth returns to Naumburg. Close friendship with Franz Overbeck and his wife.

1879 Publishes 'A Miscellany of Opinions and Maxims' as appendix to *Human, All Too Human*. Resigns from Basle University in May, citing ill health. Granted a pension of 3,000 Swiss francs for six years (later extended). Writes 'The Wanderer and His Shadow'. Suffers 118 days of bad migraine attacks throughout the year. Plans to become a gardener living in a tower in Naumburg town wall.

1880 Travels to south Tyrol, meets Peter Gast in Riva on Lake Garda. They travel to Venice. A restless year, ending in Genoa at Christmas. Writes *Daybreak*.

1881 Further travelling to Recoaro, Lake Como and St Moritz. Discovers Spinoza. Visits Sils-Maria for the first time; experiences revelation of eternal recurrence. First sketches of *Zarathustra*. Publishes *Daybreak*. Returns to Genoa; identifies with Columbus. Hears Bizet's opera *Carmen* for the first time.

1882 Experiments with typewriter. Publishes *The Gay Science*. Writes poems *The Idylls of Messina*. Travels to Messina. In April, to Rome where he meets Lou Salomé and Paul Rée; Lou proposes they live together in an 'unholy trinity' of free spirits. On Mount Orta, Nietzsche proposes to Lou; she declines. In Basle, the notorious photograph is taken of Nietzsche and Rée yoked to a cart with Lou brandishing a whip over them. Nietzsche takes Lou to Tribschen but refuses to accompany Elisabeth and Lou to Bayreuth. Meets them in Tautenburg, where he reveals the eternal recurrence to Lou. Breaks with Elisabeth and his mother. The 'unholy trinity' plan to live and study together in Paris, but Lou and Rée run away together. He dulls the pain with opium and writes of suicide.

1883 Composes the first part of *Thus Spoke Zarathustra* in January. In February, Wagner dies in Venice. Writes Part II of *Zarathustra* in Sils-Maria and Part III in Nice. Elisabeth announces her engagement to anti-Semitic agitator Bernhard Förster.

1884 Publishes Part III of *Zarathustra*. Problems with publisher: Nietzsche's books are not selling. Meets Meta von Salis-Marschlins and Resa von Schirnhofer. Adopts Polish ancestry. Reconciled with Elisabeth. Writes Part IV of *Thus Spoke Zarathustra*.

1885 Privately prints small run of *Zarathustra* Part IV. Elisabeth marries Förster. Nietzsche pays for a new headstone for his father's grave. Writes *Beyond Good and Evil: Prelude to a Philosophy of the Future*.

1886 *Beyond Good and Evil* privately published, as all his books will be from now on. Publisher Ernst Fritzsch buys the rights to Nietzsche's earlier work and publishes new editions of *The Birth of Tragedy* and *Human, All Too Human* (now with a second volume comprising 'A Miscellany of Opinions and Maxims' and 'The Wanderer and His Shadow') and *Daybreak*. Franz Liszt dies in Bayreuth. Elisabeth and Bernhard Förster travel to Paraguay to set up Nueva Germania, a 'racially pure' Aryan colony.

1887 Experiences earthquake in Nice. Reads Dostoyevsky in French translation. Lou Salomé announces her engagement to Friedrich Carl Andreas. Nietzsche sets her poem 'Hymn to Friendship' to music and has it privately printed as 'Hymn to Life'. Attempts in vain to get it performed. Hears *Parsifal* and is enraptured by the music. Publishes *On the Genealogy of Morals, a Polemic*. New, expanded editions of *Daybreak* and *The Gay Science*.

1888 Enjoys public acclaim at last after Georg Brandes lectures on his work in Copenhagen. Corresponds with Swedish playwright August Strindberg, who writes 'Nietzschean' plays. Nietzsche discovers Turin, where he writes *The Case of Wagner: A Musician's Problem*. Abandons *The Will to Power*. Completes, in quick succession, *Twilight of the Idols: or How to Philosophise with a Hammer*; *The Anti-Christ: A Curse on Christianity*; his final autobiography *Ecce Homo, or How To Become What You Are*; *Nietzsche contra Wagner: from the Files of a Psychologist*. Collects poems he wrote in 1880s into the volume *Dionysian Dithyrambs*. Beginnings of breakdown evident from increasingly bizarre letter-writing.

1889 Collapses in Turin on 3 January. Loyal friend Overbeck escorts him to Switzerland. Diagnosed as suffering from progressive paralysis induced by syphilitic infection. Committed to an asylum in Jena. *Twilight of the Idols* published on 24 January. In Paraguay, Bernhard Förster commits suicide. Elisabeth fights for survival of the colony.

1890 Discharged into his mother's care in childhood home in Naumburg.
      Sinks ever deeper into insanity and creeping paralysis, losing both his
      reason and his speech.

1896 Enthusiasm for his work sweeps the avant-garde. Richard Strauss
      composes and premieres *Thus Spoke Zarathustra*.

1897 Franziska Nietzsche dies on 20 April. Elisabeth moves Nietzsche and his
      papers to Weimar, where she founds the Nietzsche archive.

1900 Nietzsche dies on 25 August. Interred in family grave in Röcken.

1901 Elisabeth publishes first version of *The Will to Power*, concocted by her
      from fragments of Nietzsche's writings.

1904 Elisabeth publishes greatly expanded 'definitive edition' of *The Will
      to Power*.

1908 Nietzsche's autobiography *Ecce Homo* is at last published. Unflattering
      references to Elisabeth are omitted.

1919 Elisabeth's cousin Max Oehler, an enthusiastic National Socialist,
      becomes chief archivist of the Nietzsche archive.

1932 Elisabeth, an ardent admirer of Mussolini, persuades the Weimar
      National Theatre to put on Mussolini's co-authored play *Campo di Maggio*.
      Adolf Hitler visits Elisabeth in her box.

1933 Hitler visits the Nietzsche archive. Elisabeth presents him with
      Nietzsche's walking stick.

1934 Hitler visits the archive with architect Albert Speer and is photographed
      staring at the bust of Nietzsche.

1935 Elisabeth dies. Hitler attends her funeral and lays a wreath. Having
      previously disinterred her brother from his location in the centre of
      the line of family graves, Elisabeth takes up this important position for
      herself.

· NOTES ·

1 : A MUSICAL EVENING

1 Ottilie Brockhaus (1811–83), sister of Richard Wagner and wife of Hermann Brockhaus, professor and Indiologist.

2 Wilhelm Roscher (1845–1923), a fellow-student.

3 The poems of Eudocia, daughter of the Athenian philosopher Leontius. She renounced paganism to marry the Byzantine Emperor Theodosius in AD 421.

4 Autobiographical fragment, 1868/9.

5 *Rückblick auf meine zwei Leipziger Jahre*, quoted in R. J. Hollingdale, *Nietzsche, the Man and His Philosophy*, p. 36.

6 *The Case of Wagner*, Section 10.

7 *Ecce Homo*, trans. R. J. Hollingdale, intro. Michael Tanner, Penguin Classics, 2004, 'Why I am so Clever', Section 6.

8 See Michael Tanner, *Nietzsche, a Very Short Introduction*, Oxford University Press, 2000, p. 23.

9 *Ecce Homo*, 'Why I am so Clever', Section 6.

10 Nietzsche to Erwin Rohde, 20 November 1868.

11 Karl Ludwig Nietzsche (1813–49) m. Franziska Oehler (1826–97).

12 Friedrich Nietzsche, *Jugendschriften*, ed. Hans Joachim Mette et al., 5 vols, Walter de Gruyter and Deutscher Taschenbuch Verlag, 1994, Vol. I, pp. 4–5, translation by David Krell and Don Bates in *The Good European*, p. 14.

13 *Jugendschriften*, Vol. I, pp. 6–7. Translation as above. Speculation surrounds Nietzsche's two, slightly differing accounts of this prophetic dream (see Krell and Bates, *The Good European*, pp. 16–17, footnote 2). Nietzsche describes the experience as happening at the end of the year 1850 but it must have been March 1850. Confusion is compounded by the date on the tomb in which little Joseph joined his father. 'Born 27 February 1848, died 4 January 1850', reads the tombstone, though according to the parish register, Joseph died several days after his second birthday, which would

have made it in March. This would agree with the timing of Nietzsche's dream.

14 Paul Julius Möbius (1853–1907), neurologist, practised in Leipzig, published extensively. His name is given to Möbius syndrome, a rare type of palsy associated with paralysis of the cranial nerves, and Leyden-Möbius syndrome, muscular dystrophy of the pelvic region.

15 Richard Schain, *The Legend of Nietzsche's Syphilis*, Greenwood Press, 2001, pp. 2–4.

16 *Jugendschriften*, Vol. I, p. 7.

17 Elisabeth Nietzsche writing as Elisabeth Förster-Nietzsche, *The Life of Nietzsche*, trans. Anthony M. Ludovici, Sturgis and Walton, 1912, Vol. I, p. 27.

18 Förster-Nietzsche, *The Life of Nietzsche*, Vol. I, pp. 22–23.

19 Ibid., p. 24.

20 *Jugendschriften*, Vol. I, p. 8. Trans. in Krell and Bates, *The Good European*, p. 19.

21 '*Aus meinem Leben*', a brief autobiographical account of the years 1844–63. Keith Ansell Pearson and Duncan Large, *The Nietzsche Reader*, Blackwell, 2006, pp. 18–21.

22 Ibid.

23 Förster-Nietzsche, *The Life of Nietzsche*, Vol. I, p. 40.

24 *Ecce Homo*, 'Why I am so Wise', Section 5.

25 *Aus meinem Leben*.

26 *Sämtliche Werke, Kritische Studienausgabe*, Vol. XI, p. 253. Nietzsche refers to this piece of work again, towards the end of his writing life in 1887, in the third section of the Preface to *The Genealogy of Morality*.

2: OUR GERMAN ATHENS

1 Text for Wilhelm Pinder quoted in Krell and Bates, *The Good European*, p. 61.

2 Philipp Melanchthon Schwarzerd (1497–1560), Luther's principal assistant in translating the Old Testament into German, better known by his Hellenic pseudonym Melanchthon.

3 Karl Wilhelm von Humboldt (1767–1835).

4 Karl Wilhelm von Humboldt, *Gesammelte Schriften: Ausgabe der Prussischen Akademie der Wissenschaften*, Vol. II, p. 117.

5 Autobiographical fragment, 1868/9.

6 Anne Louise Germaine de Staël, *Germany*, 1813, Vol. I, *Saxony*.

7 Nietzsche to Wilhelm Pinder, April 1859.

8 Journal, 18 August 1859. Quoted in Krell and Bates, *The Good European*, p. 23.

9 Sander L. Gilman (ed.), *Conversations with Nietzsche*, Oxford University Press, 1987, p. 15.

10 The teacher was probably Professor Koberstein.

11 Nietzsche, 'Letter to my friend . . .', 19 October 1861.

12 Friedrich Hölderlin, *Hyperion*, trans. James Luchte, from *The Peacock and The Buffalo, The Poetry of Nietzsche*, Continuum Books, 2010, p. 34.

13 Empedocles, Fragment 38 and 62.

14 Nietzsche to Raimund Granier, 28 July 1862.

15 Krell and Bates, *The Good European*, p. 26.

16 Autobiographical fragment, 1868/9.

17 The Roman author Tacitus (*c.* AD 55–116) wrote the first description of Germany, *Germania*.

18 Autobiographical fragment, 1868/69.

19 Elisabeth Nietzsche writing as Elisabeth Förster-Nietzsche, *The Life of Nietzsche*, Vol. I, p. 117.

20 Autobiographical fragment, 1868/9.

3 : BECOME WHAT YOU ARE

1 Förster-Nietzsche, *The Life of Nietzsche*, Vol. I, p. 144.

2 Ibid., pp. 143–4.

3 Gilman (ed.), *Conversations with Nietzsche*, p. 20.

4 Chambers' *Encyclopedia*, 1895, Vol. IV, p. 433.

5 Nietzsche to Elisabeth Nietzsche, 11 June 1865.

6 Nietzsche to Carl von Gersdorff, Naumburg, 7 April 1866.

7 Heinrich Stürenberg, fellow-student at Leipzig University. See Gilman (ed.), *Conversations with Nietzsche*, p. 29.

8 *Pythian Odes*, 2:73.

9 Nietzsche to Erwin Rohde, Naumburg, 3 November 1867.

10 Nietzsche to Jacob Burckhardt, 6 January 1889.

11 Carl Bernoulli quoted in Hollingdale, *Nietzsche, the Man and His Philosophy*, p. 48.

12 Gilman (ed.), *Conversations with Nietzsche*, p. 62.

13 Nietzsche to Carl von Gersdorff, August 1866.

14 Nietzsche to Erwin Rohde, February 1870.

15 Richard Wagner to Franz Liszt, 15 January 1854, quoted in Barry Millington, *Richard Wagner, The Sorcerer of Bayreuth*, Thames and Hudson, 2013, p. 144.

16 Immanuel Kant, *Critique of Judgement*, 1790, trans. James Creed Meredith, Oxford University Press, 1928, p. 28.

17 It is most probably the Rigi ghost that contributed certain supernatural elements to Wagner's *Ring*: the rainbow bridge leading to Valhalla the home of the gods, the pair of giants who loom enormous and threatening through the mist at Valhalla's windows, and the specific stage direction in *Rheingold* that reads: 'The cloud suddenly lifts, revealing Donner and Froh. From their feet a rainbow bridge of blinding radiance stretches out across the valley to the castle, which now glints in the glow of the evening sun.'

18 Judith Gautier, *Wagner at Home*, trans. Effie Dunreith Massie, John Lane, 1911, p. 97.

19 Alan Walker, *Hans von Bülow, A Life and Times*, Oxford University Press, 2010, p. 98.

20 Richard Wagner to Eliza Wille, 9 September 1864.

21 Richard Wagner to Mathilde Wesendonck, 4 September 1858, cited in Walker, *Hans von Bülow*, p. 110.

4: NAXOS

1 Cosima Wagner, *Diary*, 17 May 1869.

2 Hans von Bülow, cited in Joachim Köhler, *Nietzsche and Wagner, A Lesson in Subjugation*, Yale University Press, 1998, p. 28.

3 Lionel Gossman, 'Basel in the Age of Burckhardt', University of Chicago Press, 2000, p. 15.

4 Jacob Burckhardt, 'The Civilisation of the Renaissance in Italy', Penguin, 1990, p. 4.

5 *Untimely Meditations*, 'Richard Wagner in Bayreuth', Section 3.

6 Jacob Burckhardt, *The Civilisation of the Renaissance in Italy*, Penguin, 1990, introduction by Peter Burke, p. 5.

7 Mendès, 'Personal Recollections', in Grey (ed.), *Richard Wagner and His World*, pp. 233–4.

8 Wagner to Nietzsche, 7 February 1870.

9 '*Zwei Nietzsche Anekdoten*', *Frankfurter Zeitung*, 9 March 1904, quoted in Millington, *Richard Wagner*, p. 153.

10 Letter of 29 September 1850, cited in Millington, *Richard Wagner*, p. 221.

11 Originally published in *Revue européenne*, 1 April 1861.

12 Joanna Richardson, *Judith Gautier, a Biography*, Quartet, 1986, p. 39.

13 Mendès, 'Personal Recollections', in Grey (ed.), *Richard Wagner and His World*, pp. 231–4.

14 Newell Sill Jenkins, 'Reminiscences of Newell Sill Jenkins', privately printed 1924, in Grey (ed.), *Richard Wagner and His World*.

15 Köhler, *Nietzsche and Wagner*, pp. 55–6.

16 Förster-Nietzsche, *The Life of Nietzsche*, Vol. I, pp. 230–1.

17 Nietzsche to Wilhelm Vischer-Bilfinger, Basle, probably January 1871.

18 Nietzsche to Franziska Nietzsche, headed from Sulz, near Weissenburg, in the vicinity of Wörth, 29 August 1870.

19 Nietzsche to Carl von Gersdorff, Basle, 12 December 1870.

20 Nietzsche to Carl von Gersdorff, 21 June 1871.

21 Cosima Wagner, *Diary*, Sunday 25 December 1870.

22 Wilhelm Vischer-Bilfinger (1808–74), noted archaeologist, professor and Councillor at the University of Basle.

23 Malwida von Meysenbug, *Rebel in a Crinoline*, George Allen & Unwin, 1937, pp. 194–5.

24 Förster-Nietzsche, *The Life of Nietzsche*, Vol. I, pp. 243–4.

25 Ibid., p. 246.

26 A vast hotel on the shores of the lake, now named the Residenza Grand Palace and divided up into apartments.

5: THE BIRTH OF TRAGEDY

1 *The Birth of Tragedy*, Section 1.

2 Ibid., Section 7.

3 Ibid., Section 15.

4 Ibid., Section 15.

5 Ibid., Section 18.

6 Ibid., Section 20.

7 Ibid., Section 21.

8 Cosima Wagner, *Diary*, 18 August 1870.

9 Ibid., 8 April 1871.

10 Nietzsche to Erwin Rohde, 1871.

11 Nietzsche to Carl von Gersdorff, 18 November 1871.

12 Nietzsche to Erwin Rohde, 21 December 1871.

13 Nietzsche to Franziska and Elisabeth Nietzsche, Basle, 27 December 1871.

14 Nietzsche to Gustav Krug, Basle, 31 December 1871.

15 'On the Future of Our Educational Institutions', first lecture, delivered 16 January 1872.

16 Cosima Wagner, *Diary*, 16 January 1872.

17 Nietzsche to Erwin Rohde, Basle, 28 January 1872.

18 Cosima Wagner, *Diary*, 31 January 1872.

19 Nietzsche to Carl von Gersdorff, 1 May 1872.

20 Nietzsche to Friedrich Ritschl, Basle, 30 January 1872.

21 Nietzsche to Erwin Rohde, 25 October 1872.

22 Cosima Wagner, *Diary*, 22 May 1872.

23 Walker, *Hans von Bülow*, p. 5.

24 Nietzsche to Hans von Bülow, draft letter, probably 29 October 1872.

25 William H. Schaberg, *The Nietzsche Canon, A Publication History and Bibliography*, University of Chicago Press, 1995, pp. 203–4.

6: POISON COTTAGE

1 Cosima Wagner, *Diary*, 11 April 1873.

2 Professor Hermann Carl Usener, theologian and classical philologist who succeeded Friedrich Ritschl at the University of Bonn.

3 Franz Overbeck (1837–1905).

4 Carl von Gersdorff to Erwin Rohde, 24 May 1873.

5 *Ecce Homo*, 'Human, All Too Human', Section 4.

6 *Untimely Meditations*, 'David Strauss', Section 8.

7 Carl von Gersdorff to Erwin Rohde, 9 August 1873.

8 Nietzsche to Erwin Rohde, Basle, 18 October 1873.

9 Johann Karl Friedrich Zöllner, *Natur der Kometen*, 1870; Hermann Kopp, *Geschichte der Chemie*, 1834–7, Johann Heinrich Mädler, *Der Wunderbau des Weltalls*, 1861, Afrikan Spir, *Denken und Wirklichkeit*, 1873.

10 *Untimely Meditations*, 'On the Uses and Disadvantages of History for Life', Section 10.

11 Cosima Wagner, *Diary*, 9 April 1974.

12 Nietzsche to von Gersdorff, 1 April 1874.

13 Cosima Wagner, *Diary*, 4 April 1874.

14 Richard Wagner to Nietzsche, 6 April 1874.

7 : CONCEPT-QUAKE

1 Nietzsche to Malwida von Meysenbug, 11 August 1875.

2 Samuel Roth (1893–1974), convicted pornographer, writer and publisher.

3 For Walter Kaufmann's account see 'Nietzsche and the Seven Sirens', *Partisan Review*, May/June 1952.

4 Herlossohn, *Damen-Conversations-Lexikon* (1834–8), cited in Carol Diethe, *Nietzsche's Sister and the Will to Power*, University of Illinois Press, 2003, p. 17.

5 Count Harry Kessler, Diary, 23 February 1919, in Charles Kessler (ed. and trans.), *Berlin in Lights, The Diaries of Harry Kessler, 1918–1937*, Grove Press, NY, 1971, p. 74.

6 Diethe, *Nietzsche's Sister and the Will to Power*, p. 20.

7 Elisabeth Nietzsche to Nietzsche, 26 May 1865.

8 *Ecce Homo*, 'Why I Write Such Good Books', Section 5.

9 Gilman (ed.), *Conversations with Nietzsche*, p. 69. Ludwig von Scheffler, memoir dated summer 1876.

10 *Untimely Meditations*, 'Schopenhauer as Educator', Section 4.

11 Ibid., Section 1.

12 Ibid., Section 1.

13 Ibid., Section 4.

14 Ibid., Section 7.

15 Ibid., Section 8.

16 Ibid., Section 4.

17 Ibid., Section 4.

18 Cosima Wagner, *Diary*, 8–18 August 1874.

19 Notebook, 1874.

20 Telegram, 21 October 1874.

21 Nietzsche to Mathilde Trampedach, 11 April 1876.

8 : THE LAST DISCIPLE AND THE FIRST DISCIPLE

1 *Untimely Meditations*, 'Schopenhauer as Educator', Section 4.

2 *Untimely Meditations*, 'Richard Wagner in Bayreuth', Section 7.

3 Ibid., Section 8.

4 Ibid., Section 11.

5 Gilman (ed.), *Conversations with Nietzsche*, pp. 54–60.

6 Ibid., p. 56.

7 Nietzsche to Malwida von Meysenbug, 20 December 1872.

8 Richard Wagner to Nietzsche, 13 July 1876.

9 'Der Wanderer', also known as 'Es geht ein Wandrer'. This is the meaning of the first version of the poem, which subsequently he altered.

10 Cosima Wagner, Diary, 28 July 1876.

11 Article submitted to Russky Viedomosty, quoted in Millington, Richard Wagner, p. 231.

12 Malwida von Meysenbug (1816–1903).

13 Memoiren einer Idealistin, published anonymously, 1869.

14 Alexander Herzen (1812–70), sometimes called 'the father of Russian socialism'; he worked for emancipation of the serfs and agrarian reform.

15 Von Meysenbug, Rebel in a Crinoline, p. 194.

16 Ibid., p. 196.

17 Nietzsche to Louise Ott, 30 August 1876.

18 Louise Ott to Nietzsche, 2 September 1876.

19 Louise Ott to Nietzsche, 1 September 1877, cited in Carol Diethe, Nietzsche's Women: Beyond the Whip, Walter de Gruyter, 1996, p. 39.

9: FREE AND NOT SO FREE SPIRITS

1 Malwida von Meysenbug to Olga Herzen, from Sorrento, 28 October 1876.

2 Nietzsche to Elisabeth Nietzsche, from Sorrento, 28 October 1876.

3 Human, All Too Human, Section 4, 'From the Souls of Artists and Writers', Section 145.

4 Paul Rée, Notio in Aristotelis Ethicis Quid Sibi Velit, Halle, Pormetter, 1875, quoted in Robin Small, Nietzsche and Rée, A Star Friendship, Clarendon Press, Oxford, 2007, p. xv.

5 As a student, Nietzsche gained most of his information on the subject from Friedrich Albert Lange, Geschichte des Materialismus und Kritik seiner Bedeutung in der Gegenwart (History of Materialism and Critique of its Present Importance), 1879. In 1887 or 1888, Nietzsche acquired a copy of Karl Wilhelm von Nägeli, Mechanisch-physiologische Theorie der Abstammungslehre (Mechanico-physiological Theory of Evolution), 1884, a detailed study of Darwinism. See Carol Diethe, The A to Z of Nietzscheanism, Scarecrow Press, 2010, pp. 53–4.

6 Published in Mind, 2 (1877), pp. 291–2. For comprehensive coverage of this subject see Small, Nietzsche and Rée, pp. 88–90.

7 Small, Nietzsche and Rée, pp. 72, 98.

8 On the Genealogy of Morality, Preface, Section 8.

9 Nietzsche to Richard Wagner, 27 September 1876

10 1876 notebook, quoted in Small, *Nietzsche and Rée*, p. 58.

11 Nietzsche to Richard Wagner, from Basle, 27 September 1876.

12 Cosima Wagner, *Diary*, 27 October 1876.

13 Ibid., 1 November 1876.

14 Nietzsche to Elisabeth Nietzsche, 25 April 1877.

15 Nietzsche to Malwida von Meysenbug, 13 May 1877.

16 Nietzsche to Elisabeth Nietzsche, 2 June 1877.

17 Förster-Nietzsche, *The Life of Nietzsche*, Vol. II, pp. 11–13.

18 Richard Wagner to Dr Eiser, 27 October 1877, cited in Martin Gregor-Dellin, *Richard Wagner, His Life, His Work, His Century*, trans. J. Maxwell Brownjohn, Collins, 1983, pp. 452–3.

19 Dr Eiser's report, 6 October 1877, cited in Gregor-Dellin, *Richard Wagner*, pp. 453–4.

10: HUMAN, ALL TOO HUMAN

1 Nietzsche to Ernst Schmeitzner, 2 February 1877.

2 *Human, All Too Human*, 'Of First and Last Things', Section 2.

3 Ibid., Section 2.

4 Ibid., Section 4.

5 Ibid., Section 5.

6 Ibid., Section 9.

7 Ibid., Section 6.

8 Ibid., Section 11.

9 Ibid., Section 19.

10 Ibid., 'On the History of the Moral Sensations', Section 37.

11 La Rochefoucauld, opening sentence of *Sentences et maximes morales*, referred to in *Human, All Too Human*, 'On the History of the Moral Sensations', Section 35.

12 Ibid., 'A Glance at the State', Section 438.

13 Ibid., 'A Glance at the State', Section 452.

14 Ibid., 'On the History of the Moral Sensations', Section 87.

15 Schaberg, *The Nietzsche Canon*, p. 59. See also Förster-Nietzsche, *The Life of Nietzsche*, Vol. II, p. 32.

16 Ernst Schmeitzner to Nietzsche, quoted in Förster-Nietzsche, *The Life of Nietzsche*, Vol. II, p. 32.

17 Nietzsche to Mathilde Meier, 15 July 1878.

18 'L'âme de Voltaire fait ses compliments à Friedrich Nietzsche.'

19 Cosima Wagner to Marie von Schleinitz, June 1878.

20 Wagner published three articles on Publikum und Popularität in Bayreuther Blätter, August–September 1878.

21 Nietzsche to Johann Heinrich Köselitz (aka Peter Gast), 5 October 1879.

22 Nietzsche to Malwida von Meysenbug, 1 July 1877.

11: THE WANDERER AND HIS SHADOW

1 Section 1 of the Preface to the second edition of Daybreak, 1886.

2 Electricity: see letters to Peter Gast and Franz Overbeck during August and September 1881.

3 Nietzsche to Franz Overbeck, 30 July 1881.

4 Ida Overbeck recalled Nietzsche quoting Feuerbach's ideas during 1880–3, when Nietzsche lived in the Overbeck household for several short periods; see Gilman (ed.), Conversations with Nietzsche, pp. 111–15.

5 Daybreak, Book I, Section 14.

6 Nietzsche to Peter Gast, 5 October 1879.

7 Matthew 16:18.

8 Nietzsche to Franz Overbeck, 27 March 1880.

9 In fact Böcklin's picture depicts the cemetery in Florence, also reached by water, though it was always assumed, for watery reasons, that the view depicted was the graveyard island of San Michele, Venice.

10 Human, All Too Human, Book III, 'The Wanderer and His Shadow', Section 295.

11 Nietzsche to Peter Gast, 14 August 1881.

12 According to an index of Swiss consumer prices from 1501 to 2006, the average wage of a skilled Swiss building craftsman at the time was 2.45 francs per day or 12.25 francs per week. The rent was on the low side.

13 Letter to Franz Overbeck, 18 September 1881.

14 The Gay Science, Book IV, Section 341.

15 Notebook, 1881.

16 Nietzsche to Elisabeth Nietzsche, 5 December 1880. The attic was in Salita delle Battistine 8, opposite the park of the Villetta di Negro, in which he found peace and shade.

17 Daybreak, Book IV, Section 381.

18 Lou Salomé (1861–1937), daughter of a Russian general of Huguenot stock; her mother was German.

19 Lou Andreas-Salomé, *Looking Back: Memoirs*, trans. Breon Mitchell, Paragon House, New York, 1990, p. 45.

20 Paul Rée to Nietzsche, 20 April 1882.

21 *The Gay Science*, Book IV, Section 77.

22 Malwida von Meysenbug to Nietzsche, 27 March 1882.

12: PHILOSOPHY AND EROS

1 Andreas-Salomé, *Looking Back*, p. 45.

2 Lou Salomé, writing as Lou Andreas-Salomé, *Nietzsche*, trans. Siegfried Mandel, University of Illinois Press, 2001, pp. 9, 10.

3 Andreas-Salomé, *Looking Back*, p. 47.

4 *Untimely Meditations*, 'The Uses and Disadvantages of History for Life', Section 2.

5 *The Gay Science*, Book II, Section 71, 'On female chastity'.

6 Andreas-Salomé, *Nietzsche*, p. 11. She is quoting aphorism number 338 from 'A Miscellany of Opinions and Maxims' in *Human, All Too Human*.

7 Lou Salomé, *Friedrich Nietzsche in seinen Werken*, 1894.

8 Andreas-Salomé, *Nietzsche*, p. 13.

9 Julia Vickers, *Lou von Salomé: A Biography of the Woman Who Inspired Freud, Nietzsche and Rilke*, McFarland, 2008, p. 41

10 Nietzsche to Peter Gast, 13 July 1882.

13: THE PHILOSOPHER'S APPRENTICE

1 *The Gay Science*, Book III, Section 125, 'The Madman'.

2 Ibid., Book III, Section 108, 'New Battles'.

3 Nietzsche to Reinhardt von Seydlitz, 4 January 1878.

4 Elisabeth Nietzsche to Franziska Nietzsche, 26 July 1882.

5 The story was first revealed by Martin Gregor-Dellin. He tells it in Richard *Wagner, His Life, His Work, His Century*, pp. 451–7.

6 Elisabeth Nietzsche, *Coffee-Party Gossip about Nora*, probably 1882. It can be read in its entirety in English translation in Diethe, *Nietzsche's Sister and the Will to Power*, pp. 161–93. Diethe gave the story its title.

7 Vickers, *Lou von Salomé*, p. 48.

8 Nietzsche to Lou Salomé, 4 August 1882.

9 We get Elisabeth Nietzsche's side of the quarrel from her memoir of her brother and from letters, notably to Clara Gelzer, written between 24 September and 2 October 1882. Lou, following her sound principle

of ignoring uncomfortable realities, makes no reference to the quarrel
with Elisabeth, either in her memoirs or in her book on Nietzsche. Like
the question of whether Nietzsche kissed her on Monte Sacro, she again
exercises her genius for silence.

10 Andreas-Salomé, *Nietzsche*, pp. 77–8.

11 Ibid., p. 71.

12 Ibid., p. 70.

13 Ibid., p. 71.

14 *The Gay Science*, Book IV, 'Sanctus Januarius', Section 276.

15 Nietzsche to Lou Salomé, end of August 1882.

16 Rudolph Binion, *Frau Lou: Nietzsche's Wayward Disciple*, Princeton University
Press, 1968, p. 91.

17 *Freundin – sprach Kolumbus – traue*
Keinem Genuesen mehr!
Immer starrt er in das Blaue
Fernstes zieht ihn allzusehr!
Wen er liebt, den lockt er gerne
Weit hinaus in Raum und Zeit –
Über uns glänzt Stern bei Sterne,
Um uns braust die Ewigkeit.

(Translation by Curtis Cate.)

14: MY FATHER WAGNER IS DEAD. MY SON
ZARATHUSTRA IS BORN

1 Nietzsche to Paul Rée and Lou Salomé, mid-December 1882.

2 Nietzsche to Franz Overbeck, 11 February 1883.

3 A later description of Rapallo in a letter to Peter Gast, 10 October 1886.

4 Nietzsche to Franz Overbeck, 25 December 1882.

5 *Ecce Homo*, 'Thus Spoke Zarathustra', Section 5.

6 *The Gay Science*, 'Sanctus Januarius', Section 342. This was the final
section of *The Gay Science* to that date. Later he would add the last
section of the book and entitle it 'We Fearless Ones'.

7 Nietzsche was far from the only one to be interested in Zarathustra.
Over the previous fifty years, twenty studies of the *Zend-Avesta* or its
author had been published in the German language. See Friedrich
Nietzsche, *Thus Spoke Zarathustra*, Oxford University Press, 2008,
introduction by Graham Parkes, p. xi.

8 See Mary Boyce, *Zoroastrians: Their Religious Beliefs and Practices*, London, 1979 and *The Oxford Companion to Philosophy*, ed. Ted Honderich, Oxford University Press, 2005.

9 *Thus Spoke Zarathustra*, 'Zarathustra's Prologue', Section 3.

10 *Thus Spoke Zarathustra*, Part III, 'Before Sunrise'.

11 Ibid., 'Zarathustra's Prologue', Section 4.

12 *Thus Spoke Zarathustra*, Part I, 'On Little Women Old and Young'.

13 Nietzsche to Franz Overbeck, 22 February 1883.

14 Nietzsche to Franz Overbeck, from Rapallo, received on 11 February 1883.

15 Nietzsche to Carl von Gersdorff, 28 June 1883. He is referring to the Chastè peninsula.

16 Nietzsche to Peter Gast, 19 February 1883.

17 Nietzsche to Elisabeth Nietzsche, April 1883, quoted in Binion, *Frau Lou*, p. 104.

18 Nietzsche to Franz Overbeck, 17 October 1885.

19 Nietzsche to Elisabeth Nietzsche, late summer 1883.

15: ONLY WHERE THERE ARE GRAVES ARE THERE RESURRECTIONS

1 Claude Gellée (1604/5?–82), known as Claude Lorrain, French painter of arcadian landscapes referencing the Bible, Virgil and Ovid. His pictures, often studded with classical architectural fragments, figures and animals, were the chief inspiration for the English Picturesque landscape movement of the eighteenth century.

2 *Thus Spoke Zarathustra*, Part II, Section 4, 'On Priests'.

3 Nietzsche to Carl von Gersdorff, 28 June 1883.

4 *Ecce Homo*, 'Thus Spoke Zarathustra', Section 3.

5 Nietzsche to Georg Brandes, 10 April 1888.

6 *Thus Spoke Zarathustra*, Part II, 'Of the Tarantulas'.

7 Nietzsche to Peter Gast, end of August 1883.

8 Nietzsche to Franz Overbeck, received 28 August 1883.

9 Nietzsche to Franziska Nietzsche and Elisabeth Nietzsche, 31 March 1885.

10 Elisabeth Nietzsche to Bernhard Förster, January 1884.

11 Dr Julius Paneth describing visits to Nietzsche in Nice on 26 December 1883 and 3 January 1884.

12 Resa von Schirnhofer (1855–1948), born in Krems, Austria, author of a short, unpublished memoir of Nietzsche, *Vom Menschen Nietzsche*, written in 1937.

13 Resa von Schirnhofer, 3–13 April 1884, quoted in Gilman (ed.), *Conversations with Nietzsche*, pp. 146–58.

14 The ghost of the wallpaper remains in the room of the house, now the Nietzsche-Haus Museum in Sils-Maria.

16: HE AMBUSHED ME!

1 Ernst Schmeitzner to Nietzsche, 2 October 1884, quoted in Schaberg, *The Nietzsche Canon*, p. 113.

2 Nietzsche to Franz Overbeck, beginning of December 1885, quoted in Schaberg, *The Nietzsche Canon*, p. 118.

3 Nietzsche to Carl von Gersdorff, 12 February 1885.

4 *Ecce Homo*, 'Why I am so Wise', Section 2.

5 *Human, All Too Human*, Book I, Section 638.

6 Nietzsche to Carl von Gersdorff, 12 February 1885.

7 Nietzsche to Elisabeth Nietzsche, 20 May 1885.

8 *The Times*, 1 February 1883.

17: DECLAIMING INTO THE VOID

1 Nietzsche to Franz Overbeck, 24 March 1887.

2 *Ecce Homo*, 'Beyond Good and Evil', Section 2.

3 *Beyond Good and Evil*, 'On the prejudices of philosophers', Section 14.

4 *Ecce Homo*, 'Human, All Too Human', Section 1.

5 *Beyond Good and Evil*, 'On the prejudices of philosophers', Section 5.

6 *Beyond Good and Evil*, 'On the prejudices of philosophers,' Section 9.

7 Ibid., Section 14.

8 Ibid., Section 14.

9 Ibid., Section 9.

10 'Frog perspective' is self-explanatory but it originated as an artist's term for a viewpoint taken from below.

11 *Beyond Good and Evil*, 'Our virtues', Section 232.

12 Nietzsche to Malwida von Meysenbug, 12 May 1887.

13 *Beyond Good and Evil*, 'The religious character', Section 54.

14 Ibid., 'On the prejudices of philosophers', Section 17.

15 Ibid., 'On the natural history of morals', Section 193.

16 Ibid., 'The religious character', Section 46.

17 *On the Genealogy of Morality*, Second Essay, Section 16.

18 *Beyond Good and Evil*, 'On the prejudices of philosophers', Section 19.

19 *On the Genealogy of Morality*, First Essay, Section 11.

20 *On the Genealogy of Morality*, First Essay, Section 11.

21 Ibid., Second Essay, Section 17.

22 *Twilight of the Idols*, 'Improving Humanity', Section 2.

23 Joseph Victor Widmann (1842–1911), influential Swiss literary critic. Like Nietzsche, he was the son of a pastor.

24 The review appeared in *Der Bund*, 16 and 17 September 1886.

18: LLAMALAND

1 Nietzsche to Elisabeth Nietzsche, February 1886.

2 Notebook 9, autumn 1887, note 102.

3 Notebook 9, autumn 1887, note 94.

4 Nietzsche to Franziska Nietzsche, 18 October 1887.

5 Chambers' *Encyclopedia*, 1895, Vol. VIII, pp. 750–1.

6 Ibid., pp. 750–1.

7 Ibid., pp. 750–1.

8 Klingbeil quoted in H. F. Peters, *Zarathustra's Sister: The Case of Elisabeth and Friedrich Nietzsche*, Crown, 1977, p. 110.

9 Julius Klingbeil, *Enthüllungen über die Dr Bernhard Förstersche Ansiedlung Neu-Germanien in Paraguay (Revelations Concerning Dr Bernhard Förster's Colony New Germany in Paraguay)*, Baldamus, Leipzig, 1889.

10 Letter to Franz Overbeck, Christmas 1888.

11 Ibid.

19: I AM DYNAMITE!

1 *Hymnus an das Leben für gemischten Chor und Orchester*, published 20 October 1887. For extensive details on the tortuous publishing history, see Schaberg, *The Nietzsche Canon*, pp. 140–9.

2 Resa von Schirnhofer was told this by Nietzsche, though later Elisabeth told her no such letter existed.

3 Nietzsche to Peter Gast, 10 November 1887.

4 Nietzsche to Reinhart von Seydlitz, 12 February 1888.

5 Georg Brandes (1842–1927), Danish literary critic and biographer.

6 *Qvinnans underordnade ställning*, 1869.

7 Prince Pyotr Alexeyevich Kropotkin (1842–1921).

8 Nietzsche to Georg Brandes, 2 December 1887.

9 Gustav Adolf or Gustavus Adolfus, King of Sweden and leader of the German Protestants, who lost his life in defeating the Catholic Imperial forces at the Battle of Lützen in 1632, during the Thirty Years War. Here too, in 1813, Napoleon was victorious in battle.

10 Georg Brandes, *Friedrich Nietzsche*, William Heinemann, 1909, pp. 80–2.

11 Elisabeth Nietzsche, letter quoted by Nietzsche in his letter to Franz Overbeck from Turin, Christmas 1888.

12 Nietzsche to Elisabeth Nietzsche (draft), December 1888.

13 *The Case of Wagner*, First Postscript.

14 *The Case of Wagner*, Second Postscript.

15 Ibid., First Postscript.

16 Meta von Salis-Marschlins (1855–1929), author of *Philosoph und Edelmensch* (*Philosopher and Gentleman*), 1897, an account of her friendship with Nietzsche.

17 Nietzsche to Franz Overbeck, 23 February 1887. Also, Nietzsche to Peter Gast, 7 March 1887.

18 *The Anti-Christ*, Section 7.

19 Carl Bernoulli, 6 June–20 September 1888, quoted in Gilman (ed.), *Conversations with Nietzsche*, p. 213.

20 *Twilight of the Idols*, 'What I owe the Ancients', Section 5.

20: TWILIGHT IN TURIN

1 Notes on differences between ancient metric rhythm ('time rhythm') and barbarous metric ('emotion rhythm') set out in letter to Carl Fuchs, from Sils-Maria, undated, end of August 1888.

2 Nietzsche to Franz Overbeck, 18 October 1888.

3 *The Maitland Mercury and Hunter River General Advertiser*, New South Wales, 30 October 1888. The paper takes the *Boston Herald* as the original source of the article on 'Sanitary Marriage'.

4 Alfred Ploetz, *Die Tüchtigkeit unserer Rasse und der Schutz der Schwachen. Ein Versuch über Rassenhygiene und ihr Verhältnis zu den humanen Idealen, besonders zum Sozialismus* (*The Industriousness of Our Race and the Protection of the Weak: An Essay on Racial Hygiene and its Relationship to Humane Ideals, Especially in Socialism*), 1895.

5 *The Anti-Christ*, Section 58.

6 See Herbert W. Reichert and Karl Schlechta (eds), *International Nietzsche Bibliography*, Chapel Hill: University of North Carolina Press, 1960.

7 Nietzsche to Malwida von Meysenbug, 18 October 1888.

8 Nietzsche to Franz Overbeck, describing *Ecce Homo*, 13 November 1888. He had finished the book nine days previously.

9 John 19:5.

10 *Ecce Homo*, Preface.

11 Nietzsche to Ferdinand Avenarius, published in *Der Kunstwart*, 2 (1888–9), p. 6.

12 *Ecce Homo*, 'Why I am so Clever', Section 10.

13 Ibid., 'Why I am so Wise', Section 3.

14 Ibid., 'Why I am so Clever', Section 2.

15 *Twilight of the Idols*, 'What I owe to the Ancients', Section 4.

16 Nietzsche to August Strindberg, 7 December 1888.

17 Nietzsche to Jacob Burckhardt, 6 January 1889.

18 Nietzsche to Meta von Salis-Marschlins, 29 December 1888.

19 Nietzsche to Franz Overbeck, Christmas 1888.

20 Nietzsche to Franz Overbeck, 18 October 1888.

21 Nietzsche to Meta von Salis-Marschlins, 14 November 1888.

22 Nietzsche to Franziska Nietzsche, 21 December 1888.

23 Nietzsche to Elisabeth Förster-Nietzsche, December 1888.

24 Nietzsche to Peter Gast, 9 December 1888.

25 Nietzsche to Peter Gast, 16 December 1888.

26 Nietzsche to Carl Fuchs, 18 December 1888.

27 Nietzsche to Franz Overbeck, Christmas 1888 and 28 December 1888.

28 Nietzsche to Meta von Salis-Marschlins, 29 December 1888.

29 Nietzsche to Peter Gast, postmarked Turin, 4 January 1889 and 31 December 1888.

30 Nietzsche to August Strindberg, undated.

31 Nietzsche to August Strindberg, undated.

32 Nietzsche to Peter Gast, postmarked Turin, 4 January 1889.

33 Nietzsche to Georg Brandes, postmarked Turin, 4 January 1889.

34 Nietzsche to Jacob Burckhardt, postmarked Turin, 4 January 1889.

35 Nietzsche to Cosima Wagner, beginning of January 1889.

36 Nietzsche to Jacob Burckhardt, dated 6 January 1889, but postmarked Turin, 5 January 1889.

21 : THE CAVE MINOTAUR

1 Schain, *The Legend of Nietzsche's Syphilis*, p. 44.

2 Verse 2 of *'An der Brücke stand'* ('I Stood on the Bridge'):
   Meine seele, ein Saitenspiel,
   Sang sich unsichtbar berührt,
   Heimlich ein Gondellied dazu,
   Zitternd vor bunter Seligkeit.
   — Hörte jemand ihr zu?

3 'Mother's Statement', part of health report from the clinic, January 1889.

4 Carl Bernoulli, cited in E. F. Podach, *The Madness of Nietzsche*, trans. F. A Voight, Putnam, 1931, p. 177.

5 *Human, All Too Human,* 'A Miscellany of Opinions and Maxims', Section 408, 'Descent into Hades'.

6 Dr Stutz, a director of the Basle clinic in the 1920s, discovered from the records that many cases diagnosed in the clinic as *paralytica progressiva* were in fact cases of schizophrenia.

7 Recollection of medical student Sascha Simchowitz, quoted in Krell and Bates, *The Good European*, p. 50.

8 Podach, *The Madness of Nietzsche*, p. 195.

9 Langbehn to Bishop Keppler, autumn 1900, after Langbehn received the news of Nietzsche's death. Cited in Podach, *The Madness of Nietzsche*, pp. 210–11.

10 Timothy W. Ryback, *Hitler's Private Library, The Books that Shaped His Life*, Vintage, 2010, p. 134.

22 : THE EMPTY OCCUPANT OF FURNISHED ROOMS

1 Klingbeil, *Enthüllungen über die Dr Bernhard Förstersche Ansiedlung Neu-Germanien in Paraguay.*

2 Elisabeth Förster-Nietzsche to Franziska Nietzsche, from Nueva Germania, 9 April 1889.

3 Bernhard Förster to Max Schubert, 2 June 1889

4 Elisabeth Förster-Nietzsche to Franziska Nietzsche, 2 July 1889.

5 Förster-Nietzsche, *The Life of Nietzsche*, Vol. II, pp. 400–1.

6 Elisabeth Förster-Nietzsche to Franziska Nietzsche, 2 July 1889.

7 Elisabeth Nietzsche, writing as Eli Förster, *Dr Bernhard Förster's Kolonie Neu-Germania in Paraguay*, Berlin, Pioneer, 1891.

8 Harry Kessler, *Diary*, 23 July 1891, in Easton (ed.), *Journey into the Abyss*, p. 30.

9 Cited in Laird M. Easton, *The Red Count, The Life and Times of Harry Kessler*, University of California Press, 2002, p. 41.

10 On 20 August 1891, Baron Zedlitz-Neumann shot Marie Elisabeth Meissner and then tried to shoot himself. He later became a journalist.

11 For the similar phenomenon in Norway see Sue Prideaux, *Edvard Munch: Behind the Scream*, Yale University Press, 2005, pp. 72–4.

12 Harry Kessler, *Diary*, 22 June 1896, in Easton (ed.), *Journey into the Abyss*, p. 160.

13 Harry Kessler, *Diary*, 28 January 1895, in ibid., p. 128.

14 *Die Freie Bühne* theatre was founded in 1889, the magazine in 1890. In 1893, its title was changed to *Neue Deutsche Rundschau*.

15 Fritz Kögel (1860–1904), philologist, composer and writer.

16 Built in 1889–90. Architects: Theodor Reinhard and H. Junghans.

17 Meta von Salis-Marschlins to Dr Oehler, 14 July 1898, cited in Peters, *Zarathustra's Sister*, p. 164.

18 Peter Gast to Franz Overbeck, 4 August 1900.

19 Harry Kessler, *Diary*, 7 August 1897, in Easton (ed.), *Journey into the Abyss*, p. 186.

20 'Ich habe meinen Regenschirm vergessen'.

21 Hollingdale, *Nietzsche, the Man and His Philosophy*, p. 253.

22 Fritz Schumacher, recollection of 1898, in Gilman (ed.), *Conversations with Nietzsche*, pp. 246–7.

23 Karl Böttcher, *Auf Studienpfaden: Gefängnisstudien, Landstreicherstudien, Trinkstudien, Irrenhausstudien*, Leipzig, 1900, and Walter Benjamin, 'Nietzsche und das Archiv seiner Schwester', 1932, cited in Paul Bishop (ed.), *A Companion to Friedrich Nietzsche*, Camden House, NY, 2012, p. 402.

24 Harry Kessler, *Diary*, 2 October 1897, in Easton (ed.), *Journey into the Abyss*, p. 190.

25 Harry Kessler, *Diary*, 3 October 1897, in ibid., pp. 190–1.

26 Förster-Nietzsche, *The Life of Nietzsche*, Vol. II, p. 407.

27 Anonymous, quoted in Gilman (ed.), *Conversations with Nietzsche*, pp. 260–1.

28 Förster-Nietzsche, *The Life of Nietzsche*, Vol. II, p. 410.

29 The eulogy was given by the art historian Kurt Breysig (1866–1940). The comment on the eulogy was made by the architect Fritz Schumacher. In 1923 Breysig nominated Elisabeth for the Nobel Prize in Literature.

30 Edvard Munch, *Friedrich Nietzsche*, 1906, oil on canvas, 201 x 160 cm, Thiel Gallery, Stockholm.

31 Edvard Munch, *Elisabeth Förster-Nietzsche*, 1906, oil on canvas, 115 x 80 cm, Thiel Gallery, Stockholm.

32 Elisabeth Förster-Nietzsche's nominations for the Nobel Prize in Literature: 1908, nominated by the German philosopher Hans Vaihinger; 1916, nominated by Hans Vaihinger and Harald Hjärne, a Swedish historian; 1917, nominated by Hans Vaihinger; 1923, nominated by the philologist Georg Goetz; 1923, nominated by Kurt Breysig, who gave the endless address at Nietzsche's obsequies; 1923, nominated by Hans Vaihinger (again).

33 Late notebook, W 13, 646, W 13, 645, cited in Krell and Bates, *The Good European*, p. 213.

34 As early as 1912, Mussolini wrote a biographical essay on Nietzsche, '*La vita di Federico Nietzsche*', published in the magazine *Avanti*.

35 Though it is not a direct translation, the English title of *Campo di Maggio* has always been *The Hundred Days*.

36 Elisabeth Förster-Nietzsche, unpublished letter, Weimar, 12 May 1933. Cited in Peters, *Zarathustra's Sister*, p. 220.

37 *Thus Spoke Zarathustra*, Section 29, 'Of the Tarantulas', trans R. J. Hollingdale.

38 Alfred Rosenberg, Commissar for Supervision of All Intellectual and Ideological Education of the NSDAP, 1934–45.

39 Yvonne Sherratt, *Hitler's Philosophers*, Yale University Press, 2013, p. 70.

40 *Breisgauer Zeitung*, 18 May 1933, p. 3.

41 Harry Kessler, 'Inside the Archive . . .', 7 August 1932, in Count Harry Kessler, *The Diaries of a Cosmopolitan, 1918–1937*, ed. and trans. by Charles Kessler, Phoenix Press, 2000, pp. 426–7.

42 Eyewitness account written by Ernst Hanfstaengel, Hitler's pianist, in his book of reminiscences, *The Unknown Hitler*, Gibson Square Books, 2005, p. 233.

43 See Ryback, *Hitler's Private Library*, pp. 67–8.

44 Ibid., p. 129.

45 Hanfstaengel, *The Unknown Hitler*, p. 224.

46 Ibid., p. 224.

47 Ernst Krieck, Professor of Pedagogy at the University of Heidelberg, quoted in Steven E. Aschheim, *Nietzsche's Legacy in Germany*, University of California Press, 1992, p. 253.

48 Elisabeth Förster-Nietzsche to Ernst Thiel, 31 October 1935.

49 Letter to Elisabeth Förster-Nietzsche, from Venice, mid-June 1884.

50 *Ecce Homo*, 'Why I am a Destiny', Section 1.

· SELECT BIBLIOGRAPHY ·

The standard German edition of the collected works is *Kritische Gesamtausgabe: Werke*, ed. Giorgio Colli and Mazzino Montinari, Walter de Gruyter, 1967– .

Quotations from Nietzsche are from the Cambridge Texts in the History of Philosophy Series, unless otherwise cited. Quotations from the letters, unless otherwise cited, are taken from *Selected Letters of Friedrich Nietzsche*, edited by Christopher Middleton, Hackett Publishing, Indianapolis, 1969.

Andreas-Salomé, Lou, *Looking Back: Memoirs*, trans. Breon Mitchell, Paragon House, 1990

Andreas-Salomé, Lou, *Nietzsche*, trans. Siegfried Mandel, University of Illinois Press, 2001

Bach, Steven, *Leni, The Life and Work of Leni Riefenstahl*, Abacus, 2007

Binion, Rudolph, *Frau Lou, Nietzsche's Wayward Disciple*, Princeton University Press, 1968

Bishop, Paul (ed.), *A Companion to Friedrich Nietzsche, Life and Works*, Camden House, 2012

Blanning, Tim, *The Triumph of Music: Composers, Musicians and their Audiences, 1700 to the Present*, Allen Lane, 2008

Blue, Daniel, *The Making of Friedrich Nietzsche, The Quest for Identity 1844–1869*, Cambridge University Press, 2016

Brandes, Georg, trans. A. G. Chater, *Friedrich Nietzsche*, William Heinemann, 1909

Brandes, Georg (ed.), *Selected Letters*, trans. W. Glyn Jones, Norvik Press, 1990

Burckhardt, Jacob, *The Civilisation of the Renaissance in Italy*, Penguin, 1990

Cate, Curtis, *Friedrich Nietzsche, A Biography*, Pimlico, 2003

Chamberlain, Lesley, *Nietzsche in Turin, The End of the Future*, Quartet, 1996

Detweiler, Bruce, *Nietzsche and the Politics of Aristocratic Radicalism*, University of Chicago Press, 1990

Diethe, Carol, *The A to Z of Nietzscheanism*, Scarecrow Press, 2010

Diethe, Carol, *Nietzsche's Sister and the Will to Power*, University of Illinois Press, 2003

Diethe, Carol, *Nietzsche's Women, Beyond the Whip*, Walter de Gruyter, 1996

Dru, Alexander, *The Letters of Jacob Burckhardt*, Liberty Fund, Indianapolis, 1955

Easton, Laird M. (ed.), *Journey into the Abyss, The Diaries of Count Harry Kessler, 1880–1918*, Alfred A. Knopf, 2011

Easton, Laird M., *The Red Count. The Life and Times of Harry Kessler*, University of California Press, 2002

Feuchtwanger, Edgar, *Imperial Germany, 1850–1918*, Routledge, 2001

Förster-Nietzsche, Elisabeth, *The Nietzsche–Wagner Correspondence*, trans. Caroline V. Kerr, Duckworth, 1922

Förster-Nietzsche, Elisabeth, *The Life of Nietzsche*, Vol. I, *The Young Nietzsche*, trans. Anthony M. Ludovici, Sturgis and Walton, 1912

Förster-Nietzsche, Elisabeth, *The Life of Nietzsche*, Vol. II, *The Lonely Nietzsche*, trans. Paul V. Cohn, Sturgis and Walton, 1915

Gautier, Judith, *Wagner at Home*, trans. Effie Dunreith Massie, John Lane, 1911

Gilman, Sander L. (ed.), and David J. Parent (trans.), *Conversations with Nietzsche, A Life in the Words of His Contemporaries*, Oxford University Press, 1987

Gossmann, Lionel, *Basel in the Age of Burckhardt, A Study in Unseasonable Ideas*, University of Chicago Press, 2002

Gregor-Dellin, Martin, *Richard Wagner, His Life, His Works, His Century*, trans. J. Maxwell Brownjohn, Collins, 1983

Gregor-Dellin, Martin, and Mack, Dietrich (eds), *Cosima Wagner's Diaries*, trans. Geoffrey Skelton, Vols I and II, Helen and Kurt Wolff Books, Harcourt Brace Jovanovich, Vol. I 1978, Vol. II 1980

Grey, Thomas S. (ed.), *Richard Wagner and His World*, Princeton University Press, 2009

Hanfstaengl, Ernst, *The Unknown Hitler*, Gibson Square, 2005

Hayman, Ronald, *Nietzsche, A Critical Life*, Weidenfeld and Nicolson, 1980

Heidegger, Martin, *German Existentialism*, trans. Dagobert D. Runes, Philosophical Library Inc., 1965

Hilmes, Oliver, *Cosima Wagner, the Lady of Bayreuth*, Yale University Press, 2010

Hollingdale, R. J., *Dithyrambs of Dionysus*, Anvil, 2001

Hollingdale, R. J., *Nietzsche, The Man and His Philosophy*, Cambridge University Press, 1999

SELECT BIBLIOGRAPHY

Johnson, Dirk R., *Nietzsche's Anti-Darwinism*, Cambridge University Press, 2010

Kaufmann, Walter (ed.), *Friedrich Nietzsche, The Will to Power*, trans. Kaufmann and R. J. Hollingdale, Vintage, 1968

Kessler, Charles (ed. and trans.), *The Diaries of a Cosmopolitan*, Phoenix Press, London, 2000

Köhler, Joachim, *Nietzsche and Wagner, A Lesson in Subjugation*, trans. Ronald Taylor, Yale University Press, 1998

Krell, David Farrell, and Bates, Donald L., *The Good European, Nietzsche's Work Sites in Word and Image*, University of Chicago Press, 1997

Levi, Oscar (ed.), *Selected Letters of Friedrich Nietzsche*, trans. Anthony M. Ludovici, Heinemann, 1921

Love, Frederick R., *Nietzsche's St Peter, Genesis and Cultivation of an Illusion*, Walter de Gruyter, 1981

Luchte, James, *The Peacock and the Buffalo, The Poetry of Nietzsche*, Continuum Publishing, 2010

Macintyre, Ben, *Forgotten Fatherland, The Search for Elisabeth Nietzsche*, Macmillan, 1992

Mann, Thomas, *Doctor Faustus*, trans. H. T. Lowe-Porter, Penguin, 1974

Meysenbug, Malwida von, *Rebel in a Crinoline, Memoirs of Malwida von Meysenbug*, trans. Elsa von Meysenbug Lyons, George Allen & Unwin, 1937

Middleton, Christopher (ed.), *Selected Letters of Friedrich Nietzsche*, Hackett Publishing, Indianapolis, 1969

Millington, Barry, *Richard Wagner, The Sorcerer of Bayreuth*, Thames and Hudson, 2013

Moore, Gregory, *Nietzsche, Biology and Metaphor*, Cambridge University Press, 2002

Moritzen, Julius, *Georg Brandes in Life and Letters*, Colyer, 1922

Nehemas, Alexander, *Nietzsche, Life as Literature*, Harvard, 2002

Peters, H. F., *Zarathustra's Sister: The Case of Elisabeth and Friedrich Nietzsche*, Crown, 1977

Podach, E. F., *The Madness of Nietzsche*, trans. F. A Voight, Putnam, 1931

Roth, Samuel (purportedly by Friedrich Nietzsche), *My Sister and I*, trans. Dr Oscar Levy, AMOK Books, 1990

Ryback, Timothy W., *Hitler's Private Library, The Books that Shaped His Life*, Vintage, 2010

Safranski, Rüdiger, *Nietzsche, A Philosophical Biography*, trans. Shelley Frisch, Norton, 2003

Schaberg, William H., *The Nietzsche Canon, A Publication History and Bibliography*, University of Chicago Press, 1995

Schain, Richard, *The Legend of Nietzsche's Syphilis*, Greenwood Press, 2001

Sherratt, Yvonne, *Hitler's Philosophers*, Yale University Press, 2013

Small, Robin, *Nietzsche and Rée, A Star Friendship*, Clarendon Press, Oxford, 2007

Spencer, Stewart, and Millington, Barry (eds), *Selected Letters of Richard Wagner*, Dent, 1987

Storer, Colin, *A Short History of the Weimar Republic*, I. B. Tauris, 2013

Tanner, Michael, *Nietzsche, A Very Short Introduction*, Oxford University Press, 2000

Vickers, Julia, *Lou von Salomé, A Biography of the Woman Who Inspired Freud, Nietzsche and Rilke*, McFarland, 2008

Walker, Alan, *Hans von Bülow, A Life and Times*, Oxford University Press, 2010

Watson, Peter, *The German Genius, Europe's Third Renaissance, The Second Scientific Revolution and the Twentieth Century*, Simon & Schuster, 2010

Zweig, Stefan, *Nietzsche*, trans. Will Stone, Hesperus Press, 2013

SELECT DISCOGRAPHY

Albany Records, USA, *Friedrich Nietzsche*, Vol. I, *Compositions of His Youth, 1857–63*, Vol. II, *Compositions of His Mature Years, 1864–82*.

Deutsche Grammophon, *Lou Salomé* (Opera in 2 Acts) by Giuseppe Sinopoli. Lucia Popp, José Carreras and the Stuttgart Symphony Orchestra.

· QUOTATIONS ACKNOWLEDGEMENTS ·

We are grateful to the following for permission to reproduce copyright material:

Extracts from *Nietzsche: On the Genealogy of Morality and Other Writings*, second edition, edited by Keith Ansell-Pearson and translated by Carol Diethe, Cambridge University Press, 2006, copyright © Cambridge University Press, 1997. Reproduced by permission of the publisher.

Extracts from *Nietzsche: Untimely Meditations*, second edition, edited by Daniel Breazeale and translated by R. J. Hollingdale, Cambridge University Press, 1997, copyright © Cambridge University Press, 1997. Reproduced by permission of the publisher.

Extracts from *Nietzsche: Thus Spoke Zarathustra*, edited by Robert Pippin and edited and translated by Adrian Del Caro, Cambridge University Press, 2010, copyright © Cambridge University Press, 2006.

Extracts from *Nietzsche: Daybreak. Thoughts on the Prejudices of Morality*, second edition, edited by Maudemarie Clark, Brian Leiter and translated by R. J. Hollingdale, Cambridge University Press, 1997, copyright © Cambridge University Press, 1997. Reproduced by permission of the publisher.

Extracts from *Nietzsche: Human, All Too Human. A Book for Free Spirits*, second edition, edited and translated by R. J. Hollingdale, Cambridge University Press, 1996, copyright © Cambridge University Press, 1986, 1996. Reproduced by permission of the publisher.

Extracts from *Nietzsche: Beyond Good and Evil. Prelude to a Philosophy of the Future*, edited by Rolf-Peter Horstmann and edited and translated by Judith Norman, Cambridge University Press, 2002, copyright © Cambridge University Press, 2002. Reproduced by permission of the publisher.

Extracts from *The Good European: Nietzsche's Work Sites in Word and Image*, translated by David Farrell Krell and Donald L. Bates, The University of

INDEX